Colorado

0   40 miles

0   40 km

INSIGHT GUIDES
COLORADO

APA PUBLICATIONS L

Part of the Langenscheidt Publishing Group

❋ INSIGHT GUIDE
COLORADO

Editorial

Project Editor
Alyse Dar
Art Director
Steven Lawrence
Picture Manager
Tom Smyth
Series Manager
Rachel Fox

Distribution

UK & Ireland
GeoCenter International Ltd
Meridian House, Churchill Way West
Basingstoke, Hampshire RG21 6YR
sales@geocenter.co.uk

United States
Ingram Publisher Services
1 Ingram Boulevard, PO Box 3006, La
Vergne, TN 37086-1986
customer.service@ingrampublisher
services.com

Australia
Universal Publishers
PO Box 307
St. Leonards NSW 1590
sales@universalpublishers.com.au

Worldwide
**Apa Publications GmbH & Co.
Verlag KG (Singapore branch)**
7030 Ang Mo Kio Avenue 5
08-65 Northstar @ AMK
Singapore 569880
apasin@singnet.com.sg

Printing

CTPS-China

©2011 Apa Publications UK Ltd
All Rights Reserved

First Edition (updated 2006)
Second Edition 2011

CONTACTING THE EDITORS
We would appreciate it if readers
would alert us to errors or out-
dated information by writing to:
**Insight Guides, PO Box 7910,
London SE1 1WE, England.**
insight@apaguide.co.uk
NO part of this book may be reproduced,
stored in a retrieval system or transmitted
in any form or means electronic, mech-
anical, photocopying, recording or otherwise, without prior written permission of
Apa Publications. Brief text quotations
with use of photographs are exempted
for book review purposes only. Information has been obtained from sources
believed to be reliable, but its accuracy
and completeness, and the opinions
based thereon, are not guaranteed.

www.insightguides.com

ABOUT THIS BOOK

The first Insight Guide pioneered
the use of creative full-color
photography in travel guides in
1970. Since then, we have
expanded our range to cater for
our readers' need not only for reliable information about their chosen destination but also for a real
understanding of the culture and
workings of that destination. Now,
when the internet can supply
inexhaustible (but not always reliable) facts, our books marry text
and pictures to provide those
much more elusive qualities:
knowledge and discernment. To
achieve this, we rely heavily on the
authority of locally based writers
and photographers.

How to use this book

This book is carefully structured to
convey an understanding of Colorado's people and culture, and guides

readers through its ancient sites,
modern resorts and intense capital.
   The Best of Colorado section at
the front of the guide helps you to
prioritise what you want to do.

◆ The **Features** section, indicated
by a pink bar at the top of each page,
is a series of illuminating essays
that cover the natural and cultural
history of the region, as well as daily
life, architecture and the arts.
◆ The main **Places** section, indicated by a blue bar, is a complete
guide to all the sights and areas
worth visiting. Places of special
interest are coordinated by number
with the maps.
◆ The **Travel Tips** listings section,
with a yellow bar, provides full information on transport, hotels, activities from culture to shopping to
sports, an A–Z section of essential
practical information. An easy-to-

LEFT: the Durango & Silverton Narrow Gauge Railroad.

The current edition builds on the excellent foundations created by the editors and writers of previous editions of the book, including **Richard Harris**, a native Coloradan, who is the author or co-author of more than 30 guidebooks on the American West, Mexico and Central America. When not traveling, he lives in Santa Fe, where he is president of the New Mexico Book Association and publisher of Southwest BookViews.

Claire Walter is an award-winning author of hundreds of magazine articles and many books. A resident of Colorado since 1988, she specializes in writing about the great outdoors.

Conger Beasley is the author of more than a dozen books, including a guide to the national parks of the Rocky Mountains.

Edward A. Jardim condensed three centuries of history into an engaging chronicle of Colorado's development, from pioneering expeditions like those of Zebulon Pike and John Frémont to the growth of vibrant cities like Denver and Colorado Springs.

Like all Insight Guides, this book owes much to the superb quality of its photographs, which aim not just to illustrate the text but also to convey the essence of everyday life in Colorado. Many of the images were taken by **Richard Nowitz**, a regular contributor to Insight Guides.

The book was proofread by **Pam Barrett** and indexed by **Helen Peters**.

Map Legend

▬▬ ▬ ▪ ▬	International Boundary
▬ ▬ ▬ ▬	State Boundary
▬ ▪ ▬ ▪ ▬	National Park/Reserve
▬ ▬ ▬ ▬	Native American Reserve
▬ ▬ ▬ ▬	Ferry Route
✈ ✈	Airport: International/Regional
🚌	Bus Station
❶	Tourist Information
✝ ✝ ✝	Church/Ruins
🛉	Statue/Monument
★	Place of Interest
⌂	Ranger Station
⊼	Picnic Area
△	Campground
✵	Viewpoint
⊃⊂	Pass
🎿	Skiing

The main places of interest in the Places section are coordinated by number with a full-color map (eg ❶), and a symbol at the top of every right-hand page tells you where to find the map.

find contents list for Travel Tips is printed on the back flap, which also serves as a bookmark.

The contributors

This fully revised and updated edition was commissioned, managed and edited by **Alyse Dar** at Insight Guides.

Santa Fe writer **Nicky Leach** has worked with Insight Guides for more than 10 years, creating and updating guides on the American West. She jumped at the chance to revisit her neighboring state of Colorado to update this edition. Her favorite destination in the Mile High state is Echo Canyon in Dinosaur National Monument, one of the most spectacular but least-known places in the National Park system. Nicky also wrote about Colorado's natural history and ancient cultures.

Contents

LEFT: an idyllic mountain lake in the Rockies.

Maps

Travel Tips

THE BEST OF COLORADO: TOP ATTRACTIONS

From the historic homes of Mesa Verde to the latest contemporary art in Denver, here are our top recommendations for a visit to the colorful state of Colorado

△ **Trail Ridge Road** in **Rocky Mountain National Park** offers soaring high-country views of serrated alpine peaks, sparkling lakes, glaciers, fragile tundra meadows, charismatic mega-fauna, wild flowers and pioneer cabins. *See page 195*

△▽ **Denver** is a vibrant and fast-growing city, with the largest municipal park system in the US and cultural institutions that include the pioneering Denver Zoo and the Denver Botanic Gardens. *See page 149*

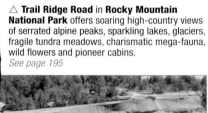

△ **Cliff Palace** is one of the most magical Ancestral Pueblo cliff dwellings in **Mesa Verde**, the nation's favorite archeological park, near Durango in the Four Corners region of southwestern Colorado. *See page 265*

▷ Combining traditional Hispanic culture, New Age retreats, hot springs, high peaks, America's tallest sand dunes, and overwintering sandhill cranes, the **San Luis Valley** surrounding Alamosa is a unique destination. *See page 185*

△ Drive, hike, or ride the Pikes Peak Cog Railroad to the top of 14,110ft (4,301-meter) **Pikes Peak**, which, among other things, inspired the writing of *'America the Beautiful'*. *See page 178*

▷ **Leadville** (elev. 10,152 ft/3,660 meters), is not only the best-preserved mining town in Colorado, with its own mining history museum, but also the highest town in the country, and possibly the most storied. *See pages 237*

◁ **Telluride** is the quintessential Colorado ski destination – an attractive Victorian mining town in a glorious box canyon setting far from anywhere, offering skiing, eclectic festivals, friendly locals, and unpretentious atmosphere. *See page 254*

▽ There are 'million-dollar' views all along the narrow, winding **San Juan Skyway** between Durango and Montrose, but keep your eyes on the road – the dropoffs are very steep. *See page 251*

▽ Ride the **Durango & Silverton Narrow Gauge Railroad** to Silverton and enjoy views of Mount Sneffels and the glorious Animas Valley, preferably during the fall when the aspens turn golden. *See page 249*

▷ A mini-Napa Valley amid the carved redrock canyons of the Colorado River, **Grand Junction** is famed for its wineries, fruit orchards, and proximity to Dinosaur and Colorado National Monuments. *See page 277*

The Best of Colorado: Editor's Choice

Colorado has a wealth of natural beauty, sophisticated culture, and historical significance. Here are the best spots to enjoy the Mile High State

Best Small Towns

● **Ouray.** The town has a well-regarded home town museum, an ice climbing festival, and Jeep drives in the nearby mountains. *See page 252.*

● **Salida.** A sporty small town with a large historic district, galleries, local food and wine, and hosts fibARK, a major whitewater celebration. *See page 180.*

● **Creede.** A remote former mining town, with an award-winning theater company and a majestic setting deep in the San Juan Mountains. *See page 258.*

● **Glenwood Springs.** The popular hot springs and spa and the historic Denver and Colorado hotels are an easy drive or train ride from Denver. *See page 225.*

● **Boulder.** Home to the University of Colorado, alternative healers and scientists, and the top farmers' market in Colorado, within view of Denver. *See page 163.*

● **Crested Butte.** Birthplace of fat tire biking and some of the state's quirkiest festivals, this mining town turned ski resort exudes Central Rockies charm. *See page 233.*

● **Paonia.** Urban refugees, creatives, outdoorsmen and farmers cluster in this little town in scenic North Fork Valley near Black Canyon of the Gunnison National Park. *See page 231.*

Best Nature Viewing

● **Rocky Mountain National Park.** Visit during the fall rutting season to view elk bugling and bighorn sheep butting heads in a competition for mates. *See page 195.*

● **San Luis Valley.** Two national wildlife refuges on the Rio Grande attract migratory elk, bison herds, and thousands of sandhill cranes in winter. *See page 185.*

● **Comanche National Grasslands.** A nationally significant birding area, southeastern Colorado's prairies host unique prairie chicken mating dances at the birds' leks in May. *See page 144.*

● **San Juan Mountains.** The remote San Juans may still support grizzly bears and have been the site of a successful reintroduction of lynx. *See page 245.*

● **Yampa Valley Birding.** The Yampa River near Steamboat Springs is an Important Birding Area, home to catbirds, orioles among others and river otters and mink. *See page 210.*

ABOVE: Ciomanche National Grassland. **LEFT:** washboard music.

BEST CULTURAL ATTRACTIONS

● **Bent's Old Fort National Historic Site.** Relive the days of the Santa Fe Trail at this former rendezvous for mountain men, traders and travelers in south-eastern Colorado. *See page 144.*

● **The Matchless Mine, Leadville.** The ghost of Baby Doe Tabor, penniless widow of Matchless Mine millionaire Horace Tabor, haunts this old cabin in Leadville. *See page 238.*

● **Denver Art Museum, Hamilton Expansion.** One of Denver's most photo-graphed new buildings, this shiny geometric DAM expansion was designed by Polish-born architect Daniel Libeskind. *See page 152.*

● **Anasazi Heritage Center, Dolores.** This state-of-the-art research center and museum holds millions of Ancestral Pueblo artifacts excavated from the Dolores River area prior to damming. *See page 267.*

● **Hovenweep National Monument, Cajone Mesa.** An outlier of Mesa Verde, Hovenweep protects unusual towers and structures on Cajone Mesa, the most arche-ologically rich area in the country. *See page 269.*

ABOVE: Bent's Fort. **TOP RIGHT:** Black Canyon of the Gunnison. **BELOW:** mountain climbing safely.

BEST SCENIC DRIVES

● **Tabegauche-Unaweep Scenic Byway.** This little-traveled highway along Colorado's western edge, where mountains meet redrocks, has mining ghosts, nature preserves, and rocky canyons. *See page 270.*

● **Silver Thread Scenic Byway, Wolf Pass to Lake City.** A lonesome highway connects the artsy mining town of Creede, the headwaters of the Rio Grande, and a Victorian belle, Lake City. *See page 256.*

● **San Juan Skyway, between Silverton and Ouray.** Linking two popu-lar small towns, this seg-ment of the highway crosses Red Mountain Pass and has views that will make you feel like a million dollars. *See page 251.*

● **Lookout Mountain Park, Lariat Loop Scenic Byway.** Visit Buffalo Bill's Gravesite and Museum at this popular scenic drive near Golden. *See page 215.*

● **Black Canyon of the Gunnison National Park Scenic Drive.** Enjoy light on schist from overlooks above this 2,000ft (610-meter) deep, dark, narrow canyon carved by the Gunnison River. *See page 233.*

● **Alpine Loop Jeep Trail.** This classic drive leaves Ouray and heads over Engineer Pass to the ghost town Capitol City and Lake City. *See page 252.*

BEST OUTDOOR ACTIVITIES

● **Mountain biking in Colorado National Monu-ment.** A mountain biking mecca set amid spectacularly carved redrock canyons along the Colorado River, west of Grand Junction. *See page 278.*

● **Rafting the Yampa River through Dinosaur National Monument.** The confluencing Yampa and Green Rivers attract river runners through Echo Canyon, scene of an anti-damming environmental victory in the 1960s. *See page 280.*

● **Climbing the Flatirons.** The distinctive reddish upended blades of this formation are a major Boulder landmark and a popular destination for climbers. *See page 163.*

● **Skiing at Steamboat Springs.** This cowboy-oriented ski resort's light, frothy Champagne powder and a renovated ski village attract winter sports enthusiasts to its runs each year. *See page 208.*

● **Hiking Maroon Bells-Snowmass Wilderness.** Twin peaks reflected in a mirror lake attract photographers and hikers who are tired of the scene in nearby Aspen. *See page 230.*

ROCKY MOUNTAIN STATE

Soaring peaks, world-class skiing and vibrant cities lure travelers to America's alpine heartland

"**T**he scenery bankrupts the English language", said Theodore Roosevelt, a man rarely at a loss for words. TR was musing about the Rocky Mountains during a visit to Colorado in 1901. Indeed, no words can capture the skyward sweep of this landscape, the heady mix of humility and exaltation one feels standing atop its legendary peaks, 54 of them soaring beyond 14,000ft (4,270 meters). It transcends them all.

Man has made his mark, of course. Roads blasted from bedrock curve heavenward. Railroads corkscrew up impossibly steep terrain. Dams restrain rivers. Bridges and tunnels span seemingly insurmountable distances. And is any feat of modern engineering equivalent in daring to the ancient cliff dwellings of Mesa Verde, laid up stone by stone in canyon alcoves without wheelbarrows, pulleys or levels?

In the 1800s, huge yields of gold and silver deep within the earth brought thousands of prospectors to Colorado. The mining boomtowns that sprang up are mostly atmospheric ghost towns now, their tumbledown saloons, cabins and headframes haunted by wind and tumbleweeds.

Elsewhere in Colorado, the bones of Diplodocus, Stegosaurus, Camarasaurus, and other dinosaurs erode from the ground. Colorado has produced more dinosaur fossils than any other state. It is a treasure trove of dinosaur trackways, embedded forever in solid rock.

And then there are the Rockies, backbone of the continent. At 30 million years old, their peaks, carved by glacial ice into cirques, hanging valleys and knife-edged aretes, retain the assertive thrust of youth.

Even on the eastern plains, where grasslands roll to the horizon, the landscape dwarfs humans, as if you are no more than a cork bobbing on the waves of a vast ocean of grasses.

Colorado has many vibrant cities, attractive towns, art and culture, great restaurants, rafting, hiking, some of the world's best skiing, and much else. But it is for its epic landscape that it is best known. That is the essence of Colorado, the magic it shares with every visitor. ❑

PRECEDING PAGES: hiking to the bowl; downtown Denver; the Otto Mears toll road in 1909. **LEFT:** a herd of elk in Rocky Mountain National Park. **TOP:** Bear Lake in Rocky Mountain National Park. **ABOVE RIGHT:** going for a ride in Estes Park.

THE CULTURAL LANDSCAPE

Hippies and yuppies, natives and newcomers – Colorado is
a mixed bag of cultures, classes and political viewpoints,
which is what makes it so interesting

The early 1970s, an era when Colorado's population was exploding, saw the birth of a bumper sticker fad so unusual that it was written up in *Time* and *Life* magazines. Created by Denverite Sandy Glade, the stickers bore the same distinctive green-and-white mountain silhouette as the state's license plates. The first ones were emblazoned with the single word "native," which spoke volumes. Everyone knew what they meant: "I'm not one of those newcomers who come here to jack up prices, pollute our pure Rocky Mountain springwater, take all the parking spaces and generally 'Californicate' our state – so don't blame me." Within weeks, new bumper stickers started popping up: "semi-native," "local," "survivor" and, yes, "tourist."

Since then, the native-versus-newcomer issue has become almost moot, as the state's population has more than doubled, largely due to the migration of an estimated one million Californians.

Denver's prominent 19th-century black residents included Barney Ford, a businessman who won the vote for black males in the West, and Aunt Clara Brown, a freed Kentucky slave and laundress who took in needy African Americans.

Colorado folks are such a diverse lot that it's hard to generalize about the characteristics that make them Coloradans. Or are they Coloradoans? They can't even agree which term is correct – just ask the news editors at the *Adams State College Coloradan* and the *Fort Collins Coloradoan*. (Merriam-Webster has it both ways.)

Coloradans are urban and rural, liberal and ultraconservative, wealthy and poor. Perhaps the best way to define how Coloradans traditionally see themselves is to look at them in the context of the state's cultural landscape – that is, how they relate to the land and face the challenges of getting along with their neighbors.

Rags to riches to rags

Much about Colorado's collective self-image is reflected in its legends. Unlike other Western states, you don't find many cowboys, lawmen, gunslingers or pioneers in Colorado's version of its own history. Although cattle ranching has been a vital part of the state's economy since the 1860s, few residents can name a single rancher, past or present. Colorado heritage is defined by tales of gold and silver prospectors, whose good and ill fortunes are a potent metaphor for many other enterprises, including tourism, land development and the ski industry.

Some are ironic stories of losers like Bob Womack, the man who first discovered gold in the Cripple Creek District in 1891. Unable to convince others that his find was anything more than a drunken fantasy, he sold his mining claim for $300. The claim became the El Paso Mine, which produced more than $10 million worth of ore. Womack died broke.

At the other end of the spectrum was Wom-

gold strike, his will endowed the Myron Stratton Home in Colorado Springs. Named after his father, it was an orphanage and old folks' home, but one unrivaled in the world for its lavish comforts. The establishment, set on a large, walled estate with lawns and bowers, tennis courts and a swimming pool, still operates today.

Some Colorado legends are just plain bizarre. Consider the case of Alferd Packer, the Lake City guide who spent a winter snowed in with six greenhorn gold prospectors high in the San Juan mountains – and survived by eating them. He was convicted twice, not of cannibalizing his companions (which wasn't a crime) but

ack's old drinking buddy Winfield Scott Stratton, a Colorado Springs carpenter who spent his summers prospecting around Cripple Creek. He returned to a claim he had twice previously explored and abandoned, after finding nothing. The third time proved to be a charm. He struck a rich gold vein that became the Independence Mine. He sold his claim for $10 million and spent the remainder of his life as a philanthropist, gifting Colorado Springs with magnificent public buildings, parks and the finest streetcar system in the state. Upon his death 11 years after his first

of killing them first. He spent the rest of his life in the old Cañon City Penitentiary, where his separate cabin is now a tourist attraction. To this day Colorado historians write papers purporting to prove his innocence. Coloradans just love Packer. At the University of Colorado, the student council voted to name a campus cafeteria after him. Trey Parker, co-creator of the raunchy television series *South Park*, wrote a stage play about Packer that was a hit in Boulder and later became a cult movie. He called it *Cannibal: The Musical*.

LEFT: Cinco de Mayo parade in downtown Denver. **ABOVE LEFT:** running Boulder Canyon. **ABOVE RIGHT:** a busker on Boulder's Pearl Street Mall.

For love or money

The legend that best symbolizes Colorado is that of Horace Tabor and his two wives.

Horace, a Leadville grocer, postmaster and mayor, grubstaked two German prospectors $17 worth of food in exchange for a one-third interest in whatever they found. They struck silver and, five months later, declared a $10,000 dividend for each partner. Horace used his share to invest in other mines around the district, including the played-out Matchless Mine. As the story goes, the seller had "salted" it with a shotgun shell loaded with gold dust, a common fraud at the time. Digging down a few feet revealed one of the richest silver veins in Colorado history, making Horace a millionaire several times over.

Money spelled trouble for Tabor. His wife Augusta, an austere New Englander uncomfortable with sudden wealth, continued to live frugally and rent rooms in their modest home. Horace liked the seemingly endless supply of money just fine and, at age 50, may have been experiencing a midlife crisis. He promptly fell in love with Elizabeth "Baby Doe" McCourt, a divorcee half his age. Horace and Baby Doe soon moved to Central City, where he lavished her with gifts and flowers to the tune of $1,000 a day. He persuaded a Durango judge to grant him a quick, secret – and illegal – divorce and later married Baby Doe.

HAVE PALETTE, WILL TRAVEL

Throughout the 1800s, as Americans set their sights on expansion west, artists were there, too, recording landscapes that defied the imagination. One of the first was George Catlin, who journeyed west in the 1830s and produced 500 oil paintings that captured the nobility of American Indian cultures. Catlin's work influenced the young Charles Deas who, in the 1840s, journeyed to the Rockies and painted *Long Jakes*, a portrait of a fur trapper whose half-wild, half-civilized appearance captured the essence of the frontier.

In the 1870s, Albert Bierstadt attempted to convey in visual terms what Romantic poets like Shelley, Byron and Wordsworth captured in verse: Nature as a religious experience, offering moral lessons for mankind. Although wildly popular, Bierstadt had his critics. "I believe this atmosphere of Bierstadt's is altogether too gorgeous," complained Mark Twain. "I am sorry the Creator hadn't made it instead of him."

In the late 1800s, a new fascination with realism emerged. In 1871, English-born Thomas Moran joined the Hayden Survey to Yellowstone. His paintings helped get the park established and paved the way for artists Charles M. Russell and Frederic Remington, who recorded a frontier way of life that is now all but gone.

Horace Tabor's bigamy became a problem when he was appointed to the seat of a deceased US Senator from Colorado. What had been viewed in Central City as everyday recklessness – perfectly understandable to anyone who saw the homely Augusta and the beautiful Baby Doe – in Washington society was a scandal of monumental proportions. To gain respectability, Horace gave Augusta the lion's share of his estimated $9 million fortune in exchange for a legitimate divorce.

Ten years passed. Horace built opera houses. Baby Doe lived lavishly. Then came the silver crash of 1893, and virtually overnight they found themselves penniless. The bank foreclosed on the Matchless Mine, cutting off their only source of income. At age 66, Horace took a job shoveling slag at a Cripple Creek mine for $3 a day. To the surprise of everybody who had regarded her as a notorious gold digger, Baby Doe stood by her man. In 1898, Horace was appointed postmaster in Denver, then died the following year.

Baby Doe Tabor spent the last half of her life in Leadville, living in a converted storage shed beside the Matchless Mine and unsuccessfully looking for a way to regain ownership. She died there at age 80, destitute. Four gunny sacks she had left at the local hospital for safekeeping were found to be filled with silks, jewelry and other treasures from her glory days. As for Augusta, she lived out her remaining years as a wealthy dowager in Pasadena, California.

The moral of the Tabors' story depends on who's telling it. What goes round comes round? Spend it while you've got it? Never give up? Take the money and run? Whatever meaning one reads into it, the tale seems strangely relevant whenever you visit one of Colorado's gold rush–era towns, whether it's now a prosperous city, a posh ski resort or a ghostly cluster of decrepit log cabins and crumbled stone chimneys still waiting for good times that may never come again.

Immigrant heritage

As gold and silver mining developed from small one- or two-man diggings into large-scale industrial operations, immigrant laborers were hired to do the dirty work. At first,

LEFT: nearly a third of the cowboys in the American West were African American. **RIGHT:** a modern cowboy at a Durango saloon.

the majority were Chinese workers, who brought experience from the earlier gold rush in California. Some 15,650 Chinese Americans live in Colorado today, just 0.4 percent of the population. Most left because of widespread persecution that culminated in the Anti-Chinese Riot of 1880. Starting as a bar brawl, the incident escalated into a mob of more than 2,000 rampaging through Denver's Chinatown, burning businesses and lynching at least one Chinese man. After that, mine and railroad jobs were filled mainly by Welsh, Cornish and Italian workers.

A more lasting impact on Colorado's cultural

landscape came with the trainloads of German-speaking immigrants from the Volga River region of Russia, who began arriving in 1880 and homesteading farms in the northeastern part of the state, growing root vegetables and winter wheat. Within two generations, many of Colorado's prominent politicians and industrialists were Russian Germans. Their greatest contribution was the introduction of sugar beet farming, one of Colorado's most important industries from 1900 to the 1960s. Most small farmers moved to the cities and towns of the Front Range during the Dust Bowl of the 1930s, but few left the region. Today, white residents reporting German ancestry make up 22 percent of the state's population.

The largest group by far are Latinos or Hispanics, commonly referred to as "Mexicans" even though their ancestors may have lived in Colorado for generations, and only three-quarters of Latinos in Colorado are actually from Mexico. As small sugar beet farms gave way to big, labor-intensive agribusiness operations, migrant labor crews were brought from Mexico. These "contract families" were encouraged to stay in the region year-round and soon developed large *barrios* in Denver and elsewhere. Today, one in five Coloradans (and more than one in three Denver residents) is Latino. Cinco de Mayo (May 5), the

annual celebration commemorating the end of French rule in Mexico, is one of Denver's biggest festivals.

The dark side of diversity

Minorities in Colorado have often been met with intolerance, bigotry and even violence. One obvious example is American Indians – the Ute, Navajo, Cheyenne, Arapaho, Kiowa, Comanche and other tribes that inhabited the region for countless centuries. Today, the percentage of American Indians in Colorado is a shade more than the percentage for the United States overall (44,241 residents, or 1 percent) but less than in any other Rocky Mountain state. Why?

On the eastern plains, the prevailing attitude toward Indians in the mid-19th century was expressed by John Chivington, the Methodist minister, political hopeful and Colorado Militia leader who led the Sand Creek Massacre, in which some 150 unarmed Cheyenne Indians – most of them women and children – were slaughtered in 1862. "It simply is not possible for Indians to obey or even understand any treaty," Chivington said a few months before the massacre. "I am fully satisfied, gentlemen, that to kill them is the only way we will ever have peace and quiet in Colorado. I say that if any of them are caught in your vicinity, the only thing to do is kill them."

Because of the massacre, Chivington was court-martialed by the Army but honored with a parade through the streets of Denver and awarded a medal of honor by the territorial governor. Within less than 10 years, all Indians had been removed from Colorado Territory except for the Southern and Ute Mountain people, whose reservations lie along the southwestern state line. Curiously, in 1992 Coloradans elected the first American Indian to serve in the US Congress in 60 years. Republican Senator Ben Nighthorse Campbell was not a native Coloradan; like many of his constituents, he moved from California. He represented Colorado from 1993–2005.

By the 1920s, the Ku Klux Klan had become a powerful force in Colorado. The *Denver Post* reported that "the KKK is the largest and most cohesive, most efficiently organized political force in the state." In 1924, riding a wave of anti-immigrant (particularly anti-Mexican) sentiment, Klan leader Clarence Morley was elected governor of Colorado by a landslide. That same year, Klansmen became secretary of state and mayor of Denver, were appointed to the state Supreme Court and seven benches of the Denver District Court, and won a majority of seats in both houses of the state legislature. In the next legislative session, 1,080 Klan-sponsored bills were introduced, but almost all of them were killed in committee by Billy Adams, a Democrat who would later take Morley's place as governor. Coloradans, it seemed, quickly got fed up with the Klan's overzealous enforcement of Prohibition laws.

Molly's crusade

As with most things Coloradan, intolerance was met with a counter-movement to encourage progressive attitudes, as illustrated by another of the state's mining camp legends. Thanks to a hit Broadway musical and motion picture, most people in the US know the rags-to-riches story of Margaret "Unsinkable Molly" Brown's rise from a one-room shack in Leadville to a Denver mansion where she reigned as a leading philanthropist, and how she survived the

> According to 2009 US Census figures, nearly 30 percent of Coloradans have an undergraduate college degree, while more than 12 percent have a graduate education.

ethnic minorities in Colorado, including American Indians, to build "villages" in a Denver park showcasing their native culture, food, arts and crafts. The two-week festival was an enormous success, though it has never been repeated.

In recent years, intolerance and prejudice have occasionally resurfaced. Colorado suffered national notoriety in 1992 when conservative Christian organizations sponsored a ballot measure prohibiting "special rights" for gays and lesbians. Designed to block ordinances such as those adopted in Boulder and Aspen that banned discrimination on sexual preference, the amendment passed with 53 percent of the vote.

Titanic disaster. What fewer people realize is that she also campaigned for an Equal Rights Amendment and ran for the US Senate three times – all before women had voting rights in most states. (In 1893, Colorado had become the second state to give women the right to vote and hold office, and the first to do so by amending the constitution in a general election in which only men could vote.) In an effort to encourage racial harmony and understanding, Molly Brown sponsored a Carnival of Nations in 1906, donating funds to representatives of 16

LEFT: enjoying a cup of herbal tea on Boulder's Pearl Street Mall. **ABOVE:** Chinese miners in the Edgar Experimental Mine near Idaho Springs, about 1920.

It prompted a nationwide effort on behalf of the gay community to boycott Colorado tourism, costing the state's hospitality industry an estimated $40 million. The Colorado Supreme Court eventually ruled the amendment unconstitutional, a decision upheld by the US Supreme Court. Although feelings still run high on both sides of the gay rights issue in Colorado, the boycott had at least one positive impact. The Adolph Coors Company, whose beer had been boycotted by gays as a Colorado symbol, began giving health insurance and other benefits to same-sex partners of employees in 1994 and launched an aggressive campaign to demonstrate its support for gay rights through advertising and donations to gay pride organizations. Coors also sponsors the Colorado Gay Ice Hockey League and funds all three teams in the league.

Changing faces

Today, more than four out of five Coloradans live in the Front Range metropolitan areas; updated US census data for 2009 indicated a 17.36 percent increase in residents from the 2000 census alone, to an estimated population of 4,328,406. Even there, the cultural climate is contradictory and as changeable as the weather. Colorado Springs, for example, is notorious for its conservatism. Local attitudes are shaped in part by a large military presence and by outspo-

ken fundamentalist religious groups. Just off the interstate, not far from the US Air Force Academy, the Focus on the Family Welcome Center greets travelers with cautions about such errors as sparing the rod and spoiling the child. Even the mansion built by General William Jackson Palmer, the city's founder, is now owned and occupied by Christian evangelists.

At the other end of the Front Range Corridor, the university town of Boulder is known as a hotbed of left-wing politics and one of the West's New Age centers. Its top visitor attraction is Celestial Seasonings, an herbal tea empire, and numerous other small family-run outdoor

POWER POLITICS IN THE NEW WEST

With its soaring Latino population and high-tech growth, the Front Range symbolizes the new politics of the Interior West. The region was a key stopover for presidential hopefuls during the 2008 election, and Denver hosted the Democratic National Convention that preceded Democrat Barack Obama's successful election as president and Colorado's first Hispanic senator, Ken Salazar's appointment as secretary of the interior in the new Obama administration. But as goes Washington, so goes Colorado, and with the economic recession showing little sign of improving, dissatisfaction with the current administration has grown, and once again in 2011 Colorado was in the national news nightly for its flip-flop politics. The midterm elections in November 2010 ush-

ered in a record number of candidates for key Colorado senate and gubernatorial races. Alongside popular Democratic candidates like Michael Bennet, appointed to fill Ken Salazar's old senate seat, are Colorado gubernatorial candidates Tom Tancredo, running as a third-party candidate, and Dan Maes, a Republican backed by the Tea Party, an ascendent anti-government grassroots organization with roots in the 1970s Sagebrush Rebellion. Whatever their political persuasion, all of the candidates have taken pains to appeal to disgruntled voters by positioning themselves as Washington outsiders. It's a scenario that's more Old West than New West and shows that states like Colorado continue to be the ones to watch in the new politics.

and eco-business enterprises can be found here. Downtown, on the Pearl Street Mall, you'll find a store that carries only left-wing political books and, a few blocks away, another that specializes in books for lesbians.

It's a wonder the two cities can exist in the same state. But then, generalizations don't always hold water. If you visit the Colorado Springs suburb of Manitou Springs, for instance, you'll find an artist colony regarded as the state's oldest "hippie" community. In Boulder, on the other hand, the intellectual University of Colorado atmosphere provides fertile ground not only for liberal thought but for such groups as the ultra-conservative America First Party and *Soldier of Fortune* magazine, which has sponsored clandestine training camps for Third World police officers in the nearby mountains. At a Pentecostal book-burning in Boulder, copies of such New Age tomes as Shirley MacLaine's *Out on a Limb* and Barbara Marx Hubbard's *Happy Birthday Planet Earth* were pitched into the flames before the event degenerated into a shouting match with protesters.

Environmental politics

Attitudes among urban dwellers, many of whom are transplants from the West Coast, often conflict with those of traditionally conservative old-timers. This is especially true in the realm of environmental protection. Activities such as mining, ranching and logging have taken a back seat to the recreational use of Colorado's vast public lands.

The trend was accelerated in 1992 when voters passed a constitutional amendment known as GOCO, which stands for Great Outdoors Colorado. The law earmarks proceeds from the Colorado Lottery for "trail construction, the purchase of parks and park enhancement, open space, wildlife and river preservation and environmental education," providing more funds for environmental causes than almost any other state. Since its inception, it has awarded funds for more than 3,000 projects in all 64 counties in Colorado.

Outdoor sports have become integral to Colorado's economy, not only promoting year-round tourism but also attracting new residents. Though they are most likely to find

employment with high-tech companies along the Front Range, most new residents cite recreation as their top reason for relocating, not jobs. Recreational opportunities range from huge events like the Bolder Boulder Marathon, in which more than 50,000 runners participate, and world-class athletic competitions such as Telluride's Extreme Ski Week and Durango's Iron Horse Bicycle Classic, to solitary expeditions into high mountain wilderness.

Recreation has also spawned a new breed of legendary figures as colorful as any from the gold rush days. Future generations may commemorate such heroes as Friedl Pfeifer, the

European ski instructor who in the late 1940s came up with the crazy idea of building Colorado's first ski slope near a down-and-out mining town named Aspen. Or Neil Murdoch, who invented and popularized the sport of mountain biking while hiding out in Crested Butte under an assumed name, dodging a federal warrant for an alleged drug offense, for 25 years.

And then there's Sandy Glade, still going strong after 30 years. Now her line of Colorado bumper stickers numbers more than 50. Still revealing a lot about contemporary Colorado culture, they include "marathoner," "mountain biker," "river runner," "catch & release," "skier" and, perhaps most telling of all, "save an elk – shoot a land developer." ❏

LEFT: a Colorado leprechaun enjoys the St Patrick's Day parade in downtown Denver. **RIGHT:** skiing fresh powder is a real thrill.

DECISIVE DATES

EARLY CULTURES

AD 1
The pithouse-dwelling Basketmaker people inhabit the Four Corners area.

c.1300
Drought forces Ancestral Puebloans to abandon *pueblos* in the Four Corners.

c.1500
Colorado is now home to the Arapahos and Cheyennes peoples in the eastern Plains and Utes in western parts of the state.

STRANGERS FROM AFAR

1682
French explorer René-Robert La Salle claims the region east of the Rockies for France.

1739
French traders the Mallet brothers pass through eastern Colorado en route to Santa Fe.

1765
Juan Maria de Rivera and fellow Spaniards explore the San Juan and Sangre de Cristo Ranges.

AMERICANS MOVE IN

1803
Most of eastern Colorado becomes American through the Louisiana Purchase.

1806
American Lt Zebulon M. Pike and a party of 22 men explores mountains west of Pueblo and Colorado Springs.

1820
Maj. Stephen H. Long and an Army force explores Colorado.

1832
During the "mountain man" era, Bent's Fort is built by the Bents and St Vrain Company near La Junta.

1842
Lt John C. Frémont leads the first of five exploratory missions to the Rockies.

1846
Gen. Stephen W. Kearney leads his "Army of the West" over the Santa Fe Trail through southeastern Colorado to peacefully take New Mexico

for the United States from Mexico. Most of western Colorado becomes American two years later.

1851
The first permanent settlement in Colorado is founded at Conejos in the San Luis Valley by six Hispanic families. The Treaty of Fort Laramie assures the Cheyenne and Arapaho tribes continued use of Colorado's eastern plain.

BOOM TIMES

1858
Small deposits of gold are found near the South Platte River and Cherry Creek, kicking off Colorado's gold rush. Denver City is founded.

1859
John Gregory's gold strike at North Clear Creek on May 6 reinvigorates the territory's mining prospects. Some 40,000 gold-diggers flock to Colorado to try their luck.

1861
The US Congress establishes the Colorado Territory (pop. 25,371).

1864
Cavalrymen slaughter about 150 Cheyenne and Arapaho men, women and children at the Sand Creek massacre.

1867
Under the Treaty of Medicine Lodge, members of the Cheyenne and Arapaho tribes agree to move to reservations in Oklahoma. Denver becomes the territorial capital.

1871
Colorado Springs is founded by Gen. William J. Palmer.

1875
Rich silver deposits are found near Leadville.

1876
Colorado is admitted to the Union.

1879
Indian agent Nathan C. Meeker is slain along with several others in a Ute uprising.

1881
Ute tribes are removed onto reservations.

1888
Two cowboys are the first Anglos to see the ancient ruins of Cliff Palace at Mesa Verde

1891
One of the world's great gold strikes is made at Cripple Creek. Gold production

FAR LEFT: an Arapaho warrior. LEFT: a newspaper article from 1879 showcases Leadville on the front page. ABOVE: Cliff House at Mesa Verde National Park. RIGHT: dancing in a traditional costume.

reaches a peak of more than $20 million annually by 1900.

1893
Congress repeals the Sherman Silver Purchase Act, wreaking havoc on the silver industry.

A NEW CENTURY

1903–4
Miners strike for better working conditions. Militia are summoned to break strikes by the Western Federation of Miners.

1914
Twenty people, including 12 children, are killed during the Ludlow Massacre, pitting miners against state militia near Trinidad.

1915
Rocky Mountain National Park is created.

1917
"Buffalo Bill" Cody dies and is buried on Lookout Mountain west of Denver.

1918
World War I stimulates molybdenum mining; coal output reaches a new high of 12 million tons.

1931
The state's population exceeds one million.

1946
Uranium is discovered near Grand Junction.

1958
The Air Force Academy opens near Colorado Springs.

1959
The Colorado-Big Thompson system brings water to the

state's populous eastern region.

1974
Huge deposits of shale oil are tapped on the Western Slope.

1982
Exxon closes oil fields in western Colorado. The 1980s bring growth in the high-tech sector.

1995
Denver International Airport opens.

2008
Denver hosts the Democratic National Convention.

2009
Colorado's first Hispanic senator, Ken Salazar, is appointed secretary of the interior in the Obama administration.

2010
Colorado's estimated population reaches 5,024,748, a 16.8 percent rise from the previous census in 2000.

NATIVE HERITAGE

For countless generations, the people of this land
hunted and farmed and fashioned intricate ways
of dealing with nature

This land was their land once. The first people to move to what would later become Colorado may have arrived from Asia some 12,000 years ago, at the end of the Ice Age. Crossing into Alaska via the exposed land mass known as Beringia, they followed big game inland, down to where the Eastern Rockies meet the Great Plains.

They found a landscape of peaks and plains and cool mountain streams capable of nourishing all living things. The hunting was good – herds of giant bison, camel, horse, elk, deer and antelope, clustered around lakes and marshes that also held 7ft (2-meter) long beavers and giant ground sloths. But the big prize was mammoths. Hunters pursued the huge, tusked creatures along the eastern Rockies, sleeping in cave shelters and flaking stone spear points around campfires. They butchered on site, leaving behind bones, chipped stone and chert spear points of a type known as Clovis, for the town in New Mexico where they were first identified.

Bison hunting

By 9000 BC, climatic warming and possibly over-hunting had doomed the large animals. Paleo hunters focused instead on one creature – the giant bison. Big-game hunting required bravery and cooperation, skills that would later characterize the tribes that wandered the Plains in search of bison in the historic period. They knapped smaller spear points from obsidian obtained from high-country sites like Black Mountain near the headwaters of the Rio Grande in the

San Juans. The Folsom, as they came to be called, were widespread throughout Colorado. Campsites have been found on the Wyoming border, near Fort Collins, and in the San Luis Valley. Anywhere, in fact, where there was grass and water to support large herds of bison.

A thousand years later, people of the Plano culture had refined bison hunting to a fine art, killing large numbers by herding them over cliffs. Some 200 bison were found at the Olsen Chabbuck "buffalo jump" in southeastern Colorado. Eventually, the giant bison, too, vanished, supplanted by modern bison of a much smaller size. And once again humans adapted, not only embracing the changing environment but

LEFT: an Arapaho Indian.
RIGHT: a painting depicts a cooperative buffalo hunt in the Wild West.

becoming expert in the great variety of plants and animals to be found there.

Man and nature

The extensive Archaic period may well have been the most successful in human history. Small bands wandered large, defined territories, stopping at favored campsites to hunt and harvest seasonally. It was a lifestyle that sustained the Utes of western Colorado for centuries – a perfect balance of man and nature.

Archaic people camped near springs, streams and rivers throughout Colorado, making use of rock shelters and portable hide tents known as

some now immersed under Curecanti Reservoir in the Gunnison River Valley, appear to date from this time. By 2000 BC, hunters were leaving split-twig fetishes of bighorn sheep in high cliffs where the sheep often traveled, perhaps hoping to attract the real thing. Shamans may also have undertaken long pilgrimages to sacred sites and painted images in red hematite on the walls: herds of bighorn sheep, flowing water and life-size, triangular figures with long thin bodies and huge, empty eyes that hovered wraithlike above dry sandy washes.

Archaic people were living in semicircular, underground homes with earthen roofs

wickiups. They hunted year-round, using snares and traps to capture small animals such as prairie dogs, rabbits and squirrels, and an atlatl, or spear-thrower, to bring down bison, deer, antelope, bighorn sheep and elk. In summer, they gathered prairie turnips, wild mustard, buffalo berries and plums on the plains, and harvested sweet, nutritious pinyon nuts from higher elevations. These wild plants were placed in woven baskets attached to a tumpline and strapped around the foreheads of women, who also carried babies this way.

A warming trend between 7,500 and 4,500 years ago may have encouraged some Archaic people to move to the Uncompahgre Plateau, where greater moisture supported more plants and animals. A number of sites, including

known as pithouses as early as 6,000 years ago. One 3,000-year-old pithouse was excavated east of Grand Junction. At this unusual site, archeologists uncovered a variety of wild ricegrass that had been cultivated to produce large seeds. By AD 100, the idea of growing food had also reached hunter-gatherers in the eastern Rockies, who were in contact with agricultural cultures in the Ohio Valley, from whom they learned home building and pottery made with a paddle and anvil.

Pueblo farmers

The tribes who lived along the Republican, Apishpa, Purgatoire, Arkansas and South Platte rivers remained hunter-gatherers until pressure from incoming tribes and European settlers doomed their way of life in the 1800s. But the Basketmakers, the first people to settle permanently among the cool mesas and perennial streams of the canyon country of the Four Corners, eagerly embraced farming.

Archeologist Christy Turner claims that Aztecs from Mexico used human sacrifice to subjugate Puebloans and engaged in cannibalism – a theory supported by the discovery of fossilized feces containing human remains.

By the early Pueblo I period (AD 700–900), extended families throughout the Four Corners were living in hamlets of above-ground houses made of sandstone and mud adobe. Pithouses were used as underground ceremonial rooms, or kivas. Here clansmen gathered to weave cotton and discuss the most advantageous times to plant and harvest. Ritual specialists tracked the daily movements of the sun, moon and planets across the sky. As the solstices approached, ceremonies were announced, and the priests quickly became the most important members of the village.

The Fremont

The people who lived in northwestern Colorado had much in common with their neighbors to the south. They too made pottery, grew corn, squash and, later, beans, and lived together in villages. But for them the hunter-gatherer lifestyle of their Archaic ancestors still beckoned. The Fremont are less obvious in the archeological record, perhaps because of their fondness for remote places. They developed a hardy strain of corn that suited the highlands, fashioned plain, utilitarian pottery, and made moccasins with the dew claw of a deer for traction.

Long after the Ancestral Puebloans of the Four Corners were building large stone villages, the Fremont found comfort in pithouses – by far the most practical shelter in the cold winters and warm summers of the high desert. Their rock art, too, echoed that of early Archaic people, with depictions of large-shouldered anthro-

LEFT: an archeological excavation of a kiva.
RIGHT: a reconstructed Basketmaker pithouse serves an educational purpose.

pomorphs and game animals and enigmatic figures like Kokopelli, the flute player. Hundreds of Fremont pictographs dot the Douglas Creek drainage, between Grand Junction and Rangely. More can be found throughout Dinosaur National Monument, in Echo Canyon and along the Green River near Dinosaur Quarry.

The Chaco phenomenon

By the Pueblo II period (900–1100), the Southwest was dominated by one major Pueblo group: the powerful Chaco civilization, centered on Chaco Canyon, New Mexico. Archeologists speculate that Chaco may have served

as a sort of Vatican City for people living in the San Juan Basin, just south of southwestern Colorado. Seasonal ceremonies at Chaco, and redistribution of trade goods from as far away as the Pacific, the Mississippi River and Mexico may have brought thousands to the remote canyon.

Satellite villages, or outliers, such as the Escalante Ruin at Anasazi Heritage Center, north of Cortez, and Chimney Rock, east of Durango, seem to have played roles in the Chaco system. Both served as pioneer Chaco communities in outlying areas, housed in typical Chaco *pueblos* with several kivas. The two distinctive rock formations at Chimney Rock seem to have been used by an isolated community of men living nearby. They apparently tracked the moon and cut high-country pines, which were floated down the Piedras River to Chaco for construction.

The Chaco culture crashed spectacularly in the early 1100s. Its leaders may have lost their power base during a long-running drought, leaving desperate farming families to their own devices. They fled to surrounding highlands, where resources were more plentiful, and clashed with existing residents. By the early Pueblo III period (1100–1300), the Montezuma Valley of southwestern Colorado had an estimated population of 30,000. Villages sprang up on every mesa with a stream. Lookout towers were built, perhaps to safeguard communities from outsiders.

These enclosed *pueblos* were hastily constructed, using large stones loosely mortared with mud, and some were now built in unusual shapes, such as the oval, circular, square and "D" shaped buildings at Hovenweep National Monument.

Mesa Verde

Just east of modern-day Cortez, Mesa Verde, an 8,517ft (2,596-meter) high plateau with warm southern exposures and stream-carved finger

MESOAMERICAN INFLUENCES

Mexican corn culture, pottery making and stone masonry construction techniques reached the Four Corners via traders from the south early in the Christian era. From the Hohokam, who practiced irrigation farming in southern Arizona, the Basketmakers may have acquired exotic goods from Mexico and learned to use check dams, ditches, and dry farming techniques. From the Mogollon of southern New Mexico, they learned how to make pots using the coiled clay method and to fire them at high temperatures to make strong, airtight containers for storing and transporting grain. The refined black-on-white pottery of the Four Corners became a prized trade item.

canyons, had been a popular farming spot for generations. When white settlers explored it in the late 1800s, they found more than 4,000 sites, from early pithouses and small *pueblos* to extensive fields and an unfinished, 12th-century ceremonial center on Chapin Mesa. Thousands of bowls, effigy pots, mugs, ladles and other black-on-white pottery lay among the ruins.

Beginning in the late 1100s and 1200s, residents of Mesa Verde left their mesa-top villages and moved into homes concealed in the cliffs. Inside warm, south-facing canyon walls, next to springs, they built some 600 cliff dwellings, ranging from small villages to major ceremonial centers, such as Cliff Palace, whose unusual tower kiva was probably used for astronomical observations. These cliff dwellings represented the last phase of Ancestral Pueblo life in the Four Corners. By 1300, the region was abandoned. Families moved south to New Mexico and Arizona to live along more reliable lands next to the Rio Grande and Little Colorado

> The prehistoric Southwest culture once known as the Anasazi are now known as the Ancestral Puebloans. Anasazi, a Navajo name meaning "enemy ancestors," is unacceptable to modern Pueblo people.

River. The inhabitants of 24 modern *pueblos* trace their ancestry to Mesa Verde.

At its height, Mesa Verde supported 5,000 people. By the end of the Great Drought of 1276–1300, Mesa Verde and the surrounding Montezuma Valley could no longer support the population. Without rain, fields didn't produce and wild foods disappeared. There must have been competition for what little remained. Violent episodes became more frequent.

The arrival of newcomers may have tipped the balance. Intriguing new evidence suggests that nomadic Athabascans from northwest Canada, who split into the Navajo and Apache tribes in the Southwest, were already in the area by the late 12th century. Utes from the Great Basin may have arrived soon after. These tribes vied for dominance in the areas abandoned by Ancestral Pueblo and Fremont farmers.

Plains culture

Just as farming transformed the lives of Pueblo people, horses revolutionized the lives of buffalo hunters on the Plains. Introduced by the Spanish in the late 17th century, horses were able to draw heavily laden sleds, or *travois*, from place to place. Men on horseback joined other groups to hunt bison over larger areas. They left for long periods, leaving behind their families to gather food, tan bison skins, and make clothing at encampments of hide-covered tents, or tipis.

A man's wealth was now counted by the number of horses he owned, and his success in

hunting bison and raiding other tribes for horses and slaves was vital to his status as a warrior. Warrior societies, such as the feared Cheyenne Dog Soldiers, grew up in Plains tribes, whose members performed feats of bravery during battle, such as touching their enemies (counting coup) and collecting scalps. Young men on vision quests fasted on mountain tops, seeking spiritual guidance. Most tribes practiced the Sun Dance, in which men fasted, danced, and pierced their flesh with hooks tied to a central pole – a sacrifice intended to benefit the whole tribe.

The first tribe to acquire horses in Colorado was probably the Ute, whose people were

widespread throughout Colorado in the 1600s. They fought the Navajo and eventually forced them to retreat into New Mexico and Arizona. In 1700, the Jicarilla Apaches in southeastern Colorado and Kansas were pushed into New Mexico by advancing Comanches from the north, armed with French guns. By 1775, the Comanche found themselves pushed south of the Arkansas River by Kiowa and Kiowa-Apaches. An alliance of Comanches, Kiowas and Kiowa-Apaches dominated the Southern Plains and inspired fear in the Pueblos of the Rio Grande as well as European settlers.

In the early 1800s, Arapahos displaced from the Great Lakes took up bison hunting on the Plains. They wandered the eastern Rockies,

ABOVE: Cliff Palace, which was abandoned in the late 13th century, is the largest cliff dwelling in North America, with more than 215 rooms and 23 kivas.
RIGHT: learning about the people of Mesa Verde.

camping seasonally in favorite spots in the Denver area and, along with Cheyenne and Sioux allies, raided Crows, Shoshones, Utes, Comanches and others.

French and American fur trappers now appeared in Colorado. Relations between traders and Indians were generally peaceful and resulted in important alliances. Trader William Bent married a Cheyenne woman. Their eastern-educated son George would survive the bloody Sand Creek Massacre of 1864 and provide an important eyewitness account of the atrocity. Another trader married a young Arapaho woman who taught English to her brother Niwot, or Left Hand. The multilingual Niwot became a highly respected leader dedicated to peaceful coexistence during the Indian Wars. It was near Bent's Fort, in 1840, that the Southern Arapaho and Cheyenne made permanent peace with the Kiowa and Comanche, following the devastating Battle of Wolf Creek in 1837.

Manifest Destiny

After Mexico ceded much of the Southwest to the United States in 1848, white–Indian relations grew increasingly strained. Over the next decade, gold was discovered in both California

NEUTRAL GROUND

No trip to Bent's Fort is complete without a stroll through the *bosque* shading the banks of the Arkansas River. It is pleasant to walk through tall grass edging the steep banks, past stands of willow and box elder, listening to cottonwood leaves fluttering overhead. A flat stem enables the leaves to turn 180 degrees in a slight breeze. In the days before air conditioning, people sat under the trees to enjoy the extra breath stirred up by the shivering leaves. The wind makes a distinctive sound as it soughs through these gnarly old trees with their stout trunks, splintered branches, and runneled bark.

It's easy to imagine hundreds of tipis pitched alongside the path of the river. William Bent reported that in the spring of 1842 thousands of Native Americans from half a dozen tribes were camped up and down the Arkansas within view of the fort. Bent's Fort was neutral ground, and all animosities, tribal and personal, were suspended for as long as the tribes were camped there.

The native people engaged in horse races, powwows, religious ceremonies and long trading sessions with the factors at the fort. Beads, blankets, kettles, knives, whiskey and guns were bartered for beaver pelts, buffalo hides, and Ute-made deerskin clothing. Young men used this lull in their normal lives to court young women, and at night the reedy tremolo of love flutes could be heard over the barking of dogs and the whinnying of horses.

and Colorado. Huge numbers of miners and settlers headed west on the Santa Fe and Oregon trails to seek their fortunes. They destroyed favorite Indian campsites with their cattle and homesteads and slaughtered buffalo by the millions, mostly for sport. Government policies instigated private ownership of what had once been communal lands, and native people were deprived of their livelihoods and forced to rely on meager handouts at government agencies. Worse still, whole bands contracted smallpox, measles and other European diseases, and warriors, unable to feed their families or hunt, became addicted to alcohol.

ple from attacking settlements, treaties were repeatedly broken by settlers. Indians had no recourse but to fight back, flee, or accept what was offered.

Tragedy followed tragedy. On November 29, 1864, trigger-happy Colorado volunteers led by Colonel John Chivington took matters into their own hands and slaughtered 137 innocent women, children and old men at Sand Creek, near the Arkansas River. Among them were chiefs Left Hand and White Antelope. The counterattacks lasted two years, until, in 1867, huge losses led Kiowa, Cheyenne, Southern Arapaho and Comanche leaders to sign the Medicine Lodge

Plains people grew increasingly desperate, and many young men turned to raiding white settlements in order to feed their starving families. The government took a hardline policy of rounding up tribes by whatever means necessary and placing them on reservations. Hunters were expected to take up farming, live with former enemies, own property, and give up their language and culture. For the nomadic tribes of Colorado, it was a disaster. As leaders such as Ouray, Black Kettle, White Antelope and Little Raven sought to restrain their peo-

Treaty confining their tribes to reservations in the Oklahoma and Kansas territories.

Many tribal members refused to go, but resistance proved futile. In November 1868, the Cheyenne leader Black Kettle, who had miraculously survived the massacre at Sand Creek, was shot down in cold blood by General George Armstrong Custer at Washita River, Oklahoma. Ten years later, the Northern Arapaho were moved to the Shoshone Reservation near the Wind River in Wyoming. The only tribe left in Colorado were the Utes, whose leaders – Ouray, Severo and Ignacio – were left with no choice but to breach the growing divide between their people and the gold-hungry whites flooding into Colorado. ❏

LEFT: mounted hunters pursue bison in Charles M. Russell's *The Buffalo Hunt No. 39*.
ABOVE: the Sand Creek Massacre.

BREAKING GROUND

From the 16th century onwards, Spaniards, the French and other strangers barged right in, reconfiguring the social landscape and rewriting a whole region's history

Colorado has plenty of spacious skies and purple mountain majesties but not a whole lot of modern history, especially as compared to a place like neighboring New Mexico. The latter was an important offshoot of New Spain, whereas Colorado was long considered remote and unpromising. Not until after the mid-19th century, when precious metals were mined and fortunes started piling up, did much development take place.

Spanish expeditions

The Ancestral Puebloan cliff dwellers of the Four Corners had abandoned the region long before, moving down to the better-watered Rio Grande and Little Colorado River by 1300. Now, only nomadic Utes and Navajos roamed the former homelands of the powerful Chaco and Mesa Verde cultures. Spanish presence was minimal, too. Some 20 years after transforming Mexico into New Spain, self-financed conquistadors arrived in North America, chasing supposedly fabulous riches. They blazed El Camino Real Trail from Mexico City to Santa Fe and Taos but did nothing to endear themselves to the numerous Indian tribes who had long used the lands, and quickly returned home.

Most famous of those Spanish pioneers was Francisco Vásquez de Coronado. In 1540, Coronado and a large force crossed into Arizona, then continued northeastward into New Mexico, seeking the supposedly fabulously wealthy "Seven Cities of C'bola." Disappointed by the modest *pueblos* they found at Zuni, Pecos,

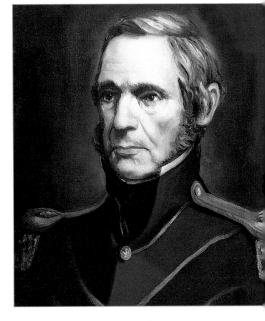

and elsewhere, they returned to Mexico City two years later, empty-handed and chastened. Misled by Pecos leaders about gold in Kansas, Coronado is thought to have traipsed across part of southeastern Colorado, leading the first recorded European expedition in Colorado.

Side expeditions covered a lot of ground, beheld wondrous sights, and bestowed place-names, including naming the great river laden with red sediments "the Colorado." But these gold-seekers were uninterested in starting settlements. That would come later, and only successfully in New Mexico. Colorado's fearsome nomadic Comanches and Utes would have not taken kindly to hewing wood, carrying water or

LEFT: a Cheyenne man, *c.*1910; the Cheyenne roamed the plains of eastern Colorado until the 1860s.
RIGHT: Stephen H. Long, leader of an 1820 expedition.

taking up farming on anyone's behalf.

Further Spanish expeditions to Colorado in the 17th century led to the discovery of various Indian settlements. Traders gradually ventured north, and by 1700 goods were being exchanged at settlements near present-day La

> In 1779, an army led by Juan Bautista de Anza pursued Comanche warrior Cuerno Verde through the San Luis Valley onto the plains below Pikes Peak. Cuerno Verde and many warriors perished in a bloody battle in the Greenhorn Mountains.

BEAVER.

Junta, a place on the Arkansas River close to the site where in later years Bent's Fort would become a landmark exchange place on the famous Santa Fe Trail for fur trappers, traders and mountain men.

The French connection

Others besides Spaniards showed up, chiefly French and English colonists, followed by representatives of the newly independent United States, a dynamic young republic which, as the 19th century dawned, began spreading across the continent.

Early on, Spain and France dueled for ownership of the region west of the Mississippi River now known as the Great Plains. This was a lot of land with a lot of natural resources, and it was claimed for France by the explorer La Salle in 1682. After leading a party of about 50 men downriver to the Gulf of Mexico, he grandly declared the entire territory between the Alleghenies and the Rockies to be the property of Louis XIV. Hence the name Louisiana.

A similar claim was made on Spain's behalf in 1706 by Juan de Uribarri, who frequently chased after Indian slaves fleeing their New Mexican masters. Concerned about possible French intrusion via the Mississippi River, Uribarri declared the region to be part of the Spanish realm.

Spanish authorities became obsessed with *voyageurs*. These were the trappers, often the offspring of French men and Indian women, who hunted beaver and other fur-bearing animals, conveying the pelts to market on canoe voyages. Fur was big business. Hats made of beaver fur were popular in Europe, and the trade played a major role in opening up the American West to settlement.

The turf was soon declared off-limits by Spanish overlords, quick to head off anything that smacked of trading activity. One such Spanish reaction in 1720 had disastrous results. An expedition under Pedro de Villasur, checking on reports that French settlers were infiltrating present-day eastern Colorado and Nebraska, was caught up in an ambush by Pawnee Indians at the Platte River in Nebraska. Villasur and almost his entire force were wiped out.

In the 18th century, French *voyageurs* roamed around a good part of the land that later was involved in the history-making Louisiana Purchase. The first known French explorers in the region were the Mallet brothers, Pierre and Paul, in 1739–41. Their expedition went from Canada to Santa Fe, where they spent nearly a year and wound up giving away all their goods, an action that has caused historians to suspect that what the Mallets were really interested in was sniffing out gold and silver mining deposits.

More Frenchmen came in the years ahead, traveling a route that, after Mexican independence in 1820, became the storied Santa Fe Trail. But overall their influence was minimal, and when the Seven Years' War was terminated in 1763, France was compelled to bow out of the American picture. The French ceded to Britain and Spain, respectively, territories east and west of the Mississippi River.

France did get back the western land, which included Colorado, in an 1801 agreement with Spain. But the restoration was short-lived. Two years later, the Louisiana Purchase brought an end to French designs on North America and the Lewis and Clark Expedition paved the way for American expansion westward.

The searchers

Colorado's awesome landscape came under scrutiny following the exploits of a couple of Franciscan friars from Santa Fe who embarked on a memorable if foolhardy journey to Monterey, California, in 1776. Padres Francisco

other activities, including searches for precious metals. Mining was key to their economic success elsewhere in the New World, so Spanish authorities made it a priority to seek out evidence of precious metals in the greater New Mexico territory.

An early effort at prospecting was made in 1765 when a group headed by Juan Maria de Rivera came north from Santa Fe to search for gold in the San Juan and northern Sangre de Cristo mountain ranges. Although unsuccessful, they were the first known outsiders to explore what eventually became known as the Gunnison River.

Dominguez and Silvestre Escalante, accompanied by eight friends, set off from Santa Fe in search of a shorter route between the missions of New Mexico and California. They roamed southwest Colorado and later described in print such vividly named places as the Sangre de Cristo (Blood of Christ) Mountains and El Rio de Las Animas Perdidas en Purgatorio (River of Lost Souls in Purgatory).

Spain's claim to the Colorado territory was reinforced through military expeditions and

LEFT: a common beaver, painted in 1814. ABOVE: Bent's Old Fort National Historic Site is a reconstruction of the original fort, built on the Arkansas River in 1832 as a trading center.

Westward ho!

Colorado's story takes a great leap forward with the Louisiana Purchase. That big deal added most of what is now eastern Colorado to the fledgling nation, although exactly where the boundary lay between the Spanish and American realms was left in doubt – was it the Arkansas River or was it the more southern Red River? It would take until 1850 for Colorado's physical shape to be configured once and for all.

One of those who went forth to chart the West's topography was a young army officer named Zebulon Montgomery Pike. In 1806, he headed a 22-man expedition instructed to gather information on the source of the Arkansas and Red rivers and on Spanish settlements in New Mexico. Traveling up the Arkansas to the vicinity of present-day Pueblo, the explorers spotted in the distance a tall snow-covered mountain later named Pikes Peak. It took them two weeks to reach the mountain, and when they tried to climb to the top, Pike and his men were unsuccessful.

Arrested by a Spanish military force, the Americans were interrogated and held for a time in Santa Fe and Chihuahua, Mexico. Pike was freed in July 1807. He died five years later in the War of 1812 in Canada. Another expedition led by a US Army officer, Major Stephen H. Long, went forth in 1820, this time at the bidding of President James Monroe. The instructions were to explore the southwest boundary of the territory acquired in the Louisiana Purchase. Long's group entered Colorado via the South Platte River and explored much of the Rockies' eastern flank.

The Long expedition's botanist and historian, Dr Edwin James, became the first to successfully scale Pikes Peak, which was given the name James Peak, but hunters and trappers persisted in calling it Pikes Peak and that name stuck.

Climb every mountain

The true western pioneers were trailblazers who operated as scouts and trappers. Known as plainsmen or mountain men, these rugged individualists pushed deep into the wilderness in search of beaver and other fur-bearing animals, and becoming the stuff of frontier legend.

Their names are well-known, among them Jim Bridger, Jim Beckwourth and Jim Baker, Tom "Broken Hand" Fitzpatrick and "Uncle Dick" Wootton, and the legendary Kit Carson, that all-purpose scout, fighter and Indian expert. Traversing a wide expanse, these prototypical free-traders forded streams and climbed mountains for furs and other items and in the process became intimate with the native inhabitants of the Colorado Rockies. Prices for beaver pelts soared in the 1820s and remained high until supplies diminished and the market collapsed in the late 1830s.

Carson was a familiar figure at one of the most famous of the western trading posts: Bent's Fort. The first Anglo settlement in what became Colorado, it was built in 1832 by William Bent, his three brothers and their partner Ceran St Vrain near the present-day city of La Junta. Indians, too, traded at this early mercantile establishment, and it was here in 1840 that an enduring peace agreement was hammered out at an extraordinary meeting of Arapaho, Kiowa, Cheyenne and Comanche chiefs.

Another busy trading post was Fort Vasquez, built for the Rocky Mountain Fur Company on the South Platte River north of what became the city of Denver. It was frequented by American trappers and hunters as well as members of Cheyenne and Arapaho tribes. In 1842, however, it was looted by Indian raiders. After the demand for beaver dried up, trading posts were generally abandoned. To protect isolated frontier settlements and trading routes, the federal

FRÉMONT AND THE BEAR FLAG REVOLT

Explorer John C. Frémont's task was to chart the West's virgin lands and note natural boundaries but he was something of a renegade hero. On June 13, 1846, he incited a home-grown Anglo–American rebellion in Mexican-owned Sonoma, California. Known as the Bear Flag Revolt, for the home-made flag depicting a grizzly bear flown by the republicans, the rebellion led to the rebels declaring a 26-day California Republic and installing a president. On June 23, Frémont took charge in the name of the United States, unaware that the US–Mexico War was already underway. In July, the US Navy sailed to California, captured Monterey, and took command. Frémont was court-martialed.

government put up a string of military forts.

Kit Carson lived for many years in Colorado. Having commanded a Union force in the Civil War, he was named to head Fort Garland, in the San Luis Valley, in 1866. He died two years later at nearby Fort Lyon. Carson served as guide to a public figure whose name ranks high in western annals, the flamboyant explorer John Charles Frémont.

Ah, wilderness!

Frémont's published reports, in lively and picturesque prose, excited curiosity about the nation's vast western expanse and natural wonders. Among their avid readers were Henry David Thoreau and the Mormon leader Brigham Young. Frémont's enthusiasm in print countered a kind of badlands view of Colorado that had taken hold in the public imagination since the days of Zebulon Pike and Stephen Long. The latter had basically written off the Colorado plains as a "Great American Desert" unfit for exploitation.

This appraisal was at odds with the grand vision of such as La Salle and the expansionist sensibility of Thomas Hart Benton, the senator from Missouri famously associated with the "Manifest Destiny" imperative – and father of the vivacious teenager with whom Frémont eloped. Jessie Benton Frémont, furthermore, turned out to be a talented writer who would greatly enhance her explorer husband's published reports and, later, his memoirs.

Thus – once he got over the shock of the elopement – was Senator Benton's purpose well served. Frémont's reportage excited interest in the edenic myth of the western landscape and its material promise. (It was the memoirs, so ably edited by Jessie Frémont, that served to fix Kit Carson's place firmly in the pantheon of American heroes.)

Sadly, Frémont's fourth expedition, in 1848, took a fearful toll in human life. Searching for a railroad route through the Rockies on Benton's behalf, he and his men became snowbound high in the La Farita Mountains of southern Colorado, and there were 11 deaths by starvation or freezing. Frémont's final expedition occurred in 1853, through the San Luis Valley and into the

Gunnison River country. Earlier that year the ill-fated Captain John W. Gunnison had come by while surveying a railroad route westward through the Colorado Rockies for the US War Department, before he and all but four of his men were slain in an attack in Utah attributed to Utes but likely orchestrated by Mormons.

In 1851, Hispanic settlers took advantage of Mexican land grants and moved into southern Colorado. They put down roots in Conejos in the San Luis Valley and this gave rise to the first permanent town of non-Indian origin in Colorado's history. Unfortunately, such manifestations of encroachment were embittering relations

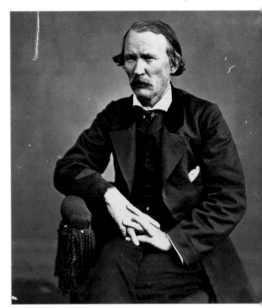

with native people, and in that valley Fort Massachusetts was established to protect settlers.

In 1848, thanks to the Treaty of Guadalupe Hidalgo, Mexico gave up most of the Colorado territory that was not acquired by the United States in the Louisiana Purchase. The territory figured only slightly in the US–Mexico War itself – in 1846 General Stephen W. Kearney's army used the Santa Fe Trail, in southeastern Colorado, en route to the annexation of New Mexico.

Colorado took final shape in 1850, when the federal government bought out the last of the territorial claims on it – in this case by Texas – and entered a volatile new era marked by extraordinary cycles of boom and bust. ❏

Left: John C. Frémont planting an American flag in the Rocky Mountains in an 1856 campaign illustration. **Right:** Kit Carson served as Frémont's guide.

STRIKING IT RICH

Eureka! A well-endowed territory yielded its treasures in the most boisterous chapter in Colorado history. Some got very rich indeed; many more were disappointed

The big discovery was that there was "gold in them thar hills" and streams out West, including Colorado, with its boulder-strewn creeks and mountains. The era began famously in early 1848 when a gleaming nugget was pulled from a ditch at John Sutter's mill in California, and a decade later it was Colorado's turn – gold dust was panned from the creeks. Suddenly, what had been a so-called Great American Desert that fronted on an enormous mountain range now was looking like some luxuriously enticing El Dorado.

Going for gold

It was about time. Treasure-hunters had been coming up dry here ever since Coronado's expedition. But intimations of gold persisted. Traces were reported here and there, such as along the Rio Grande south of present-day Colorado, by early Spanish colonizers. Precious metal and minerals were sought in the 18th century in places like the Sangre de Cristo and San Juan mountain regions. Early in the 19th century a trapper told Zebulon Pike, the Army officer who had been sent forth to map the Louisiana Territory, of gold traces spotted in the South Platte River area.

Nuggets plucked from streams were reportedly shown to William Bent by passers-by at Bent's Fort, that prototypical rest stop on the Santa Fe Trail. William Gilpin, who later became Colorado's first territorial governor, searched Rocky Mountain streams for it as a young man. But few people stayed for long,

LEFT: a Denver & Rio Grande locomotive steams through Royal Gorge. **RIGHT:** panning for gold near Clear Creek, *c.*1890.

at least until 1851 when some New Mexicans put down roots on fertile land in the San Luis Valley and injected an Hispanic-Catholic flavor into the southern Colorado region that has resonated ever since.

Also coming by were hordes of Forty-niners with pans and pickaxes and a bad case of that "California fever" sweeping the world. Making their way across the Plains, these gold-diggers either tried to skirt the obtrusive Rockies blocking their path or else seized the opportunity to poke around in the region while en route to the promised land. One particular group came from the east in 1850 via the Santa Fe Trail to the Pikes Peak region, sifted some gold dust at a creek off the South Platte River close to today's downtown Denver, and then decided to keep pressing on to California.

The latter experience partly inspired an 1858 expedition involving William Green Russell that was considerably more successful. A native

> The 1858 discovery of gold in Cripple Creek in Colorado was especially welcome to Americans. It came on the heels of the economic panic of 1857, which brought hard times as banks and factories were forced to shut down.

Georgian who had been in the Forty-niner quest, Russell was accompanied by two brothers and some other prospectors. Setting out from Georgia, where one of the early gold rushes had taken place in 1828–30, Russell and the others panned doggedly at a place off the South Platte called Cherry Creek before hitting "pay dirt." Before long, they were piling up bags of gold dust.

The news spread fast. Pikes Peak in what was then known as the Kansas Territory became fixed in the public imagination, a bit imperfectly, as the place where all the gold was. Fortune-seekers began flocking there, most of them from east of the Great Plains. Many of their wagons were emblazoned with banners: PIKES PEAK OR BUST. Inevitably, perhaps, a

measure of disbelief set in and the euphoria dissipated as a reverse wave of luckless prospectors headed back home, their banners now telling a different story: BUSTED, BY GOD.

Nonetheless, there were two new discoveries made in 1859 about 40 miles (64km) to the west, at a place called Clear Creek, in a canyon of the Rockies' Front Range. The excitement started all over again.

One discovery was by George A. Jackson, a Missouri trader – and cousin of Kit Carson – who in January stumbled upon a gold nugget and some gold dust near a place called Idaho Springs. The second and more substantial strike was by John H. Gregory, another native Georgian. He and his comrades dug out crumbled rock and earth while picking and shoveling along the sides of a stream on May 6, 1859. Immersed in the icy stream water, the cleansed dirt yielded a pan of gleaming gold amid much jubilation.

The place quickly boomed into Central City. For a time it rivaled Denver itself, before fading as a ghost town. Prospectors poured into the region from the Mississippi Valley, the Midwest, the East, everywhere. What became Denver grew almost overnight from the crude settlement at the juncture of the South Platte River and Cherry Creek into a major supply center. It took its name from the governor of the Kansas Territory, James W. Denver.

It was General William H. Larimer Jr, a native Pennsylvanian following on the heels of William Green Russell's expedition, who laid out "Denver City" by picking a tract on the east side of Cherry Creek and marking its center with cottonwood sticks. The date was November 22, 1858. On the other side of the creek was the rival camp of Auraria – Latin for "gold" – named after Russell's home town in gold-infused Georgia. Both camps grew rapidly.

Going with the flow

Within a year some $18 million in gold was extracted in the Clear Creek area. Middlemen profited by supplying the food, clothing and liquid spirits it was necessary to stock up on while roughing it in the hills, not to mention wagons, lumber, tools and much more. Denver and Auraria prospered. They merged in 1860 to become the "Queen City of the Rockies," the mile-high Denver destined for status as the leading urban center in the western expanse that stretches from Plains to Pacific.

Tent stores and log saloons sprang up along the muddy streets of raw new towns. Visitors from the East attracted by word of the so-called "camp cure" were fitted out in Denver with wagons, tents and bedding for their sojourn into the mountains. There were exotic street scenes and types – band music, spectator sports, Native Americans, nattily garbed English sportsmen, urbane dudes from Eastern cities. Population mushroomed – Leadville's hitting a peak of 40,000 by 1880; Denver's more than tripling by 1890 to 106,000.

Saloons, dance halls, gambling parlors and brothels became commonplace. Prospectors prospectors. Starting in the late 1860s and into the 1870s, rich veins of silver – "white metal" – were discovered. One early locale was Georgetown, west of Denver. It was the most important silver camp in Colorado before the fabulous discovery at Leadville in 1878.

Still more lay ahead – copper, lead, zinc, iron, bismuth, manganese, molybdenum. Like the old-time mountain men, prospectors followed icy streams into high terrain. Water was always necessary for cleaning and, more importantly, smelting, as that vital mining process was introduced. Costs grew as the focus shifted from sifting in streams to locating and extracting veins

who worked with single-minded diligence in less than healthful conditions came out of the hills for rest and recuperation, seeking spirits and scant lodging at inflated prices – $1 to share a bed in a makeshift room of beds at a flophouse. Gold detritus was a common currency – a pinch of gold dust between thumb and forefinger equaled 25 cents.

More gold brought more boomtowns – Golden, Gold Hill, Boulder, Fairplay, Colorado City. And when the easy-to-find surface deposits became exhausted, fortune kept smiling on

LEFT: miners in Ouray County, c.1920.
ABOVE: pioneers make camp in the foothills of the Rocky Mountains near Colorado Springs, c.1875.

of ore often deeply embedded in the earth. This required the kind of capital best provided by large financial interests. Smelters were installed and railroad tracks put down in usually difficult, high-altitude terrain. Single-gauge railways of narrower dimension were introduced for shipping ore and moving supplies to high-altitude locales. It was hard, dangerous work. Avalanches were one hazard, fire another – towns of wood-frame structures hastily thrown together were subject to conflagration.

Railroads became an important factor in conveying men and metals and opening up the territory to wider and wider development. Although the all-important Union Pacific line was routed through Cheyenne, Wyoming, 12 miles (19km) to the north, a spur was constructed to link Colorado with that transcontinental rail corridor in 1870. This was the Denver Pacific Railroad. Two years later came completion of another important line, the Denver & Rio Grande, which connected central and southern Colorado.

In the San Juan region, the Rio Grande Southern and the Silverton Northern railroads were built under the leadership of Otto Mears, a Russian-born immigrant who had come to America as a 10-year-old orphan. Mears also constructed a toll road over Poncha Pass to the Arkansas River valley and went on to erect

Madams and millionaires

Immigrants came to Colorado from many points, domestic and foreign, as towns arose out of the wilderness, places such as Creede, South Park, Telluride, Silver Plume, Silverton and, most famously, Leadville. At 10,188ft (3,105 meters), fairly high up in the Rockies of central Colorado, Leadville came to be called "Cloud City."

It was at the center of an area where first gold and then, in the 1870s, huge slabs of silver carbonate were discovered. Before the good times ran out, the silver yield alone was worth hundreds of millions of dollars. Such a

hundreds of miles of roads, notably the "Million Dollar Highway" over Red Mountain Pass, connecting Silverton and Ouray. He became known as the "Pathfinder of the San Juans" and went on to serve in the Colorado legislature.

The railroads tended to lessen the immensity of the nation's western region in the public's imagination. In addition, they lowered travel costs as well as the time it took to traverse distances once regarded as virtually insuperable. Land became cheaper, too, as railroads publicized the availability of large tracts in order to stimulate settlement. Agricultural settlements were planted throughout the South Platte Valley, and railway extension into the territory also had the effect of mitigating the threat posed by hostile Indians.

bonanza attracted thousands of settlers. In just a few months the population shot up to 24,000, including a good number of millionaires and madams – Leadville at one point had a bordello for every 148 inhabitants.

One of the most famous of the Leadville success stories was Horace Tabor, a Vermont-born miner whose good luck brought him a fortune. He took up with and then married the divorcee "Baby Doe", served in the US Senate, built opera houses that presented such headliners as Lily Langtry, Sarah Bernhardt and Oscar Wilde – and then lost everything in the crash of 1893. By the time of his death six years later his wife and family were living in a much diminished state.

Getting organized

Meanwhile, political jurisdictions were being carved out as early as 1858, when Miners' Courts were set up to resolve the inevitable and often violent disputes over land, stakes and claims. A part of the Kansas Territory was carved out as Arapahoe County, followed by a short-lived entity variously known as Jefferson Territory or Jefferson State. In 1859, Congress responded to pleas that Colorado be admitted to the Union by establishing the Colorado Territory as a prelude to statehood.

Official status as a territory was proclaimed on February 28, 1861, by Abraham Lincoln, whose presidency was about to be burdened with a ferocious Civil War. Lincoln handed the reins of office to William Gilpin as Colorado's first governor. Seventeen counties were created and Colorado City was designated the capital, a distinction that soon passed to Denver and has stayed there since 1867.

On native ground

The Civil War proved to be an aggravating factor in the relationship between native and settler. That relationship was already strained with the influx of fortune-seekers that was transforming the environment. In 1860, the first enumeration of Colorado's highly fluid population counted some 34,000 people. In just two years of the 1860s, the mining rushes brought an estimated 100,000 newcomers to the Colorado plains and mountains. They overran the land, destabilized old ways of life and added insult to injury by disdaining native culture.

The preoccupation with military engagement in other theaters, compounded by the absence of miners who had returned home for army service, left isolated ranches and settlers in the Colorado Territory unprotected from attack by hostile Plains Indians. Hostility intensified in 1862 as Cheyenne and Arapaho warriors harassed settlers and prospectors, attacking wagon trains and ranches and disrupting traffic and supplies on overland corridors like the Santa Fe Trail.

An attempt was made to bring together tribal chiefs for a peace council to iron out differences. What resulted instead was the Sand Creek Massacre of 1864, one of the most notorious of the bloody incidents recorded in the annals of western history.

Sand Creek was a small stream marking the boundary of a barren patch of land that served as an Indian reservation southeast of Denver. Encamped at the reservation in the autumn of 1864 was a band of Cheyenne people under Black Kettle as well as Arapaho natives led by Left Hand. Both chiefs had disdained the violent acts committed by native marauders and sought the help of Fort Lyon's commander, Major Edward Wynkoop. He promised protection while terms for better relations were worked out, and gave them food and supplies.

THE CIVIL WAR IN COLORADO

Colorado governor William Gilpin was a staunch supporter of the Union during the Civil War, but his loyalty proved costly. He was forced out in 1862 for exceeding his authority in issuing drafts on the national treasury on behalf of a military force – largely raised by himself – to represent the territory in the war. (Gilpin was replaced by John Evans, who himself would be ousted after the notorious Sand Creek Massacre of 1864.) Later, the First Regiment of Colorado helped resist Confederate advances, especially in the important engagement at Glorieta Pass in New Mexico, near Santa Fe, that put an end to the South's designs on the West's gold.

LEFT: the Silverton toll road connected mining camps in the San Juan Mountains to the outside world.
RIGHT: the ill-fated silver baron Horace Tabor.

But peace was not the goal of officials more in sync with a public mood enraged by the depredations of Native Americans, especially officials with political ambitions like Colorado's Territorial Governor John Evans or Colonel John M. Chivington, the "fighting parson." Chivington, a Methodist minister and Colorado hero for his resistance to Confederate incursion at Glorieta Pass in New Mexico, is said to have preached with Bible and six-shooter at hand.

Chivington launched a severe anti-Indian policy, eschewing any distinction between peaceful or hostile natives. The sympathetic Wynkoop was replaced, and Black Kettle was

GOLD DIGGERS OF 1859

The flow of people moving West as precious metals were unearthed in California, Colorado, and elsewhere constitutes one of the great American migrations. Horace Greeley, editor of the *New York Tribune*, reported on Colorado's lively camp scene for his readers. The sobersided editor, while inspecting the "Kansas gold fields," wrote with dismay in June 1859 of the "log city" of 150 dwellings at Cherry Creek (Denver) that was the scene of "more brawls, more fights, more pistol shots with criminal intent" than any place of comparable size. He found similar frenzy elsewhere in that hectic year of 1859 when fortune-seeking prospectors swamped the territory.

forced to confine his Cheyenne band to the Sand Creek strip. This was for the tribe's own safety, the chief was told. In fact, a force of about 700 volunteer soldiers was on the way from Denver, under Chivington's command.

At dawn on November 29, the Third Colorado Volunteers launched a surprise attack on the Sand Creek encampment, gunfire awakening most of its inhabitants. What followed was the slaughter of some 150 people, mostly women and children. Their mutilated body parts would be waved triumphantly in Denver to raucous cheers.

Elsewhere in the nation, however, there was outrage and widespread condemnation over the wanton massacre. Chivington's expedient resignation from the Army saved him from punishment, and Governor Evans resigned as well.

End of the trail

One final obstacle remained before fortune-seekers could exploit the land for all it was worth: the Ute Indians. They comprised several bands whose traditional native habitat was western Colorado and eastern Utah, and their turf was increasingly being overrun by miners. Skillful both as equestrians and mountain people, they hunted deer, elk and antelope, roamed east across the Rockies to pursue buffalo on the Plains, and delighted in racing huge herds of horses across the open landscape.

Their isolation ensured a peaceful existence, until the inevitable conflict caused by a wave of prospectors at once determined and fearful of the "savages" blocking progress. Acts of horse thievery and murderous atrocity by lawless native people fed resentment in mining-suffused places like Denver, and the press helped foster a public sentiment whose undisguised message was "the Utes must go!"

A treaty was negotiated in 1863, thanks largely to the efforts of Chief Ouray, the exceptionally talented Ute leader. It promised 16 million acres (6.5 million hectares) for a vast Ute reservation in western Colorado. With the occurrence of rich new strikes, however, this was reduced when the Utes were prevailed on to sell back 4 million acres (1.6 million hectares) at a bargain price. The treaty was again undermined when strained relations between the federal Indian Bureau and the Utes turned deadly.

As agents persisted in efforts at domesticating and reining in these seminomadic people, a band of northern Utes in 1879 took out their frustration on Indian Bureau agent Nathan C. Meeker at the White River Agency. Originally one of Greeley's editors at the *New York Tribune*, Meeker had been the guiding force behind the establishment of Union Colony, a farming cooperative northeast of Denver that established the first irrigation project in Colorado.

Meeker and six others were killed and three women taken as hostages. The marauding Utes then took on a detachment of army cavalry that had been sent to help Meeker with his domestication effort. Fourteen soldiers were killed and many wounded. Chief Ouray and Otto

economic enterprises: cattle raising. Cattle men took their herds north from Texas to Colorado's eastern plains, where the animals grazed before being shipped to meatpacking centers, Chicago in particular. One emerging entrepreneur was John Wesley Iliff, "cattle king of the Plains."

Iliff had some 50,000 head of cattle grazing over a wide region along the South Platte River. A thirst for western adventure had propelled this native Ohioan to the fledgling Cherry Creek gold camp in 1859, and shortly afterward he decided to invest in a small herd of cattle.

Iliff's fortune grew, as did that of another cattle baron, John Wesley Prowers. A native

Mears worked out a truce, and the hostages were released, unhurt though not unmolested. Federal officials used the incident to lay aside the treaty and confine the Utes to small holdings in Utah and eventually southwestern Colorado. By the time of Chief Ouray's death in 1880, of natural causes, the days of an unbridled way of life for Colorado's native people were effectively over.

On the cattle trail

The gold rush of 1859 indirectly provided the stimulus for another of Colorado's important

LEFT: John Chivington led an unprovoked attack on Cheyenne and Arapaho Indians at Sand Creek in 1864. **ABOVE:** the aftermath of the Meeker massacre.

Missourian, Prowers went to work, while still in his teens, for William Bent, who had set up a trading center in 1832, and became a successful stock raiser and dealer who controlled 400,000 acres (162,000 hectares), opened a slaughterhouse in southern Colorado, and shipped meat to the East. Also emerging in this period was the Denver Union Stockyards, established in 1886 and quickly becoming the nation's largest sheep market.

Population grew steadily as the 19th century wound down, reaching 413,249 by 1890 – more than twice what it had been a decade earlier and a far cry from the 1870 total of 39,864. Railroads were an important stimulus, as reflected by the terminals that went up in a wave of emerging structures and institutions. Denver got a telegraph link with the East in 1863, phones in 1878, electric lights in 1883. Colorado Seminary, forerunner of the University of Denver, was established in 1864, while Colorado State University at Fort Collins dates

> British investors were attracted to the Colorado cattle industry, which thrived in the Arkansas and South Platte river valleys. Cattle kingdoms evolved by the 1880s into large ranch companies with operations from Texas to Colorado.

to 1870. Then came Colorado College at Colorado Springs in 1874. Still another new school, the University of Colorado at Boulder, held its first classes in 1877.

The booming prosperity brought theaters, hotels, commercial emporiums, and public buildings. Grandly constructed opera houses went up in mining towns such as Leadville and Aspen as well as in Denver. President Ulysses S. Grant signed the legislation which on August 1, 1876, granted Colorado admission to the Union as its 38th state. It thereupon became known as the "Silver State" and, more officially, the "Centennial State" – the nation was celebrating 100 years of independence that summer.

The first governor was John L. Routt, for whom Routt National Forest in central Colorado would be named. The state was entering its headiest period between 1876 and 1893, when suddenly everything fell apart.

The big chill

Silver prices took a nose-dive in that panic year of 1893, and Colorado took it especially hard. The problem was that huge amounts of the precious metal coming out of western mines were flooding the world's markets, undermining price stability by putting the gold standard in jeopardy. This did not sit well with the power brokers in the big financial houses back East and elsewhere.

For them, gold was the only measuring stick that mattered. Impassioned arguments for a policy of bi-metallism – silver and gold – by such as Henry Moore Teller, who represented Colorado in the US Senate, failed to persuade his Republican colleagues. In an attempt to rejuvenate the national economy, Congress in November 1893 repealed the Sherman Silver Purchase Act it had approved just three years earlier. That policy, which authorized the US Treasury to purchase so much silver per month, had raised the white metal's price to more than $1 an ounce.

Congress's action crippled the mining industry, worsened the state's already severe rate of unemployment, and brought an end to the heady prosperity that marked the 1880s in Colorado. Newly coined millionaires in towns like Aspen, where silver had been discovered in 1879, saw their fortunes wiped out.

In disgust, Teller deserted his Grand Old Party for the Democrats, who made the whole money question a potent, though unsuccessful, campaign issue in 1896 under presidential contender William Jennings Bryan. "You shall not crucify mankind upon a cross of gold!" Bryan thundered in his famous speech accepting the nomination.

The only silver lining – gold, actually – was the bonanza that occurred at Cripple Creek. A mining probe at Bob Womack's cattle ranch there in 1891 unearthed a fabulous lode that would soon make the place famous as one of the world's richest gold centers. Eventually, gold production amounted to half a billion dollars.   ❏

LEFT: Ouray (center) and other Ute leaders, c.1868. Ouray led the efforts to live peacefully with the US Government.

Wild About Oscar

In one of the strangest lecture tours in literary history, celebrated wit Oscar Wilde toured America in 1882 and drew appreciative audiences in Colorado's mining towns

I t was a most unlikely gathering that took place on April 13, 1882, in Leadville, Colorado. Here was the young Oscar Fingal O'Flahertie Wills Wilde, aesthete and rising star of London's smart set, putting away drink after drink with the working-class guys down in the depths of the Matchless Mine owned by Horace ("Silver King") Tabor.

The bibulous Mr Wilde emerged from his underground experience no worse for wear. The miners pronounced the Irish visitor "a perfect gentleman," while Tabor opened a new shaft in his honor – "The Oscar." Of the many memorable moments in Wilde's year-long safari through darkest America in 1882, this one surely ranked high.

Oscar Wilde's outlandish garb and wit had attracted public notice in Britain, and he and theatrical impresario Richard D'Oyly Carte were seeking to capitalize on it with an American lecture tour. Wilde arrived in New York after his maiden voyage across the Atlantic, claiming he found the ocean "disappointing" and telling the customs officer he had nothing to declare "but my genius."

Wilde jested his way cross-country, reportedly saying of the tempestuous Mississippi, "No well-behaved river ought to act that way." He reached Colorado on April 12, lecturing that night from the stage of Tabor's new opera house, then it was on to Leadville, Colorado Springs and back to Denver again for a fourth straight night of preaching on the importance of being artful. In Leadville, he stayed next door at the Clarendon Hotel where Tabor had installed his young paramour, Baby Doe, in an elegant suite.

A standard lecture topic was "The Practical Application of the Aesthetic Theory to Exterior and Interior House Decoration, with Observations on Dress and Personal Ornament." Gaudily attired in frilly white neck-handkerchief, silk knee breeches, silk stockings and patent-leather pumps, Wilde poked fun at American sartorial drabness by declaring the

miners "the best dressed men in America." Visiting a Leadville saloon, he remarked favorably on a sign reading: "Please do not shoot the pianist. He is doing his best." Here, he said, was succinct recognition "that bad art merits the penalty of death... the only rational method of art criticism I have ever come across."

How much his creative flair and poetic license colored the remembrances he later put to paper is uncertain, but there were some good lines all the same. Wilde claimed that he read from the pages of the autobiography of Benvenuto Cellini, the Renaissance artisan, and was pressed by the unlettered miners as to why Cellini had not come

along on the tour. Told that Cellini was long dead, the miners are supposed to have asked: "Who shot him?"

Wilde was the object of a prankish diversion at the start of his Colorado visit, courtesy of the muck-raking *Denver Tribune* editor Eugene Field. As interest in Wilde's impending visit mounted, Field took it upon himself to deflate some of the mystique surrounding this reputedly cultured visitor. He donned longish wig and fur-trimmed overcoat and arrived at the Denver railway station just ahead of Wilde's scheduled time of arrival.

Field was thus mistaken for Wilde and whisked off grandly through town in a carriage. By the time the real Oscar Wilde arrived, no crowd was on hand to greet him. ❑

RIGHT: Oscar Wilde was a hit with Colorado miners.

CHANGING FORTUNES

Beyond mines and metals lay other natural resources,
and they were cultivated in a variety of ways
as a fledgling state invented itself

Colorado has a checkered history. Plenty of ups and downs, boom and bust. Gold and silver camps flourished, then faded into ghost towns when the treasure ran dry or the bottom dropped out of the market. To survive it was necessary to adapt, which is what Coloradans did, and still do, as they seek new ways to take advantage of their plentiful resources.

In the early years of the 20th century, agriculture surpassed mining as the state's chief economic enterprise. There was abundant fertile farmland in Colorado's eastern plains region, land that would yield a bounty of wheat, corn, soybeans and much else. What was always crucial was water, brought in by irrigation systems devised to overcome the problem of insufficient rainfall and the inconvenient fact that so much of the moisture needed was far off in the headlands of the western slope.

Tapping water

Irrigation schemes were undertaken, from simple diversion of water in streams and creeks to large-scale projects requiring heavy outlays of federal money and local labor. Thus did agriculture and animal husbandry flourish. Wheat was sown, fruits and vegetables grown, cattle raised, dairy goods produced. One important crop was potatoes. They burgeoned in the mid-1880s, and by 1890 more than 2,000 carloads of potatoes were being shipped by rail each year to the crowded East. Beet sugar became important, too, after a couple of pioneer Lead-

ville merchants, Charles Boettcher and John F. Campion, got together with some others and formed the Great Western Sugar Company. A refinery was built in 1899 at Grand Junction, soon followed by another one at Fort Collins. Sugar beets were cultivated on thousands of acres in Colorado's northeastern and east-central sections. Greeley and Fort Morgan were two other important centers.

Great Western was a bustling agribusiness by the 1920s, and Boettcher prospered as a builder and industrialist. Born in Germany in 1852, he had come to America as a teenager, later purchasing the landmark Brown Palace Hotel in Denver, among many ventures. He died in Den-

---

LEFT: miners in the Ajax Mine near Cripple Creek, posing in and around an elevator, or cage.
RIGHT: dancers pose at Denver's amusement park, Elitch Gardens, *c.* 1930.

ver in 1948 after a long life that spanned the years from Andrew Jackson to Harry Truman.

Meanwhile, the first major federal reclamation project in Colorado got under way in 1903. Its chief feature was the horseshoe-shaped Gunnison Diversion Tunnel, which conveyed water several miles from the Gunnison River to the Uncompahgre Valley.

By 1910, Colorado had more than 46,000 farms and the state ranked first in the nation in land under irrigation – nearly 2.8 million acres (1.1 million hectares). Agriculture remained the leading economic money-maker until it was surpassed in later years by manufacturing.

The state did benefit, at least, from relief programs in the 1930s and beyond. One big undertaking was the Colorado-Big Thompson Project carried out by the US Bureau of Reclamation. Relying on a system of dams, the project diverted water from the headstreams of the Colorado River and across the Continental Divide to irrigate about 720,000 acres (291,400 hectares) of land in the state's northeastern area and supply power for the region. The work went on from 1938 to 1956. Another major enterprise was the Fryingpan-Arkansas Project, authorized in 1962 and also conveying water over a long distance to the Arkansas River valley for public use.

The Gunnison Diversion Tunnel took six years to build and cost $2.9 million. On hand for the tunnel's opening in 1909 was William Howard Taft, who was at that time the nation's chief executive.

There were, however, some lean years for farmers after the inflationary euphoria of World War I. In the early 1920s, prices dropped sharply and rural areas suffered. They suffered again in the 1930s thanks to a lengthy spell of rough weather. Extended drought and high winds, for example, caused severe soil erosion in southeastern Colorado, compounding Depression misery.

Metals and minerals

Mining remained an important activity even though the fervor of the early gold and silver rushes abated. There were some new gold strikes, and fulsome discoveries of zinc and copper. In 1918, miners from nearby Leadville dug into deposits of molybdenum – "moly," as everybody called it. Mistaken at first for lead, it is in fact valuable as a hardening agent in the production of steel. The mine at Climax, near Leadville, accounted for a big part of the total world output of molybdenum before the decline of steel production shut it down in the 1990s.

Many other minerals and fuels were extracted, including tungsten, uranium, petroleum and natural gas. Petroleum, the state's leading fuel resource, was found on both the eastern and western slopes. Coal was abundant, too, in both northern and southern Colorado. A record amount of it was dug up in 1918 – 12½ million tons. Unfortunately, coal mining was at the center of increasingly strained relations between corporate overlords and earthy miners, many of the latter being foreign immigrants.

Resentment festered in the early part of the 20th century over wages and workplace hazards, especially involving laborers in mine operations. For example, two mine disasters in 1910, at Primero and Delagua, took 153 lives. Bitterness simmered, sometimes spilling over

coal miners evicted from company homes for striking, and John D. Rockefeller's Colorado Fuel & Iron Corporation.

National Guardsmen and security guards employed by Rockefeller and associates attacked a colony of coal miners and their families holed up in tents at Ludlow, near Trinidad, in southern Colorado. The strike by thousands of workers had begun in September 1913 following the murder of a labor organizer. The tent camp was set ablaze by the attackers, who then opened fire on its panicky inhabitants, levying the deadly toll. News of the onslaught spread quickly among labor circles, and 10 days of gunfire

into deadly violence, as in a strike at the Cripple Creek gold field in 1903. The worst moment came in 1914 with the Ludlow Massacre.

Massacre at Ludlow

The trouble started just before dawn on April 20, the day after Easter Sunday. Before it was over, 20 people lay dead, including two women and 11 children who suffocated in a makeshift cellar beneath a tent. It was the climax of a bitter seven-month strike and one of the blackest days in Colorado's history. The antagonists were

LEFT: ore processing factory, c.1905.
ABOVE: Miners widen the Breast of Gold Standard Tunnel in Teller County, c.1900.

followed. The final toll in the savage 1913–14 Colorado Coal Field Strike was 74 dead.

It was widely perceived as unbridled class warfare, which shocked newspaper readers across the country. The only saving grace, as historians see it, was that the bloodshed probably helped inspire reforms in labor-relations practice and influenced management to begin looking more benignly on collective bargaining and negotiation as a necessary means to resolving workplace issues.

Making progress

Reform was in the air in that progressive era, and Colorado seemed a likely proving ground for its propositions. It had already, in 1893, become the second state in the nation to approve women's suffrage – the right to vote – as in 1924 it would become the second state to approve the federal child-labor amendment. The city of Denver in 1907 instituted the first Juvenile Court in America. In 1910, Colorado voters added the good-government principle of initiative and referendum to the state constitution. And the period brought other such innovations, including workers' compensation and, for state employees, civil service status.

Physical improvements were being made, too, as the state began rolling out the welcome mat for visitors. Denver banker David H. Moffatt and

began construction of concrete highways along its main travel corridors.

A fortress state

The military presence in Colorado went back to the frontier forts charged with protecting traders, travelers and settlers. But it was the military presence that resulted from World War II that most affected the state's development. More than 70,000 residents were inducted into the armed services, and the private sector kept busy meeting the nation's extraordinary need for metals, minerals and manufactured goods, as well as agricultural products. But it was Colo-

associates began pressing in 1902 for a rail line traversing the Continental Divide. It led 25 years later to completion of the 6.4-mile (10.3km) Moffatt Tunnel, at an altitude of 9,094ft (2,772 meters), beneath James Peak on the Continental Divide, west of Denver. Used by the Denver & Rio Grande Railway, it put Colorado for the first time on a direct transcontinental rail route.

A toll road for motorists intent on ascending Pikes Peak was built in 1915, two years before Colorado issued its first automobile license. The year 1915 also saw the creation of Rocky Mountain National Park as a federal preserve. In 1918, the Denver city administration set aside Overland Park as an auto campground for free use by tourists. And in 1921 the state

rado's emergence as a base of defense-related operations that transformed its socioeconomic profile. In 1937 the federal government opened a field school near Denver for Army Air Corps training in aerial photography and bombing in an area that encompassed 64,000 acres (26,000 hectares). It became Lowry Field. Then, during the war, more bases and installations sprang up – including, unhappily, a camp on the Kansas border where some 10,000 Japanese-Americans were interned for the duration of the war.

Camps, arsenals, ordnance centers and aviation bases were created. Fort Carson was established as an Army reservation in 1942 on an enormous tract of land at the southern edge of Colorado Springs. A dozen years later, Colorado was chosen as the site for an Air Force Academy to complement the traditional Army, Navy and Coast Guard institutions. It was based at Lowry Air Force Base in Denver until relocating to Colorado Springs in 1958 and graduating its first class there a year later.

Colorado Springs became the base of operations as well for the North American Air

> American poet Katharine Lee Bates, moved by her experience atop Pikes Peak in 1893, penned her classic America the Beautiful.

has led to major cleanup efforts to ease the fear of contamination from chemicals and other hazardous waste at places like Rocky Flats near Boulder and elsewhere, an ongoing situation.

Fun and majesty

In the years after World War II, the state began to enjoy an enhanced reputation as a recreational haven. Visitors had long been inspired by the majestic landscape. Among them were 19th-century artists like Albert Bierstadt, famous for his idealized depictions of western landscapes in paintings like *Storm in the Rocky Mountains*.

The creation of national parks such as Mesa

Defense Command, established in 1957 and hunkering down in a cave burrowed into Cheyenne Mountain. The state, a third of whose land is owned by the federal government, is home to many scientific enterprises, including the National Center for Atmospheric Research at Boulder, and leading schools like the University of Colorado, the Colorado School of Mines, Colorado State University and the University of Denver. Concerns about pollution arising out of the weapons plants and military-related manufacturing activity of the post-war period

LEFT: striking miners armed for confrontation with National Guardsmen during the Ludlow Massacre.
ABOVE: cowboys in the San Luis Valley, 1909.

Verde (1906) and Rocky Mountain (1915) and Dinosaur National Monument (1915) stirred public interest, and the designation of land for recreational purposes encouraged such pursuits as fishing, hunting, canoeing, camping and mountain climbing. Colorado was attracting health-seekers, outdoors enthusiasts and antiquarian-minded vacationers curious about the old mining camps and Gilded Age glamour evoked by historic restorationists.

What most famously put Colorado on the map as a vacationer's mecca, however, was its emergence as a favored location for skiing. Such activity began taking off in popularity most decidedly in the 1950s. Crude skis had been used in earlier times by pioneers and prospectors for such basic needs as laying in food and delivering mail. The year 1914 saw a ski jump built at Steamboat Springs and the start of a winter festival that has persisted ever since.

Around the same time, skiing began as a popular pursuit at Denver, Boulder and Colorado Springs. A ski run with a jump was created on Genesee Mountain west of Denver, while in the other two towns ski clubs were formed. It was also the city of Denver that in 1938 established a ski area at Winter Park near the Moffatt Tunnel, with trains soon hauling skiers to the slopes. Colorado's first rope tow was installed in 1937

at nearby Berthoud Pass, and other communities began designating ski areas.

Two places that have become exceptionally well known in the public imagination as Colorado skiing centers are Aspen and Vail. Aspen was a roaring silver camp that made men rich in the 1880s before its luck changed. It was rejuvenated in the 1940s by the industrialist Walter P. Paepke and his wife, Elizabeth. She had taken a fancy to the shabby town high up on the Continental Divide and induced her husband to invest in its potential. They developed it into a mountain resort that became doubly famous for winter skiing and summer cultural seminars.

A MASSACRE AND A HOAX

There's a Spielbergian dark side to the American Dream in the Interior West. It's easy to feel hemmed in by the cookie-cutter suburbs and dwarfed by the beautiful yet impersonal landscape. Some people flame out in spectacular ways. The Columbine High School Massacre in Littleton, on April 20, 1999, is perhaps the most sobering example of what happens when parents and teachers ignore festering youth problems. Bullied by high-school jocks, and caught up in goth culture, the internet, video games, and revenge fantasies, seniors Dylan Kliebold and Eric Harris shot and killed 12 students, one teacher, and wounded 24 other students, before turning the guns on themselves and entering the history books. A decade later, an incident dubbed the Bal-

loon Boy Hoax again shone a media spotlight on Colorado's Front Range. On October 15, 2009, handyman, actor, and amateur storm chaser Richard Heene and his wife Mayumi reported that they suspected their six-year-old son was aboard a runaway home-made weather balloon. Pursued by live TV cameras, National Guard helicopters, and patrol cars, the balloon blew 50 miles (80km) across three counties and caused the closure of Denver Airport. When the boy was not found inside, a manhunt ensued, called off when he was "found" in the attic of the family's Fort Collins home. The ruse was revealed on *Larry King Live*, when the child let slip that the whole thing had been a publicity stunt for a proposed reality TV show.

A similar enterprise came into being at Vail, which was developed in the late 1950s by a master skier named Pete Seibert, and Earl Eaton, a uranium prospector. Taking note of the sport's growing popularity, they began acquiring land in the area and opened their resort in 1962. Seibert had served during World War II with the new Tenth Mountain Division based at Camp Hale high in the Rockies. Recruits were trained there for eventual ski-clad combat in the Italian Alps. The division suffered heavy losses in the war.

Tourism in Colorado has grown to huge proportions – an estimated one-tenth of the state's population is involved in the industry. Probably the most telling sign of its strength came in 1995 with the opening, after much delay, of the expansive Denver International Airport. One of the world's busiest airports, covering an area twice the size of Manhattan in New York City, it aptly represented Colorado's bullish spirit on the eve of the 21st century.

Runaway growth

From the mid-1960s on, the state's most rapid growth has occurred in the crowded eastern sector that runs from Fort Collins, north of Denver, to Pueblo in southeastern Colorado, a region known as the Front Range Urban Corridor. The boom in computer-related technology intensified in the 1980s and gave rise to many high-tech businesses in the 1990s. As a result, the suburban landscape around the Denver Metro Area has been transformed and afflicted with such headaches as snarled highways, sprawling subdivisions of identical tract housing, and pollution. Public concern about managing infrastructure was serious enough to cause voters to decline to foot the bill when Denver was selected to host the 1976 Winter Olympics, forcing the IOC to move the event to Innsbruck, Austria.

Until the global Great Recession began in 2008, which saw record foreclosures in the Denver suburbs, contraction of the once-thriving jobs market, and a Colorado unemployment rate of 8 percent, young adults had been attracted to Colorado in droves. The state is highly educated, with the second highest population of BAs in the country. The majority of new residents are California transplants, drawn by high-tech jobs,

a healthy climate and Colorado's recreational charms, bringing with them a liberal political mind-set that has rearranged the political map in Colorado. The once Republican state went Democrat in 2008, largely on the strength of Front Range liberalism and the influx of Latino immigrants into the Denver metro area; rural parts of the state remain largely Republican.

Today, a major preoccupation is how best to cope with an accelerated growth whose roots lie in the 1950s, fueled by tourism and federal expenditures on generally defense-related enterprises. By 2010, Colorado's growth rate was four times the national average. The state that counted

539,700 residents a century earlier is now, as of 2011, home to more than 5 million people.

Public agencies and citizen groups continue to seek ways to lessen the problem of metropolitan sprawl associated with rising population. Although a light rail in Denver has proved successful, public transportation is still hit or miss, and other than a few pedestrian-friendly spots such as Boulder, most Front Range residents spend hours in their cars getting from A to B and looking longingly at the mountains as their weekend escape route. Small wonder many folks end up moving to the delightful small mining towns dotted throughout the Rocky Mountains, whose populations have begun to swell. ❏

LEFT: demonstrators protest a Durango water project.
RIGHT: subdivisions crowd the boundaries of Colorado National Monument outside of Grand Junction.

THE BACKBONE OF THE CONTINENT

The Rockies run through Colorado like a crooked spine, with more than
50 peaks soaring beyond 14,000ft (4,270 meters). The state is called
America's Switzerland, but it has a character that is all its own

It's called the Rocky Mountain State, and mountains are its primary attraction – range after range of big, beautiful, skyscraping peaks laid down in ancient seas, rivers, floodplains and deserts over millennia, thrust up and tilted by volcanism, etched by glaciers, and eroded away by time. In few other places is alpine scenery so alluring. Frigidly beautiful throughout the snowy winter, when skiers flock to the slopes. Gray and austere on the windy summits after spring melt, when nature slowly begins to wake up. Skirted in phosphorescent green meadows and brilliant wild flowers in summer, and splashed with aspen golds in fall, when warm temperatures attract hikers, campers, bikers, horseback riders and four-wheel-drivers.

Perhaps it is because there are so many of them that Colorado's numerous mountain ranges seem so majestic. That, and the fact that 54 of the state's peaks top 14,000ft (4,270 meters), with many more clearing 12,000ft (3,660 meters). No doubt about it, this is America's Switzerland.

Varied terrain

Other than the mountains, what is less known about Colorado's geography is that it is remarkably diverse. The state is shaped like a large rectangle. To the east, the Great Plains meet the sawtooth peaks of the Front Range like an ocean lapping against the wall of a giant medieval fortress. At the southeastern end of the Rockies, between the plains and the San Juan Mountains, stretches the massive San Luis Valley, an extension of the volcanic Rio Grande Rift Valley which lies to the south, in New Mexico.

Most dramatic of all is the meeting of two geological provinces on the Western Slope: the Rocky Mountains and the 130,000 sq miles (340,000 sq km) of horizontal sedimentary rocks that make up the Colorado Plateau. Cracked by faults, uplifted by volcanism and downcut by the river system for which it is named, this unique mile-high plateau of redrock mesas, buttes and deep, shadowy canyons makes a spectacular counterpoint to the Rocky Mountains, rising to the east.

PRECEDING PAGES: leading to the Black Canyon of the Gunnison. **LEFT:** cycling through the Garden of the Gods. **RIGHT:** San Juan Mountains scenic byway.

Rocky Mountain high

At 100,000 miles (260,000 sq km), Colorado is the eighth largest state in the Union. It is joined by Wyoming to the north, Utah to the west, Arizona to the southwest, New Mexico to the south, and Kansas to the east. The different ranges that make up the Rocky Mountains cover much of the state. Running through Rocky Mountain National Park and down through the central San Juan Mountains of the Southern Rockies is the nation's Continental Divide, where major river systems flow east or west. The Colorado River and its tributaries – the Green, Yampa, Dolores, Gunnison and Ani-

mas rivers – flow west to the Pacific Ocean. The Arkansas and North and South Platte rivers and the Rio Grande flow east to the Atlantic.

The towering Rockies on view today have their origins in geologic events that go back to the dawn of life on earth. The oldest rocks in Rocky Mountain National Park and Dinosaur National Monument, for example, were laid down at least 1.8 billion years ago as sea sediments, which then hardened into horizontal sedimentary limestone strata. These Precambrian Era sedimentary rocks were later subjected to a long period of volcanism. Intense heat and pressure forced the soft sedimentary

NATURAL RESOURCES

Colorado is rich in gold, silver, lead, coal, oil, gas and uranium and has long attracted miners to its lands. Early prospectors concentrated on extracting placer deposits of native gold flakes found in stream gravels and sands in the South Platte River near Denver. When these deposits played out, the prospectors sold their stakes to large mining companies with the deep pockets and latest equipment to reach lodes, or veins, of gold deep underground. Silver was discovered in the 1860s, creating overnight boomtowns in places like Silverton and Creede, followed by veins of lead and zinc, uncovered during searches for gold and silver in the San Juan Mountains. Uranium, found in western Colorado near Paradox, is associated with the fossil-rich Chinle

and Morrison formations. Following World War II, company towns like Unavan became one of the country's major producers of carnotite, which yields uranium as well as vanadium. Unavan and other uranium towns remained in business until the 1980s, when local production was no longer profitable. Small, rich deposits of oil, gas and coal have also lured energy companies to western Colorado since the early 1900s. The Piceance Basin, north of Grand Junction, contains huge quantities of oil shale laid down in the mud of a lake 50 million years ago. Extracting the oil by crushing the shale and heating it to high temperatures has never proved economical, despite a major effort during the oil crisis of the 1970s.

rocks to undergo a metamorphosis into hard gneisses and schists. Later intrusions of hot magma formed a core of crystalline igneous granite intrusions in these rocks. During the next 1.5 billion years, they were uplifted repeatedly, worn down into plateaus by erosion, and covered by sediments.

The Ancestral Rockies did not make their first appearance until the Pennsylvanian Period (325 to 280 million years ago), when a phase of mountain building, known as the Colorado Orogeny, lifted up two huge mountain islands – Frontrangia and Uncompahgria – in the midst of another inland sea. These Ancestral Rockies were

much higher than the modern Rockies, with huge basins between and west of the ranges.

As the climate warmed and dried, during the Permian Period (280 to 240 million years ago), the inland sea withdrew to the west, leaving behind salt deposits several miles thick. Rainwater attacking the new mountains created streams and rivers that abraded red iron-rich sediments, carrying them from the highlands into the basins, initially mingling with the salt in colorful bands and later forming thick redbed deposits.

ABOVE: sandstone formations rise above the Yampa River in Echo Park, part of the Canyons section of Dinosaur National Monument.

One of these huge basins, the Paradox, straddled what is now the Colorado–Utah border on the edge of what's called Canyon Country. Its basement formation, the "Paradox salt formation," became so compressed by later sedimentary deposits, the salt actually became plastic and began to move away from the overburden, doming up along faults, entering joints in the rocks, and dissolving in groundwater. As joints widened, groundwater created long fins in the sandstone that wind and ice sculpted into the arches and other famous landmarks in Colorado National Monument and Utah's Arches National Park. In Colorado, the eroded sandstone formations at Red Rocks Park, west of Denver, are far older, part of the original redbed deposits shed from the Ancestral Rockies, 300 million years ago.

Dinosaur haven

Throughout the Triassic period (240 to 200 million years ago), erosion continued to wear down the Ancestral Rockies, and the warming climate and withdrawal of the sea left behind broad floodplains and deltas. The Age of Fishes now gave way to the Age of Reptiles – huge dinosaurs such as the platey-backed Stegosaurus, the state emblem. Large and small dinosaurs sloshed about in the floodplains and marshes of northwestern Colorado, which, as the continents drifted on their red-hot sea of magma, far below the surface, was close to where West Africa is today.

Enormous conifers and cycad ferns grew in the humid conditions, becoming compressed into soft shales that would eventually yield some of the country's largest deposits of oil,

> *Little-visited Dinosaur National Monument in northeastern Colorado preserves not only one of the country's largest caches of dinosaur fossils but also 2 billion years of geological strata, the most intact record in the national park system.*

gas and coal in northwestern Colorado. During a major flood at a river crossing near the location of present-day Green River, hundreds of dinosaurs were wiped out as they tried to ford the swollen waterway. These unfortunates were buried in the river sediments where they died, gradually becoming entombed in the pale crumbly Morrison Formation. The skeleton of one of these dinosaur casualties – a brontosaur – was discovered in the early 1900s by Carnegie Museum paleontologist Earl Douglass (*see page 281*), just north of Jensen, Utah. Other museums quarried specimens for display until, in 1906, President Theodore Roosevelt set aside

> Carved by the Gunnison River through the Gunnison Plateau a million years ago, Black Canyon of the Gunnison National Park is deeper, narrower, steeper and younger than the Grand Canyon, Yosemite or Yellowstone.

Dinosaur National Monument to halt the removal. The embedded bones of other dinosaurs, long on display at the Dinosaur Quarry Visitor Center, are temporarily closed to visitors while the National Park Service stabilizes and reconstructs the structure protecting them. Some exhibits are on view in a temporary visitor center.

The modern landscape

The contemporary Rockies arose just as the Age of Dinosaurs was giving way to the Age of Mammals at the end of the Cretaceous period, 65 million years ago. In a now familiar ritual, giant blocks of ancient crystalline rock, overlaid by younger sedimentary rock, broke and were thrust upward. The origins of this major mountain building period lay to the west, off the present-day California coast, where the oceanic Pacific Plate continues to dive under the North American Plate, forcing up the Sierra Nevada and coastal mountains.

These distant seismic movements substantially changed the topography of the Interior West. Stretching and thinning of the earth's surface east of the Sierra Nevada created the Basin and Range topography of the Mojave Desert around Death Valley. In the Southwest, reverberating plate movements wrinkled the earth's surface into huge sedimentary uplifts known as monoclines, such as Utah's Waterpocket Fold, and in Colorado created the Rockies. Although they would be leveled once more by erosion, most of the structure of the Rockies came into being during this period of intense mountain building, known as the Laramide Orogeny. Now,

GETTING INTO HOT WATER

Although they are found all over the state, hot springs abound in the western Rockies, where they have long been sacred to Native Americans. In southwestern Colorado, Pagosa Springs was used by the prehistoric Pueblo residents living at nearby Chimney Rock. Later, it was called pagosa, or "big healing waters," by Southern Utes who revered the steaming pools. Utes and Arapahos laid down their arms and bathed together at Manitou Springs in northwestern Colorado. And in the western San Juan Mountains, Ouray, chief of the Northern Utes, frequently bathed in the hot springs in the town that now bears his name, in order to ease his arthritis.

Some 50 known hot springs can be found throughout the Colorado Rockies. These thermal springs, which rise along faults in volcanically active mountains, range from a tepid 68°F (20°C) to a scalding 181°F (83°C). A century ago, rustic resorts grew up around many of these hot spots. Some, such as clothing-optional, family-run Orvis Hot Springs, south of Ridgway, remain pleasantly low-key and down home, while others, such as those in Steamboat Springs, Ouray and Pagosa Springs, have been developed into popular public facilities with attached therapy rooms. Colorado's best-known hot springs are Glenwood Springs, where the 90°F (32°C) pool is two soccer fields long, the largest in the world. It made headlines during the 2000 Winter Olympics, when the Olympic torch was swum through the pool en route to Salt Lake City.

where a great sea had lain 100 million years ago, the Great Plains appeared. As rivers and streams eroded materials from the highlands, it shed into this vast basin to the east. Eventually, sediments more than 13,000ft (4,000 meters) thick would cover what is now Kansas and the other Midwestern states.

The Rockies that are visible today did not appear until between 30 and 5 million years ago, during the Miocene-Pliocene Uplift, when faulting and regional upwarping lifted the Rocky Mountain Front Range as much as 5,000ft (1,500 meters) to its present height. In southwest Colorado, ongoing volcanism during the

Corners its distinctive appearance. In western Colorado, the ancient Uncompahgre Uplift that created the Ancestral Rockies forced up the Uncompahgre Plateau, which has been gradually exposed as the Colorado River and its tributaries cut into it. Where hot lava reached the surface within the last couple of million years, it frequently sits atop sedimentary rocks from eons of inland seas, beaches, rivers and streams. Southwest of Grand Junction, Grand Mesa is the largest lava plateau in the world. Just to the south, the Gunnison River has carved a pathway through an enormous lava dome at Black Canyon of the Gunnison National Park and created an awe-

Oligocene Epoch, 28 million years ago, created the San Juan Mountains, or Southern Rockies. This volcanism, which formed the major peaks of the San Juans and San Luis Valley, continues to affect western Colorado and accounts for the numerous geothermal hot springs found along faults in the western San Juans.

Lava lands

It is hot magma rising along faults at the edge of the Rocky Mountains and Colorado Plateau that has helped give the landscape of the Four

LEFT: dinosaurs are exhibited and explained at the Museum of Nature and Science. **ABOVE:** the glacier-carved peaks of Maroon Bells.

inspiring, black chasm nearly a mile deep.

Where overlying sedimentary rocks were thickest, hot magma welling up along faults domed up the landscape but never reached the surface. The resulting humped formations, known as laccoliths, encircle the large basins adjacent to uplifted areas. One good place to see them is at Far View Visitor Center at Mesa Verde National Park in southwestern Colorado. Nearby Sleeping Ute Mountain and more distant Navajo Mountain have been sacred landmarks for native people for centuries. In some instances, erosion has completely stripped away the sedimentary rocks, revealing the volcanic cores of these formations. Ship Rock, which plays a major role in the origin stories of the

Navajo, is clearly visible in the 25,000 sq mile (65,000 sq km) San Juan Basin, south of the San Juan River.

Ice sculpture

In the Rockies, the main erosional force has been four periods of glaciation, which began during a cooling trend early in the Quaternary Period, 2 million years ago, and continued until the end of the Ice Age, 10,000 years ago. In Colorado's higher valleys, snow became compacted into rivers of ice, or glaciers, which began to flow down the narrow valleys. Telltale signs of their passage can be seen throughout

the Rockies. River-cut V-shaped ravines have been widened into characteristic U-shaped valleys. Peaks have been carved into jagged pinnacles, knife-edge aretes and bowl-like depressions known as cirques that frequently fill with meltwater.

The relentless grinding of glaciers scoured the valleys, leaving behind striations, grooved and polished surfaces caused by transported rocks. Some boulders, aptly known as erratics, were marooned atop smooth granite in the high country. Other rock debris, called moraine, was carried into the lower valleys. A distinctive feature of glaciated valleys is the way glacial moraines have been deposited. As the glaciers made their way down the valleys, debris (or till) has left behind lateral moraines. Glacial till is most visible at the bottom of valleys, where melting glaciers finally drop their largest load of eroded material as a terminal moraine. Frequently in such places, glacial meltwater has created crystal-clear lakes filled with blue-green glacial flour, made up of suspended ice particles.

Not all lakes in the high country were created by glacial moraines. The lake that gave Lake City in the San Juans its name was formed when a mud slide, the Slumgullion Earthflow, slid off the mountains and blocked the Gunnison River. Rock slides are common throughout the high country of the Rockies, where flows of massive boulders spill down steep mountainsides.

Most mobile of all are the soils that have shed from the San Juan Mountains and been carried through San Luis Valley by the Rio Grande. As the river changed course, the sandy deposits were left victim to the powerful southwesterly winds that blow through the valley. Sometimes reaching more than 40mph (64km/h), these winds scoop up the grains of sand and buffet the 14,000ft (4,270-meter) Sangre de Cristo Mountains. The sand is too heavy to funnel through the mountain passes. As the winds continue their passage out of the valley their sandy cargo is left cradled at the base of the foothills, creating sand dunes 700ft (215 meters) high, the tallest in America. The area is preserved within Great Sand Dunes National Monument. ❏

THE GEOLOGY OF BUILDINGS

Ever wondered about the geology of buildings? David Williams has. In *Stories in Stone*, he devotes one chapter to William Brown's gas station in Lamar, Colorado. Built in the 1930s, the 15 by 35ft (4.5 by 10.5-meter) structure is made of 100 pieces of petrified wood gathered from a wash south of town and set in a castellated pattern reminiscent of a miniature castle. The *Lamar Daily News* raved: "Here is a building worthy of study... observe these marvelous trees... they stand to remind you of the ancient ages long ago, and to serve you with the modern fluid which is the vital touch of our ultra-modern motor-age."

LEFT: the ever-shifting dunes of Great Sand Dunes National Monument at the base of the Sangre de Cristo Mountains.

Heritage Tourism

Today, Colorado is renowned as much for its family farms and markets, and ancient cultural attractions, as for its superb skiing

For struggling farmers, ranchers and others in Colorado's rural areas, many of whom have worked the land for generations, ecotourism has become an important lifeline during tough times. Assisted by an innovative state heritage program, regional tourism hubs, and direct marketing on the internet, many have taken control of their own destinies, offering numerous interesting activities, from horsemanship, cattle drives and trail maintenance to you-pick produce, egg gathering and harvest dinners featuring local food and wine.

Southwestern Colorado is famous for its archeological heritage. At Crow Canyon Archeological Center near Cortez, you can take part in an ongoing archeological dig at a significant Pueblo site near Mesa Verde National Park. Kelly Place, a very reasonably priced bed and breakfast in McElmo Canyon, has 25 archeological sites on its 40-acre(16-hectare) property and offers professionally guided tours of other archeological sites in the area. At the other end of the spectrum, Canyon of the Ancients Guest Ranch rents luxury vacation homes and you can even pick your own produce for supper. After the Pueblo people moved on in the late 1200s, they were supplanted by Ute Mountain Utes whose reservation abuts Mesa Verde just south of Cortez. Regular tours to Pueblo ruins on the reservation are conducted by tribal guides. It's a unique and rugged way of viewing less well-known ruins and learning about Ute culture.

Southern Colorado's San Luis Valley, southeast of Salida, is one of the most isolated areas of Colorado. It remains a tightly knit Hispanic region, in the shadow of the Spanish Peaks, where many inhabitants still speak an archaic form of Spanish and live in adobes, grow beans and grain, and ranch cattle. Its main attraction is Great Sand Dunes National Park, which protects the tallest sand dunes in North America and is a migratory corridor for sandhill cranes and other birds. An unusual way to enjoy the valley is to stay at the Nature Conservancy-owned

Zapata Ranch, a working cattle and bison ranch adjoining the park. Visitors learn about the wildlife, horsemanship, and assist with the herds.

With 400 of 625 North American bird species using Comanche National Grasslands, Southeast Colorado is an important birding destination. It is also a magnet for historians interested in the Santa Fe Trail. The Cimarron Cutoff branch of the trail passed directly through here, and Bent's Fort was located directly on it to take advantage of trail traffic. Picketwire Canyon, known for its unusual dinosaur tracks, and Picture Canyon, a rock art site, are both scenic and historic attractions. Canyon Journeys Tours can arrange hiking and driving tours and

lodging in the area. Estelene Bunkhouse, in the former early-1900s log post office in Estelene, is right on the birding trail.

Park County, located in the central Rockies, contains the highest gold and silver mines in the country, as well as a variety of historic ranches, mining towns and scenic railroads. An hour from Denver, it is immensely popular for driving tours amid spectacular scenery. Como, Breckenridge, Fairplay, Alma, and other communities offer a taste of mountain living. Historic bed and breakfasts like the Como Depot Hotel, built by the railroad, have high-country character to spare, while an increasing number of historic ranches, including the 1880s Tarryall Ranch, have been restored and now welcome visitors. ❑

RIGHT: hiking the dunes at the Great Sand Dunes National Park in southern Colorado.

MOUNTAIN AND PRAIRIE LIFE

From alpine tundra to shortgrass prairie, Colorado's
varied terrain sustains a fascinating variety of plants
and animals in eight distinct ecosystems

With an average elevation of 6,500ft (2,000 meters), Colorado is the highest state in the country. It's also one of the most diverse. Elevations range from 3,300ft (1,000 meters) along the Arkansas River to 14,443ft (4,402 meters) at Mount Elbert, the state's highest point. Within that 11,000ft (3,350-meter) gain are eight distinct ecosystems, supporting 900 species of wildlife from rattlesnakes, jackrabbits and deer mice to black bear, ptarmigans and bighorn sheep. Seventy-four Colorado species are listed as state or federally endangered or threatened. These include humpback chub and other native fish affected by damming of the Colorado River, as well as boreal toad, lynx, wolverines, river otters, and lesser and greater prairie chickens, whose numbers have shrunk due to habitat loss.

Sea of grass

Colorado is famous for awe-inspiring peaks, but nearly 40 percent of the state is grasslands. The plains are found at elevations of less than 5,500ft (1,700 meters) and roll for hundreds of miles east of the Rocky Mountains, which cast a rainshadow, limiting average annual rainfall in the region to a scant 14in (36cm). Dominating the landscape are perennials such as buffalograss, western wheatgrass and blue grama. The native plants of the shortgrass prairie rarely exceed 2ft (60cm) in height. Their vertical blades maximize light absorption in the cooler part of the day and minimize the effects of midday radiation. Most of their biomass is contained in the root system, meaning

that fire and cropping is essential for regenerating vegetation.

Grassland animals have adapted to prairie conditions. Among them are pronghorn, erroneously dubbed antelope. Pronghorn became swift runners to escape their enemy, the now-extinct North American cheetah. Family groups of pronghorn are common on the prairie.

Eastern Colorado is a historic home of another significant native species: the American bison. Millions of bison – incorrectly dubbed buffalo by the Spanish – once roamed the plains, seasonally grazing grasslands and churning the ground underfoot into a fertile mulch. Bison sustained the Plains Indians. Their entire

LEFT: Boulder Creek flows down Boulder Canyon.
RIGHT: the Pawnee National Grassland.

culture centered on hunting bison, an animal that provided for much of their needs, from meat and clothing to glue, bone and sinew.

Wildlife watchers are well rewarded at Pawnee and Comanche National Grasslands, large federally managed tracts in the northeast and southeast corners of the state, respectively. Both are good for viewing badgers, foxes, mule deer and pronghorn. Black-tailed prairie dogs are a common sight, too. These highly social creatures live in underground burrows to stay cool and avoid predators such as coyotes and red-tailed hawks, eagles, owls and other raptors that patrol the skies.

Comanche National Grassland supports some

grounds in the world for mountain plovers. Cliff swallows and white-throated swifts are common around the buttes, and the cascading song of the canyon wren reverberates from the walls of the escarpment.

As in all dry places, water attracts life. Cottonwoods, willows and tamarisk grow along the South Platte, Purgatoire and Arkansas rivers and their tributaries, offering shade and important nesting habitat on the otherwise treeless prairie. Small ponds and reservoirs, most intermittent in nature, lure migrant shorebirds, which pause to refuel for their long journey north in spring.

273 bird species, including specially adapted species such as scaled quail, pheasant and grouse, which build nests directly on the ground. Burrowing owls have an additional specialty: they prefer to nest in abandoned prairie dog colonies. The most famous of the grassland birds are the threatened lesser and greater prairie chickens whose frenetic mating dance in open areas called leks takes place in spring. The two units of Pawnee National Grassland, 90 miles (145km) northeast of Denver, have even more birds – 296 species at last count. Cliff-dwelling raptors such as prairie falcons and golden eagles inhabit the twin Pawnee Buttes, a geological landmark consisting of sedimentary rocks that rise above the plains, and this is one of the primary breeding

In the 1800s, free-roaming bison herds were exterminated by settlers monopolizing lindigenous hunting grounds. Today, large ranches east of Denver raise them for the exploding bison meat market.

Between prairie and mountains

The canyons and foothills of the eastern Rockies and the high plateau country of western Colorado, between 5,000 and 7,000ft (1,500–2,000 meters), encompass dry shrublands, a transition zone between the mountains and the open grasslands. Directly in the shadow of high mountains, these areas are even drier than the plains, with 10in (25cm) or less of precipitation, falling mostly as snow in winter. These areas are hot in summer and frigid in winter. To survive, plants and animals have to be able to manage on little or no water for long periods.

Sandy soils are stabilized by perennial native grasses such as galleta and Indian ricegrass, whose nutritious seeds were once gathered by wandering indigenous peoples. Overgrazing has all but destroyed many native grasses, allowing woody shrubs such as sulfur-colored rabbitbrush and pungent sagebrush to take over. The montane shrublands of the Front Range are home to Gambel oak and mountain mahogany.

In summer, early-morning hikers may glimpse brightly hued collared lizards, horned toads and rattlesnakes basking on warm rocks. Cottontails, jackrabbits, ground squirrels and mice are the most active in the daytime. By dusk, they are safe in their burrows, avoiding crepuscular hunters like coyotes and gray foxes.

As elevation rises, dwarf forests of stunted pinyon pine and juniper trees appear. The round-topped pinyon tree bears nutritious nuts that have been valued by animals and humans for centuries. Pinyons rarely grow over 30ft (9 meters) tall and are more cold tolerant than junipers, a drought-resistant shaggy-barked

The semidesert shrublands of the West Slope are a region of dry washes and low shrubs.

Prickly pear and other cactus are well suited to the aridity. Cactus have done away with leaves altogether and photosynthesize food from sunlight along thick, waxy pads covered in spines that keep away predators. Bright flowers attract bird and insect pollinators in spring. Animals return to eat the juicy fruits in late summer, and spread seeds through their digestive tracts. Semidesert conditions mean plenty of reptiles and rodents make their home here.

shrub that is more at home in lower elevations. The pinyon pine-juniper woodlands zone, which now dominates much of the Colorado Plateau, supports numerous wildlife species, including noisy pinyon jays, little gray tits, and ground squirrels. In northwestern Colorado, look for herds of elk and mule deer and wild horses in the vicinity of Dinosaur National Monument, in the White River region between Rangely and Meeker.

Cathedral of trees

More moisture and cooler temperatures above 7,000ft (2,100 meters) allow trees to grow taller. In the transition life zone, ponderosa pine begins to appear, a tall tree with platey

LEFT: an abandoned farm on the Pawnee National Grassland. **ABOVE:** flowering cactus on the Northeast Plains of Colorado.

bark that smells of vanilla. The odd ponderosa grows among pinyon and juniper at first, then becomes the dominant tree, forming thick stands separated by natural "parks," or open meadows. Scrub oaks can often be found growing in the shade of ponderosa at lower elevations. Fast-growing, arrow-straight Douglas fir is also found in this life zone. It prefers hillsides with northern exposures where temperatures are cooler and moisture is more plentiful.

Among the birds that make their home in the ponderosa zone are bluebirds, sparrows, juncos, chickadees and Steller's and scrub jays. Jays, a relative of the crow, flash through the branches and often cause a commotion fighting over seeds. Larger mammals include mule deer and their natural predator, mountain lions, shy felines that are rarely seen. Tassel-eared squirrels and ponderosa pines have evolved an interesting symbiotic relationship. Squirrels dig around the base of ponderosas in search of fungi that grow on the roots. As they dig, they inadvertently mulch the soil and release nutrients that benefit the tree. The needles of the ponderosa are born in long bunches, which gives it an airy, umbrella shape that allows a lot of light to penetrate the forest floor. Lupine, scarlet gilia, Indian paintbrush and other wild flowers

THE ROLE OF FIRE

Fire is essential to the health of western forests. Unfortunately, 150 years of fire suppression, poor logging practices and drought have allowed forests to become overgrown and weakened. In recent years, thousands of pinyon and ponderosa pines, and other evergreens, have died in the West, as bark beetles bore into drought-ravaged trees, multiply rapidly, and kill their hosts. The problem has been particularly acute in ponderosa forests choked with young, small-diameter blackjack pines that have not been selectively pruned by fire or logging. Natural forest fires in this ecosystem historically burned slowly and remained low on the forest floor, allowing pine cones to open, spill seed and germinate. There was plenty of time for wildlife to escape. But as a thick duff of dried needles has built up, fires caused by lightning strikes or human carelessness have become deadly, racing up into the canopy during periods of hot, dry, windy conditions and obliterating every living thing in their path. In the summer of 2002, Durango's devastating Missionary Ridge Fire charred nearly 71,000 acres (28,700 hectares) north of town and claimed 56 homes, while the Hayman Blaze, the most extensive fire in state history, ravaged 138,000 acres (55,800 hectares) on the southern edge of Denver and destroyed 133 homes. Thinning the forests is only one solution to the problem. Home building in the so-called urban-wildland interface, an area where 30 percent of Coloradans live, also jeopardizes the ecosystem.

do well here. Only trees that are over 25 years old reproduce seeds, and then only in enough quantity to germinate every three to five years, during a particularly moist year.

Aspens aquiver

At higher elevations, between 8,000 and 10,000ft (2,400–3,000 meters), where precipitation averages 25in (64cm) a year, limber pine, blue spruce and aspens appear. Limber pine, a tall straight tree often used by Utes for tipi poles, and quaking aspen, a relative of the willow, are pioneer species, meaning they are the first to take root in clearings created by fire, logging and other

One reason for the aspen's endurance is its dual reproductive strategy. In spring, flowering catkins produce small cones, which release cottony seeds that are dispersed on the wind and root in moisture-rich soils. Where moisture is abundant, this strategy works well, but dry conditions in the West necessitate a different tactic. Western aspen groves reproduce almost entirely vegetatively, sending out suckers, or ramets, from existing root systems into areas disturbed by fire, logging or avalanches – in effect, cloning.

A mature root system can put out a million shoots per acre, which then grow 3ft (1 meter)

disturbances. New groves of aspens take five to 10 years to establish themselves, and reach their maximum density in 25 to 50 years.

Once mature, an aspen forest creates enough shade to allow conifer seedlings such as Douglas fir, Engelmann spruce and subalpine fir to take root. From then on, it's downhill for the aspens, which become crowded out by conifers and susceptible to disease, insect infestation and browsing elk and deer. For decades, spruce-fir forests dominate the scene. Eventually, they, too, fall prey to wildfire, clearing the way once again for an aspen forest to take hold on the forest margin.

every season, outcompeting forest species that rely on seed regeneration. Aspen clones are extraordinarily long-lived. The giant Pando clone in south-central Utah, which covers 106 acres (43 hectares) and contains more than 47,000 individual stems, may be at least 10,000 years old. So, take another look at that aspen grove. It's no accident that the trees look so alike.

Between 10,000 and 11,000ft (3,000–3,350 meters), where snowfall is heavy, tall narrow conifers with waxy needles that shrug off snow form climax forests of several-hundred-year-old Engelmann spruce and subalpine fir that cloak the mountain sides in miles of soothing velvety green. Though rarely seen,

---

LEFT: a Rufus Hummingbird in bright plumage.
ABOVE: golden aspen leaves in the fall.

wolverines and Canada lynx and black bears also live at this height. In the mountains near Pagosa Springs, there are tales, too, of grizzly bears, long thought extirpated from the region.

At the highest elevations, thin air, rocky soils and frigid winds are as stressful for trees as the hot, dry conditions at low elevations. This is the province of specially adapted trees, such as the bristlecone pine, which can live for thousands of years by shutting down parts of itself and bowing into the wind to form krummholz, a German word meaning "crooked wood."

Tundra peaks

In the alpine zone, above 11,000ft (3,350 meters), life is harsh. Intense solar radiation, gusty winds and scant oxygen are constant challenges. Even so, a surprising number of living things have adapted to the rocky soils that are buried under 40 to 60in (100–150cm) of snow each winter.

Just above the treeline, alpine meadows provide some of Colorado's most spectacular hiking areas. Places like Yankee Boy Basin in the San Juan Mountains are a riot of color come June, when snow gradually melts and livings things race to reproduce in the abbreviated summer. Bluebells, sneezeweed, lupines, sunflowers and Colorado's state flower, the spurred Rocky

Mountain columbine, form a colorful tapestry among lush green grasses fed by snowmelt.

Picnic here after a long hike and your companions will be sleepy yellow-bellied marmots, perhaps a pine marten, pika, vole or snowshoe hare. If you're really lucky, you may spot bighorn sheep grazing in the meadows or lounging on rocky ledges in the distance. In late fall, rutting males assert their dominance by crashing into each other's horns at speeds of up to 55mph (90km/h). This is also the territory of mountain goats, whose shaggy white coats protect them from the elements, and highly specialized hooves allow them to clamber up impossibly steep terrain.

Plants at the highest elevations keep a low profile but are surprisingly numerous. Perhaps the most fascinating are the brightly colored lichens that splotch gray granite boulders throughout the alpine zone. Colorado's high mountains support 450 species of lichen. Lichen actually consists of two mutually beneficial organisms – fungi and algae – that live together and survive by making use of wind-blown particles, minerals in the rock and occasional moisture. Lichens are another important pioneer species. They secrete acids that help to break down rock into soil.

Eventually, tiny plants take root in crevices. Many, such as pink moss campion and sunny snow buttercup, look surprisingly delicate. Like the environmentally stressed plants at lower elevations, this pincushion-sized flora survives by staying low to the ground and attracting pollinators with bright colors, retaining water through woody stems, and employing a vast

The American dipper is a wren-like bird with specialized feeding habits. It plunges into raging rivers and picks insect larvae from the bottom. How such a tiny creature can withstand strong currents is a bit of a mystery.

underground root system to collect nutrients. Like desert flora, they are easily destroyed by careless human activity. Walk lightly in the lowest and highest elevations and respect life at these outer margins. ❑

LEFT: a black bear at the Denver Zoo. **RIGHT:** sunset at the Pawnee National Grasslands.

FOUR SEASONS

Primarily a state of high mountain ranges, valleys and rich wildlife, Colorado attracts outdoors lovers who enjoy hiking, biking, skiing and nature at any time of year

For many people, winter ski season is the only season in Colorado. Former mining towns-turned-ski resorts swing into action, advertising the deepest, softest, fluffiest snow, gnarliest slopes and best facilities for skiing and snowboarding. In the San Juans, cross-country skiers and snowshoers make their way from hut to hut; there's extreme ice jeeping in Georgetown and ice climbing in Ouray, and other oddities, while down in the San Luis Valley wetlands, sandhill cranes stop over on their migrations. Spring arrives late, often bringing the heaviest wet snowfalls. At lower elevations, warmer temperatures swell rivers and wetlands, and courtship and reproduction begin. Prairie chickens perform their odd dances in prairie leks while fawns, bighorn lambs, elk calves and other youngsters debut. Summer is precious for its brevity and beauty in the Rockies. Travelers on the trails and scenic byways leave behind the torrid low-elevation areas around Grand Junction and Denver and head for the high country to view Rocky mountain columbine and other stunning wild flowers in now passable mountain basins. Everything races to bloom, reproduce, and set seed before fall swoops in in September. Aspens shimmer gold across the mountain sides and bring out legions of leaf peepers on the passes, trams, scenic railroads and ski lifts. Listen carefully and you'll hear bugling elk and head-butting bighorn sheep, heralding winter's imminent arrival.

ABOVE: hiking to Flat Top Mountain and Hallett Peak in Rocky Mountain National Park can be cold at any time of year.

ABOVE: it is illegal to pick the Blue Columbine, Colorado's state flower

ABOVE: skiers often climb to remote spots to ski out of bounds

ABOVE: only male elk have antlers, which are grown each year in the spring and shed by early winter.

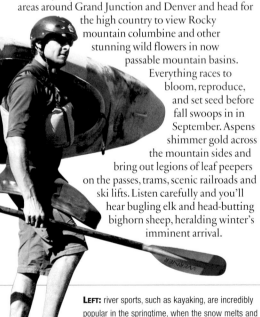

LEFT: river sports, such as kayaking, are incredibly popular in the springtime, when the snow melts and rivers run at their peak.

BELOW: Colorado has more than 300 days of sunshine every year, making it the ideal place to get outside.

THE WINTER HOLIDAYS

Christmas in the Rockies. It's a fairy-tale setting of deep white snow, toboggans, horse-drawn sleigh rides, twinkling lights, roaring fires, cozy comforters, ear muffs, hot toddies and caroling. Estes Park, gateway to Rocky Mountain National Park, offers a panoply of seasonal attractions, including the Catch the Glow Parade the Friday after Thanksgiving, caroling, Christmas lights and visits with Santa. In Snowmass, Telluride and Crested Butte, there's a torchlight parade across the mountain side on Christmas Eve. In Glenwood Springs, the Hotel Colorado has a life-size gingerbread house, tree lighting, a visit with Santa and a hotel pageant, while ski resorts like Breckenridge pull out all the stops, turning the entire town into a Victorian Christmas Village. In pretty Durango, kids all get gifts from Santa on the special Polar Express train, which runs to Silverton amid icicles and snowy mountains just like the Swiss Alps. Lights, of course, are aglow in towns throughout the state. The whole of Tenderfoot Mountain in Salida is lit up each year, while in Denver, more than a million Christmas lights adorn the Botanic Gardens.

BELOW: extreme mountain biking in Telluride is a popular summer activity. **BELOW RIGHT:** rock climbing near Sprague Lake.

RIGHT: "snowpack" in Colorado refers to the accumulation of snow over a winter season.

OUTDOOR ADVENTURE

Whatever your passion – rock climbing, backpacking, mountain biking or whitewater rafting – Colorado offers room to roam and stunning scenery to enjoy

In surveys of American health, Colorado routinely ranks first in fitness, last in fatness. It's not difficult to see why. Coloradans are always out running, biking, hiking, skiing, paddling and otherwise enjoying life in the great outdoors – when they're not working out in the gym, that is. With an inviting climate and an unsurpassed wealth of mountains, rivers and lakes to play on, Coloradans find little excuse to stay indoors.

High-country scenery

There is no finer way to discover the state's magic than on foot. From easy ambles in urban parks to grueling scrambles up steep slopes to sky-high summits, Colorado offers trails for hikers at every level of conditioning and experience. High-country scenery is breathtaking, and the opportunity to explore wild areas is abundant. Mountains invite exploration and encourage people to put one foot in front of the other until they reach a goal – a panoramic viewpoint, an alpine lake, a ghost town, a windswept peak.

Front Range trails are often snow-free through much of winter, but conditions are best from late spring to early fall. Wild flower season begins with avalanche lilies sprouting in the wake of melting snowfields, reaches a climax in July, and tapers off in September. Wildlife watching is best in spring and fall, at dawn or dusk.

Trails crisscross the state. Many are near major highways or on the outskirts of cities and resort towns; others branch off from harrowing four-wheel-drive roads and lead deep into the wilderness. Trails vary in length and difficulty from handicapped-accessible paths of less than a mile to arduous treks along the crest of the Rockies. Many ski areas operate at least one lift in summer, so visitors who want a shortcut can ride up and hike down.

Far more challenging is scaling the hundreds of peaks that rise from mountain ranges throughout the state. The degree of difficulty varies considerably from one mountain to another, but some require no special skills or equipment and can be climbed in a single day. There are oxygen-sapping heights and often violent summer storms to contend with, but most mountains have at least one hike-up route.

LEFT: Akiti Arch in Colorado National Monument.
RIGHT: climbing at Ouray's annual Ice Climbing festival.

Hikers with little or no experience may want to set their sights on a modest goal – say, 9,250ft (2,820-meter) Crozier Peak near Estes Park. On the opposite side of the scale is a lung-searing trek to the top of one of the state's 54 "fourteeners" – mountains 14,000ft (4,270 meters) or higher – regarded with a certain reverence by avid hikers.

Be prepared

Whatever your route, thoughtful preparation is the key to a successful outing. Sunscreen, sunglasses, a broad-brimmed hat (or peaked cap and bandana protecting the neck), pants and shirts with sleeves that can be rolled down for sun protection, and comfortable wool socks and hiking boots, sturdy shoes or outdoor sandals are the minimum equipment for even a moderate hike; veteran hikers often use a single walking stick or pair of trekking poles. If you intend to reach elevations of 8,000 to 10,000ft (2,400–3,000 meters), pack a fleece jacket, waterproof shell, and a high-energy snack. Above 10,000ft (3,000 meters), you'll need cold-weather gear, including long johns, a warm hat, gloves, an emergency blanket and extra food, even in midsummer.

A trail map is a good idea even if you intend to follow a well-marked route. In remote areas, it's essential to carry a topographical map and

CLIMB EVERY MOUNTAIN

When most people say they've "climbed" a mountain what they really mean is that they've "hiked" it. The term "peak bagging" refers to a successful summit ascent, and bagging "fourteeners" – mountains 14,000ft (4,270 meters) or higher – is the ultimate goal of the hardiest hikers. Although some 200,000 people a year reach the state's highest peaks, fourteeners have achieved mythic status. While some hikers are content to have done just one, others are compelled to ratchet up the challenge by, for example, climbing all 54 in Colorado, climbing them all in a year, on consecutive days, in winter, or all of the above. Every fourteener, whether it's your first or your 54th, offers a sense of being on top of the world and of having gotten there one step at a time.

Difficulty ranges widely. Some peaks, like Mount Sherman, a short drive from Denver, are a good choice for beginners. A trail leads to the summit, making for a fairly easy walk-up, though hikers unaccustomed to the elevation should take it slow. Others, like Capitol and Pyramid peaks, involve traversing knife-edge ridges, loose talus and extremely steep slopes. They should be attempted only by those with excellent route-finding skills and in top physical condition.

Fourteeners can be climbed in all seasons, but the best time for casual hikers is between late June and September. Afternoon electrical storms are common in summer. Start early and get below treeline before 2pm.

compass and know how to use them. GPS units are handy too, but should be used in addition to a compass, never as a substitute for one: satellite information is not the same as on-the-ground information and you may find yourself going off a cliff if you're not careful. Other basics for wilderness travel include a Swiss army knife, matches in a waterproof case, a flashlight, a whistle, a space blanket, and turned-off cell phone at the bottom of your day pack, in case you're on the trail longer than expected or need to signal for help. Most important, carry a gallon (4 liters) of water per person per day (at least a liter or 2 pints) for short jaunts). Stay hydrated by sipping at regular intervals, even if you don't feel thirsty, and avoid hyponutremia (an electrolyte imbalance) by eating salty nutritious snacks like trail mix and drinking water.

Altitude sickness is another concern, especially if you're coming from sea level. Symptoms include headache, shortness of breath, fatigue, dizziness and loss of appetite. The best preventative is to spend a couple of days adjusting to the elevation. Avoid overexertion, lay off alcohol and coffee (both are dehydrating), and drink more water than you think you need. Lastly, leave a travel plan with someone at home, so they know when and where to start looking if you don't turn up.

On the rocks

Rock climbing epitomizes confident partnering in a vertical world. One climber moves up the rock; the other provides protection via the rope. Only when the lead climber is secure does the second climber begin to move. The process has been compared to chess in terms of concentration and the importance of small, critical moves. The satisfaction and the self-confidence gained from rock climbing are so deep that it has become a popular component of team-building and self-esteem workshops.

The learning curve is quite precipitous for rock climbing, although even in this sport, in which technical skill and strength are paramount, the opportunities for beginners are expanding. Not too many years ago, the only practical way to learn rock climbing was to tag along with experienced climbers. Today, it's

much more common for newcomers to hone their skills at climbing gyms before they actually put flesh to rock.

Beginners can learn a few basic maneuvers in just four or five hours, but there's only so much you can do without being out in the field. For that, it's best to contact organizations like the Colorado Climbing School (722 North 31st Street, Colorado Springs, CO 80904; tel: 719-650-1026; www.coloradoclimbingschool.com) or the Colorado Mountain Club (710 10th St, Suite 200, Golden, CO 80401; tel: 303-279-3080; www.cmc.org), which run courses covering the fundamentals of climbing technique, equipment and,

LEFT: a perfect sky in Rocky Mountain National Park.
RIGHT: always practice safe climbing techniques, and never climb alone.

LIGHTNING SAFETY

Lightning isn't just a great light show; it's potentially lethal and, above treeline, there are few places to hide. If you're in the mountains when a storm moves in, descend from high, open terrain. If you can't get away from an exposed area, make yourself as small as possible, crouching down on the balls of your feet, or perching on a small rock with insulation such as a poncho or a foam pad under you, with your feet touching rock and your hands clasped around your knees. Stay clear of tall objects such as isolated trees as well as depressions, shallow caves and rock overhangs. Ground currents can be dangerous.

above all, safety. Such classes are a great place to meet climbing companions and learn about organized field trips.

Ice is nice

For an even greater challenge, consider ice climbing, which involves scaling a cascade frozen to a steep rock wall. To gain purchase on the slippery surface, ice climbers use axes and spiky footgear called crampons. The climber maneuvers upward in a manner similar to that of a rock climber scaling a cliff. Unlike rock climbers, however, ice climbers create their own routes by choosing where to place their tools.

Out for the night

If you like hiking, you'll love multiday excursions, which are the logical next step. A longer backpacking trip provides the opportunity to really experience the high country, to study the wild flowers, photograph the scenery and generally steep yourself in the beauty and tranquility of the mountains.

Overnight trips are naturally more complicated to plan and require a rather daunting list of additional equipment, including a backpack, sleeping bag, tent, water-purifying kit and camping stove. The design and quality of camping gear has never been better, though choices (and prices) can

Despite this flexibility, ice climbing contains a constant element of insecurity because the very surface on which the climber depends can melt, shatter or break away. The changeable nature of ice also means that the same climb can vary radically from one day to another. A route's difficulty is often impossible to predict.

The premier site for ice climbing in Colorado – and perhaps the entire western United States – is the Ouray Ice Park, an area of "cultivated" ice flows in Uncompahgre Gorge. Climbing routes, including some with safety ropes and bolts set in the rock, range in difficulty from easy to expert. The Ouray Ice Festival, usually held in mid-January, features gear demonstrations, competitions and free instruction.

quickly become overwhelming. Unless you have an experienced friend to show you the ropes, the best advice is to start by doing a little research in books, magazines and on the internet, then go to a reputable camping-supply retailer such as REI and work with a salesperson who is willing to take the time you need to make the right decisions. Remember: comfort is key. Roughing it in the outdoors shouldn't be rough at all. The idea is to simplify your life, unload stress, and enjoy the place, people, and moment, not aggravate yourself with ill-fitting or poor-quality equipment that leaves you cold, hungry, achy and miserable.

Once you're properly equipped, you can begin making the tough decisions about where to go. Colorado has 30,000 campgrounds in locations ranging from the deepest wilderness to the outskirts of cities. Choosing how and where to camp is a function of taste, budget and availability of sites. Consider why you want to camp and how rugged you want the experience to be. In general, you'll find that the more conveniences a campsite offers and the easier it is to reach, the less privacy and scenic beauty it has to offer.

For maximum ease, pull in to a road side campground and use your tent, trailer or motor home as a base for day hikes. Most drive-in campgrounds have basic sanitary facilities as well as picnic tables and grills. Private facilities may also have utility hookups (electricity, water and

if you're adequately prepared, camp at large in a wilderness area designated for the purpose. If that sounds like a daunting prospect, consider hiring a guide or outfitter to help you. At the most basic level, outfitters assist with trip planning, provide the necessary equipment, and perhaps shuttle your party to and from a trailhead. At the opposite extreme, many outfitters script every inch of your trip in high style – toting your gear, setting up camp, and even capping each day with dinner beneath the stars. Most of all, outfitters can share the knowledge they've acquired over years of travel. Going with an expert is a great way to learn about a place and

sewerage), showers, a laundry, a grocery, a playground and other amenities. Electricity brings with it television, stereos, bright lights and other "conveniences" that, in the view of many campers, spoil the point of being outdoors. Campsites at national parks, national forests and other public lands tend to be more laid-back and often feature rangers giving campfire talks or leading guided hikes.

If you want a real back country experience, however, you will have to leave the road behind and set out on foot to a primitive campsite or,

> When nature calls, answer with a trowel. Dig a cathole at least 6in (15cm) deep for human waste and bury or carry out toilet paper. Pick a site at least 200ft (60 meters) from water sources.

acquire new skills – and, if you choose, sweeten the adventure with a touch of luxury.

Wet and wild

The possibilities for outdoor adventure become even more enticing when you consider alternative modes of transportation such as biking and rafting, which often free you from the burden of

LEFT: a climber at Ouray's Box Canyon digs into a wall of ice with axe and crampons. **ABOVE:** camping grounds in Rocky Mountain National Park.

Extreme Sports

Testing one's mettle against the elements is an essential part of outdoor adventure. Numerous Colorado sporting events push human limits of strength and endurance

For marathon runners, the **Bolder Boulder** 6-mile (10km) road race in May is a major event on the calendar. With categories for professional runners, elite runners, citizen run-

ners, walkers and wheelchair participants, more than 50,000 entrants took part in 2009, a record turnout. For scenery, it's hard to beat the **Steamboat Marathon, Half-Marathon, and 10K** held in Steamboat Springs in early June. It has been listed as one of the most scenic marathons in North America and a Top 10 Destination by *Runner's World*. The **Leadville Trail 100** is a 100-mile (160km) run nicknamed "the race across the sky," because it takes place at elevations of 10,000ft (3,050 meters) or higher. Events added since the first 100-miler in 1983 are a full marathon, 100- and 50-mile (160 and 80 km) mountain bike races, and a 6-mile (10km) run. Another popular road race, the **Pikes Peak Marathon** takes place in Manitou Springs in August. Competitors in this

half-marathon follow the 13-mile (21km) Barr Trail to the summit of Pikes Peak, an elevation gain of 7,815ft (2,382 meters). A full marathon to the summit and back is run the next day.

If you don't fancy Shank's mare, opt instead for a burro or llama. **World Championship Pack Burro Races**, a team event, are held in Fairplay in July and are surprisingly demanding. Described as the world's "highest, longest, roughest, and toughest" race, the course is 29 miles (47km) long and climbs to an elevation of 13,000ft (915 meters).

For mountain bikers, the **Montezuma's Revenge** 24-hour race, held in Montezuma County in August, is a popular outing. The race is divided into seven loops that cross the Continental Divide 10 times. Those who finish the race rack up more than 200 miles (320km) and an elevation gain of 35,000ft (10,700 meters). The world's oldest mountain bike event, **Pearl Pass Ride** is a two-day, 38-mile (61km) ride from Crested Butte to Aspen via 12,700ft (3,870-meter) Pearl Pass that takes place in September. For extreme cyclists, the **Iron Horse Bicycle Classic**, between Durango and Silverton, receives top billing. The 47-mile (77km) road race for ranked and non-ranked racers with 5,500ft (1,680 meters) of elevation gain over two 11,000ft (3,350-meter) passes takes place over the Memorial Day weekend and includes in-town criteriums, circuit races, road races, tours, BMX races, dual slaloms, team trail rides and mountain bike races. The **Elephant Rock Ride** held in Castle Rock in June includes four road cycling events, from 25 to 100 miles (40–160km), plus a 26-mile (42km) off-road ride, and attracts more than 7,000 participants.

Auto races also go to the extreme in Colorado. The famous **Pikes Peak International Hill Climb** in Manitou Springs in June follows a serpentine, 12-mile (19km) gravel road to the summit of Pikes Peak, maneuvering through 156 hairpin turns with no guardrails. Vehicles include stock cars, sport cars, diesel trucks and motorcycles.

And, of course, it wouldn't be Colorado without winter sports. During the 24 Hours of Aspen event in December, billed as the "most grueling endurance ski race in history," men and women skiers race for 24 consecutive hours. Also in December, the Leadville Ski 100 Nordic Ultra-Ski Race attracts soloists and relay teams who enter this 100-mile (160km) cross-country ski race. ❑

LEFT: mountain biking in the Leadville Trail 100 race.

lugging a backpack, and open up territory that may be unreachable on foot. If you enjoy water sports, for example, you'll get a kick out of white-water paddling. Colorado's 13 river systems provide everything from boat-bashing rapids in early spring to gentle summer floats that can be safely done in an inner tube. The rafting season begins in May, peaks in mid-June, and typically ends in early October. Snowmelt feeds Colorado's rivers, so the biggest water and best paddling follow winters when the skiing was great.

The real beauty of rafting is that just about anybody can do it. Licensed outfitters handle all provisions and equipment. All you have to do –

the Animas, Blue, Cache la Poudre, Colorado, Green, Gunnison, Yampa and Rio Grande. River rafting contributed $142 million to state coffers in 2008. The government licenses all commercial raft companies, 55 of which belong to the Colorado River Outfitters Association, a trade group that serves as a clearinghouse for information on whitewater adventures (tel: 1-800-COLORADO; www.croa.org).

For those who crave even more action, Colorado's fast-flowing rivers are best experienced in a kayak or canoe. Mobility, freedom and the thrill of constantly testing yourself against the elements are the appeals of the sport. Kayakers

aside from paying the bill – is show up. More than half a million people a year put themselves in the hands of Colorado boatmen trained in whitewater navigation, first aid and rescue. The best river guides know a great deal about history and nature, too. Trips range from calm half-day floats suitable for families with small children to multiday expeditions with camping, cook-outs and plenty of opportunities for exploring the surrounding terrain in depth.

The Arkansas River between Buena Vista and Royal Gorge is reportedly the most-rafted river in the western United States, but there are more than 10 others to choose from, including

ABOVE: a river guide leads a family rafting trip.

UP, UP AND AWAY

For a real "Rocky Mountain high," consider taking to the skies. Tandem hang-gliding and skydiving, where students and instructors soar together, offer the experience of free flight without training. For a scenic view of Colorado at a slow pace, consider a hot air balloon ride. Pilots use propane heaters to adjust altitude and fine-tune the flight, but the balloon essentially rides air currents. Upon landing, you are served champagne and transported back to your car. Ultralights, which look something like motorized hang-gliders or parachutes, are another option. You can do a tandem flight with an instructor at the controls, or spend a few hours learning to fly solo.

talk about "playing" the water, not just navigating rapids but performing an aquatic ballet of "cartwheels," "enders," "pirouettes" and other tricky maneuvers.

Unless you already have a good deal of experience under your belt, instruction is essen-

> *Even clear streams can harbor parasites that cause severe gastro-intestinal illness. All water from wild sources should be boiled for at least a minute, treated with iodine, or passed through a portable filter.*

tial. Kayaking schools throughout the state offer clinics in basic skills such as proper paddle strokes, rolls and water safety as well as advanced "playboating" and whitewater rescue. Most introductory courses are divided into pre-river and on-river segments. The pre-river curriculum may include pool or lake instruction.

If whitewater is for thrill-seekers, flatwater canoeing has the opposite appeal – a calm, often meditative activity as well as an efficient mode of transportation. Canoes have more room for gear than kayaks and are better suited for camping and fishing trips, especially if you're traveling with kids. Basic canoeing doesn't take extraordinary skill either, just a little practice to paddle efficiently.

Pedal power

Colorado is cycling central. Local riders pedal everything from beat-up clunkers to mountain bikes and state-of-the-art touring bikes with four-figure price tags. You'll find them pedaling on thousands of miles of city streets, mountain passes, bike paths, mining roads, abandoned railroad beds and single-tracks (trails wide enough for only one bike). The number of designated trails and suitable routes is increasing so quickly that keeping track is virtually impossible.

Every Colorado resident seems to have a bike or two, and visitors often bring their own. Many resort towns have as many bike shops as T-shirt emporiums, so if you are of average size you'll have no trouble finding a rental, even if you're looking for a tandem or other specialty bike. Children's seats and trailers make cycling a family sport even if the kids aren't old enough to ride by themselves. Guided rides and overnight trips are available, too, often with van support. Special events ranging from modest bike festivals to big-time road cycling and mountain biking competitions are held throughout the summer.

Recreational paths in (and sometimes between) urban areas welcome cyclists. Some are paved; others are gravel. Cycling is permitted on unpaved roads and some trails in national forests and Bureau of Land Management (BLM) regions but only on paved roads in national parks. Networks of old mining roads lead deep into the mountains and make for excellent bike routes.

Bike maps are usually available at visitor centers, ranger stations and other tourist information facilities. Bicycle Colorado (1525 Market Street, Suite 100, Denver, CO 80202; tel: 303-417-1544; www.bicyclecolo.org) promotes bicycling in Colorado, lobbies for improved conditions and gives Colorado cyclists a voice.

In the end, it doesn't really matter how you experience the outdoors. The important thing is to spend time outside – to feel the sun on your face, the earth beneath your feet, the flow of a mountain stream. And to understand, as Colorado naturalist Enos Mills did, that enjoying the outdoors "will develop a love for nature, strengthen one's appreciation of the beautiful world outdoors, and put one in tune with the Infinite."   ❏

LEFT: canoeing on Lost Lake near Kebler Pass.
RIGHT: biking in Rifle Gap State Park.

POWDER TO THE PEOPLE

Experts and novices alike are drawn to the
deep powder, long season and huge vertical drops
of this high altitude kingdom of snow

If any place on the planet is designed for skiing, it's Colorado. And it didn't take early settlers long to discover it. It is thought that skis were first used in a mining camp along the Blue River near present-day Breckenridge during the winter of 1859–60. Father John L. Dyer, the most famous of the 50 or so stalwarts contracted to carry mail over the mountains, used skis to deliver letters and the word of God to remote mining camps.

Miners from Irwin and Crested Butte challenged each other to downhill races as early as 1886. In 1911, Norwegian ski jumper Carl Howelsen – dubbed the "Flying Norseman" during a brief stint with Barnum & Bailey's circus – thrilled crowds in Hot Sulphur Springs by soaring 79ft (24 meters) through the air. Two years later, when Denver was blanketed by one of the worst blizzards of the century, Howelsen and a handful of other skiers impressed local sportsmen by sliding down Capitol Hill. The episode inspired the formation of the Denver Rocky Mountain Ski Club, which soon became an avid promoter of the sport.

Birth of an idea

It wasn't until the 1930s, however, that the concept of the "ski area" came into its own, thanks largely to the advent of the rope tow, which had its Colorado debut at Berthoud Pass in 1937. The first chair-lift, constructed in the fashion of a mining tram, was installed at the Pioneer Ski Area near Crested Butte in 1939. Colorado's first double chair-lift was erected nine years

LEFT: powder flies as a back country skier slices through fresh snow. **RIGHT:** skiers on a snow path in Genesee Park, 1940.

later at Berthoud Pass. World War II naturally put a hold on ski area development, but not on skiing. Thousands of "ski troops" were trained at Camp Hale near Leadville during the war. Afterwards, veterans of the camp's 10th Mountain Division were a prime force in creating the post-war ski boom.

The Colorado ski industry contributes $2.6 billion annually to Colorado tourism. Twenty-six full-fledged ski areas operate in the state and attracted 11.86 million skier visits for the 2009–10 season, 20 percent of the national total. Choices range from low-key ski centers where prices are moderate and the atmosphere is relaxed, to ritzy, world-class resorts where the facilities are state-of-the-art, the clientele is chic, and the prices are stratospheric. Regardless of size, they all enjoy some of the world's finest snow conditions. Winter storms barrel down on the Rockies from the Pacific, losing moisture over the deserts of Utah, Nevada and Arizona before unloading tons of light, dry powder on Colorado. What Mother Nature is slow to deliver, technology provides. Snowmaking systems at most ski areas ensure an early start to the season and, coupled with expert grooming, an adequate surface throughout the winter.

Large or small, just about every ski area offers runs for skiers of all abilities, halfpipes and terrain parks for snowboarders and freeriders, rental equipment, instruction, day care, and a ski patrol trained in rescue and first aid. Major ski areas may have larger and faster chair-lifts than their smaller counterparts (and perhaps a gondola or two), but everything else is merely a matter of scale. What you'll find at the biggest and most elaborate resorts – and here we're talking about world-class destinations like Aspen, Vail, Steamboat and Telluride – is vertical drops of 2,500 to 4,400ft (750–1,350 meters), high-capacity lifts that speed thousands of skiers up the slopes, lodgings for thousands of vacationers and a rollicking après-ski scene. The

SOLDIERS ON SKIS

Taking a cue from the snow-savvy Finns and Scandinavians who had outmaneuvered their respective Russian and German antagonists in winter hostilities, the US military decided in mid-1941 to create its own special fighting force. General George C. Marshall gave the go-ahead to a project that would give birth to the storied 10th Mountain Division – and, indirectly, the Colorado skiing industry as we know it.

The site the Army chose as a training center was an obscure place named Pando high up in the heart of the Colorado Rockies. Here, in a mountain valley 6 miles (10km) north of Leadville, was established Camp Hale. From it would emerge an entire division of troops trained to ski,

climb and fight in harsh weather and on rugged turf by a cadre of mixed American and European experts.

There was plenty of frostbite and other ailments before the 10th Division was put to the test in Italy, starting in November 1944. Its warriors engaged in a series of encounters with Nazi forces in the Po Valley as they cleared a path for the US Army stretching north to the Alps. The cost was high: 992 American war deaths.

The division was eventually disbanded in October 1945. But fond memories of life in Colorado, augmented by a strong bond among comrades, brought many back. They carved out new lives in a skiing industry they did so much to energize.

giants among them rack up a million or more skier visits every winter and are popular summer resorts. Those closest to Denver, including Keystone, Breckenridge, Copper Mountain, Vail and Winter Park, are jammed with both day-skiers and vacationers. Others are far enough afield to be purely destination resorts.

The Colorado ski season extends over an extraordinary eight months a year. It starts in late October or early November, when Arapahoe Basin and Loveland compete for first-to-open honors, and finishes in June or even July, though most skiers agree that prime time is between Thanksgiving and Easter. Prices for lift tickets and lodging vary widely depending on when you go. Expect the best deals early and late in the season as well as in January. The Christmas holiday and Presidents Week (in late February) command the highest prices and biggest crowds.

The I-70 corridor

Driving west out of Denver along Interstate 70, the first major ski area west of the Eisenhower Tunnel is Keystone. Established in 1970, it burst on the scene with a network of mostly mild runs etched through the trees, a brand-new luxury hotel that stood in sharp contrast to the primitive ski lodgings of the day and, soon after, clusters of condominiums tucked into the woods. Keystone's trail system now includes 135 routes spread across three mountains. It is Colorado's only resort with two high-speed gondolas and the state's only major destination to offer night skiing on a large scale. The Keystone Lodge, an early bastion of ski-country luxury, has been refurbished more than once over the years and is still a fine place to stay.

Next is the exit for Breckenridge, a 19th-century gold-mining boomtown set against the soaring 10 Mile Range – a dramatic north–south chain of 10 mountains named Peak 1 through Peak 10. When it opened in 1961, with one double chair-lift and a short T-bar, Breckenridge welcomed 17,000 skiers during the first season. Today, it hosts the same number on a busy Saturday. In 1981, Breckenridge installed the world's first detachable quad chair-lift which, with a capacity of 2,800 skiers per hour,

is credited with launching the sport's high-speed quad revolution. Three years later, Breck became Colorado's first major resort to allow snowboarding. Another lift innovation followed in 1999 with the installation of a double-loading, six-passenger chair-lift.

Copper Mountain, directly south of I-70, was developed 10 years after Breckenridge. Like Keystone, it was a built-from-scratch ski resort, with lodging as well as lifts. Its mountain and big backside bowl regularly win kudos for their intelligent layout, and its resort base has been totally remade in the successful formula developed by corporate giant Intrawest, which

acquired it in 1997. Copper has more skiable terrain than any other area in Summit County – which means it's bigger than Keystone, Breckenridge and Arapahoe Basin.

High and mighty

Farther along I-70 is Vail, America's largest ski area in terms of skiable acreage and lift capacity, and arguably its most successful resort. Vail was the brainchild of 10th Mountain Division veterans Pete Seibert, Bill "Sarge" Brown and Bob Parker, who shared an audacious vision for a grand, European-style resort. When Vail opened in 1962 with the nucleus of an Alpine-style village, a long four-passenger gondola, two chair-lifts, and a Pomalift, it became the most

---

LEFT: skiers with wooden skis and a single pole at Steamboat Springs, *c.*1916. **RIGHT:** kids learning at ski-school at Copper Mountain Resort.

talked-about ski area in the country. Skiers haven't stopped talking since – or visiting.

Vail's mammoth ski terrain stretches 7 miles (11km) from east to west, and encompasses nearly 5,300 acres (2,200 hectares), 33 lifts (14 of them high-speed quads) with a mind-boggling hourly lift capacity of 51,781, and snowriding on 193 named trails. In addition to frontside runs cut through the trees, Vail has seven side-by-side backside bowls. Across the valley is Blue Sky Basin, added in the winter of 1999–2000. Vail Village takes in half a dozen development pods on both sides of I-70, and what is now known promotionally as the Vail

Valley stretches all the way from the west side of Vail Pass to Edwards. Vail is just about as far from Denver as most people are willing to drive for day skiing.

Beaver Creek, 10 miles (16km) to the west, was to have been developed for the 1976 Winter Olympics. Colorado refused the Games, however, giving time for the Beaver Creek plan to mature. Since it opened in 1980, Beaver Creek has grown into the state's most up-market resort, with gated entrances, monumental architecture and some of the most pleasant cruising terrain in Colorado. The resort's legal beagles copyrighted the term "village-to-village skiing"

CRISSCROSSING COLORADO

With hundreds of miles of groomed trails and virtually limitless back country terrain, Colorado is perfect for cross-country skiers. But where to start? A logical choice is one of 14 Nordic centers and three guest ranches that offer groomed trails for both cross-country skiers and snowshoers and access to challenging back country terrain. Most have classes for skiers at every level of experience, including children, as well as special nature tours and guided treks. For information, contact the Colorado Cross Country Ski Association, PO Box 8937, Keystone, CO 80435; www.coloradocrosscountry.com. For a full-blown Western experience, you may want to check into one of several dude ranches that trade horses for skis during the winter months. Sleigh rides, sledding and horseback riding are just a few of the supplemental diversions you'll find at the ranches, most surrounded by thousands of acres of national forest. For multiday journeys there's a network of 29 cabins linking 350 miles (560km) of back country in the Central Rockies between Aspen, Crested Butte, Leadville and Vail and throughout the San Juan Mountains of the Southern Rockies. It's known as hut-to-hut travel among enthusiasts, and trekking between huts requires both navigation skill and skiing ability, so skiers with less experience tend to spend one or more nights in a single hut rather than travel from one to another. For further information, contact the 10th Mountain Division Hut Association, 1280 Ute Ave, Suite 21, Aspen, CO 81611; tel: 970-925-5775.

in order to stress that its three lodging "villages" – Beaver Creek, Bachelor Gulch and Arrowhead – are connected by trails, a fairly unusual arrangement in the United States.

Winter Park and Steamboat

If you exit I-70 at Empire and head north over Berthoud Pass, you come to Winter Park, an area popular with both vacationers and day-trippers. This is the only resort in the Rockies served by a dedicated "ski train," which departs from Union Station in Denver. Winter Park's 3,060 skiable acres (1,238 hectares) encompass four summits, 143 runs and 25 lifts. Groswold Discovery Park

Steamboat's pioneering Kids Ski Free program lures thousands of families. The traditional ranching town of Steamboat Springs is just 3 miles (5km) from the sprawling resort at the base of the mountain.

Aspen and Crested Butte

Among skiers, "Aspen" refers to four ski areas under one ownership near the chic mountain town of the same name. Aspen Mountain, the granddaddy of them all, sprang to life in 1941 with a 10-passenger "boat" tow, comprised of an old mine hoist powered by a truck engine. A chair-lift was installed in 1946, and Aspen

is an exceptional beginner area, situated well up the mountain but isolated from faster skiers and snowboarders. The Mary Jane sector offers legendary mogul-dotted steeps; Parsenn Bowl has gobs of high-elevation powder; and the Cirque offers fly-on-the-wall pitch.

Far to the northwest, Steamboat occupies a beautiful west-facing massif near the Wyoming state line. The resort's marketing department coined the phrase "champagne powder" to describe the deep, soft snow that accumulates on broad slopes and drifts into aspen glades.

LEFT: snowmobiling through the forests near Vail.
ABOVE: a Winter Park instructor encourages a student; children's programs are available at most resorts.

SILVERTON MOUNTAIN, ANTI-RESORT

The biggest little ski area in America, Silverton Mountain is not your average resort. It opened in 2000 in southwestern Colorado, the antithesis of the megaresorts that sprawl across the Rocky Mountains. This back country, experts-only ski area is best defined by what it does not have – no conventional amenities, no novice or intermediate terrain, no trail map, no ski school, no frills. Not surprisingly, it quickly developed a cult following among some of the best skiers and snowboarders in the land. Among the resorts big selling points is Silverton, an old mining town filled with character, reached via narrow-gauge railway or the winding San Juan Skyway from Durango.

Mountain has set the gold standard for ski-borne excitement ever since.

Three other resorts – Aspen Highlands, Buttermilk and Snowmass – were developed later, each with a distinct personality. Snowmass is by far the largest of the trio, with 5,300 skiable acres (2,144 hectares) second only to Vail, and features a wicked 4,406ft (1,343-meter) vertical drop, Colorado's biggest. A million-acre (404,685-hectare) new base village at Snowmass is currently being developed by Related Westpac, complete with hotels, condos, restaurants, shops, and other visitor facilities, all with a sustainable design. The new Snowmass will include a children's center and mountain improvements.

Just 25 miles (40km) from Aspen as the crow flies, but an epic drive in winter, is Crested Butte. The enchanting Victorian town nestles in the valley; a separate resort area is set at the base of the lifts. The terrain is varied and quirky, wrapping part-way around a signature peak. Crested Butte offers everything from beginner slopes that are smooth as a table top to some of Colorado's gnarliest terrain, including an area dubbed Extreme Limits, described by one writer as "a staircase of huge, staggered headwalls that drop off the north side of the moun-

SKI COUNTRY, INCORPORATED

The consolidation rampant in corporate America has invaded ski country, providing capital for large-scale improvements at big resorts but homogenizing the ski experience. Vancouver-based Intrawest developed Keystone's Village at River Run and owns Steamboat Ski and Resort and Winter Park. Vail Resorts, Inc., operates some lodging and all on-mountain facilities at Vail, Beaver Creek, Breckenridge and Keystone, as well as Heavenly in California; Rockresorts luxury properties and golf resorts; and Colorado Mountain Express. Aspen Skiing Company controls on-mountain facilities at Aspen Mountain, Buttermilk, Aspen Highlands and Snowmass, and operates some Aspen lodging.

tain." Though Crested Butte is relatively modest in overall size, an elevation gain of 3,062ft (933 meters) from base to summit puts it in Colorado's top 10 of vertical drop.

The San Juans

Durango Mountain Resort and Telluride are the top destinations in the snow-rich San Juan Range of southwestern Colorado. Telluride is the name of a gussied-up mining town as well as a nearby ski area, which encompasses a posh development called Mountain Village and an expanded terrain of 2,000 skiable acres (809 hectares). Linking the old town and Mountain Village is a gondola, affording breathtaking views of the valley and surrounding peaks. Telluride's expert runs are among Colorado's most challenging, but its novice and intermediate terrain are top-notch, too.

Durango Mountain Resort (dubbed Purgatory by locals) is smaller and far less exclusive than Telluride, with 1,200 skiable acres (485 hectares), 10 lifts and a vertical drop that's a hair over 2,000ft (600 meters). In 2008, the resort opened its luxury $50-million Purgatory Lodge, anchor for the new Purgatory Village, followed, in 2009, by the unveiling of expanded acreage with 125 acres (50 hectares) of expert terrain. The town of Durango is about 30 minutes away.

skiers and families with school-age children may prefer Sunlight Mountain Resort near Glenwood Springs or Powderhorn Resort on the north side of Grand Mesa east of Grand Junction.

Just because a ski area is small doesn't mean it's not challenging. In fact, some of Colorado's most exciting slopes are found at half a dozen sites that are short on size but long on action. Five of the six are situated on high passes along the Continental Divide, where snow falls frequently, piles up deep, and lasts late into the season. These areas are ideal for people who miss the ambience of old-time skiing, don't give

Good things, small packages

In addition to the mega-resorts is an array of mid-sized ski areas, where the prices are reasonable, the atmosphere is low-key, and the conditions, while not superlative, are adequate for novice and intermediate skiers. SolVista Golf & Ski Ranch, for instance, is the odd name for a pleasant little ski resort north of Winter Park, near Granby. It consists of an easy hill and an easier hill – a snooze if you're an experienced skier but a good choice if you're just learning or traveling with small children. Intermediate

a fig about fashion, and prefer snow as nature makes it. They have day lodges instead of slopeside villages, free parking instead of pay lots, and their collective 33 lifts don't include a single high-speed chair. They're decent places for beginners, but have plenty to offer intermediate and advanced skiers and snowboarders.

Loveland straddles I-70 about an hour from Denver. It has two pods: Loveland Valley for beginners and the larger Loveland Basin, which has trails woven through evergreens topped by expansive ski-anywhere terrain. Its fixed-grip quad, which unloads at 13,010ft (3,965 meters), is the world's highest four-place chair-lift.

Just over the west side of Loveland Pass is Arapahoe Basin. With a summit elevation of

LEFT: hiking to the perfect spot high above Telluride.
ABOVE: preparing to go over the edge at Copper Mountain Resort, on ski and snowboard.

13,050ft (3,980 meters), A-Basin is the country's highest lift-served ski area. A spring-skiing center, the lifts regularly operate into June, often July, and with snow-making finally installed, the season launches in October. Set in a cirque beneath the brow of the Continental Divide, half the ski terrain is above timber line, providing vistas of treeless, craggy peaks etched in high relief against an azure sky. Steep snowfields and relentless chutes give it a reputation as an experts-only area, but milder slopes are available, too. Beginners have free use of the Molly Hogan novice hill at the base.

Situated just east of Monarch Pass near Sal-

ida, the Monarch Ski Area snares an average of 350in (890cm) of powder annually from the "Monarch Cloud." Nearly all the acreage is skiable, including areas that don't appear on the trail map – uncharted powder shots through a mature forest of well-spaced pine and fir. A lodge is a couple of miles away, but there are ample accommodations in Salida.

Ski Cooper, high on Tennessee Pass, is the true heir to World War II's Camp Hale. This family-friendly, low-cost ski area remains a rustic outpost of casual, spirited, rarely crowded skiing. The site encompasses 26 runs on two mountain faces with a modest 1,200ft (365-meter) vertical drop. There are two longish chair-lifts and two short surface lifts. The front side offers easy to mid-level skiing, with slightly steeper runs on the backside.

Wolf Creek, between South Fork and Pagosa Springs, has a 465in (1,180cm) average annual snowfall, nearly 100in (250cm) more than any other ski area in Colorado save Silverton Mountain. The prodigious powder and laid-back ambience appeal to deep-snow addicts. The area is comprised of a long ridge that drapes down into mountain top bowls, superlative glades and wide cruising runs. Advanced skiers and snowboarders seeking a back country experience can traverse to Alberta Peak, Step Bowl and Knife Ridge, true havens of the steep and deep in southern Colorado.

Home town advantage

The small fry in Colorado's ski scene are the modest, often municipally owned ski slopes. Many are run by volunteers and open only on weekends and school holidays for the benefit of local youngsters. These include Kendall Mountain in Silverton, Chapman Hill in Durango and Hesperus between Durango and Mancos.

Among the largest sites in this category is Eldora Mountain Resort outside Boulder, which has 680 skiable acres and a dozen lifts. Another small ski area that casts a big shadow is Steamboat Springs' Howelsen Hill. It is the town's main winter amenity, offering night skiing, ski jumping, freestyle and race training, cross-country skiing and ice-skating – all at a rock-bottom price. If you ski Steamboat and want to meet the locals, including a few candidates for the USSki Team, Howelsen Hill is the place to be.

Colorado Ski and Snowboard Museum and Hall of Fame in Vail chronicles the history of Rocky Mountain skiing from postmen who trekked over mountain passes on primitive skis in the mid-1800s to 21st-century Olympic hopefuls.

Despite their diminutive size, these local ski hills are guardians of Colorado's ski legacy, and they are just as important as the giant resorts that pull in millions of skiers and riders from around the world. ❏

LEFT: carving through the powder at Steamboat Springs. **RIGHT:** young children enjoy the snow under almost any condition.

GHOST TOWNS

Visions of bygone days are evoked by former mining camps – some
in ruins, others reborn as tourist havens – mementoes of those
who came here seeking their fortunes

Here today, gone tomorrow... then, frequently, back again, in a completely different form. Colorado's many mining ghost towns are the shape-shifters of the architectural world. From potential state capital to tourism and gambling at Central City. Silver mining to celebrity skiing at Aspen, Breckenridge and Telluride. Rough mining camp to ghost town museum at Fairplay. Abandoned mountain town to vacation paradise in artsy Creede. All of these ghosts, and many more, have roared back to life, blurring the line between past and present in entirely new ways.

They are the lucky ones, the rediscovered gems of Colorado's rich and rowdy mining history. Hundreds of other mining camps and towns, with populations that once numbered in the thousands, slumber on in mountain valleys and hillsides throughout the Rockies. Today, their only inhabitants are deer and chipmunks and the occasional tourist in search of Colorado's colorful past.

Former lives

Once these towns were spectacularly alive, swarming with miners and merchants, clergymen and saloon-keepers, lawmakers and lawbreakers. Well-dressed dudes from back East brought capital for the expensive machinery required to dig deep into the earth for hidden and elusive riches. But many of the towns they created were destined to fail. When all the precious stuff was tapped out, the settlements were doomed. The bonan-

LEFT: an actor dressed up for the wild west at Buckskin Joe at the Royal Gorge in Cañon City. **RIGHT:** handcart passengers on the Cripple Creek Short Line in one of the state's richest mining districts.

zas that fueled boomtowns were dramatic, the decline often catastrophic. As mineral deposits played out and miners moved on to new fields of dreams, fortunes won turned quickly to fortunes lost, and boomtown became ghost town.

Those towns built to serve surrounding mining camps never really died. Lake City, Ouray, Silverton, Telluride, Durango and Denver were close to mines that yielded billions of tons of gold, silver, lead and other precious metals. They grew into the largest and wealthiest towns in the state and became politically important as supply centers and seats of local and state government. Today, they are undergoing a metamorphosis. Whole districts of Victorian mansions, company buildings, hotels, bars and bordellos are now on the National Register of Historic Places. Many have been restored by artists, retirees and local historical associations and turned into quirky home-grown museums, art galleries, bed and breakfasts, bars and restaurants filled with mine memorabilia.

Colorado's mining boom began late, nearly a decade after the California Gold Rush, mainly due to the inaccessibility of the 14,000ft (4,270-meter) Rocky Mountains. The 1859 gold strike in Gregory Gulch attracted fortune hunters who traveled to north-central Colorado's high-altitude mining camps by whatever means they

could, some hauling their worldly possessions up mountain sides in handcarts. It was the construction of toll roads and narrow-gauge railroads in the 1870s that made mining economically viable, linking remote mining settlements with smelter towns like Durango. Today, these historic roads, Jeep trails and narrow-gauge railroads have been restored and are the mainstay of a new economy – tourism – that has helped revive ghost towns throughout the Rockies.

There are more than 700 ghost towns in Colorado, by some estimates the greatest number in the West. A true ghost town has two characteristics: Its population has precipitously decreased, and the initial reason for its settlement, usually a mine, no longer supports the community. Scores are no more than mysterious names on a topographical map, completely unpopulated, with dilapidated buildings, empty schools, churches and collapsed headframes. Most, though, have a few residents who look after the buildings, conduct tours, and keep alive those forgotten places.

Frozen in time

The quintessential Colorado ghost town is a highly photogenic mining camp at the foot of breathtaking mountains, the faded timbers of its cabins and false-front buildings creaking in the wind and nearby mining tackle falling into a steep ravine filled with wild flowers. Your best bet in Colorado for this type of experience is St Elmo, 24 miles (39km) southwest of Buena Vista in the South Park mining region. Founded in the 1880s, St Elmo was typical of gold and silver boomtowns: it grew so fast that tents standing one day were replaced by hand-hewn

---

HAUNTED COLORADO

From ghostly beauties tempting train engineers, to dripping mine shafts echoing with the banter of men long dead, Colorado echoes with tales of unexplained phenomena. Leadville historian Roger Peterson has had several close encounters over the years.

His most powerful experience took place in Silverton, where he recorded noises in an old miners' boarding house. In the night, he was awakened by the sound of someone slamming books on a coffee table in an empty adjoining room. Playing back the tape the next day, he heard a menacing voice, sounding as if it came from inside a well, saying "Share the loot."

Cheryl Lloyd, caretaker of the Matchless Mine Museum,

also tells of strange goings-on at the 1880 silver mine that made millionaires – then paupers – of Horace and Baby Doe Tabor. After Horace's death, Baby Doe occupied a shack at the worthless mine, surviving on charity from townsfolk and unrequited hope of a new silver boom. In March 1935 she was found frozen to death at the age of 81. But Lloyd says she is still very much present.

Visitors send Lloyd photos taken here, showing unexplained waves, lights and reflections in the shack. Lights flick on and off, even after light bulbs are removed.

And after visitors tried to sit in an empty rocking chair that already seemed occupied, Lloyd placed a sign on it: "Please don't sit on me."

log cabins within the week. A few months later, many cabins were supplanted by milled-lumber false-front buildings. In the early days, if a guest arrived at a not-quite-complete hotel and asked for a private room, the hotelier drew a chalk line around one of the beds and told him that he had even given him a suite.

A supply center for nearby mines, St Elmo was a favorite Saturday night "blow off" town for miners, freighters, railroad workers and other passersby. When Mark Twain rode the railroad down to St Elmo, the brakeman "had some difficulty" after the perilous journey, and Twain declined a return trip. Now the town is somnolent. Miners'

from St Elmo on the outskirts of the former mining camp of Fairplay, founded in 1859 by miners who found themselves shut out of diggings at Tarryall. Opened a century after the first gold strike in Colorado, South Park City is an authentic restoration of a Colorado mining town. Some 28 of its 35 buildings were brought here from all over Colorado, restored, and filled with mining-era artifacts. A schoolhouse straight out of *Little House on the Prairie* has desks, chairs and a blackboard. A drug store is so well stocked with remedies, it looks like the movie set of *Dr Quinn, Medicine Woman*. In all, some 60,000 mining-era artifacts fill the buildings.

cabins have become summer residences and the main activity centers on insatiable chipmunks cadging handouts from visitors. Eccentric brothers Roy and Tony Stark and their sister Annabelle owned the Comfort Home Hotel and protected the town for decades. Tony and Annabelle were among the last residents of the crumbling ghost town. Since she died in 1960, Annabelle's ghost has been seen or felt at times, still watching over the town from the hotel windows. The town is now a national historic site.

A ghost town of a different type lies not far

In summer, the Alpine Loop links Silverton to communities in the central San Juans, such as Lake City , and the San Juan Skyway – connecting the western San Juans – brings thousands of drivers into the mountains annually.

Nearby Cripple Creek's restoration was funded in an entirely different way: casino gambling. Slot machines and blackjack tables now fill the historic buildings in this 1890s gold-mining town, which once had a larger population than Denver. For a glimpse of what Cripple Creek once looked like, visit Victor, 6 miles (10km) to the southwest. This

LEFT: a ghost town with a few modern touches.
ABOVE: the Ghost Town Museum in Colorado Springs is a collection of old buildings from around the state.

former gold town has rare brick-and-mortar buildings, including a two-story school, depot, church, newspaper office and a once-elegant miners' club. Its paved streets, dug up during the Depression, were literally "paved with gold" – mine waste from local diggings. Boxing legend Jack Dempsey, who grew up in Colorado, was a mucker at the Portland Mine before becoming heavyweight champion of the world. To view more former mining towns, drive the 122-mile (196km) Gold Belt Loop between Cripple Creek and Cañon City, which winds among the steep gulches of the south slope of Pikes Peak.

Vanished communities

St Elmo and Victor are two of Colorado's best ghost towns, but even deserted, decrepit ghosts offer much to see and photograph. Some showcase old railroad depots. Others feature mills, smelters, headframes, tramways and other mining-related buildings and equipment. Often a boarded-up courthouse or school dominates the site. In many cases, the sole reminder that a town ever existed is its forlorn cemetery, with weathered markers and picketless fences.

The 65-mile (105km) Alpine Loop Back country Byway linking Lake City, Silverton and Ouray in the San Juan Mountains of southwest-

ALL ABOARD!

Colorado's narrow-gauge railways have added an element of romance to visiting ghost towns in the Rockies. The 45-mile (72km) Durango & Silverton Narrow Gauge Railway brings passengers by steam train from Durango into the heart of Silverton twice a day in summer. The 6-mile (10km) Georgetown Loop Railroad carries passengers between Georgetown and Silver Plume on an hour-long trip on a 1920s-era steam locomotive. The railway links two 1859 mining towns that boomed for 30 years, first with the discovery of gold, then large quantities of silver. Georgetown today is undergoing a renaissance as an expensive retreat for the wealthy, and its downtown historic district has the largest number of preserved historic buildings in Colorado. Several of the more than 200 buildings are now museums recounting the area's rich mining history. The historic railroad through Royal Gorge, the 1,053ft (321-meter) deep canyon cut by the Arkansas River, begins in Cañon City, about 35 miles (56km) from Cripple Creek. The 24-mile (38km) round-trip offers amazing views of Royal Gorge, one of Colorado's deepest canyons, and views of the world's highest suspension bridge, built in 1929. Outside the entrance to Royal Gorge is Buckskin Joe, a movie-set town recreated with buildings from the original mining town of Buckskin Joe, northwest of Cañon City. Ghost town experiences in Colorado don't come more authentic than Buckskin Joe, with its stagecoach rides, shootouts and costumed actors.

ern Colorado is filled with abandoned ghost towns. Capitol City, a few miles southwest of Lake City and reachable by passenger car, briefly boomed in the 1870s, when the Galena Mining District brought untold silver wealth to the area. One entrepreneur, George Lee, was so convinced the town was set to become the state capital, he built smelters and a governor's mansion at the remote site. With the silver crash of 1893, the town was quickly left to the elements and has never been reoccupied.

There are people in the buildings at Animas Forks, but only for a few days each summer, when this abandoned 1870s town, located at an elevation of 11,200ft (3,415 meters) 12 miles (19km) north of Silverton, offers living-history days. Costumed interpreters, including a doctor's wife, a teacher, pioneer children and the town sheriff, serve lemonade and apple-sauce cake and chat with visitors who arrive by Jeep, mountain bike or hiking trail.

Animas Forks was once a bustling mining community of 450 people with 30 cabins, a hotel, general store, saloon and post office. An important mining mill and processing center, it was the San Juan County seat, where court cases were heard. One man who didn't like the outcome of his trial promised, "I'll take this to a higher court!" Responded the wry judge, "There is no higher court in Colorado."

In 1884, Animas Forks suffered a blizzard that lasted 23 days and dumped 25ft (7 meters) of snow on the town. Residents dug tunnels to get from building to building. Silverton, 2,000ft (610 meters) lower, was considered positively balmy and became a popular place to spend the winter. Laid out along the Animas River in Baker's Park in 1874, Silverton soon became the mining center of the San Juans. The arrival of the Denver & Rio Grande Railroad linked it to the new smelter town of Durango, 45 miles (72km) away, in 1882, and Otto Mears' new toll road allowed auto traffic to continue north to Ouray and Ridgway. Eventually, Silverton was incorporated and became the county seat. Among the many buildings in its authentic downtown historic district (complete with saloons, hotels, stores and a redlight district) is a lavish courthouse next door to the county museum.

LEFT: the Durango & Silverton Narrow Gauge Railroad.
RIGHT: waste ponds from the uranium mines in Western Colorado.

Glowing ghosts

Despite their scenic locations, authentic ghost towns are frequently homely affairs. Colorado's 20th-century mining boom netted a number of forgettable company towns dedicated to extracting copper, radium, vanadium, uranium and oil shale to suit the energy and defense needs of an entirely different new century.

The town of Uravan on the spectacular Unaweep–Tabegauche Scenic Byway, which follows SR 141 between Naturita and Whitewater, was built in 1936 by the US Vanadium Corporation. Until the declining market forced the town to close down in 1984, some 42 million lbs (20

million kg) of uranium and 220 million lbs (100 million kg) of vanadium were extracted from carnotite rocks here. Today, the place is abandoned, and Umetco Minerals Corporation is undertaking a 15-year, $70 million reclamation project to clean up the mine site.

The fate of Parachute, just east of Grand Junction, is still in the balance. Built by Union Oil Company during the energy crisis of the 1970s to mine oil shale, the multimillion-dollar company town and processing plant was one of the largest employers in the Grand Junction area. All but abandoned since the 1990s, it now sits beside roaring traffic along I-70, a forlorn testament to modern boom-and-bust economics in Colorado's energy-rich northwest corner. ❑

RIDING THE RAILS

It took master builders to lay track over forbidding terrain,
connect Colorado with the rest of the world,
and leave a steel trail for vacationers to pursue

ioneers would be puzzled by our modern romance with that clanking, smoky, iron contraption: the 19th-century steam engine. They would see an automobile as being so much cleaner, so much more comfortable than a hard-backed seat on wheels. For that matter, the diesel locomotives of today are a great improvement – quieter, more powerful, pulling clean air-conditioned cars on welded tracks. You can imagine an old-timer shaking his head, wondering why people would want to get cinders in their hair.

On the other hand, even the toughest old miner working his diggings in a high-country camp must have got excited seeing that column of smoke moving up the canyons of the Colorado Rockies. With their whistles sounding, freight cars full of fancy goods from back East, visiting relatives and hardware for the mines, the steam trains that huffed their way through Colorado's mining country were a vital link with the outside world. Back then, passengers probably leaped aboard with the same enthusiasm as the 700,000 tourists who today line up to ride one of the 10 scenic railroads that, since the 1990s, have been revived throughout the Rockies.

United by iron

Although they seem quaint to us now, the 5,739 miles (9,236km) of railroad track that once linked the far-flung communities of Colorado were a miracle of American can-do technology and entrepreneurial vision in the second half of the 1800s, when most of it was laid. What

LEFT: christening the Colorado Springs & Cripple Creek train No. 2 in 1900. **RIGHT:** the engineer of the Royal Gorge Scenic Railway.

started out as a grand political move to build a transcontinental railroad, linking East and West, was quickly taken on as a local cause among the movers and shakers within the states the American railroad crossed. Once a cross-country railroad became a reality, in the 1880s, businessmen like Union Pacific Railroad's Jay Gould, the Denver & Rio Grande's General Palmer, Denver Pacific Railroad's David Moffat, and Colorado Central Railroad's William Loveland competed to build branch lines that would tie remote mining towns in Colorado to the main route, and to markets back East. Over nearly a century, fortunes were made and lost, as the markets for gold, silver, coal and, in the 20th century, uranium, rose and fell and railroads changed ownership as fast as a game of Monopoly.

In 1848, remote, mountainous Colorado seemed like the other side of the moon to the US government in Washington DC, which had just taken ownership of the West from Mexico. From the reports of Spanish and American explorers, politicians and businessmen were keenly aware that vast mineral wealth lay under unsettled lands out there. Colorado's rugged topography presented a formidable obstacle to American settlement. It was territory known only to Utes and other native people and a few mountain men and adventurers.

try again, this time as part of a major railroad survey authorized by Congress, which had fast-tracked its plans following the discovery of gold in California in 1848. Congress allocated $150,000 for four separate surveys and sent Captain John Gunnison to survey a potential route through the Central Rockies. Following part of Spanish friar Escalante's route, Gunnison traveled through the Gunnison River valley, staying north of the San Juan Mountains. He made it as far as Utah, where he and seven others, including well-known surveyor Richard Kern, were killed in the desert, apparently by Utes at war with Mormons during the Walker War (although this is by no

One American explorer, John C. Frémont, had already made three overland trips to California, using famed scout Kit Carson to guide him through the Rockies. Late in 1848, a cabal of St Louis railroad promoters paid Frémont to make a fourth cross-country trip to investigate a possible transcontinental route through Colorado. After getting a late start, the expedition turned deadly in the San Juan Mountains, when Frémont and the 33 men in his party found themselves trapped by deep snows in the high country surrounding the headwaters of the Upper Rio Grande. Frémont and his men were eventually rescued, but not before 11 had died in the treacherous mountains of the Continental Divide.

It would be five years before surveyors would

means certain: anti-government feeling by Mormon militants may have played a part).

Gunnison's second-in-command continued to Salt Lake City and eventually returned to Washington with a favorable report of the route. Not to be outdone, in the winter of 1854, John C. Frémont returned to Colorado, retracing Gunnison's route, proving that a year-round railroad was indeed viable.

A national depression, in-fighting over which towns would host the new railroad, and the Civil War delayed construction of the transcontinental railroad for a decade. But the discovery of gold in 1858, followed by a silver bonanza, finally forced the government to act. In the late 1860s, Congress chartered the Union Pacific to build a transcontinental line, and to the chagrin of the fledgling state capital of Denver, UPR chose a route through Cheyenne, Wyoming, that avoided the Rocky Mountains.

Left out in the cold, Denver businessmen hatched plans to build their own railroads

> Riding the train through Black Canyon of the Gunnison in 1889, Rudyard Kipling noted: "There was a glory and a wonder... about the mad ride... I had to offer prayers for the safety of the train."

north to tie in with the transcontinental line. The first to act was William Loveland, whose Colorado Central Railroad Company built track north from Golden to Cheyenne. Denver rival David Moffatt formed the Denver Pacific Railroad in 1870, linking Denver with Cheyenne. By the end of that year, 157 miles (253km) of track had been laid. The race was on.

Narrow gauge debut

Early railroads all ran on standard gauge track, but Colorado's steep mountain and canyons required a different kind of railroad. In 1870, General Palmer, former director of the Denver Pacific, founded the Denver & Rio Grande Railroad, which, from the beginning, was designed to serve the remote mining country of Colorado. An empire builder by nature, Palmer's genius was to conceive of a railroad with many feeder branches linking Colorado's far-flung mining communities. The Denver & Rio Grande operated on the 3ft (1-meter) wide narrow gauge as opposed to the standard gauge, which allowed steam trains and their cars to better negotiate narrow curving canyons in the mountains. "It doubles in, doubles out, leaving the traveller still in doubt whether the engine on the track is going, or coming back," wrote one commentator. Palmer's line was hailed as a resounding success.

Mining communities along the way, such as Animas City in southwestern Colorado, worked closely with the Denver & Rio Grande, realizing the railroad would give them an important competitive edge in business. But Palmer proved a

fickle business partner. Once he had gained local support for the railroad, he drove a hard bargain with local communities that hoped to host a D&RG rail depot. When, inevitably, local burghers balked, he would lay out his own company town nearby, complete with smelters, banks, hotels, saloons, mercantiles and other businesses. Colorado Springs, Pueblo, Durango, Salida and Gunnison were all Palmer towns that became important commercial centers. Once established, Palmer then created subsidiary businesses to serve the mines. One, the Colorado Coal and Iron Company, supplied coal that ran the smelters and trains. Coal mining became an impor-

tant component of smelter towns like Durango, which, by the late 1800s, were wreathed in the dark smoke of coal-fired boilers.

Palmer wasn't the only one to benefit from the flurry of railroad building. By the 1880s, Denver had maneuvered itself to the center of the Union Pacific Railroad, Denver & Rio Grande, and Kansas Pacific lines, and had quickly taken over from Golden as Colorado's main supply center. In Golden, William Loveland regrouped and built a line from Golden to Denver to take advantage of its central position on the railroad. He now concentrated on building a railroad to the major producing mines of the South Slope of Pikes Peak in Clear Creek Canyon, Black Hawk and Georgetown, and laid track to Fort Collins,

---

LEFT: an 1894 wreck on the Florence & Cripple Creek Railroad near Anaconda. **RIGHT:** the distinctive yellow carriages of the Durango & Silverton Railroad.

due north of Golden. Other companies moved to monopolize the southern routes. In 1889, the Atchison, Topeka & Santa Fe Railroad consolidated its hold on eastern Colorado by constructing what came to be called the Banana Line (for its yellow coaches) through the San Luis Valley to Pueblo. Pueblo became a major railroad center for points south. One line, dubbed the Chili Line, was built through the agriculturally rich Rio Grande Valley of New Mexico to Española. Another went from Pueblo to the mining town of Trinidad, over Raton Pass, the gateway to the Pecos Valley, to Lamy, near Santa Fe, and continued to points south and west.

THE DURANGO & SILVERTON LINE

A visit to southwest Colorado isn't complete without an excursion through the San Juan Mountains aboard the Durango & Silverton Narrow Gauge Railroad. Two 1920s steam trains pulling yellow parlor cars and open gondolas travel through the lovely Animas River canyon. The 45-mile (72km) journey takes in breathtaking redrock cliffs, epic views of 14,000ft (4,270-meter) mountains in the Weminuche Wilderness, the rapids of the Animas River 400ft (120 meters) below, and the 1905 Tacoma Hydroelectric Power Plant, the nation's oldest. Trains arrive in Silverton around noon. Explore Silverton's historic district before returning by train or taking a chartered bus back to Durango.

Silver roads

The short, savvy Russian immigrant they called the "Pathfinder of the San Juans," Otto Mears, benefited twice over from the arrival of the railroad. Mears was instrumental in pressuring the Utes to sign the Brunot Treaty of 1873, which forced the majority to vacate western Colorado and move to the Uinta Basin of northeastern Utah. Within the year, he had built the San Juan Skyway from Durango to Ridgway. A few years later he sold Palmer the railroad rights-of-way for the D&RG. In just nine short months, the Durango to Silverton line through the Animas Valley had been blasted out of sheer cliffs above the Animas River, allowing Silverton to become the Silver Capital of the San Juans. By 1887, the D&RG had reached the mining town of Ouray. Two years later, it connected with Lake City in the central San Juans.

The late silver rush continued the railroad building throughout Colorado. A number of smaller spurs tied into the D&RG. The County Midland built a line to Aspen in 1890. The Silverton Railroad, linking Silverton with mineral-rich Red Mountain, was built in 1889. In 1899, the Silverton, Gladstone & Northerly Line reached Gladstone. Then in 1904, the Silverton Northern Line reached Animas Forks. In 1892, David Moffatt's Denver to Creede line through Wagon Wheel Gap took advantage of the late silver rush in the Upper Rio Grande area. That same year, Otto Mears himself built the 172-mile (277km) Rio Grande Southern Railroad, linking Durango and Ridgway with the remote mining towns of Rico, Telluride, and nearby mines. Mine profits went up 90 percent overnight.

It didn't last long. Silver prices plummeted during the Silver Panic of 1893, and many of Colorado's smaller railroads went bankrupt and were bought out by the Union Pacific and Denver & Rio Grande. The days of small-time mining were over. Corporations now used expensive new technologies to dig deeper into veins of precious metals, and to intensively cyanide-leach gold and other minerals out of previously mined areas.

With the Depression, numerous companies went bankrupt and miles of railroad track fell out of use. In the 1930s, Rio Grande Southern and Denver & Rio Grande Western converted automobiles to run on narrow-gauge railroad tracks in the western San Juans. The hybrid auto/train, fondly known as the Galloping Goose because of its odd swaying gait on the tracks, once again linked remote communities in the Dolores River valley and the Lake City to Sapinero route. Today, examples can be seen at railroad museums in Ridgway and Dolores. Short excursions in a Galloping Goose car are a highlight of the Durango & Silverton Narrow Gauge Railroad's annual Railfest in August, along with special trips to Silverton in brightly painted 19th-century wood-powered and steam-powered locomotives.

Tourism

Set in some of the most dramatic and beautiful scenery in the country, Colorado's railroads

track would often report sightings of mysterious ghosts, such as beautiful women who beckoned from the side of the tracks, and naughty children who skipped right onto tracks and taunted engineers. Engines themselves sometimes acted as if possessed, racing behind trains and mysteriously jumping tracks, crashing into snowbanks, and causing problems for drivers. One of Colorado's worst train wrecks occurred in August 1904, when the Missouri Pacific Express derailed in a gulch north of Pueblo, killing 96 people. Heavy rains, not ghouls, were responsible for the disaster.

Today, thanks to the commitment of numer-

have always been popular with tourists. In the late 1800s, ordinary folks, not just miners, rode the trains as day-trippers on their days off. In the late 1880s, people from Leadville traveled to Colorado Springs, via Manitou, Ute Pass and South Park, and enjoyed a thrilling ride through a tunnel and along a huge trestle. In 1891 a cog railway was completed to the top of 14,110ft (4,301-meter) Pikes Peak.

As more people rode the rails, a lively folklore grew up around Colorado's trains. Train drivers engulfed in darkness on lonely sections of

ous railroad enthusiasts, historic railroads are again doing a lively business, linking former mining towns all over Colorado. Today, train fans are spoiled for choice. For those with little time, one-hour excursions aboard historic trains are available between Cripple Creek and Victor and on the Georgetown & Silver Plume Loop, linking former mining towns in Colorado's most extensive historic mining district. Not far away, short trips of a very different type are offered up Pikes Peak aboard the historic Pikes Peak Cog Railway, and on the newly opened Cañon City–Royal Gorge scenic train ride, where you can ride in air-conditioned comfort aboard a diesel locomotive to view Colorado's deepest gorge and the country's highest trestle bridge. ❏

LEFT: engine 42 at the Durango Railroad Museum.
ABOVE: a 1900 "flower excursion" on the Colorado Midland Railway.

HOME ON THE RANGE

For a taste of the real West, would-be cowboys eagerly
mount a horse, learn to rope or join a cattle drive,
and don't mind being called dudes

Give us your tired, your upper middle class, your city slickers with caffeine nerves and commuter jitters, and we'll turn them into ridin' and ropin' buckaroos. That was, and still is, the promise of the dude ranch, as unique an institution as ever set up house-keeping in the American West. What other vacation spot would ask guests to help water the horses and round up the heifers – and then ask them to pay for the privilege? But so strong is the American admiration for the cowboy lifestyle that people have spent a century's worth of summers at these homes away from home on the range.

Dude ranches began as a mix of roman-tic escapism and economic necessity. In the late 19th century, cattle ranchers in the newly opened frontiers of Colorado, Wyoming and the Dakotas found Eastern friends and family – and sometimes perfect strangers – arriving at their doorsteps in droves. The visitors needed a base while they hunted buffalo and explored the sce-nic wonders. Such was the code of hospitality that the ranchers felt obliged to board and bed these guests for free and soon found that they were being eaten out of house and home

Though they hated charging visitors, they hated going broke even more. And so, starting in the late 19th century, some ranchers accepted paying guests. Ironically, it was those guests that saved them from economic disaster. While the vagaries of the cattle business drove other ranches into bankruptcy, those with paying guests managed to hang on. The idea caught

LEFT: cowboy portrait, *c.*1880. **RIGHT:** visitors can take a horseback ride from Aspen Lodge, near Estes Park, whether they are experienced or not.

on and before long dude ranches were opening throughout the West.

Westward, ho!

Meanwhile, the railroads had discovered that a dude-ranch vacation could lure paying pas-sengers on westbound trains. They promoted the ranches in their tourist brochures. Popular magazines like *Ladies' Home Journal* and the *Saturday Evening Post* published paeans to the ranch vacation. As cities in the East and Mid-west grew more crowded and industrialized, Western ranch life was seen as an ideal anti-dote to the strains of urban living. During the golden age of dude ranching, from about 1910 to World War II, guests would head west on the train to spend entire summers learning to rope and ride. On the ranch, tired businessmen swapped boardroom pressures for bunkhouse pleasures. Children got to live the life they saw in Tom Mix or Gene Autry movies. Women, in particular, were seen to benefit. Back East they might be condemned to enduring social chit-chat on the porch of a staid resort while their husbands played golf. Out on the ranch, they could ride and hike and fish, just like the men.

By World War II, dude ranches had blossomed throughout Colorado and the West. Most of the ranches offered the basics: lots of horseback riding, including lessons and guided pack trips into the back country, wholesome entertainment like rodeos, square dancing, hay rides and campfire singalongs and great quantities of hearty food.

Dude, where's my horse?

Naturally, there were a few bumps along the trail as Easterners got a crash course in Western ways. The very name "dude ranch" hinted at one difficulty. Was being a dude a matter of pride or shame? To many, the term carried definite connotations of Eastern effeteness, like the pair of ranch visitors described this way by a grizzled wrangler: "One wore lavender angora chaps, the

RIDING, ROPING AND RESTORATION

For a ranch vacation with an environmental difference, consider the 103,000-acre (41,682-hectare) Zapata Ranch adjoining Great Sand Dunes National Park and Preserve in the San Luis Valley of southern Colorado. It is owned by the Nature Conservancy and managed as a unique conservation partnership with the Phillips ranch family, and guests learn traditional and modern ranching practices and enjoy exceptional views of wildlife and the surrounding high-desert landscape. The ranch accommodates 30 guests, housed in the lodge's 1800s log ranch house, a bunkhouse, or a separate building. For more information, visit www.zranch.org.

other bright orange, and each sported a tremendous beaver sombrero and wore a gaudy scarf knotted jauntily about his throat."

But, fearful that the paying guests might take offense, ranch owners took pains to say that "dude" was not an insult but simply a description of anybody who was not a native of the Rocky Mountains. Many dudes, they maintained, could outride Westerners – and that went for women and children, too.

Westerners had to make some adjustments, too. Ranchers had to learn how to manage herds of tourists instead of herds of cattle, and ranch wives had to cook for more demanding Eastern palates. Even the horse underwent some changes. A good dude horse possessed a capable trot and gallop and, most important of all, a good disposition. Some dude ranches began to breed their own horses to promote those traits.

In some ways, a dude ranch was a boon to the working cowboy: as working cattle ranches became fewer and farther between, the dude ranch provided a place where cowboys could still be paid for their skills. As one ranch manager said, "There is a real future here for a cowhand who can ride, play the guitar, and still smell nice." An able dude-ranch wrangler had to be charming to the ladies, pals with the men, and a hero to the children. The duties could be arduous indeed, as one cowboy song laments:

honed their horsemanship skills as children came back to work as wranglers on summers off from college. And an experience – seeing Colorado from the back of a horse – that had once been limited to ranch owners or to the very wealthy, became accessible to millions of middle-class Americans.

That's still true today. Dude ranches may have more competition for vacation time and money than they once did; few people take more than a week or two at a time for vacations. But the dude ranch has learned to change with the times and remain competitive by catering to the needs of family vacationers.

I'm a tough, hard-boiled old cow-hand with a weather-beaten hide,
But herdin' cows is nuthin' to teachin' dudes to ride.
I can stand their hitoned langwidge and their hifalutin' foods,
But you bet your bottom dollar I am fed up on wranglin' dudes.

Still, despite a few burrs under the saddle, dudes and wranglers and ranchers all generally got along fine. Many families returned to the same dude ranch summer after summer, generation after generation. Teenagers who had

ABOVE: cowboys round up a herd near Yellow Creek in Rio Blanco County, 1911; a typical salary was $25 a month plus "all the horses you can ride."

Today's dude ranches are more plush than the ranches of yore. Some have added healthful spa cuisine to the old standards of barbecued steak, beans, corn on the cob; others entertain guests with swimming pools, tennis and volleyball courts, square dancing and even dinner theater. Yet many others stick to their roots, focusing on horseback riding, pack trips and riding lessons.

Saddle up

Horseback riding is still the main activity at most dude ranches. But you don't have to be an expert rider – in fact, you don't have to have ever climbed into a saddle at all. A good ranch will maintain a stable of horses suited to all levels of riding ability. It will also have an ample number of wranglers capable of instructing riders from novice to expert. Some even give advanced riders a chance to try out rodeo events.

Most ranches offer daily trail rides; many also offer longer two- or three-day horse-packing trips for guests who really want to gallop far from the madding crowd. While guests at the earliest ranches regularly herded dogies, rode fences, and performed other ranch chores, such work is harder to come by these days. But some ranches still let guests who are good riders participate in the working life of the ranch. A few, like Colorado Trails in Durango and Sylvan Dale near Estes Park, even hold cattle drives that qualified guests can join.

Freedom of choice

Although horses still reign at the dude ranch, many ranches offer other activities. The popularity of fly fishing in the West has inspired some ranches – especially those along trout streams – to offer instruction in the sport. Other outfits offer whitewater rafting, mountain biking, Jeep tours, big-game hunting and courses in bird-watching, photography, even geology. Children's programs are also offered at many ranches.

As for amenities, those can vary greatly. Some

CHOOSING A DUDE RANCH

Dude-ranch vacations don't come cheap. A stay at a reputable ranch costs a couple of thousand dollars a week for each adult during peak season. Ask around for personal recommendations, but in the absence of first-hand information try searching the web or calling the ranches directly. Two good sources of information are the Dude Ranchers Association (PO Box 2307, Cody, WY 82414; tel: 307-587-2339) and the Colorado Dude and Guest Ranch Association (PO Box D, Shawnee, CO 80475; tel: 1-866-94-CDGRA). Be sure to ask whether the ranch has cabins, a bunkhouse, or a lodge? Are meals are included? Is there a children's program? And is accessibility an issue?

old-time ranches maintain a simple but comfortable rusticity. That may mean cozy cabins grouped along a stream and grub that tends towards the Western classics. The emphasis at these places is on an authentic ranch experience and as much outdoor activity as you can handle. Other Colorado dude ranches are more akin to resorts, with tennis courts, golf courses and cocktails by the pool. Some of the newest ranches – places like the Home Ranch near Clark and the Kessler Canyon Ranch near Rifle – are downright luxurious, with guest suites that rival those of the finest hotels and the kind of haute cuisine you'd expect to savor in Beverly Hills. ❏

ABOVE: MacGregor Ranch, near Estes Park.

Colorado Cowboys

Ranching in Colorado produced several famous cowboys, from cowboy-archeologist Richard Wetherill to Bose Ikard, the black cowboy portrayed in the Western classic *Lonesome Dove*

The American cowboy has his roots in the Spanish cowboys, or *vaqueros*, who worked on ranches throughout the Southwest in the colonial era. Many cowboy terms in use today derive from Spanish words of this era: buckaroo from *vaquero*, lariat from *la reata*, and chaps from *chapareras*. Spanish missionaries in New Mexico, Texas and California converted Indigenous farmers and taught them ranching, using hardy longhorn cattle and churro sheep from Africa. Nomadic Western Utes, Jicarilla Apaches, Navajos and Plains Indians in and around Colorado were more interested in Spanish horses, which they quickly adopted for hunting buffalo and raiding Spanish settlements. By the early 1900s, after they had been forced to settle on reservations, many of them became expert stockmen, hiring themselves out as cowboys to the Anglo ranchers who took over their lands.

The first rancher in Colorado, Colonel John D. Henderson, established a ranch on the South Platte River in 1859 and began selling meat to mining camps, after discovering that cattle could survive on the prairie year-round. In 1866, Texan Charles Goodnight drove 2,000 head of cattle north through New Mexico on the Goodnight-Loving Trail and sold them to Denver merchant John Wesley Iliff, Colorado's first cattle baron. Iliff eventually bought 30,000 head of cattle from Goodnight and supplied not only miners but workers building the transcontinental railroad. The completion of the railroad linked ranchers with markets back east and made ranching economically viable.

By 1884, there were 58 cattle companies in Adams County alone. But they didn't last long. In 1886–7, 80 to 90 percent of ranches failed as overstocked ranges depleted grasslands and caused what came to be known as the "Big Die-Up." The days of open range were over.

One in three cowboys in the late 1800s was African American or Hispanic. Black cowboys like Bose

Ikard, who rode for Charles Goodnight, were skilled stockmen, many of whom started their own ranches out west. "Bose surpassed any man I had in endurance and stamina," Goodnight once said. "There was a dignity, a cleanliness and reliability about him that was wonderful... I have trusted him more than any man."

Nor were all cattle barons men. Cattle queen Ann Bassett ran her family's ranch in remote Browns Park in northwest Colorado in the 1880s and was a match for any man, rolling her own cigarettes and drinking whiskey straight. In 1889, Butch Cassidy courted her sister Josie, and Ann herself was engaged to rustler Matt Rush. "I've

done everything they said I did and a helluva lot more," boasted Bassett.

Remote canyons were a favored hideout for cattle rustlers. Sewemup Mesa, in the redrock country of the Dolores River, got its name for the outlaw practice of cutting off brands on rustled cattle, sewing them up with baling wire, and rebranding them with another rancher's brand.

One of Colorado's most famous cowboys gained fame for something else entirely. During a snowstorm in 1880, rancher Richard Wetherill stumbled on Cliff Palace in Mesa Verde, and a whole new career. He led excavations of Mesa Verde, Chaco Canyon and other remote areas. Wetherill coined the Navajo word Anasazi to describe the Ancestral Puebloans and named their immediate predecessors the Basketmakers. ❑

RIGHT: a Colorado cowpoke in his finest gear, 1911.

ROCKY MOUNTAIN CUISINE

From true grits to nouvelle cuisine, Colorado has been
changing its menu to satisfy budding tastes for all
kinds of savory dishes

Not long ago, Colorado cuisine was strictly
meat and potatoes. Steak was considered
a good meal; a big steak was considered
a great one. Fortunately, times have changed.
Thanks largely to a wave of hot new chefs in the
1990s, an epicurean fever has taken hold in
Colorado's cities and mountain resorts. Restau-
rateurs are bolder, chefs more eager to extend
their creative reach, and customers more willing to sample cutting-edge foods.

A key element of this gastronomic shift is a
rediscovery of foods associated with the state's
history and landscape stretching all the way
back to its earliest inhabitants. What was on
the menu in old-time Colorado? Fruits and
vegetables, of course, plus game meat, fish and
whatever else nature could serve up to sustain
the native people, most of whom were superb
hunter-gatherers. Such was the case with the
nomadic Utes, who inhabited the high country
west of the Front Range, as well as the Arapaho,
Cheyenne, Kiowa and Comanche tribes who
followed the bison herds across Colorado's
eastern plains.

Early days

The state's first farmers were the ancestors of
today's Pueblo people who, beginning in AD
700, built large, complex communities in the
Mesa Verde canyon country of southwestern
Colorado. Their predecessors in the area were
nomadic hunter-gatherer Archaic people, and
the Basketmakers, the first to stay put, build
pithouse villages and experiment with agriculture during the early Christian era. Wild foods
and game were abundant in this high-elevation
mesa country, and Ancestral Pueblo people
hunted small game such as deer and rabbits,
using bows and arrows. But they were primarily farmers, who settled in and around well-
watered tributary canyons, building villages on
the mesa tops and, finally, in the 13th century,
cliff dwellings in the protective canyon walls.
They dammed streams and husbanded springs
and rainwater to irrigate staple crops of corn,
beans and squash that they dried and kept in
stone granaries and beautifully made black-on-
white pottery containers.

By the early 1800s, Spanish settlers had fil-
tered up from New Mexico and put down roots
in the San Luis Valley, where they raised grains,
beans and chile peppers. After them came Anglo
explorers, mountain men and prospectors, who
hunted and traded for food as they went along

at such rendezvous places as Bent's Fort in south-eastern Colorado. In the late 1800s, a rudimentary food industry sprang up to nourish hungry miners struggling to wrest gold and silver from the ground. Local farms and ranches supplied the basic foods. Luxury items were shipped into the territory by rail and snapped up by the nouveau riche, who wanted to prove that there was indeed civilization on the frontier.

Although Colorado had its share of ethnic diversity among the miners and other immigrants who settled here, this particular smorgasbord of nationalities didn't make much of a dent in the culinary landscape. The diets of Colo-

farming heritage as well as its long tradition of hunting and fishing. What's been touted as "Colorado cuisine" or "Rocky Mountain cuisine" has developed into an eclectic style utilizing ingredients that thrive in the state's high, dry climate. It's not unusual to find menus featuring ranch-raised elk and venison, Colorado lamb and local trout, artisan goat cheese and pasture-raised free-range farm eggs accompanied by fresh organic produce from local growers – lush peaches, baby squash, heirloom tomatoes, exotic mushrooms, designer asparagus, Japanese eggplant, field greens, and fresh herbs.

radans tended to be blander than those in America's big coastal cities and industrialized states, where whole families from the Old World settled in dense clusters and assimilation proceeded at a slower pace. No regional style developed to produce anything distinctive like the chowders of New England, the gumbos of New Orleans, or the fiery specialties of the Southwest.

Home-grown flavor

What contemporary chefs are doing instead is reinterpreting the region's ranching and

LEFT: at work in the kitchen. ABOVE LEFT AND RIGHT: enticing entrées from Restaurant Kevin Taylor at Hotel Teatro in downtown Denver.

FARMERS' MARKETS

Farmers' markets are found from Denver to Ridgway and have become bona fide community attractions. Usually held once a week, they are a great way to connect with local communities; sample regional foods; learn how to cook them; and enjoy home-grown entertainment as well as delicious prepared foods. Most also sell handmade products, from wine to soap and clothing, that make usual and inexpensive gifts. The best-known farmers' market is the Boulder County Farmers' Market, the largest in the state and one of the Top 25 in the nation. It takes place Wednesdays and Saturdays, May to October, next to Boulder's Central Park.

These products have graduated from oddities to staples. To raise Colorado foods up a few more notches, chefs have been busy developing distinctive salsas, marinades, glazes, infusions, vinaigrettes, spice rubs and other such flavorful enhancements. Ingredients from the Southwest, including beans, chiles, tortillas and tomatillos, have made their mark on Colorado kitchens but are prepared and presented with far more sophistication than typical Tex-Mex fare.

Imaginative cooks can also count on the availability of fresh, non-traditional ingredients considered vital to a rich cuisine. Fresh mozzarella, lemongrass, pancetta, miso, sesame oil, cilantro, sticky rice and other former exotica have become commonplace as restaurants serving up French, Italian, Mediterranean, Thai, Japanese, Southwestern and various combinations of so-called "fusion" fare pop up all over the place.

The trend hasn't gone unnoticed. The best of the Colorado restaurants have been singled out for diamonds from AAA, stars from Mobil, huzzahs from *Wine Spectator* and plaudits from such trade groups as Distinguished Restaurants of America. One of the singular honors for an American chef is an invitation to cook at the James Beard House in New York. There, fussy foodies regularly gather to sample the best of

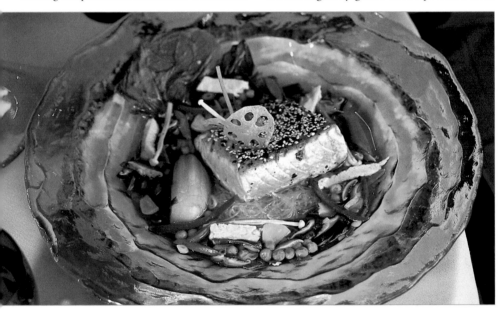

UP WITH ORGANICS

Health-conscious Boulder is home to the country's first and most famous herbal tea company: Celestial Seasonings. It was started in the late 1960s by Mo Siegel and sold teas made from plants gathered in the foothills of the Rockies in folksy packaging. Now owned by Hain Foods, its factory tour is Boulder's most popular visitor attraction. Boulder is also home to White Wave organic tofu, Coleman natural beef, Redbird chicken, Earth's Best baby foods, Westbrae Natural Foods, Spectrum Oils, Rudi's organic bakery and Great Range bison products. Organic foods and personal products are a booming business.

the best. At last count, more than two dozen Colorado chefs have cooked there and been shortlisted for annual awards. In 2009, Hosea Rosenburg, executive chef of Jax Fish House in Boulder, won the Bravo cook-off reality show *Top Chef*. In 2010, Vail chef Kelly Liken and Telluride chef Kenny Gilbert were among the 17 chefs competing on the show.

Bread and cheese

Nowhere in the Colorado food firmament have the changes been more dramatic, and more welcome, than in the kingdom of breads. At artisan bakeries all over the state, from Paonia's chef-owned Flying Fork Café and Bakery to Rudy's Organic Bakery in Boulder, ovens produce well-crusted loaves in a variety of shapes, sizes and colors destined for restaurant tables and serving as foundations for tasty sandwiches. Today, in addition to the homespun white, rye and whole wheat of Colorado's traditional bread lexicon are such novelties as focaccia, boule, bâtard and pain au levain.

Food & Wine magazine's Classic at Aspen is the star of culinary festivals, a three-day extravaganza featuring the most celebrated culinary talents from Colorado and beyond.

the region and at its new cheesery in Longmont near Boulder.

Birgit S. Halbreiter and Robert Poland established the MouCo Cheese Company, a micro-cheesery in Fort Collins, in 2001. Birgit grew up in Germany and is the daughter of a master cheesemaker (her father is a consultant to the company), and the cheeses, made from local milk, follow a strong European tradition. MouCo's camembert was an instant hit, soon followed by the company's other cheese, ColoRouge. You will find both these products on fine restaurant menus, in cheese stores and delicatessens, in Colorado health food stores

Colorado has also made great strides in the field of cheesemaking. In 1989, a lapsed educator named Jim Schott bought a farm in Niwot, northwest of Boulder, added some goats and started learning the craft of cheesemaking. Schott's Haystack Mountain Goat Dairy was Colorado's first artisanal cheesery and garnered seven medals, including one gold, in the first national cheese competition it entered. Now under new management, and minus its own goat herd, it continues to make six award-winning artisan cheeses available in stores in

like Vitamin Cottage, and at farmers' markets.

Cheesemaking is also making inroads on the Western Slope. In 2009, Rocking W Ranch in the Uncompahgre Valley hired a Wisconsin cheesemaker and began making farmstead cheeses using milk from the pioneer Webb family's own herd of grass-fed cows. Members of the extended James clan living on 400-acre(160-hectare) James Ranch in the Animas Valley are also dipping their toes into the artisanal cheese market. Their farmstead cheeses are made in the Dutch and Italian styles from raw milk from the family's grass-fed Jersey cows. The hand-crafted cheeses are currently only available in local stores and farmers' markets and direct from the ranch.

LEFT: well-prepared dishes appeal to the eye as well as the taste buds. **ABOVE:** hearty camp cooking is a Colorado tradition.

"Field to Fork"

High and dry as Colorado is, the state's short, intense growing season is well suited to cultivating a cornucopia of delicious fruits and vegetables, which comes as a delightful surprise to visitors who associate Colorado mainly with spectacular mountains and outdoor sports. In fact, Colorado is first in the nation for organic vegetable acreage in cultivation, ahead even of California. Colorado farmers plant and pick stone fruits in the Grand Valley, sweet corn around Olathe, various vegetables and herbs – many organic – from small farms around Palisade, Paonia and Hotchkiss (all in western Colorado), potatoes in the San Luis

> *A locavore is someone who prefers to eat locally grown food. In 2009, eating local was cited as the top dining trend by the National Restaurant Association. Locavore was the Oxford American English Dictionary's "word of the year" in 2007.*

Valley, and organically grown tomatoes, herbs and vegetables in what remains of agricultural areas on the Front Range.

"Fresher is better" is the new mantra and increasingly a high priority for residents and visitors concerned about their health, food safety, long-term sustainability, and supporting the people who grow our food. One of the big new trends among Colorado's top chefs, whether they work in kitchens at high-end luxury resorts or in their own small venues, is to "grow your own," cutting out the middleman to provide fresh, local, organic, and sustainably grown food that is truly "locavore." Among those now experimenting with growing their own produce are Justin Cicci, chef-owner of Root Down in Denver, which has a "field to fork" menu; and Max Mackissock, co-owner of the Squealing Bean, an ambitious cafe/bakery/cocktail bar/locavore restaurant in a former 1930s soda fountain, also in Denver.

At the last count, there were some 37,000 farms in Colorado, nearly half of them small family concerns. Of those, about 679 welcome visitors for tours, farm stays, special harvest dinners and educational programs. An increasing number of farms in Colorado offer Community-Supported Agriculture programs (CSAs), which allow you to invest in the farm's yield for the year and receive regular boxes of pro-

duce. Some ranches also now offer herd-share programs, which under new state regulations allow people to buy a share of an animal and receive raw goats' and cows' milk products and reasonably priced grass-fed meat.

It goes without saying that one of the growth areas in Colorado is its farmers' markets. There are currently 110 such markets all around the state offering an array of fresh, Colorado-grown ingredients, from the flowers, lettuces and herbs of spring and summer to Olanthe corn, Rocky Ford melons and Palisade peaches of late summer, and the squash and apples of fall. Many growers' markets also feature the output of local baker-

ies, plus small-batch preserves, pickles, salsas and other condiments. Come hungry on market day and enjoy breakfast pastries, sandwiches, wraps, roasted corn, salads, tamales, burritos, Asian specialties, pasta dishes, baked goods and other eat-on-the-spot treats as well as locally made wines.

Wine, too

In 1890, George A. Crawford, who had founded Grand Junction in the fertile Grand Valley of western Colorado, planted 60 acres (24 hectares) of fruit, including grapes, along Rapid Creek above Palisade. Within a decade, Colorado reported a grape harvest of 586,300 lbs (266,000kg) and wine production of 1,744 gallons (6,600 liters). This hardly made Colorado an important wine grower, but it was a good start. Nearly seven decades later, the first modern winery appeared when Gerald Ivancie opened Ivancie Cellars in the Grand River Valley. In 1990, when there were only four wineries in the state, the Colorado Wine Industry Development Board (www.coloradowine.com) was established, shifting the Colorado wine business into overdrive.

Colorado now supports more than 100 wineries in five different growing regions, with some 89 percent located in the Grand Valley. The gentle beauty of rows of vines is no longer a rare sight on Colorado hillsides, and wineries and tasting rooms are scattered around the western and central regions of the state as well as, increasingly, in the Front Range. When the climate is suitable and space allows, wineries grow all or most of their own grapes. Merlot and Chardonnay predominated during the infancy of Colorado's wine industry. These have been joined by Cabernets, Rieslings, honey wines (meads), fruit wines, port wines and other fortified wines, as well as Champagne-style sparkling wine. The oldest and largest winery is award-winning Colorado Cellars, harvesting 450 acres (182 hectares) in the Grand Valley. It is on the site of one of the first test plots for wine-making and makes the full spectrum of wines from Colorado grapes.

> Low in fat and high in essential fatty acids bison meat is enjoying a revival, both for its delicious taste and health benefits. Colorado's prairies are studded with ranches raising bison meat for sale to Whole Foods and other outlets.

(For more information about Colorado wine-making, see Colorado Wine Country on p.272.)

Beef and buffalo

For a taste of what Coloradans ate in the old days, stop at The Fort, a landmark restaurant serving heritage cuisine just west of Denver. It was opened in 1963 by history buff Sam Arnold, a former reporter, radio announcer and adman who became enamored of Bent's Fort, the fur-trading post dating from the early days of the Santa Fe Trail. He purchased 7 acres (3 hectares)

LEFT: teatime at Denver's Brown Palace Hotel, an experience of Victorian refinement. **RIGHT:** bottles filled with local wine from Palisade.

north of Morrison, where, against a backdrop of dramatic redrock formations, he built an adobe re-creation of the historic fort.

Buffalo dinners are served there at a rate of 50,000 a year, more than anywhere else in the country. They include such classic cuts as steak and prime rib and some you would be hard-pressed to find elsewhere, such as buffalo hump, barbecued ribs, center-cut shank prepared osso buco-style, or tongue, a 19th-century gourmet specialty. In addition to buffalo, elk and other big game, quail and guinea fowl remain on the menu as a tribute to the game birds prepared in the 19th century. Chilled rattlesnake cocktail

is the restaurant's most popular appetizer, and Rocky Mountain oysters are perhaps the best known. The oysters, which have never been near any ocean, are the testicles of bison, calves or sheep, rolled in bread crumbs and deep-fried. The restaurant's annual "awful offal" dinner features exotic innards that people either love or loathe.

Sam Arnold died in 2006 but still remains Colorado's best-known restaurateur. He produced and hosted food shows on radio and television, wrote many magazine articles, pitched commercials and authored such books as *Taste of the West*, *Frying Pans West* and *The Fort Cookbook: New Foods of the Old West from the Famous Denver Restaurant*. ❏

PLACES

A detailed guide to the entire state, with principal sites
clearly cross-referenced by number to the maps

Most of Colorado is in the legendary Rocky Mountains, the tallest range in the continental United States. And mountains attract dreamers eager to match themselves against the craggy peaks, rushing rivers, or "parks."

Denver founder General William Larimer gambled that his new town in the foothills would emerge a thriving capital, and won the bet. Today, the Denver Metro Area monopolizes the Front Range, bringing its top attraction, Rocky Mountain National Park, ever closer to millions of urban dwellers.

In the eastern third of Colorado lie the Great Plains. Famed as a birding area, its rolling grasslands are grazed by cattle and bison herds all the way to the San Luis Valley. Here, in the shadow of the Spanish Peaks, Hispanic ranchers mingle with New Agers, and sandhill cranes overwinter near Great Sand Dunes National Monument.

The country's greatest concentration of Ancestral Pueblo Indian ruins are preserved in the Four Corners country near Durango in southwestern Colorado, at Mesa Verde National Park, and on adjoining Ute Indian lands.

Casino gambling has revived the fortunes of the Utes, and of played-out mining towns like Victor and Cripple Creek in the Northern Rockies where ritzy Aspen and Vail are now celebrity ski resorts. In contrast, ski resort towns in the Southern Rockies trade on authenticity and remoteness. Pretty Telluride and feisty Silverton, Creede, and other captivating former ghost towns are an independent bunch, attracting ranchers, artists, writers, scientists, and outdoor lovers.

The West Slope is farm and ranch country. Below lofty Grand Mesa, set in a valley carved by the Colorado River into the dramatic redrocks at Colorado National Monument, the Grand Junction area thrives as a fruit-growing area. Two billion years of geology are displayed at nearby Dinosaur National Monument. The Colorado, Green, and Yampa rivers thrill river runners, but the real sparks fly in Black Canyon of the Gunnison National Park, where the Gunnison River has carved a precipitous canyon. ❑

PRECEDING PAGES: Book Cliffs; National Western Stockshow; sculpture in Denver Botanic Gardens. **LEFT:** Rocky Mountain National Park. **ABOVE RIGHT:** skulls decorate Glenwood Caverns Adventure Park. **ABOVE LEFT:** a male elk looks into the distance.

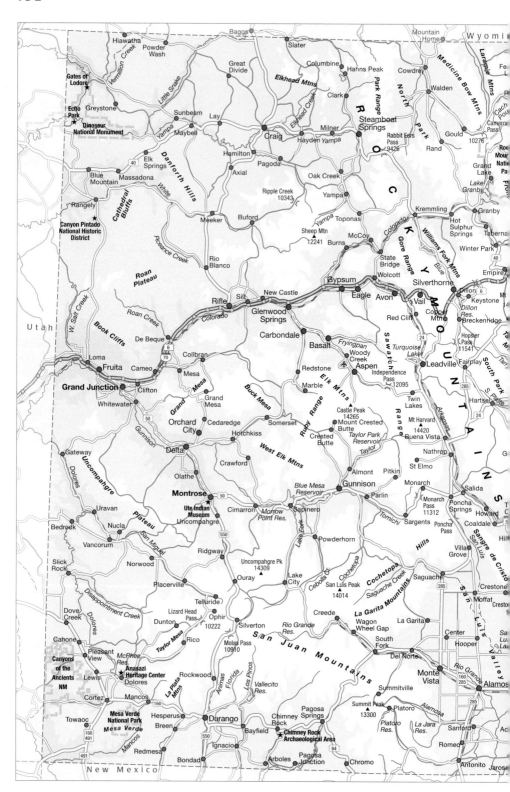

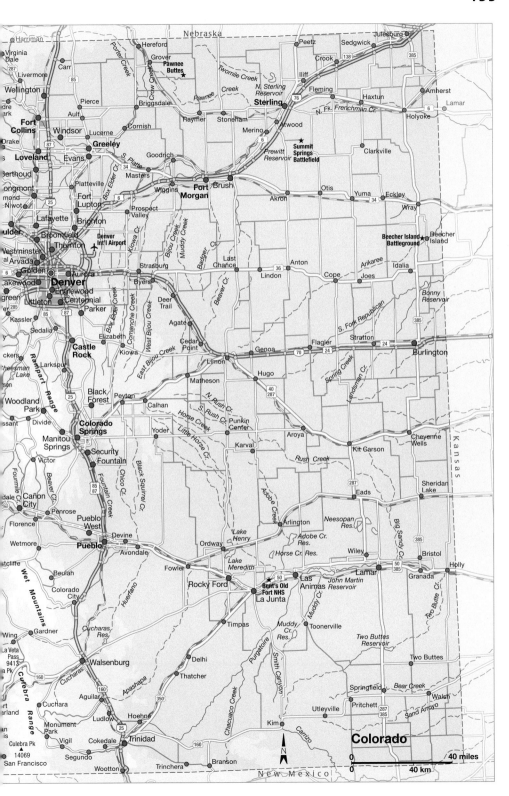

Colorado

THE FRONT RANGE AND EASTERN PLAINS

Colorado's largest metropolitan areas are strung along the foothills between the Rockies and Great Plains

Flying over eastern Colorado at night, you look down and see a string of lights running north to south in a sometimes thin, sometimes clotted line. This is the sprawling Denver Metro Area, strung along the foothills of the Rocky Mountains like a snarl of Christmas lights.

Denver, home to 610,345 people, now makes up just a fraction of the busy Front Range Urban Corridor (pop. 2.7 million), which includes miles of suburbs, such as Englewood and Lakewood. Denver grew by 10 percent in the first decade of the 20th century, the vast majority of new residents from California and Hispanic in origin. The demographic shift has reinvigorated politics and the once-decaying urban core: 16th Street is a pedestrian mall; historic Larimer Square has been restored; the industrial no-man's land of LoDo, has been re-imagined as a hip SoHo-style neighborhood, and Denver International Airport has been built.

To the north is Boulder, home of the University of Colorado. Progressive and youthful, Boulder is famous for its innovative small businesses focusing on health and healing, for its spiritual centers and pedestrians-only Pearl Street Mall, and its proximity to recreation in the surrounding wilderness and parkland.

Conservative Colorado Springs, south of Denver, sits below Pikes Peak, an equally gorgeous setting. The town's right-leaning inclinations are rooted in a large population of active and retired military personnel. Fort Carson, Peterson Air Force Base and the US Air Force Academy are located in Colorado Springs, as are numerous conservative Christian organizations.

Fringing the Front Range are railroad towns like Pueblo, Trinidad, and Fort Collins, still focused on a traditional farming and ranching lifestyle. The vast shortgrass prairie is inhabited by rare birds, and revived herds of bison – once the mainstay of Cheyenne, Arapaho, and Comanche people. Quiet and little traveled, the plains offer subtle landscapes, fascinating natural and cultural history, and a sweeping sense of space. ❏

PRECEDING PAGES: sunlight illuminates the Capitol rotunda in Denver; the exterior of the dome is wrapped in gold leaf. **LEFT:** the Daniels & Fisher Tower, a landmark on the 16th Street Mall, is lit up at night. **ABOVE LEFT:** a local musician tunes up. **ABOVE RIGHT:** leading the way to Kendall Mountain.

THE EASTERN PLAINS

Complementing the alpine spectacle of peak and
precipice is a wide-open expanse of rolling prairie and
flatland where Colorado's history was writ large

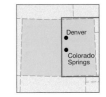

High plains occupy the eastern third of Colorado – a sea of grass surmounted by buttes and soaring ridges, wrinkled with creeks and shallow canyons. Cattle dot the landscape, along with the occasional antelope. Solitary ranch houses look tiny and shrunken, as if viewed through the wrong end of a telescope. Roads run at right angles, following property lines to what appears to be the edge of the earth.

A land of delicate colors and subtle contrasts, this part of Colorado contains its own allure. Mountains overwhelm, but flatlands tug seductively at the senses. Amid all this space, details tend to catch the eye: an abandoned schoolhouse standing on a lonely hill, or the spectacle of thunderstorms brooding on the skyline, or the vertical effrontery of a creaking windmill.

Bad company

If you're in a rush, I-70, I-76 and I-25 will get you across the Colorado flatlands in a hurry. These busy thoroughfares lead inexorably to the major cities that sprawl across the foothills of the Front Range. But if you've got the time and a meandering spirit, the lightly traveled roads that thread these wide-open spaces lead to interesting spots that are too often overlooked.

Take, for example, the **Beecher Island Battleground ❶**, situated near the Kansas line about 12 miles (19km) north of US 36. One of the epic struggles between native Americans and whites in the settling of the West was fought here during nine days beginning on September 17, 1868. A party of 51 frontiersmen under the command of Major George A. Forsyth was besieged on an island in the Arikaree River by hundreds of Cheyenne, Arapaho and Lakota warriors. Again and again the Indians attacked, only to be

Main attractions
BEECHER ISLAND BATTLEGROUND
OVERLAND TRAIL MUSEUM, STERLING
SOUTH PLATTE RIVER TRAIL
SUMMIT SPRINGS BATTLEFIELD
PAWNEE BUTTES
CENTENNIAL VILLAGE, GREELEY
KOSHARE INDIAN MUSEUM
COMANCHE NATIONAL GRASSLANDS
BENT'S OLD FORT
PICKETWIRE CANYON DINOSAUR TRACKS
PICTURE CANYON
TRINIDAD HISTORY MUSEUM
A.R. MITCHELL MUSEUM OF WESTERN ART

LEFT: wild flowers near Grand Lake.
RIGHT: Generals Merritt, Sheridan, Crook, Forsyth, and Custer around a table.

The Eastern Plains

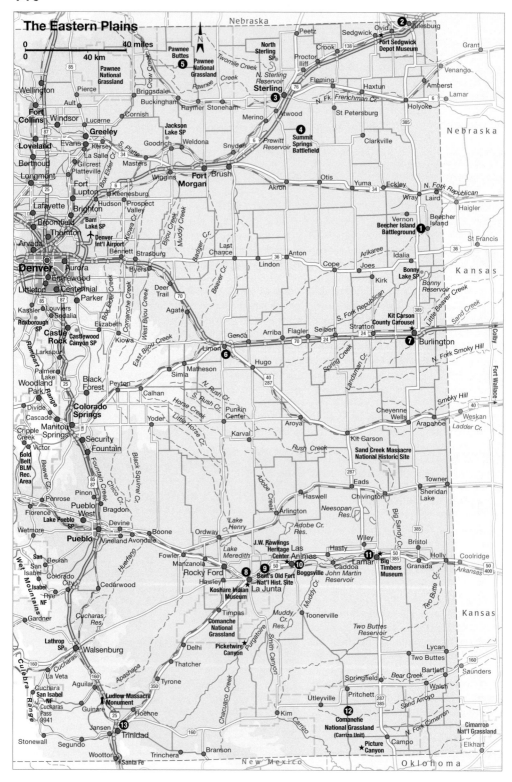

0 _____ 40 miles
0 _____ 40 km

Nebraska

Grant

Nebraska

Kansas

Kansas

New Mexico   Oklahoma

repulsed by deadly fire from the company's lever-action rifles.

Colonel Forsyth was badly wounded; Lieutenant Frederick Beecher, second in command, was killed. For two nights running, barefoot volunteers, crawling on their hands and knees, slipped between enemy lines and made their way to Fort Wallace in northwest Kansas. The siege was lifted on September 26, when a relief column reached the site. A whitewashed obelisk marks the spot today. Every year since 1899, a reunion has been held on the premises. The grounds are open to the public year-round.

In the extreme northeast of Colorado, about 70 miles (110km) away, is the town of **Julesburg** ❷ (pop. 1,500). It was founded in 1859 by a mixed-blood trader named Jules Beni at a ford of the South Platte River, where the California, Overland and Pony Express trails converged. From the beginning the post had an unsavory reputation. Beni fought openly with his boss, Jack Slade, until Slade could stand no more and killed him. Legend has it that Slade celebrated the victory by slicing off Beni's ears, tacking one to a fence post and fashioning the other into a watch fob. In 1865, Indians enraged by the Sand Creek Massacre *(see page 48)* torched the fledgling town. Later, in the 1870s, it was a favorite stopover of railroad workers who patronized the bars and bordellos, earning it a reputation as "the Wickedest City in the West."

The nearby **Fort Sedgwick Depot Museum** (114 First Street; tel: 800-777-9075; late-May–early-Sept Mon–Sat 9am–5pm, Sun 11am–5pm; charge), housed in a former Union Pacific station, displays railroad equipment, pioneer tools and Pony Express memorabilia as well as artifacts from Fort Sedgwick, which was established in 1864 to protect wagon teams and travelers.

The mountain goat was introduced to Colorado in the 1940s to expand hunting opportunities. It was declared native to the state in 1993.

Buttes and battles

You'll find an even greater variety of pioneer artifacts at the **Overland Trail Museum** (US 6; tel: 970-522-3895, Apr–Oct Mon–Sat 9am–5pm, Sun

BELOW: Centennial Village in Greeley.

Remembering Sand Creek

At dawn on November 29, 1864, 700 US volunteer soldiers led by Col. John M. Chivington attacked 500 Cheyennes and Arapahos led by Chief Black Kettle, encamped along the banks of Sand Creek in southeastern Colorado. Seven hours later, the troops had killed at least 150 people, mostly children and the elderly, and mutilated many bodies. The atrocities committed by Col. Chivington and his men were decried by the public and resulted in three federal investigations. Approximately 12,500 acres (5,000 hectares) in Kiowa County, Colorado, are authorized for a planned Sand Creek Massacre National Historic Site (see Striking It Rich), symbolizing the struggle of American Indians to stay on their ancestral lands. The massacre site is currently closed to visitors.

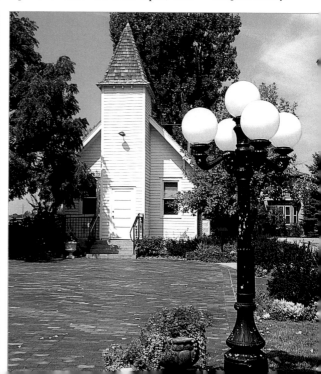

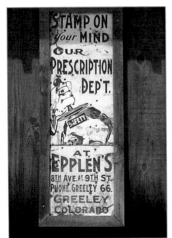

A vintage billboard brings the past to life at Centennial Village.

BELOW: Plains Indians pinned down a party of frontiersmen and soldiers at the 1868 Battle of Beecher Island.

1–5pm, Nov–Mar Tue–Sat 10am–4pm; free) about 55 miles (90km) away in the trim little town of **Sterling ❸**. The grounds include a replica of an Old West fort as well as a schoolhouse, church, country store and barn. Exhibits range from antique farm equipment and a stagecoach to wedding dresses, sun bonnets and household items.

About 35 miles (56km) away, in the prairie southeast of Sterling, is the **Summit Springs Battlefield ❹**, site of a clash between Cheyenne Indians and US soldiers in 1869. Cheyenne dog soldiers raiding deep into Kansas in the spring of that year killed several settlers and captured two women. The Fifth Cavalry under Major General Eugene A. Carr, 250 strong with 50 Pawnee Scouts, including Buffalo Bill Cody, rode off in pursuit.

On Sunday morning, July 11, scouts discovered a Cheyenne camp along White Butte Creek, which flows out of Summit Springs. First to see the army was a 15-year-old boy, who swung onto his horse and raced for the village to sound the alarm. The troopers charged, but their horses were exhausted, enabling many Cheyennes to escape. One of the captive women was killed, as was Tall Bull, the Cheyenne chief. The soldiers burned the native lodges, along with possessions and supplies. There are two monuments at the site, one describing the battle, the other commemorating the Cheyennes who died there.

Farther west, about 40 miles (65km) outside Sterling, the **Pawnee Buttes ❺** (off CR 110) tower in lonely splendor over **Pawnee National Grassland** (660 O Street, Greeley; tel: 970-346-5000; www.fs.fed.us.r2/arnf). It takes a bit of navigating to reach the buttes, but it's worth it. The squat sandstone formations rise side by side to a height of 250ft (76 meters). Archeologists trace human occupation of the region to 12,000 years ago, the end of the last Ice Age. A 1½-mile (2.5km) hiking trail leads over eroded *arroyos* (gulleys) to the foot of the west butte. As well

as numerous bird species, a variety of mammals, including pronghorn antelope, mule deer, prairie dogs, badgers and coyotes, are found in the area.

For a glimpse of prairie life from the 1860s to the 1920s, stop at **Centennial Village** in **Greeley** (1475 A Street; tel: 970-350-9220; May–Sept Tue–Sat 10am–4pm; charge). Living-history demonstrations bring the past alive at a collection of more than 30 buildings on the 8-acre (3 hectare) property, including a blacksmith shop, church and schoolhouse.

Frontier life

All roads lead to **Limon** ❻ (pop. 2,071), nexus of the regional highway system. Originally a railroad town, now an agricultural hub, Limon (rhymes with "Simon") was devastated in 1990 by a tornado that caused $20 million of damage. About 70 miles (110km) east via I-70, **Burlington** ❼ (pop. 3,048) features the **Old Town Museum** (420 S. 14th Street; tel: 719-346-7382; Mon–Sat 9am–5pm, Sun noon–5pm; charge), a facsimile of an early 20th-century high-plains community, complete with a blacksmith shop and a saloon that in our more temperate age sells mostly lemonade. Burlington is also home to the **Kit Carson County Carousel** (5th Street at Colorado Avenue; Memorial Day–Labor Day daily 11am–6pm; charge), a fully restored 1905 merry-go-round built by the Philadelphia Toboggan Company and now designated a National Historic Landmark. A small museum is open the same hours.

From Limon, Route 71 makes a beeline from the South Platte watershed, over a barely detectable hump known as the Palmer Divide, into the Arkansas River valley. In the 1870s and 1880s, Hispanic settlers from Santa Fe and Taos introduced a system of *acequias* (irrigation canals) in the fertile bottomlands along the Arkansas River and began growing the excellent agricultural produce for which the region is famous. **La Junta** ❽, the major town in this cluster of agricultural communities, is home to the **Koshare Indian Museum and Trading Post** (115 W. 18th Street; tel: 719-384-4411; www.rurainet.net/koshare, Mon–Sun 10am–

TIP

In Vogel Canyon in Comanche National Grasslands, four hiking trails lead from the picnic area past canyon walls etched with Indian rock art to two spring-fed pools at the canyon bottom.

BELOW: the entrance to Pawnee National Grassland.

Pawnee Buttes Bird Tour

Pawnee National Grassland attracts some 250 bird species, including grassland birds, migrant waterfowl, and shorebirds, and is popular with birding enthusiasts from all over the world. On the 36-mile (58km) self-guided auto tour of Pawnee Buttes, which begins in Briggsdale, you can enjoy the "larking" (singing courtship flight) of lark buntings, horned larks, meadowlarks and longspurs from late May through June. Prairie birds include mountain plovers, chestnut-collared and McCown's longspurs, burrowing owls and long-billed curlews. The box elder/willow riparian area at Crow Valley Campground attracts a variety of eastern and mountain birds from April through June, and late August through October. Murphy Reservoir offers good shorebird and waterfowl viewing.

5pm; charge), on the Otero Junior College Campus, which contains one of the largest collections of American Indian artifacts in the region.

South of La Junta lies the **Timpas Unit of Comanche National Grassland** (1420 E. 3rd Street, La Junta; tel: 719-384-2181). With more than 400,000 acres (160,000 hectares) of range land, the area abounds with wildlife, including 275 species of birds, 40 species of reptiles, and mammals such as mountain lion, black bear, pronghorn, coyote, fox and bobcat.

Traders of the plains

The crown jewel of the eastern plains is **Bent's Old Fort National Historic Site ❾** (35110 Highway 194; tel: 719-383-5010; www.nps.gov/beol; daily May–Aug 8am–5pm, Sept–Apr 9am–4pm; charge), just east of La Junta. The fort was built in the 1830s by three St Louis fur traders – brothers Charles and William Bent and Ceran St Vrain – and became a major stop on the Mountain Route of the Santa Fe Trail. William Bent was married to a Cheyenne woman, and so effective were

his peacekeeping skills that each year thousands of Indians from all over the plains gathered in the *bosque* along the Arkansas River to parly and trade.

The Mexican War brought soldiers into the region and upset the delicate balance. A cholera epidemic broke out, the bison herds dwindled, and both settlers and natives cut down the cottonwood groves along the river. In 1849, with the world crowding in, William Bent set fire to the fort and moved downstream to Big Timbers, near present-day Lamar.

The reconstructed fort is now a living-history museum, run by the National Park Service depicting frontier life during the heyday of the Santa Fe Trail. Guided tours in summer are often led by costumed interpreters. Annual events include the three-day **Santa Fe Trail Encampment**, a re-enactment featuring mountain men, dragoons, explorers, merchants and Indians.

For a detour, follow US 50 east to Las Animas, then 2 miles (3km) south on Route 101 to the ghost town of **Boggsville ❿**. Founded in 1862 by

BELOW: Bent's Old Fort National Historic Site.

Prairie Chicken Dances

If you visit the Comanche National Grasslands *(see text above)* in spring, you might see the courtship ritual of the lesser prairie chicken. Male chickens arrive on the leks (elevated dancing grounds) to establish their territory. To attract females, the males dip their heads, bob their wings, hackle their feathers, and stomp their feet, all the while emitting a gobbling sound from the reddish air sacs on their necks.

Thomas O. Boggs (William Bent's son-in-law), the town served as a trading center and county seat until the construction of the railroad farther north in 1873. Legendary scout Kit Carson moved here in 1868. Exhibits chronicling Boggsville history, from Carson's days through World War II, are on display at the new **John W. Rawlings Heritage Center** (560 Bent Aveune, Las Animas; tel: 719-456-6066; Mon–Sat 1–4pm; charge).

Big Timbers

To the east, a dense growth of trees known as the Big Timbers once stretched along the Arkansas River for 45 miles (72km). Composed mainly of cottonwoods, the *bosque* provided refuge for Indians and settlers from the harsh winters of the southern plains. William Bent built his new fort in 1853 about 6 miles (10km) west of present-day **Lamar** ⑪ in the heart of the Big Timbers country. Despite social upheavals, many Indians remained loyal to Bent, and in the spring and fall they pitched their lodges nearby. Bent later sold the fort to the US government.

Big Timbers Museum (7515 W. US 50, Lamar; tel: 719-336-2472; summer Mon–Sat 10am–5pm, winter 1–5pm; charge) is one of those small-town, grab-bag repositories that feature a little bit of everything – guns, wedding gowns, spinning wheels, dolls, quilts, surgical instruments, farm tools, battle flags and more. A display of newspapers and photos recounts the 1928 murder of prominent father and son bankers by the notorious Fleagle Gang, sparking one of Colorado's greatest manhunts.

US 287-385 drops south from Lamar, toward the **Carrizo Unit of Comanche National Grassland** ⑫ (27204 US 287-385, Springfield; tel: 719-523-6591; www.coloradodirectory.com/nationalparks/comanche.html). Here the east fork of Carrizo Creek flows through a small canyon of the same name, shaded by juniper and cottonwood trees. An impressive array of prehistoric Indian petroglyphs – images of mountain goats, elk and deer – are etched on the canyon walls. **Picture Canyon**, south of Springfield, is also filled with fine examples of rock art, several of astro-

TIP

Picketwire Canyon (off CR 25), carved by the Purgatoire River, has a unique feature: some 1,300 dinosaur tracks run for about ¼ mile (½km) along the river. Created 150 million years ago, they are the largest aggregation of Jurassic footprints in North America.

BELOW:
schoolmarm and students at Centennial Village's one-room schoolhouse.

A lone church beckons to the faithful of the high plains.

BELOW: the lavish Bloom Mansion in Trinidad.

nomical significance. For directions to the petroglyph sites, inquire at the ranger station in Springfield.

Undiscovered treasure

It's a long and lonely ride west on US 160 from Springfield to **Trinidad** ⑬ at the foot of the Sangre de Cristo Mountains. The Spanish Peaks rise in the distance, spangled by the late afternoon sun. Mesa de Maya – dark, hulking, heaped with volcanic cinders – looms on the left. From this vantage, little seems to have changed since the 1870s, when cattle baron Charles Goodnight led his herds on a secret trail over the mesa in search of pastures lusher than those in Texas or New Mexico.

Back then, eastern Colorado was poised on the cusp of momentous change. The 1862 Homestead Act, which famously offered newcom-

ers 40 acres (16 hectares)and a mule, attracted swarms of settlers, who sallied forth from the green hills of the Midwest hoping to find the same sort of arable land west of the 100th meridian. The days of land barons comfortably ensconced on Spanish land grants were quickly coming to an end. The beckoning spaces of eastern Colorado were on the verge of being snapped up by hordes of land-hungry immigrants.

Trinidad (pop. 11,000) lies at the junction of US 160 and I-25, at the foot of Raton Pass, near where the Purgatoire River debouches onto the plains from its headwaters in the Culebra Range. Prior to 1860, Trinidad was little more than a way station on the mountain branch of the Santa Fe Trail that wound slowly up to the summit of Raton Pass and the dividing line between the territories of Colorado and New Mexico.

In the early 1860s, *comancheros* (traders) from Taos and Santa Fe began hauling supplies north over the pass to the boisterous town of Denver, where gold had been discovered. Impressed with the productivity of the soil along

the Purgatoire River, 12 families from the town of Mora, in northern New Mexico, settled there in 1862. Officially incorporated in 1876 (the year Colorado became a state), Trinidad underwent a remarkable transformation in a few short decades from a rustic adobe village to a brick and iron city graced with stately Victorian houses.

By the turn of the century Trinidad was a polyglot community of many nationalities, drawn from all over the world by the coal seams that glistened in the foothills like dark ribbons. Labor unrest between owners and miners festered for years, culminating in the brutal Ludlow Massacre of 1914. The massacre site, about 10 miles (16km) north of Trinidad (via I-25, Exit 27) is commemorated by an impressive statue erected by the United Mine Workers of America.

Trinidad today is one of the unspoiled gems of the American West. Handsome structures such as the **Trinidad Opera House**, the **Columbia Hotel** and **Temple Aaron** (one of Colorado's oldest synagogues) line the brick streets of the Corazon de Trinidad Historic District. The town has attracted more than its share of idealists and desperadoes. Mother Jones once walked these streets, clamoring for workers' rights. It's the place where train robber Black Jack Ketchum ordered a doctor to cut off his arm without an anesthetic because he didn't want anyone to take advantage of him while he was unconscious. Legendary labor organizer Louis Tikas was buried here after dying at the hands of the Colorado State Militia during the Ludlow débâcle. It's said that his funeral cortege stretched more than a mile, and that all you could hear in the cold gray air was the muffled clump of marching feet and the ruffle of black bunting.

Landmark homes

Two historic residences are lovingly preserved onsite by **Trinidad History Museum** (312 E. Main Street; tel: 719-846-7217: May–Sept Mon– Sat 10am–4pm, Sept–Apr Tue–Sat 10am–4pm; tours every 30 minutes in summer; charge). **Baca House** is a Territorial-style adobe dwelling built in 1870 and purchased in 1873 by rancher Felipe Baca for $7,000 of wool. Period furnishings reflect a mixture of traditional Hispanic and Victorian styles. The 1882 **Bloom Mansion** is constructed in comparatively lavish Second Empire style, with ornate furnishings reflecting high Victorian fashion and the availability, via railroad, of imported goods. **Santa Fe Trail Museum**, housed in an adobe outbuilding, chronicles the homestead period with old wagons, cowboy gear and other artifacts. **Historic Gardens** around the buildings are planted with heirloom varieties similar to those tended by Hispanic and Anglo settlers. The **Louden-Henritze Archaeology Museum** (Trinidad Junior College; tel: 719-846-5508; Mon– Fri 1–4pm; free) specializes in the prehistory of the region, with exhibits of fossils, geologic samples and Indian artifacts. A free trolley carries visitors around the historic Downtown. ❑

TIP

Artwork by celebrated western illustrator A.R. Mitchell is displayed in the splendid former 1907 Jamieson Department Store in Trinidad. The A.R. Mitchell Memorial Museum of Western Art museum is at 150 E. Main Street; tel: 719-846-4224; www.ar mitchell.org and is open Monday to Saturday 10am to 4pm, Sun noon to 4pm; charge.

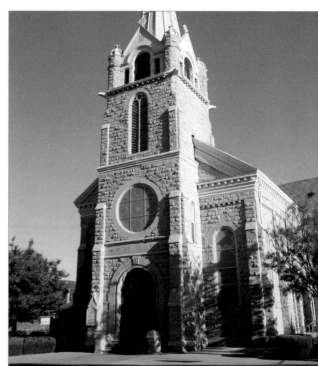

BELOW: a church in historic Trinidad.

DENVER

There's much to experience in this sprawling Western metropolis that fortune spawned from a ragged mining camp along the banks of a lowly creek

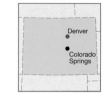

Writing to his wife in Kansas, General William H. Larimer, the self-proclaimed founder of Denver, bluste red that "Everyone will soon be flocking to Denver for the most picturesque country in the world, with fine air, good water, and everything to make a man happy and live to a good old age."

A natural-born finagler, Larimer had actually claim-jumped a little settlement established in 1858 by a party of Georgia prospectors who found a few flakes of gold in Cherry Creek. Hoping to curry political favor, he named the fledgling town after territorial governor James Denver, unaware that the governor had already resigned. Realizing that the place needed links to the civilized world, he bribed a stagecoach company to establish its headquarters there. Faced with competitors from three nearby settlements, each vying for recognition as the territorial capital, he bought them off with a barrel of whiskey.

Like the gold fields that spawned it, Denver was a gamble. It lacked most of the basic requirements of a city, such as a navigable waterway, and was isolated by hundreds of miles of dry, treeless prairie. Its own gold deposits proved paltry, and when a huge strike was reported at Central City, the town was nearly deserted. A catastrophic fire in 1863, a flash flood in 1864 and Indian hostilities in the late 1860s nearly wiped it out. It seemed Denver's fate was sealed when the Union Pacific bypassed Colorado in favor of a transcontinental route through Cheyenne, Wyoming. Larimer, failing to become the mayor of Denver or the governor of Colorado, abandoned the place.

Tested by hardship

But Denverites were not so easily defeated. They raised funds and

Main attractions
COLORADO STATE CAPITOL
UNITED STATES MINT
DENVER ART MUSEUM
DENVER HISTORY MUSEUM
DENVER PUBLIC LIBRARY
MOLLY BROWN HOUSE MUSEUM
16TH STREET MALL
BROWN PALACE HOTEL
DENVER PERFORMING ARTS
  COMPLEX
LARIMER SQUARE
UNION STATION
MUSEUM OF CONTEMPORAY ART
CHILDREN'S MUSEUM OF DENVER
DENVER ZOO
DENVER MUSEUM OF NATURE AND
  SCIENCE
DENVER BOTANICAL GARDENS

LEFT: the Denver Public Library with the sculpture *Lao-Tzu* in the foreground. **RIGHT:** the Colorado Rockies at Coors Field.

Denver

Black American West Museum

BENEDICT FOUNTAIN PARK

Molly Brown House Museum

State Capitol

Cathedral of the Immaculate Conception

St Paul's Lutheran Church

Central Presbyterian Church

Trinity United Methodist Church

One Corporate Center

Wells Fargo

Lincoln Center

Denver Post Tower

RTD Civic Center Bus Station

Amoco Bldg

WAR MEMORIAL PARK

Colorado Veterans' Monument

State Judicial Building

History Colorado Center

Lincoln Park

Brown Palace Hotel

Holy Ghost Church

US Custom House

Federal Bldg & Courthouse

Main Post Office

Denver Bus Terminal

Sakura Square

Denver Place

LOWER DOWNTOWN (LoDo)

Coors Field

Wynkoop Brewing Company

Ice House

Union Station (Amtrak)

Oxford Hotel

RTD Market St Bus Station

Tattered Cover Book Store

Museum of Contemporary Art Denver

Tabor Center

D&F Tower

Shops at Tabor Center

Writer Square

Larimer Square

16th Street Mall

Paramount Theatre

Denver Club Bldg

Masonic Bldg

Denver Pavilions

Denver Dry Bldg

US Bank Tower

Federal Reserve Bank

Denver Conv. & Visitor Bureau

World Trade Center

Republic Plaza Tower

Petroleum Bldg

Pioneer Monument

Greek Theater

Denver Art Museum

Byers-Evans House

Clyfford Still Museum

Bronco Buster

Civic Center Bldg

Camera Obscura

Indigos

Native American Trading Company

US Mint

Firefighters Museum

Colorado Convention Center

Colfax at Auraria

AURARIA

Pepsi Center/Six Flags

Pepsi Center

Point the Creek

Denver Tramway Power Co.

Helen Bonfils Theater Complex

Auditorium Theatre

Temple Buell Theatre

Boettcher Concert Hall

Curtigan Exhibition Hall

University of Colorado at Denver

EVent in Denver

Science

Emmanuel Gallery

Library & Media Center

St Elizabeth's Church

St Cajetan's Center

Metropolitan State College

St Francis Center

Denver Community College

Metropolitan State College Arts

Tivoli Student Union

King Center

Golda Meir House

Bentero Office

Child Development Center

Campus Police & Security Office

Facilities Management

Administration

West Auraria

Walnut Street

Parking & Transportation Office

9TH ST PARK

LINCOLN PARK

Printing and Distribution Center

Downtown Aquarium

Elitch Gardens Amusement Park

Children's Museum of Denver

COMMONS PARK

CONFLUENCE PARK

REI

CENTENNIAL PARK

FISHBACK PARK

GATES CRESCENT PARK

PLATTE RIVER GREENWAY

Invesco Field at Mile High

Riverside Baptist Church

New Life in Christ Church

JEFFERSON PARK

500 yds
500 m

Skyland

Denver Zoo

CITY PARK

Denver Museum of Nature & Science

Denver Botanic Gardens

Cherry Creek North

Tattered Cover Book Store

CHEESMAN PARK

City Park

Cheesman Park

Congress Park

Country Club

Curtis Park

Denver Performing Arts Complex

State Capitol

University of Colorado

Capitol Hill

Golden Triangle

Lincoln Park

Baker

Byers

1000 yds
1000 m

donated labor to build their own railroad, the Denver Pacific, which in 1870 was linked to the Cheyenne line. Not long after, the Kansas Pacific reached town, and Denver became the hub of a rail network that stretched in all directions. The railroad brought gold, minerals and coal to the town's smelters, agricultural products from the plains, and immigrants from Europe. In 1878, Leadville mines yielded the richest silver strikes in the nation's history, and Denver once again was at the crossroads of a prospecting frenzy. By 1900, 100 trains a day steamed in and out of Union Station.

Other hardships befell the fledgling city, as the cycle of boom and bust alternately yielded riches and ruins. Through it all, Denver kept its nose to the grindstone, diversifying into light manufacturing, military facilities, aviation, energy and, in recent years, high-tech industries. In 2009, Denver's population surpassed 600,000, one of the highest growth rates in the nation. Ironically, many people are relocating here from California in a kind of reverse migration.

Mile-high sightseeing

Start your tour of Denver at one of the city's most photographed spots – the 18th step of the **Colorado State Capitol ❶** (203 E. Colfax Avenue; tel: 303-866-2604; summer Mon–Fri 9am–3.30pm, 9.15am–2.30pm winter; free tours every 45 minutes), where a plaque informs visitors that they are standing one mile above sea level. Patterned after the US Capitol, the Colorado State Capitol is built in the shape of a Greek cross, with Corinthian columns, a central rotunda and other neo-classical features. Construction of the 18-story structure began in 1886 and took 22 years and nearly $3 million to complete. All the stone used in the building – granite, sandstone, marble – was quarried from locations around the state. The crowning glory is the dome, wrapped in gold leaf donated by Colorado miners in 1908.

The interior is equally impressive, with stained-glass portraits of Colorado pioneers, and murals chronicling key moments in state history. The rose onyx wainscoting is from Beulah, Colorado, and is the world's entire supply of this rare stone. Four full-time employees are responsible for polishing the ornamental brass railings around the rotunda. From the third floor, you can climb 93 steps to the dome's observation deck for a panoramic view of the city.

Descend the front steps of the Capitol, pass the red sandstone Colorado Veterans Monument, and cross Civic Center Park. To the far right, the **Pioneer Monument ❷** commemorates the end of the Smoky Hill Trail, a stage road connecting Denver with the Missouri River. The fountain, which depicts a pioneer mother, a miner and a trapper, sparked some controversy when it was erected in 1911; a figure of an American Indian that originally

The interior of the State Capitol Building, the construction of which consumed the entire known supply of Colorado rose onyx, a rare red marble from the small town of Beulah.

We Were Here, Too

The **Black American West Museum** (3091 California Street; tel: 720-242-7428; www.blackamericanwestmuseum.com; Tue–Sat 10am–2pm; charge) is dedicated to chronicling the role of African Americans in the settling and shaping of the American West.

The museum was founded by Paul W. Stewart, who as a child had been told that there was no such thing as black cowboys. In fact, nearly a third of the cowboys in the American West were black, and when Stewart grew up he met one who had led cattle drives at the turn of the 20th century. To set the record straight, Stewart set about compiling this eye-opening collection of artifacts, clothing, photographs, oral histories and documents that tell the story of black Western heroes such as Nat Love (alias Deadwood Dick), mountain man James Beckwourth, and rodeo riders Bill Pickett and James Arthur Walker as well as other African-American pioneers who became miners, ranchers, military heroes and millionaires. A homestead exhibit depicts Deartown, a black pioneer town founded in 1910 by O.T. Jackson near Greeley. The museum itself is housed in the one-time home of black physician Justina L. Ford who, despite the challenges of race and gender, established a successful medical practice here from 1902 to 1952.

topped the piece was replaced with a statue of frontiersman Kit Carson.

On the south end of the park is the lifelike *Bronco Buster* (1920), a statue by Alexander Proctor. The cowboy Proctor used as a model was arrested for horse rustling after posing for the artist. Nearby, the open-air **Greek Theater** ❸ (1919) is used for a variety of performances and public gatherings; it is adorned with murals by Alan True, whose work is also found in the Capitol. Bracketing the park on the west side is the grand semicircular **City and County Building**, a government building completed in 1932.

Behind the City and County Building is the **United States Mint** ❹ (320 W. Colfax Avenue; tel: 303-405-4761; www.usmint.gov/minttours; Mon–Fri 8am–2pm; free tours by reservation only). One of only two mints in the United States, it churns out $6 million daily in small change, a total of 52 million coins, about 40 percent pennies.

About three blocks away, just south of Civic Center Park, is the **Denver Art Museum** ❺ (100 W. 14th Avenue; tel: 720-865-5000; www.denverartmuseum.

org; Tue–Sun 10am–5pm; charge). The original North Building was designed by Gio Ponti in 1971.

The spectacular Frederic C. Hamilton Building is the most recent extension. It has doubled the size of the museum, creating much-needed space for more than 40,000 works of pre-Columbian, Spanish Colonial, Asian and modern American and European art. The collection of Western and Native American art is incomparable, with objects representing tribes throughout North America and works by such Western masters as George Catlin, Frederic Remington, Charles Russell and Alfred Jacob Miller. Designed by celebrated Polish-born architect, Daniel Libeskind, the building is covered in 9,000 titanium panels that reflect the Colorado sunshine and recall the peaks of the Rocky Mountains, and the geometric rock crystals found in the foothills near Denver.

Another landmark art museum building is currently being constructed nearby. Once completed, it will house the 2,000-piece private personal collection of works by famed American abstract Expressionist artist Clyfford Still, which was bequeathed to the city of Denver by his widow in 2004. The $7 million **Clyfford Still Museum** is due to open sometime in 2011 and will consist of a 28,500 sq ft (2647 sq meter), two-story, poured-concrete building with a cantilevered lobby leading to open-plan galleries displaying Still's works made between the 1920s and 1979.

Behind the Denver Art Museum is the historic **Byers-Evans House** ❻ (1310 Bannock Street; tel: 303-620-4933; Tue–Sun 10.30am–2.30pm; half-hour guided tours; charge), built in 1883 by *Rocky Mountain News* founder William Byers and later purchased by businessman William Gray Evans. A 30-minute guided tour is preceded by a film detailing the history of these prominent families. Visitor numbers are limited, so arrive early if you haven't booked in advance. The former

carriage house contains the **Denver History Museum**, which chronicles the development of the city from the gold rush to World War II.

Across the courtyard from the museum is the **Denver Public Library** ❼ (10 W. 14th Avenue; tel: 720-865-1111; www.denverlibrary.org), housed in a distinctive contemporary building designed by architect Michael Graves and Denver firm Klipp Colussy Jenks DuBois. This is the largest library between Chicago and Los Angeles and contains the highly regarded Western History Collection of rare books, maps and photos. A Western gallery is on the sixth floor; changing exhibitions are on the eighth.

The **Colorado History Museum** ❽ (1560 Broadway, Suite 400; tel: 303-866-3682; www.coloradohistory.org; Mon–Sat 10am–4.30pm, Sun noon–4.30pm; charge) is currently housed in the old Denver Post building pending its move to the newly built **History Colorado Center** at 1200 Broadway planned for late 2011. Exhibits range from Ancient Puebloan artifacts and Plains Indian art to mining equipment and memo-rabilia belonging to ill-fated silver king Horace Tabor.

It's a six-block walk through the Capitol Hill neighborhood to the **Molly Brown House Museum** ❾ (1340 Pennsylvania Street; tel: 303-832-4092; www.mollybrown.org; Tue–Sat 10am–3.30pm, Sun noon–3.30pm; charge), former home of the celebrated Margaret Brown, survivor of the *Titanic* disaster and subject of the popular musical and film *The Unsinkable Molly Brown*. A costumed guide recounts Margaret's rags-to-riches story as you tour the 1889 Queen Anne–style residence. Never fully accepted by high society, Margaret was self-educated, spoke five languages, and was an avid campaigner for women's and children's rights. Ironically, she was never known as Molly during her lifetime. Meredith Willson, the musical's composer and lyricist, bestowed the name upon her because he thought it would be easier to sing.

16th Street Mall

In the early 1980s, a mile-long stretch of 16th Street between Broadway and

Donald Lipski's whimsical The Yearling *stands outside the Denver Central Library.*

BELOW: the Denver post office; philanthropist Andrew Carnegie famously complained that the city's neoclassical architecture had "too many pillars."

TIP

The small but highly regarded **Museo de las Americas** (861 Santa Fe Drive; tel: 303-571-4401; www.museo.org; Tue–Fri 10am–5pm, Sat–Sun noon–5pm; free) south of Downtown is dedicated to Latino culture, ranging from Pre-Columbian civilizations to contemporary works.

Market Street was bulldozed to make way for the **16th Street Mall** ⑩. This popular thoroughfare – pedestrian-only except for free shuttle buses – launched the revitalization of downtown Denver. Today, the Mall, which was designed by famed architect I.M. Pei, is one of the liveliest urban spaces in the state. In summer, its shady central boulevard comes alive with bubbling fountains and some 50,000 flowers, and folks lounge on benches and at outdoor cafés or play chess under the trees.

Starting near the top of the Mall, at 16th Street and Tremont Place, is the glitzy **Denver Pavilions**, a two-block-square, open-air complex of shops, restaurants and movie theaters linked by the "Great Wall," a neon-lit, upper-story marquee that straddles Glenarm Place with its signature DENVER sign.

A block from the Mall is the landmark **Brown Palace Hotel** ⑪ (tel: 303-297-3111; www.brownpalace.com), which stands on a triangular lot at 17th and Tremont. The hotel was built by Henry Cordes Brown, a carpenter-turned-entrepreneur who settled in Denver in

the 1860s. Brown donated land for the Capitol, then made a fortune selling off his property on Capitol Hill. But he reserved the three-sided pasture where he grazed his cow to build a grand hotel. Designed in Italian Renaissance style by Frank E. Edbrooke, architect of the State Capitol and much else, the hotel was completed in 1892 at a cost of $1.6 million after four years of construction. It was worth every penny. The Palace rivaled the splendor of the finest eastern hotels, impressing guests and residents alike with its red granite and sandstone facade, soaring eight-story atrium, golden onyx pillars and stained-glass ceiling. Luminaries such as Theodore Roosevelt, Dwight Eisenhower and Harry Truman were frequent guests. Even if you can't stay here, don't pass up an opportunity to see the lobby, join a historic tour (Wed and Sat at 3pm), or enjoy the sumptuous afternoon tea.

If time permits, consider another detour on Tremont Place for a self-guided tour of the **Denver Firefighters Museum** ⑫ (1326 Tremont Place; tel: 303-892-1436; www.denverfirefighters

BELOW RIGHT: the grand atrium of the Brown Palace Hotel, designed by architect Frank Edbrooke and completed in 1892.

The LoDo District

The restoration of Larimer Square in the 1970s started a revitalization movement that culminated some 25 years later with the resurrection of a blighted warehouse district known as Lower Downtown, or LoDo. Encompassing about 25 square blocks from Larimer Street to Union Station, and Cherry Creek to 20th Street, LoDo contains a remarkable concentration of early 20th-century industrial buildings. During its heyday, LoDo was a bustling commercial district full of sprawling warehouses and showrooms that were the forerunners of modern department stores.

Denver was a major rail center, and the warehouses were packed with goods for distribution throughout the West. By the early 1990s, however, LoDo had been all but abandoned – a haven for drug dealers and the homeless that was strictly off-limits after dark. All that changed in 1995 with the opening of the 50,000-seat Coors Field baseball stadium at Blake and 20th streets. Suddenly thousands of people were trooping through LoDo, and their potential custom sparked the regeneration of the neighborhood. Within five years, LoDo went from having no taxpaying residents to about 5,000, a number that has grown steadily ever since. Dozens of bars, restaurants and brewpubs, as well as some 30 galleries, keep the place buzzing year-round, though summer evenings – when the young and beautiful go club-hopping – tend to be the liveliest.

museum.org; Mon–Sat 10am–4pm; charge). The museum is set in a historic firehouse and displays an array of steam pumpers, fire trucks and other equipment dating back to the 1860s. Children can try on firefighting equipment and slide down a pole.

The **Masonic Building** (1889), also by Frank Edbrooke, stands at Welton Street. Gutted by fire in 1985, its stone facade was rescued by erecting a new steel skeleton within. Next door, the **Kittredge Building** (1891) houses the **Paramount Theatre ⑬**, Denver's only surviving movie palace, which opened in 1930. It's worth catching a performance if only to view the Art Deco interior.

Two blocks farther on, a detour to the left leads to the **Denver Performing Arts Complex ⑭** (950 13th Street; tel: 720-865-4220; www.artscomplex.com). Encompassing four city blocks and eight theaters, it is the world's largest center of its kind under one roof – an impressive glass arch 80ft (24 meters) high and two blocks long. Drama, musicals, cabaret, opera, ballet and concerts are staged here.

At Arapahoe Street the view opens onto distant mountains. On the right is one of the city's oldest landmarks, the **Daniels and Fisher**, or **D&F, Tower ⑮**. Colorado's first "skyscraper" is 330ft (100 meters) tall – 375ft (114 meters) to the top of the flagpole – and was the highest building west of the Mississippi when it was completed in 1909. Modeled after the campanile in St Mark's Square in Venice, the tower has its original clockworks, thought to be the largest of their kind in the country. The weights are wound by hand several times a week. The lobby displaying the mechanism is open to the public, and the five floors are often used for parties, weddings and corporate events.

Rest in **Skyline Park**, a leafy plaza rescued from neglect by an ambitious redevelopment plan in 2003. On the next block is the glass-walled **Tabor Center**, a lively shopping mall with more than 50 retailers and restaurants, wandering entertainers and a visitor information booth. Opposite is **Writers Square**, a complex of shops, offices and apartments built around a

The dome of the Capitol Building in Denver is covered in real gold leaf.

BELOW: Union Station in LoDo.

The Denver Art Museum has an extensive collection, but is known primarily for its American Indian art.

BELOW: the Hamilton wing of the Denver Art Museum, designed by Daniel Libeskind.

central plaza.

Cut through Writers Square to **Larimer Square** , a block of restored Victorian-era buildings on Larimer Street between 14th and 15th streets. The Granite Building at 1228 15th Street stands on the site where General William H. Larimer built his log cabin, using coffin lids for doors. Western legends like Bat Masterson and Buffalo Bill Cody also had Larimer Street addresses at one time or another during their Western sojourns.

On the north side is the square's trendiest hang-out, **The Market**, where you can soak in the scene over coffee, pastries, sandwiches or ice cream. Horse-drawn carriages depart from the Square for rides along the 16th Street Mall. At the end of Larimer Street, on the banks of Cherry Creek, you can buy tickets to **Punt the Creek** (tel: 303-893-0750)– a relaxing 75-minute float trip on a flat-bottomed boat, or punt, propelled by a long pole.

LoDo a-go-go

Anchoring the restored Lower Downtown (or LoDo) on Wynkoop Street is **Union Station** ⑰, built in 1881 and still serving as a railroad terminal. Amtrak runs two cross-country lines through Union Station as well as the weekend Ski Train to Winter Park. Modern restaurants have been added to the wings, but the central waiting room is still a vision from an Edward Hopper painting, with tall-backed wooden benches, overhead reading lights and arched windows.

Next to the station, the 1903 **Ice House**, a former cold storage plant for the Littleton Creamery, is said to have stored furs and corpses as well as dairy products. The spooky basement level lends credibility to the tale, but otherwise the building sports a smart lobby, a restaurant, and a deli. Across the street, the **Wynkoop Brewing Company**, Colorado's first brewpub and a LoDo pioneer, occupies the beautiful turn-of-the-20th-century J.S. Brown Mercantile. Around the corner, at 17th and Wazee streets, is yet another Frank Edbrooke creation,

the **Oxford Hotel**, built in 1891 and embodying all the grand aspirations of Colorado's silver boom.

The **Museum of Contemporary Art Denver** ⑱ (1485 Delgany Street; tel: 303-298-7554; www.mcadenver.org; Tue–Sun 10am–6pm; charge) is currently Denver's only contemporary art museum, housing works by modern masters such as Damien Hirst. The building itself is a work of art, a sustainable structure on a former brownfield site that has just won gold LEED designation. It was designed in 2006 by Tanzania-born David Adjaye, one of Britain's leading architects, and contains five galleries, a store, a café, and a lecture hall.

On the north side of LoDo is **Coors Field** ⑲, home of the Colorado Rockies. Opened to much acclaim in the mid-1990s, the $215 million stadium was designed in the spirit of the classic ballparks of the 1940s and 1950s. The **Sandlot Brewing Company**, owned by the corporate giant that sponsors the park, provides appreciative fans with specialty beers.

A three-block walk fom the stadium is the small Japanese enclave of **Sakura** Square (19th and Larimer streets). During World War II, when people of Japanese descent faced hostility in the United States, Governor Ralph Carr welcomed them to Colorado. A bronze bust honors his memory. The **Pacific Mercantile Company**, which sells Asian foods and gifts, opened here in 1942. Otherwise, there's not a great deal of interest for tourists.

South Platte Valley

Due west of LoDo, where Cherry Creek flows into the South Platte River, is **Confluence Park** ⑳. Kayakers can often be seen testing the rapids above the confluence, and kayaks can be rented on nearby Platte Street. For decades this stretch of the South Platte was an industrial wasteland – polluted, cluttered with trash and prone to flooding. A reclamation project launched in the 1970s has worked a marvelous transformation, and today the river front is a popular public space, with some 12 miles (19km) of biking trails, picnic

The Denver Art Museum has more than 4,500 works of modern and contemporary art.

BELOW: climbing the wall at REI's flagship sporting goods store.

Tattered Cover Bookstore

Denver's Tattered Cover Bookstore is one of the West's great independent bookstores. The historic LoDo shop (1626 16th Street; tel: 303-436-1070) occupies the former Morey Mercantile building. It contains a huge selection of books on two cavernous floors and hosts numerous author readings, The Colfax Avenue Store (2526 East Colfax Street; tel: 303-322-7727) is located in the historic Lowenstein Theater and contains some 150,000 titles, an extensive news stand, a coffee shop, and reading nooks and comfy chairs. A third branch opened in modern Highlands Ranch Town Center (9315 Dorchester Street; tel: 303-470-7050) in 2004. It has a large children's section. All three branches have coffee and tea shops, great places for refreshments. Call for store hours, author reading schedule, and other information.

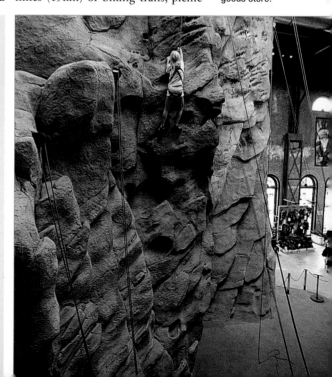

The Museum of Nature and Science has more than 1 million artifacts, ranging from Egyptian mummies to dinosaurs.

BELOW: dinosaur exhibit at the Museum of Nature and Science's *Prehistoric Journey*.

areas, even wetlands where native species like beaver thrive.

The **Children's Museum of Denver** ㉑ (2121 Children's Museum Drive; tel: 303-433-7444; www.mychildsmuseum. org; Mon–Fri 9am–4pm, Sat–Sun 10am–5pm; charge) has interactive exhibits that encourage kids to play the role of storyteller, artist, scientist and more. An outdoor challenge center gives children an opportunity to try skating, snowboarding and skiing in safety. Outside the museum is a stop for the **Platte Valley Trolley**, an open-air streetcar reminiscent of those operated by the Denver Tramway Company in the early 20th century. It follows a scenic route along the South Platte on railroad tracks dating to the 1890s.

Across the river is **Elitch Gardens Amusement Park** ㉒ (I-25 and Speer Boulevard; tel: 303-595-4386; www. elitchgardens.com; daily June–Aug 10am–9pm, hours vary in Apr, May, Sept and Oct; charge). The park was originally located in northwest Denver, where in 1890 John and Mary Elitch started a "pleasure garden" in an orchard. Moved to a much larger

site on the South Platte in 1995, it currently has four steel and wooden roller coasters and nine other thrill rides, including the highest free-fall drop swing in Colorado and a white water rafting ride, a 300ft (90-meter) observation tower, a 100ft (30-meter)high Ferris wheel, and a 10-acre (4-hectare) water park.

The large soda-can-shaped building near Elitch Gardens is the **Pepsi Center**, a top concert venue and home of the Colorado Avalanche hockey team. **Invesco Field**, where the Denver Broncos play soccer, is on the opposite side of the river, off I-25.

City Park

With more than 4,000 acres (1,620 hectares) of traditional parks and parkways, including 2,500 acres (1,012 hectares) of urban natural land, more than 300 acres (121 hectares) of parks, designated rivers and trails, and an additional 14,000 acres (5,666 hectares) of spectacular mountain parks, Denver has the largest municipal park system in the United States. One of the oldest is **City Park**, created in

1881 when 314 acres (127 hectares) of sagebrush were transformed into a sanctuary of green lawns and rose gardens. The **Denver Zoo** ㉓ (2300 Steele Street; tel: 303-376-4800; www.denverzoo.org; daily 10am–5pm, extended summer hours; charge) was founded here a few years later. Its first exhibit was an orphaned black bear named Billy Bryan, who was tethered to a tree. Bear Mountain, built in 1918, was the first naturalistic habitat – an enclosure without bars – an idea that wouldn't catch on at other zoos for another 50 years. Today the zoo is home to about 4,000 animals representing 700 species. Among the zoo's highlights are the Primate Panorama, a habitat for some 29 primates, ranging from pygmy marmosets (which weigh as much as an airmail letter) to 600lb (270kg) lowland gorillas; Tropical Discovery, a simulated rain forest; and a pack of Arctic wolves.

On the east side of the park is the **Denver Museum of Nature and Science** ㉔ (2001 Colorado Boulevard; tel: 303-322-7009; www.dmns.org; daily 9am–5pm; charge), the fifth largest natural history museum in the United States. Exhibits cover familiar territory – mummies, meteorites, totem poles, tepees, wildlife dioramas and much else. Where the museum really excels is in the field of paleontology. *Prehistoric Journey*, an exhibit on the third floor, chronicles 3½ billion years of life on earth. The highlight is a collection of dinosaur fossils, including an 80ft (24-meter) long Diplodocus and an Allosaurus and Stegosaurus engaged in battle. In the next room is a diorama of a nightmarish creature known as a Dinohyus, nicknamed the "terminator pig," stalking its prey about 20 million years ago. The museum is also home to the **Gates Planetarium**, which features daily star shows, and an **IMAX** theater.

Denver Botanic Gardens

Denver Botanic Gardens ㉕ (1007 York Street; tel: 720-865-3713; www.botanicgardens.org; daily 9am–5pm, summer until 9pm; charge) is rated one of the top botanical gardens in the country. It encompasses 23 acres (9 hectares) planted with over 16,000 examples of more than 250 plant species at its York Street gardens and two satellite locations: Chatfield, a picturesque nature preserve along the banks of Deer Creek, and Mount Goliath, which showcases alpine tundra. The misty Tropica Botanic collection is housed in the only major tropical conservatory in the Rockies. For the best view, ascend to the overhead platforms on an elevator disguised as a banyan tree. Plants from all over the world are featured in 30 outdoor gardens, including a Japanese garden with a teahouse, and the Monet Garden, with flowers and water lilies inspired by the canvases of French Impressionist Claude Monet. Colorado plants take pride of place in gardens of rare wild flowers, alpine species, medicinal plants used by native Americans, and heirloom varieties brought to Colorado by Anglo pioneers. Special events are held throughout the year, including summer garden strolls and a concert series. ❑

Some rides were relocated from their home at the original Elitch Gardens in northwest Denver to the current site in the Platte River Valley.

BELOW: spring arrives with a riot of colorful blossoms at Denver Botanic Gardens.

FESTIVALS

Colorado is famous for the sheer number of its festivals. Almost every community has a festival during the year – some of which fall on the odd side of the spectrum

When you have a spectacular setting like the Colorado Rockies, you like to show it off to its full advantage. Some communities in Colorado, though, have hit on some unique festivals to attract visitors. Manitou Springs has not one, but two, weird festivals: the Great Fruitcake Toss in early January, celebrating the famous American dislike of Grandma's Christmas fruitcake, and the Emma Crawford Coffin Races in October, a blackly humorous race up Pikes Peak commemorating the 1890 death of Emma Crawford, her burial on Red Mountain, and the subsequent refusal of her remains to stay buried there. Just as macabre is Frozen Dead Guy Days in Nederland, near Boulder, in March, which culminates in an excursion to a wooden shed to view the remains of an elderly Norwegian man whose remains were unable to be repatriated and instead were frozen here forever. Mike the Headless Chicken Festival in Fruita in May is equally strange, celebrating a chicken that managed to live after its head was cut off. Compared with these fests, fibARK, the biggest whitewater convocation in the country, on the Arkansas River in downtown historic Salida in early September, is fun in the sun, as is Rolling River Raft Race, in Pueblo in July. And the International Rhubarb Festival in July celebrating Silverton's only crop. Positively mainstream.

ABOVE: mummers perform at Vinotok, wearing medieval attire and dancing with drums through the streets and stages of Crested Butte.

ABOVE: the coffin races at Frozen Dead Guy Days are a spectacle unto themselves. The event also features a polar plunge.

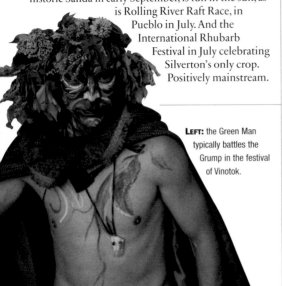

LEFT: the Green Man typically battles the Grump in the festival of Vinotok.

ABOVE: FibARK, the whitewater festival in Salida, has been attracting kayakers since 1949. It is America's oldest kayak festival.

FUN IN THE MOUNTAINS

Tucked away in a gorgeous box canyon in the Western San Juans, Telluride is decidedly off the beaten track. Until a few years ago, it was mainly popular as a destination ski resort in winter but welcomed fewer visitors during the summer. Until, that is, local tourism boosters hit upon the brilliant idea of turning the small town into a summer festival destination. Today, throughout the summer and at other times of year, there is always something going on in Telluride, from its Blues and Brews Festival, Bluegrass Festival, International Film Festival and Mountainfilm Festival to more obscure offerings such as the Telluride Mushroom Festival and the tongue-in-cheek Nothing Festival, a weekend when everyone stays home for a change (tagline: "Thank you for not participating"). Telluride is not unique in the community fun stakes. The tiny ski resort town of Crested Butte also has quite a roster of home town festivals, including Flauschink, an off-the-wall, end-of-ski-season celebration in March; Fat Tire Bike Week in June; the Rubber Duckie fund-raiser in July; and Vinitok, celebrating the change in season in September.

ABOVE: dressing in costume to celebrate Frozen Dead Guys Days is a popular activity in Nederland, where the locals always join in.

LEFT: Vinotok is Crested Butte's celebration of the changing of the seasons, from summer to fall to winter.

RIGHT: the chainless bike race in Crested Butte, where some contestants lose more than their chains.

BOULDER AND ENVIRONS

The mind-set is strictly forward-looking in this quintessential college town set amid the scenic splendors of the Rocky Mountain foothills

"Twenty-five square miles surrounded by reality." That's how some Colorado pundits describe **Boulder ❶**. Though only 30 miles (48km) from downtown Denver, this city of 102,800 people is a world apart. Both unapologetically New Age yet fast-paced and intellectual (the average age of the population is 29), Boulder is a place where past, present and future co-exist quite happily, with former hippies now running some of the city's most successful health products businesses, alternative health and meditation schools, science think-tanks and outdoor companies. Boulderites are liberal in outlook, with a penchant for political correctness. Residents share a fanatical commitment to fitness and a strong interest in educational, spiritual, alternative health, environmental and social issues.

The city has been focused on education ever since the University of Colorado was established here in 1876, the year Colorado achieved statehood. One-third of the city's population is now connected to UC Boulder, famed for its science programs, and the city hosts several major science research centers, including the National Center for Atmospheric Research, the Space Science Institute, and the Rocky Mountain Institute.

Boulder Mountain Parks

Etched into the national consciousness along with other such "progressive" towns as Austin (Texas), Berkeley (California), and Madison (Wisconsin), Boulder arguably has the most scenic location. The tilted rock slabs known as the **Flatirons** and a procession of nearby peaks form a splendid western backdrop that captures the light and lifts the spirit. These formations comprise the heart of **Boulder Mountain Parks** (tel: 303-441-3440; www.boulder colorado.gov), part of the city's 45,000-

Main attractions
BOULDER CREEK
COLORADO CHAUTAUQUA
PEARL STREET MALL
BOULDER COUNTY FARMERS' MARKET
UNIVERSITY OF COLORADO CAMPUS MUSEUMS
BOULDER MOUNTAIN PARK AND THE FLATIRONS
NATIONAL CENTER FOR ATMOSPHERIC RESEARCH
ELDORADO SPRINGS
CELESTIAL SEASONINGS TEA TOUR
LONGMONT MUSEUM AND CULTURAL CENTER
NEDERLAND
BRAINEARD LAKE RECREATION AREA
INDIAN PEAKS WILDERNESS

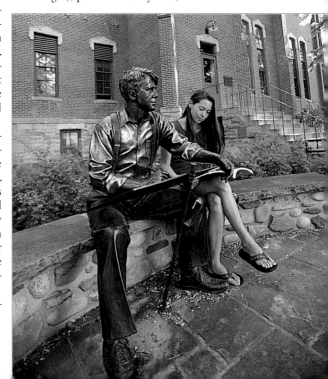

LEFT: a student from Boulder.
RIGHT: University of Colorado campus.

Boulder has more than 100 miles (160km) of bikeways.

plus acres (18,211 hectares) of open space and parks. Open space in general and the mountain parks in particular are more than a buffer against suburban sprawl. They are laced with hiking, biking and equestrian trails that form part of a 300-mile (480km) urban trail system.

Urban park

The 7-mile (11km) stretch of **Boulder Creek Path** that follows the contours of the creek roughly east–west across the city is a gem. This meandering path, paved through the city's core, is crowded with cyclists, in-line skaters, runners, walkers and parents pushing baby carriages. Majestic cottonwoods shade the creek banks, and benches, kids' fishing and fish-spotting areas, historic markers, and sculptures are diversions along the way. Kayakers navigate Boulder Creek's rapids just upstream from the mouth of **Boulder Canyon**, while tubing is a cool way to enjoy the creek between pretty **Eben Fine Park** (at the west end of Arapahoe Avenue) and **Central Park** (Broadway between Walnut and Canyon). The Boulder

Creek Festival takes place here every Memorial Day weekend.

Credit for these amenities goes to the foresight of city officials. They purchased thousands of acres of open land as early as 1967 and adopted stringent zoning and growth control in the 1970s. Boulder's policy has been to reuse existing buildings and fill in empty lots, rather than endlessly sprawl outward, with a few new carefully thought-out subdivisions on the edge of town. What Boulder has done for decades other cities are now, often belatedly, envying and emulating.

An enlightened colony

Boulder lies in a broad open valley, with the Flatirons and foothills to the west, Davidson Mesa to the south, and a gentle, nameless ridge to the north. From this high perch, it seems like a small settlement tucked among the trees, especially in summer when they are fully leafed out. On a clear day in any season, the eye is drawn above the trees and rooftops to the majestic mountain backdrop, culminating in 14,255ft (4,325-meter) Longs Peak, the

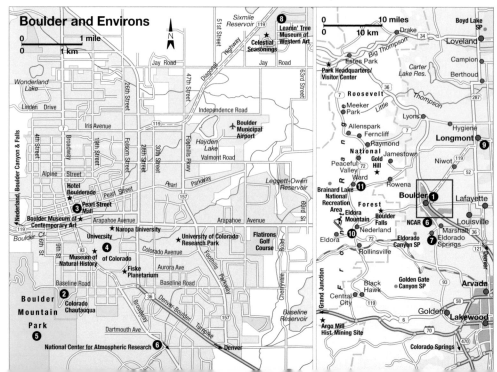

highest along the Front Range, just 40 miles (64km) northwest of Boulder.

When the Southern Arapaho wintered here, the valley was high prairie virtually devoid of trees. On October 17, 1858, the first Anglo settlers established a rough camp below Red Rocks at the mouth of **Boulder Canyon**. A plaque at **Settlers Park** commemorates their arrival. Just four months later, the Boulder City Town Company was organized, with A.A. Brookfield as president and 56 shareholders. They platted 4,444 parcels of land priced at $1,000 each. Encompassed by Kansas Territory until February 28, 1861, when Congress created the Territory of Colorado, Boulder City became a supply town for prospectors seeking gold and silver in the mountains to the west. Residents, longing for respectability, opened the territory's first school in 1860, created a stable town government in 1871, and cheered the arrival of the railroad in 1873.

By 1900, such residential neighborhoods as Goss Grove, Whittier and Mapleton Hill had taken shape around the downtown commercial core. Now designated as historic districts, they have the patina of old Boulder, albeit far leafier than the city's founders could have envisioned. **Historic Boulder** (1123 Spruce Street; tel: 303-444-5192; www.historicboulder.org; Mon–Fri 9am–4pm) sponsors guided tours of the neighborhoods (charge) and sells inexpensive pamphlets for self-guided walking tours.

In 1898, Boulder was chosen by Texas educators and local citizens as a location for the Chautauqua movement, a summer colony devoted to educational enrichment, spiritual enlightenment and physical health. The **Colorado Chautauqua** ❷ (tel: 303-441-3282; www.chautauqua.com) was founded on a hillside southwest of town, where the wooden Auditorium, the Dining Hall and tent cabins were erected. Quaint wood-frame cabins long ago replaced the tents as popular vacation rentals; the Auditorium is now home of the summer **Colorado Music Festival** (tel: 303-449-1397), while the **Dining Hall** (tel: 303-440-3776) is a fine, year-round restaurant. The expansive lawn is popular with picnickers and

The Pearl Street Mall in Boulder is the perfect place to go shopping for an unusual or handmade item.

BELOW: a harpist entertains passersby on the Pearl Street Mall.

The campus of the University of Colorado at Boulder has all been designed in the same architectural style.

BELOW RIGHT: a busker entertains.

Frisbee-throwers. Trailheads for three of the best trails in the Boulder Mountain Parks are on the perimeter. Hiking information is available at the Ranger Cottage in Chautauqua Park (Baseline and Grant; tel: 303-441-3440; Mon–Fri 9am–4pm, Sat–Sun 8am–6pm, park events have various hours). The cottage stocks maps and is the departure point for ranger-guided hikes and interpretive programs.

Around the Mall

In 1977, four blocks in downtown Boulder between 11th and 15th streets were set aside as a pedestrian mall. The town's commercial district and much of its public life centers around the **Pearl Street Mall ❸**, one of the country's first (and still one of the most successful) pedestrians-only zones. Gradually, most traditional stores and services moved elsewhere, replaced by trendy boutiques, art galleries, craft shops, restaurants and nightclubs. Beautifully landscaped, it is the perfect place for strolling, shopping, dining or sitting at a sidewalk café and watching the world go by. With warm, sunny days common even in winter, outdoor tables at south-facing establishments are popular throughout the year.

"The Mall" attracts jugglers, musicians and other buskers, but it's also the setting for many special events, including the **Downtown Boulder Food and Wine Festival** in April; the **BoldBoulder 10K** marathon over Memorial Day weekend; the **Downtown Art Festival** in late September; and **Switch on the Holidays** on the Friday after Thanksgiving. (Tel: 303-449-3774 for details.)

Just a block from the Mall is the 1909 **Hotel Boulderado** (2115 13th Street; tel: 303-442-4344; www.boulderado. com), which has a gorgeous *fin-de-siècle* lobby topped by a soaring stained-glass ceiling. Around the corner, **Boulder Theater** (2034 14th Street; tel: 303-786-7030), an Art Deco landmark, hosts concerts, dance, films and the weekly

Higher Learning

Naropa University (2130 Arapahoe; tel: 303-444-0202) in Boulder isn't an ordinary college. For starters, mindfulness training, through daily meditation, is as important as traditional Western studies. While coeds at other schools study chemistry, calculus and macro-economics, Naropa's 1,000 international students develop skills in Tai-Chi, contemplative psychology and Tibetan Thangka painting. It is one of only two Buddhist universities in the United States. Naropa's approach emphasizes intellect and intuition. It is rooted in six elements: awareness of the present moment, learning in community, cultivating openness, the Buddhist educational heritage, world wisdom traditions, and nonpartisanism. First developed at India's Nalanda University, founded by Buddhist scholar Naropa in the 11th century, the concept was introduced to the US in 1974 by Tibetan Buddhist teacher Chogyam Trungpa Rinpoche. A sartorial figure with a taste for sharp suits and high living, Trungpa Rinpoche is today acknowledged as a key popularizer of Buddhism in the West. Following his exile, he attended Oxford University, then founded meditation centers in North America and Europe. Although he died in 1987, he lived to see Naropa become an accredited institution of higher learning, with a faculty that included Beat poet Allen Ginsberg for whom the school library is named, and popular teachers like Pema Chodron, abbot of Gampo Abbey, Nova Scotia.

broadcast of National Public Radio's *e-Town*. Nearby, the **Boulder Dushanbe Tea House** (1770 13th Street; tel: 303-442-4993; www.boulderteahouse.com) is an exotic polychrome tile structure from Dushanbe, Tajikistan, one of Boulder's six sister cities.

Just south of the teahouse, **Boulder Museum of Contemporary Art** (1750 13th Street; tel: 303-443-2122; www.bmoca.org; Tue–Fri 11am–5pm, Wed until 8pm, Sat 9am–4pm, Sun noon–3pm; charge) features shows by visiting artists and a series of lectures and workshops. **Boulder County Farmers' Market** (tel: 303-910-2236; www.boulderfarmers.org; Apr–Nov Sat 8am–2pm, May–Oct Wed 4–8pm) occupies 13th Street between Canyon Boulevard and Arapahoe Avenue. An on-ramp to the Boulder Creek Path is just steps away at 13th and Arapahoe.

School days

In 1874, Boulder donated 45 acres (18 hectares) to the **University of Colorado ❹** for the purpose of establishing an institution of higher learning on the wild frontier. **Old Main**, built in 1877 for classrooms, offices and the president's living quarters, now houses the **Heritage Center** (tel: 303-492-6329; Mon–Fri 10am–5pm, summer 10am–4.30pm, free), a museum devoted to the university's history and traditions. One room honors CU's 15 alumni astronauts, including Kalpana Chawla, who perished in the Columbia explosion.

The **Colorado Museum of Natural History** (Henderson Building, 15th and Broadway; tel: 303-492-6892; Mon–Fri 9am–5pm, Sat 9am–4pm, Sun 10am–4pm; charge) houses more than 4 million artifacts in the fields of paleontology, zoology and anthropology, including exhibits of Ancestral Puebloan art, dinosaur fossils and specimens of native species. The Discovery Corner is a hands-on section designed especially for children. Three galleries offer changing exhibitions.

Fiske Planetarium (Regent Drive;

Naropa University offers classes in Eastern spiritualism.

BELOW: picnickers gather in Boulder Creek Park.

A fanciful street sign guides visitors to Celestial Seasonings, the country's largest producer of herbal teas.

BELOW: the afternoon sun is reflected on the clouds.

tel: 303-492-5002; call for show times; charge) is the largest facility of its kind between Chicago and Los Angeles. It presents star shows, workshops and labs as well as laser shows set to pop music. Amateur astronomers can gaze at the heavens through 16-, 18- and 24-in telescopes at **Sommers-Bausch Observatory** (Regent Drive and Kittridge Loop; tel: 303-492-6732; public viewing Fri night). Weekly stargazing sessions focus on such themes as black holes, extraterrestrial life and planetary exploration.

The southern fringe

Begin exploring the outskirts of town by driving south on Broadway to Baseline Road, then west up steep, tortuous Flagstaff Road into **Boulder Mountain Park ❺**. Pullouts along the way offer panoramic views of Boulder, the Front Range and the Continental Divide. Hiking trails cross the road at various points, and at the summit of

Flagstaff Mountain are picnic tables, an amphitheater built in the 1930s by the Civilian Conservation Corps, and a rustic cabin with nature exhibits.

Return the way you came, turning south on Broadway to Table Mesa Drive for a winding uphill ride to the **National Center for Atmospheric Research ❻** (1850 Table Mesa Drive; tel: 303-497-1000; www.ncar. ucar.edu; Mon–Fri 8am–5pm, Sat–Sun and holidays 9am–4pm; free guided tour weekdays at noon). Designed by architect I.M. Pei and set dramatically at the base of the Flatirons, the facility's sandstone walls and rectangular masses recall the ancient cliff dwellings of Mesa Verde. A series of interactive exhibits explores weather and the science of climatology.

About 8 miles (13km) south of Boulder, in the hamlet of **Eldorado Springs ❼**, the area's best outdoor swimming pool is operated by water-bottling company **Eldorado Artesian Springs** (tel: 303-499-1316; daily June–Aug 10am–6pm; charge). The pool is all that remains of the ritzy Eldorado Springs Resort, which opened in 1905

Celestial Seasonings Tea

Celestial Seasonings (4600 Sleepytime Drive; tel: 303-581-1202; www.celestialseasonings.com; Mon–Sat 10am–4pm, Sun 11am–3pm; tea shop: Mon–Sat 9am–6pm, Sun 11am–5pm; Celestial Café: Mon–Sat 7.30am–2.30pm; free tours), is the country's largest producer of herbal teas and Boulder's top visitor attraction. Enjoy samples and learn how the teas are grown, dried, blended and packaged on free tours (an astounding 8 million teabags are produced every 24 hours.) A visit to the aromatic Mint Room – one of the tour highlights – is an olfactory tour de force. A gallery displays the original paintings for the folksy tea packaging. Red Zinger, Grandma's Tummy Mint and other popular teas are sold at a discount in the tea shop.

and hosted such luminaries as boxer Jack Dempsey, Dwight and Mamie Eisenhower, and actor W.C. Fields, the well-known tippler, who famously declared "I never drink water because of the disgusting things fish do in it," who reluctantly tried a sip of spring water. **Eldorado Canyon State Park** (tel: 303-494-3943) is Boulder's premier rock-climbing area, with 500 routes, picnic sites and 12 miles (19km) of hiking trails. During the resort's heyday, daredevil Ivy Baldwin entertained guests by walking a tight-rope across the canyon. He made the trip 86 times – the first in 1906, the last, at age 82, in 1948.

Tea time and more

On the north side of town, just off the Diagonal Highway (CO 119), is **Celestial Seasonings**, the country's top herbal teas producer *(see panel)*, and nearby **Leanin' Tree Museum of Western Art** ❽ (6055 Longbow Drive; tel: 303-581-2100; www.leanintree museum.com; Mon–Fri 8am–5pm, Sat–Sun 10am–5pm; free), which features the private collection of Ed Trumble,

founder of a greeting card company specializing in Western themes. Scores of paintings and bronze sculptures – nearly all created after 1950 – are jammed into a handful of galleries.

Northeast of Boulder, in the town of **Longmont** ❾, is **Longmont Museum & Cultural Center** (400 Quail Road; tel: 303-651-8374; Mon–Sat 9am–5pm, Sun 1–5pm; free), a striking contemporary structure inspired by the region's agricultural heritage. Two galleries display permanent exhibits chronicling the city's growth with such quotidian objects as hair driers, an icebox, a telephone switchboard and a variety of office equipment. Traveling shows, including, in 2010, an exhibition called "From Swords to Ploughshares: Metal Trench Art of World Wars I and II," are presented in the other two galleries.

Rugged and funky

The region's hardscrabble mining era reveals itself as you travel into the mountains west of Boulder via Canyon Boulevard. Eight miles (13km) up the twisting, rock-rimmed road is **Boulder Falls**, a 70ft (21-meter) cascade that's

Boulder topped a 2010 study of the Brainiest Cities in America, conducted by social demographer Richard Florida. Businessweek also ranked it the Best City for Startups, and USA Today judged it the Happiest City in America.

BELOW: Boulder's 30,000 acres (12,000 hectares) of parkland offer plenty of opportunities for rest and recreation.

Inner tubing down the creeks and rivers of Colorado is a popular way to spend a hot summer's day.

been called, with considerable hyperbole, "the Yosemite of Boulder." Eight miles (13km) farther on, **Boulder Canyon** opens into a wide valley occupied by Barker Reservoir, a good trout fishing spot, and the town of **Nederland** ❿, a former mining camp known today for its hippie-ish, New Age ambience, funky shops and eateries, and four summer festivals: Frozen Dead Guy Days in March *(see panel)*, the Summertime Fun Fair & Artisan Show in June, Old Timers' and Miners' Days in July and NedFest in August. Information on all events is available by calling 303-258-3936.

Summer visitors may enjoy **Nederland Mining Museum** (200 Bridge Street; tel: 303-258-0567; www.nederlandmuseums.org; May–Sept Sat 10am–4pm, Sun 11am–4pm, Oct–Apr by appointment only; free), a collection of artifacts and hands-on exhibits that highlight life in a 19th-century mining camp.

From Nederland, head north about 12 miles (19km) on CO 72 (also known as the Peak-to-Peak Highway) to **Ward** ⓫, a former silver mining town now best known as a high-country outdoors retreat. Eight miles (13km) west of town, on Brainard Lake Road is **Brainard Lake National Recreation Area**, popular for summer hiking, winter cross-country skiing and snowshoeing and jaw-dropping views of the Indian Peaks in any season *(see page 171)*.

The only downward route out of Ward is **Lefthand Canyon Drive**. About 7 miles (11km) along, turn right onto Lick Skillet Road, a steep dirt track that twists into the **Gold Hill** mining district. In the quaint village of **Gold Hill** (10 miles/17km northwest of Boulder) are log cabins, mining artifacts, and the **Gold Hill Inn** (tel: 303-443-6461), built as a hotel in 1872 and now an atmospheric seasonal restaurant (May–Dec). From the crossroads, take Sunshine Canyon Road directly to Boulder's fancy Mapleton Hill neighborhood. The route is downhill all the way. ❏

Frozen Dead Guy Days

Nederland is internationally famous for what may be the oddest home town festival anywhere. Frozen Dead Guy Days is held annually over an early March weekend to commemorate the 1989 death (and future reanimation) of Bredo Morstoel, an elderly Norwegian gentleman whose body resides in the world's only "do-it-yourself cryogenic facility" – a garden shed packed with dry ice. The scheme was hatched by Bredo's grandson, Trygve Bauge, who was deported back to Norway before he was able to find his grandfather more suitable lodging. The event features a coffin race, Grandpa look-alike contest, a frozen salmon toss, an evening dance known as Grandpa's Blue Ball, a midnight visit to the shed and a pancake breakfast. For more information, tel: 720-374-6742.

Indian Peaks Wilderness

Rising from Boulder's back yard, and within easy driving distance from Denver, the Indian Peaks soar to 13,000ft (3,960 meters) and rank as a Colorado back country favorite

Some 41 designated wilderness areas in Colorado are protected islands of scenic beauty within the state's vast sea of publicly owned lands, accessible only on foot. The 73,391-acre (29,700-hectare) Indian Peaks Wilderness, straddling the Continental Divide, isn't close to being the state's largest wilderness area, but it is accessible to more people than any other.

Of the more than 70 mountains in the Wilderness, seven soar to 13,000ft (4,000 meters) or higher, 23 to at least 12,000ft (3,660 meters), and 32 to 11,000ft (3,350 meters). The Indian Peaks' northern anchor is 14,255ft (4,345-meter) Longs Peak, just outside the Wilderness in adjacent Rocky Mountain National Park. At the southern end looms massive James Peak. Between them are such commanding summits as round-topped Mount Audubon, the twin summits of Arapaho Peak, pointy Mount Toll, and Apache Peak, a giant bracketed by three enormous ridges.

An important chunk of land immediately east of the Continental Divide is owned by the City of Boulder and permanently closed to the general public. Giving the peaks the names of Indian tribes was the idea of botany teacher Ellsworth Bethel in the spring of 1914. Of the 11 he named, the US Board on Geographic Names kept six. The Indian Peaks included in Enos Mills' *(see page 200)* original proposed boundaries for Rocky Mountain National Park but were removed from the proposal to avoid conflicts with mining interests and local development.

National forest land serves as the gateway to the Wilderness. Fourteen trailheads provide access even to the most remote and seldom visited areas. More than 100,000 people enter the Wilderness each year. Judging by the number of cars parked at popular trailheads, you might wonder how such a heavily used area could possibly be called a wilderness. The answer lies in the hidden peaks, high lakes and surprisingly secluded valleys deep within the Wilderness, far from the trappings of civilization.

Among the easiest places to get a flavor of the region is Brainard Lake National Recreation Area, just beyond the Wilderness's eastern boundary. A paved road circling the lake leads to picnic sites and a campground. Reaching nearby Long Lake within the Wilderness requires only a gentle, half-mile hike, though the trailhead elevation of 10,500ft (3,200 meters) makes it a lung-buster for those who aren't yet acclimated to the elevation. In midsummer, open meadows and stream banks are ablaze with wild flowers, and in fall stands of aspen glow gold against the clear blue sky.

Splayed above Brainard Lake is one of Colorado's most enticing panoramas. This craggy landscape, formed by a vast geological uplift and carved by glaciers whose remnants cling to the highest summits, is as stunning to look at as it is alluring for hikers, climbers and photographers. Fans of back country skiing and snowboarding ascend year-round snowfields packed into vast glacier-carved cirques, and anglers head to more than 50 frigid, cobalt lakes.

Roads closed by heavy snowfall effectively expand the Wilderness boundaries and serve as a back country getaway for Nordic skiers and snowshoers. The first heavy snow usually arrives in October, and a sufficient cross-country skiing base is soon deposited. Permits are required for overnight campers June to September. Contact the Boulder Ranger District (tel: 303-541-2500) for information. ❑

RIGHT: fly fishing is a popular activity.

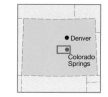

COLORADO SPRINGS AND ENVIRONS

Growth is a constant here, practically from the moment a one-time general laid the foundation for a city in the shadow of Pikes Peak

Colorado Springs ❶ owes much of its flair to William J. Palmer, railroad baron and Civil War general. In 1871, Palmer bought 10,000 acres (4,000 hectares) in the Pikes Peak foothills, where he laid out a spacious, progressive city with plenty of schools, parks and churches. He discouraged heavy industry as well as bars and gambling houses. So successful were his strictures that Colorado Springs remained "dry" until the repeal of the 18th Amendment in 1933.

Nearby Manitou Springs, with its clamorous bawdy houses, attracted a rougher clientele. Thirsty miners, down from the diggings around Victor and Cripple Creek, much preferred the raucous joints where they could drown their woes in a flood of rotgut and soothe their aching limbs in the bubbling springs that trickled from the mountain sides. Meanwhile, General Palmer's straightlaced community in the foothills to the east enjoyed some of the purest air in the nation, and it wasn't long before the railroads were transporting hordes of people out to Colorado from back East to take the waters and breathe the salutary air.

Mining wealth

The city's economic fortunes were intimately tied to the health of the nearby mining communities, the most prominent of which was Cripple Creek, set high in the mountains behind Pikes Peak. Many of the miners who struck it rich built lavish homes in Colorado Springs and established a solid social base still evident in the mansions around the Broadmoor Hotel and the sturdy domiciles in the old residential districts Downtown. From 1900 to 1910, Colorado Springs had the highest per-capita income of any comparable town in the country.

Main attractions
COLORADO SPRINGS
MANITOU SPRINGS
CAVE OF THE WINDS
PIKES PEAK COG RAILWAY
FLORISSANT FOSSIL BEDS
  NATIONAL MONUMENT
WESTCLIFFE
ROYAL GORGE
CAÑON CITY
CRIPPLE CREEK
PUEBLO

LEFT: rafting the Arkansas River.
RIGHT: the bridge over the Royal Gorge sits 955 feet above the Arkansas River below.

*By the 1890s,
Colorado Springs had
become so popular
with the chic,
international crowd
that it came to be
known as "Little
London."*

World War II stimulated growth, particularly in the military sector. Fort Carson was built south of town in 1942; the US Air Force Academy opened in 1954; and NORAD, a vast air defense command center within Cheyenne Mountain, became operational in 1966. Growth in recent years has been a mixed blessing. While the downtown core around Acacia Park has been preserved, suburban sprawl has resulted in a familiar glut of strip malls and tract housing.

Downtown and beyond

Start your visit in the downtown area. The **Pioneers Museum ❷** (215 S. Tejon Street; tel: 719-385-5990; Tue–Sat 10am–4pm; free), housed in the former county courthouse, showcases a first-rate sampling of historic artifacts from the Pikes Peak area, including guns, mining equipment and household items as well as a restored 1903 courtroom. The **McAllister House Museum** (423 N. Cascade Avenue; tel: 719-635-7925; www.mcallisterhouse. org; tours May–Aug Tue–Sat 10am–4pm, Sept–Dec, Feb–Apr Thur–Sat

10am–4pm; charge), built in 1873 by civic leader Henry McAllister, is one of Colorado Springs' historic landmarks. Original furnishings give visitors a glimpse of life in a well-to-do 19th-century household.

A few blocks away, **Colorado Springs Fine Arts Center ❸** (30 W. Dale Street; tel: 719-634-5583; www. csfineartscenter.org; Tue–Fri 9am–5pm, Sat 10am–5pm, Sun 1–5pm; charge) features a wide array of 19th-century, modern and postmodern artworks housed in a distinctive 1930s Pueblo Deco building. The museum shows works by Peter Hurd, Georgia O'Keeffe and Edward Hopper. Of special interest to aficionados of Western art is the Charles Russell Room, with a collection of sketches and letters by the "cowboy artist."

East of Downtown, the **US Olympic Training Center ❹** (1750 E. Boulder Street; tel: 888-659-8687; www. teamusa.org; Mon–Sat 9am–4pm, Sun 11am–6pm; free) occupies a 37-acre (15-hectare) complex, including the headquarters of the US Olympic Committee, and receives 140,000 visitors

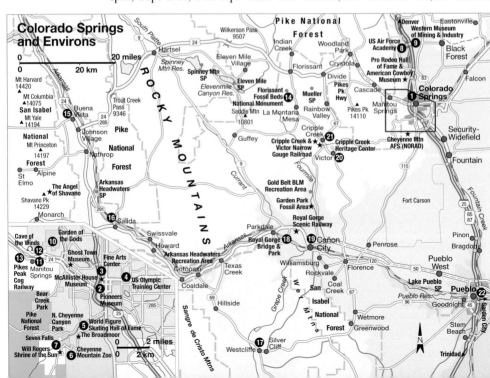

a year. Visitors are welcome to watch the athletes work out in a wide range of sports, including fencing, gymnastics, volleyball and swimming. Hourly tours begin with an inspirational film on Olympic history. Those who prefer winter sports may be intrigued by the **World Figure Skating Hall of Fame and Museum** ❺ (20 1st Street; tel: 719-635-5200; www.worldskatingmuseum.org; Tue–Fri 10am–4pm; charge) in the southwest corner of town, which commemorates the history of ice skating and celebrates such well-known skaters as Sonja Henie and Peggy Fleming.

Cheyenne Mountain

Cheyenne Mountain Zoo ❻ (4250 Cheyenne Mountain Zoo Road; tel: 719-633-9925; www.cmzoo.org; daily late May–early Sept 9am–6pm, early Sept–late-May 9am–5pm; charge), situated high on the slopes of Cheyenne Mountain, overlooking the city. Giraffes and elephants have long been the zoo's mainstays and are now showcased in the naturalistic African Rift Valley exhibit, part of a $50 million renovation that also includes the Mountain

Sky Ride chair-lift. The zoo is home to about 500 animals in all, including a variety of rare and endangered species such as snow leopards, orangutans, lowland gorillas and Amur tigers.

Admission to the zoo includes entry to the **Will Rogers Shrine of the Sun** (4250 Cheyenne Mountain Zoo Road; tel: 719-578-5367; daily late May–early Sept 9am–4pm, early Sept–late May 9am–3pm), a slim granite tower that clings to a steep slope. The structure was built in 1937 in honor of the folksy entertainer, who died in a plane crash in 1935. The remote, aerie-like location offers stupendous views of Colorado Springs.

Equally stunning is **Seven Falls** ❼ (2850 S. Cheyenne Canyon Road; www.sevenfalls.com; daily May–Sept 8.30am–9.30pm, Oct–Apr 9am–4.15pm; charge), set at the end of a narrow redrock canyon at the foot

The Will Rogers Memorial offers beautiful views of the Colorado Springs area.

BELOW: the Pioneers Museum chronicles the region's colorful past.

Van Briggle Pottery

Van Briggle Art Pottery (1024 S. Tejon Street; tel: 719-633-7729; www.vanbriggle.com; Mon–Sat 9am–5pm, Sun 1–4pm; free), the oldest continuously operated pottery in the United States, was founded in 1899 by Artus Van Briggle, a brilliant American artist of Dutch descent who trained in Paris and Italy and worked with the famed Rookwood Pottery in Ohio. Van Briggle developed a sensuous pottery style influenced by natural forms and glazed with a beautiful satin matte colored with natural earth minerals. His health failing due to tuberculosis, he took a train out to Colorado Springs and continued making his unique pottery before succumbing to the disease. Tour the pottery to watch ceramicists produce Art Nouveau-inspired designs, then shop in an enormous showroom.

A youngster practices his lasso throw.

of Cheyenne Mountain. Seven ribbony cataracts spill 181ft (55 meters) down the face of a billion-year-old rock mass into a clear pool of plump, basking trout. If you are reasonably fit, climb the 200-plus steps to the observation platform. Otherwise, take the elevator. American Indian dances are performed several times a day at the base of the falls.

Top guns

The biggest attraction in Colorado Springs is the **US Air Force Academy** ❽ (2304 Cadet Drive; tel: 719-333-2025; www.usafa.af.mil; visitor center daily 9am–5pm; free), off I-25 about 12 miles (19km) north of Downtown. Founded in 1954, the academy is situated on 18,000 acres (7,000 hectares) of preserved land in the foothills of the Rocky Mountains. Most of the campus is off-limits to civilians, but visitors can take a self-guided tour starting at the

BELOW: steel, aluminum and glass define the soaring interior of the Air Force Academy Chapel.

Visitor Center, which features exhibits and films on the academy's history. The highlight is the Cadet Chapel, a daring contemporary structure whose 17 aluminum spires evoke both the heavenly aspirations of the faithful and the sleek soaring figures of jets in flight. If you time your visit right, you may see cadets drilling on the parade ground or parachuting over the Thunderbird Airmanship Overlook.

Near the North Gate of the academy, the **Western Museum of Mining & Industry** ❾ (225 Northgate Boulevard; tel: 719-488-0880; www.wmmi.org; Mon–Sat May–Sept 9am–5pm, Oct–Apr 9am–4pm, guided tours 10am and 1pm; charge) brings the history of Colorado mining to life with exhibits of more than 3,000 artifacts, including a re-created assay office, a wide array of machinery and equipment, a simulated mining tunnel and tableaux illustrating life in a 19th-century mining camp. Visitors can try panning for gold, too.

Another mainstay of Western lore is celebrated at the **Pro Rodeo Hall of Fame & American Cowboy Museum** (101 Pro Rodeo Drive; tel: 719-528-4764; www.prorodeohalloffame.com; Wed–Sun 9am–5pm; charge), south on I-25 at Exit 147. Exhibits chronicle the evolution of the cowboy from hired hand to Hollywood icon; rodeo stars are honored in the Hall of Champions.

Rock garden

For another taste of the Old West, head south on I-25 then west on US 24 to the **Ghost Town Museum** (400 S. 21st Street; tel: 719-634-0696; www.ghosttown museum.com; Mon–Sat 10am–5pm, Sun 11am–5pm; charge), a collection of vintage buildings relocated from various parts of the state and reassembled in an indoor hall.

Just across US 24, along Colorado Avenue, is **Old Colorado City**, a mining camp founded in 1859 and notorious for its saloons and brothels. It was later annexed by the city of Colorado Springs and designated a National Historic Landmark District, and is best known today for its galleries and boutiques.

Farther west on US 24 is the turnoff for **Garden of the Gods** ⑩ (1805 N. 30th Street; tel: 719-634-6666; visitor center daily late May–early Sept 8am–8pm, early Sept–late May 9am–5pm; free), a 1,300-acre (500-hectare) park renowned for its dramatic sandstone formations. Millions of years ago, when the Rockies rose through the earth's crust, it tilted horizontal slabs of sedimentary rock into bold, vertical angles. Today, these "blades," as they're called, catch and reflect the colorful hues of morning and evening light. For hundreds of years, the site was an important Indian gathering place. It's said that old people, knowing their time had come, would position themselves on the high shelves and ledges so they could draw their last breath as the first rays of dawn warmed their faces. Today, a series of loop roads and trails enables motorists, bikers, joggers and walkers to explore just about every corner of the park. It's a popular spot among rock climbers, too, and they are often seen scaling the walls. The visitor center presents exhibits on the area's human and natural history, and naturalists are usually on hand for free nature tours and brief lectures.

At the east entrance to the park is **Rock Ledge Ranch Living History Site** (30th Street; tel: 719-578-6777; www.rockledgeranch.com; June–Aug Wed–Sun 10am–5pm; charge), an assembly of late 19th- and early 20th-century buildings staffed in summer by interpreters in period costume who work the ranch in traditional fashion.

Manitou Springs

Just west of Garden of the Gods is **Manitou Springs** ⑪, a pretty little town known for its effervescent mineral springs, elaborate Victorian architecture and abundant art galleries and interesting shops. Among the most notable buildings in town is **Miramont Castle** (9 Capitol Hill Avenue; tel: 719-685-1011; www.miramontcastle.org; late May–early Sept daily 9am–5pm, early Sept–late May Tue–Sat 10am–4pm, Sun noon–4pm; charge), an 1895 stone mansion constructed in an eccentric combination of styles by a wealthy French priest who had come

BELOW: the Garden of the Gods.

Galleries, boutiques and cafés line the streets of downtown Manitou Springs.

to Manitou Springs in search of a cure for his tuberculosis. It now serves as a museum, with exhibits of period furnishings, antique toys and an elaborate toy train collection.

Cave of the Winds ⓬ (Cave of the Winds Road, off US 24; tel: 719-685-5444; www.caveofthewinds.com; daily late May–early Sept 9am–9pm, early Sept–late May 10am–5pm; charge) has been a top tourist attraction for more than a century. A 45-minute guided Discovery Tour leads visitors through passages "decorated" with bizarre limestone formations – stalagmites and stalactites, icicle-like soda straws, smooth flowstone and myriad delicate crystals. Other options include a Lantern Tour, in which visitors equipped only with a hand-held lantern see the cave much as 19th-century tourists did; and the green Eco-Venture Tour, where the lights in the cave are turned off after 5pm and flashlights only are used.

The Ancestral Pueblo ruins at **Manitou Cliff Dwellings** (US 24; tel: 719-685-5242; www.cliffdwellingsmuseum.com; daily May–Sept 9am–6pm, Oct–Nov, Mar–Apr 9am–5pm, Dec–Feb 10am–

BELOW: exploring Cave of the Winds.

4pm; charge) are real, though they were relocated from a site in southwestern Colorado and are completely out of place on the Front Range. Skip this one if you plan to visit Mesa Verde National Park or other Ancestral Pueblo sites. American Indian dances are held daily in summer.

America's mountain

Towering above Manitou Springs is 14,110ft (4,301-meter) **Pikes Peak**, not the highest mountain in Colorado but surely the most famous. Named after explorer Zebulon Pike, who never actually reached the summit, and associated with the gold fever that swept the Central Rockies in the late 1800s ("Pikes Peak or bust!" declared thousands of hopeful prospectors), the mountain's most enduring role has been that of a tourist attraction. Despite Pike's proclamation that the mountain would never be climbed, tourists in the 1870s routinely scaled the peak. In 1891, a cog railway reached the summit, followed in 1916 by an auto road.

The **Pikes Peak Cog Railway** ⓭ (515 Ruxton Avenue; tel: 719-685-5401; www.cograilway.com; Apr–Nov; charge) departs from Manitou Springs for a breathtaking 9-mile (14km) ascent to the summit. The tracks follow a cascading creek through Englemann Canyon before climbing precipitously (the grade reaches 25 percent in some spots) above timber line into alpine tundra, a boulder-strewn expanse where bighorn sheep are often seen grazing on thin mosses, grasses and wild flowers. A round-trip takes about three hours and 10 minutes, including a 30-minute stopover at the summit house. Be sure to bring warm clothes. Frigid winds and violent electrical storms, often accompanied by hail or snow, are common even in summer.

About 5 miles (8km) northwest of Manitou Springs, at the little town of Cascade, is the entrance to the famous **Pikes Peak Highway** (tel: 719-473-0208; www.visitpikespeak.com; year-round, weather permitting; toll), a 19-mile (31km) auto route to the summit. This

is decidely not a drive for the faint of heart. The curves are sharp, the slope is precipitous, there are no guard rails, and only the first 7 miles (11km) are paved. However, the views from the peak are truly spectacular. On a clear day, you can see west to the Continental Divide, east across the plains to Kansas and Nebraska, and south to New Mexico. It's the same view that inspired poet Katharine Lee Bates, after visiting in 1893, to write the lyrics of the popular anthem *America the Beautiful*.

Blast from the past

Continuing west, US 24 soars up through **Ute Pass** (9,165ft/2,794 meters) toward the hamlet of Florissant and the turn-off for **Florissant Fossil Beds National Monument** ⓴ (15807 Teller County 1; tel: 719-748-3253; www.nps.gov/flfo; daily late May–early Sept 9am–5pm, early Sept–late May 8am–4.30pm; charge). Set aside in 1969, the park is dedicated to the preservation of fossil deposits and petrified redwood from the Oligocene Period. About 35 million years ago, volcanic eruptions blanketed what was then a lush and humid forest with lava and ash, preserving an invaluable fossil record of ancient plants and insects. Brief orientation talks and a 60-minute Petrified Forest tour are offered daily.

At **Wilkerson Pass** (9,507ft/2,898 meters), US 24 seems to sail off into thin air as magnificent vistas of **South Park** open up below. Bison and other wildlife followed the same route through Ute Pass to this vast high-elevation meadow on the backside of Pikes Peak. Paleo-Indians armed with stone-tipped spears tracked the game, as did their successors – Ute, Comanche, Arapaho – mounted on Spanish horses. Later came white men clad in furs and buckskin searching for beaver.

The town of **Buena Vista** ⓯, founded by silver miners in 1879, sits in shady repose at the west edge of South Park. The town is aptly named – residents enjoy some of the finest views in the state. West of town stands a dense cluster of "fourteeners" known as the **Collegiate Peaks** – Mount Yale (14,194ft/4,326 meters), Mount Princeton (14,197ft/4,327 meters), Mount Harvard (14,420ft/4,395 meters), Mount

BELOW: the petrified trees at the Florissant Fossil Beds

The Incline Railway at Royal Gorge was contructed in 1931.

BELOW: once a boisterous railroad town, Salida is known today as a gateway to the Arkansas River.

Oxford (14,153ft/4,314 meters) and Mount Columbia (14,075ft/4,290 meters). At the foot of this majestic range lies the valley of the Arkansas River, which rises farther north near Leadville. Depending on the quantity of the spring melt-off, the north Arkansas River in the Buena Vista area runs hard and fast through toothy rapids, giving whitewater enthusiasts an exhilarating ride.

At **Salida** ⑯ the river turns east toward Royal Gorge and the town of Pueblo, where it debouches onto the Great Plains and is transformed from a frothy mountain stream to a placid rill. Salida was founded in 1880 as a railroad town and, like Buena Vista, had a reputation for the rowdiness of its bars and bordellos, a quality that is noticeably absent from the sedate historic district today. The river is as rambunctious as ever, though, and there are plenty of experienced outfitters in this increasingly hip little town who can make the necessary arrangements for a whitewater trip. The **Arkansas Headwaters Recreation Area** stretches 48 miles (77km) along the river on either

side of Salida and has put-ins, hiking trails, campsites and picnic areas.

Southeast of Salida, CO 69 angles through the Wet Mountains Valley to the town of **Westcliffe** ⑰, founded in 1885 by Englishman Dr J.W. Bell, and regarded by some Coloradans as one of the state's few remaining unspoiled locations. It's not difficult to see why. Situated between the Wet Mountains and the mighty Sangre de Cristos, the town sits in a broad valley generously watered by snowmelt and filled with lush meadows and pastures.

Across the great abyss

About 48 miles (77km) east of Salida is **Royal Gorge Bridge and Park** ⑱ (off US 50; tel: 719-275-7507; www.royalgorge-bridge.com; daily late May–early Sept 10am–7pm, early Sept–late May10am–4pm; charge), a deep and narrow fissure carved through the mountains by the Arkansas River. Don't be put off by the site's theme-park atmosphere. Once you get past the billboards, the gorge itself is quite spectacular. For those with nerves of steel, an aerial tram glides across the abyss on a slender cable.

Only slightly less exhilarating is walking across what is said to be the world's highest suspension bridge (1,053ft/321 meters), peeking between the wooden slats, and feeling the structure sway beneath your feet. For a closer view of the canyon, consider a ride on the incline railway, which plummets more than 1,500ft (460 meters) at a 45 degree angle to the river's edge. Other attractions at the gorge include a carousel, a petting zoo, mule rides and the Royal Rush Skycoaster, a gargantuan sling-like contraption that swings riders over the gorge at the end of a tether.

Just before reaching **Cañon City** 19, look for **Skyline Drive**, a 3-mile (5km) scenic route that leads motorists up an 800ft (240-meter) high ridge before depositing them in a leafy residential neighborhood. The road was built in 1906 with convict labor – fitting for a town that describes itself as the "prison capital of Colorado." There are 13 correctional facilities in the area.

Housed in a former women's prison, the **Museum of Colorado Prisons** (201 N. Street; tel: 719-269-3015; www. prisonmuseum.org; daily late May–early Sept 10am–5pm, early Sept–late May 8.30am–6pm; charge) chronicles life behind bars since territorial days, with an often grisly collection of artifacts. Included are pictures of Alferd Packer, who served 17 years for murder and cannibalism; Anton Wood, the youngest inmate in the state's history who, at the age of 11, was sentenced to 25 years for murdering a neighbor in a dispute over a watch; a gas chamber last used in 1967; and the "Old Grey Mare," a flogging post used to temper the spirits of rebellious inmates.

You'll find Indian artifacts, vintage firearms, mining equipment and other Old West artifacts at the **Cañon City Municipal Museum** (612 Royal Gorge Boulevard; tel: 719-269-9018; Tue–Sun 10am–4pm; charge). An authentically furnished 1860 log cabin and a stone Victorian-era house are also on the grounds. Also in town is the **Dinosaur Depot Museum** (330 Royal Gorge Boulevard; tel: 719-269-7150; www. dinosaurdepot.com; Wed–Sun 10am–4pm; charge), where you can view fossil exhibits, watch technicians remove stegosaurus bones from a rock matrix,

The Museum of Prisons in Cañon City is appropriately placed, as there are nine state and four federal penitentiaries in town.

BELOW: onlookers watch from a distance as an 1899 blaze consumes downtown Victor.

In its long, riotous history, Cripple Creek produced twice as much mineral wealth as California's famed Mother Lode, and nearly $100 million more than Nevada's Comstock Lode. No single geological deposit has produced as much gold as Cripple Creek.

or join a tour of the Garden Park Fossil Area north of town.

Behind the Dinosaur Depot is the boarding station for the **Royal Gorge Scenic Railway** (401 Water Street; tel: 303-569-2403; www.royalgorgeroute.com; charge), a two-hour, 24-mile (38km) journey through the Royal Gorge on tracks laid by the Denver & Rio Grande Railroad more than 120 years ago.

Gold strikes and jackpots

A few miles east of Cañon City, Phantom Canyon Road turns north off CO 50 and snakes for about 30 mostly unpaved miles (48km) through the **Gold Belt BLM Recreation Area** to the old mining town of **Victor ⑳**. During its heyday in the 1890s, Victor was home to 18,000 people, though costly strikes in the early 1900s reduced the number by half. Attempts by the miners to unionize were met with hostility by the owners, who called out the dreaded Colorado State Militia in September 1903. Rioting erupted in the aftermath of a bloody mine accident in 1904, resulting in the deaths of several miners.

Policing the Skies

Deep inside a Colorado mountain is a small army of men and women on perpetual guard against an attack on North America. The place is the Cheyenne Mountain Air Force Station, about 6 miles (10km) outside the city of Colorado Springs and tucked securely below almost 2,000ft (610 meters) of granite. It is like a small city itself.

At the heart of the 15-building complex is the North American Aerospace Defense (NORAD) command center. Here, eagle-eyed military personnel keep tabs on just about anything that moves in the skies above the US and Canada, including the shuttles launched into outer space.

The actual address is 1 NORAD Road, and the joke is that armed guards won't let anybody in but the local pizza deliveryman. There are, in fact, tour programs for the public. And the base has its own major eatery and much else – chapel, barbershop, gym, softball field, medical clinic and more. Built to absorb a nuclear attack, the installation was opened in 1966.

With the end of the Cold War, NORAD's focus narrowed to such relatively minor concerns as stemming drug traffic. But the worry over international terrorism fueled by the events of September 11, 2001, has brought renewed reliance on its defensive value.

Fewer than 300 people live in Victor today. It's a quiet, rather forlorn town, notable primarily for the **Victor-Lowell Thomas Museum** (3rd St at Victor Avenue; tel: 719-689-5509; www.victorcolorado.com; late May–early Sept Wed–Sun 10am–6pm; charge), dedicated to the life and career of the journalist and radio broadcaster who grew up here and cut his teeth professionally at the *Victor Record*.

The scene is livelier at nearby **Cripple Creek ㉑**, a busted-out gold town that was given a second lease on life when gambling was legalized in 1991. Most of the original buildings were gutted for casinos; vacant land was paved for parking lots. For an overview, check out the new **Cripple Creek Heritage Center** (9283 S. CO 67; tel: 719-689-3315; www.visitcripplecreek.com; daily Apr–Oct 9am–5pm, Nov–Mar 10am–4.30pm, free), which has state-of-the-art exhibits that are family-friendly. Then mosey over to the **Outlaws and Lawmen Jail Museum** (126 W. Bennett Avenue; tel: 719-689-6556; daily; free) housed in a restored red-brick museum that served as the Teller County jail for 90 years. Among the infamous occupants was Robert "Kid" Curry, a member of the Wild Bunch. Two museums offer a glimpse of Cripple Creek's glory days: **Cripple Creek District Museum** (5th and Bennett; tel: 719-689-2634; daily late May–early Sept 10am–5pm, early Sept–late May 10am–4pm; charge) and the surprisingly elegant **Old Homestead House Museum** (353 Myers Avenue; tel: 719-689-3090; June–Oct daily 10am–5pm; charge); which occupies a former brothel.

Just outside town, visitors can take an elevator 1,000ft (300 meters) underground for a look at the **Molly Kathleen Mine** (CO 67; tel: 719-689-2466; www.goldminestour.com; daily May–Sept 9am–5pm, Mar, Apr, Oct 10am–4pm; call for reservations; charge). The **Cripple Creek & Victor Narrow Gauge Railroad** (5th and Bennett; tel: 719-689-2640; www.cripplecreekrailroad.com; May–Oct daily 10am–5pm; charge) makes a narrated, 45-minute run through the gold-mining district, where more than 600 tons of the precious stuff was extracted from the earth.

Between mountains and plains

Thirty-five miles (56km) south of Colorado Springs via I-25 lies **Pueblo ㉒**, one of Colorado's most underrated cities. Geography played a pivotal role in its development – the town sits on the plains at the confluence of Fountain Creek and the Arkansas River but lies close enough to the mountains to have benefitted from trapping and mining. Native people found the area a productive place to hunt. Spaniards traipsed through in the 18th century, looking for gold. Comanche, Kiowa and Arapaho warriors terrorized the region in the latter part of the 18th century, until they were crushed by a Spanish military force led by Juan Bautista de Anza at the foot of nearby Greenhorn Mountain in 1786.

In 1842, famed trapper Jim Beckwourth built a trading post where Fountain Creek flows into the Arkansas. Over the next decade, Pueblo attracted a mix of Mormon settlers, Indian agents, trappers and traders. A disaster occurred at Christmas 1854, when drunken pioneers allowed a party of Utes inside the stockade; the Indians massacred all but one man and three children.

The post languished for over a decade. Settlers came and went, but few tried to make a life there. Turmoil on the frontier during the 1860s drove more people to the settlement, and Pueblo was officially incorporated as a township in 1870. The Denver & Rio Grande Railroad arrived two years later, followed in 1876 by the Atchison, Topeka & Santa Fe. Coal smelters were built over the next few decades, and steel mills came shortly after.

The newly completed **River Walk** with its bike paths, pedestrian walkways and landscaped gardens is the locus around which the city fathers have placed their hopes for the rejuve-

nation of Downtown. Other attractions include **El Pueblo Museum** (324 W. 1st Street; tel: 719-583-0453; Mon–Sat 10am–4.30pm; charge), built on the site of the 1842 trading post, which displays Indian artifacts and equipment from the iron and steel industry.

The **Sangre de Cristo Arts and Conference Center** (210 N. Santa Fe; tel: 719-295-7200; www.sdc-arts.org; Mon–Sat 11am–5pm; charge) is the cultural hub of South Colorado. It encompasses six galleries, a 500-seat theater and a hands-on children's museum. The **Pueblo Weisbrod Aircraft Museum** (31001 Magnuson Avenue; tel: 719-948-9219; www.pwam.com; daily 9am–sunset; free), at the airport east of town, has a fine collection of World War II aircraft and early jets. During the war, the airport served as an air base to train B-24 Liberator crews – a slice of history preserved at the **International B-24 Museum** (tel: 719-948-9219; Mon–Fri 10am–4pm, Sat 10am–3pm; charge) just across the street. Pueblo is also the site of the **Colorado State Fair** (tel: 719-561-8484; www.coloradostatefair.com), which is held at the end of August. ❑

Slot machines crowd a Cripple Creek casino.

BELOW: a colorful dinosaur greets visitors at a Cañon City tourist information center.

SAN LUIS VALLEY

Between two mountain ranges lies this region, known best for its deeply rooted Hispanic heritage and one of Colorado's most unusual geological phenomena

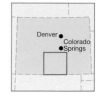

Denver • Colorado • Springs

America's Tibet, it's been called. And it's easy to see why. The San Juan and Sangre de Cristo Mountains rise in snowcapped majesty on the flanks of the San Luis Valley, a remote, sparsely populated basin in south-central Colorado. It's a place of startling contrasts. The valley encompasses Colorado's only true desert but sits atop an aquifer brimming with water. It is situated in a depression between two mountain ranges but rises in places to nearly 8,000ft (2,400 meters). Agriculture is the primary industry, but annual precipitation rarely exceeds 8in (20cm). It's the site of North America's tallest sand dunes but is 600 miles (950km) from the nearest sea.

Early inhabitants

Utes roamed the region centuries ago, when it was occupied mostly by wetlands. Later came Plains Indians – Arapaho, Kiowa, Comanche, Jicarilla Apache – riding mounts descended from Spanish herds. The Spanish were the first Europeans to venture into the area. Diego de Vargas led a foray north from Santa Fe in 1694 and dubbed the region Sierra de las Grullas – Mountains of the Cranes. Though the Spanish never actively settled the valley, they guarded it jealously as a buffer against foreign incursion. The first Anglo American on the scene was explorer Zebulon Pike after whom Pikes Peak is named, who stumbled out of the Sangre de Cristos with 10 hungry men in 1807, built a stockade in a cottonwood grove on the Rio Grande and was promptly arrested by the Spanish as a trespasser.

Anglo mountain men like Jim Bridger and Tom "Broken Hand" Fitzpatrick quickly arrived, scouring the Sangre de Cristos for beaver. They were followed in 1820 by entrepreneurs like William Becknell, who pioneered

Main attractions
CRESTONE
GREAT SAND DUNES NATIONAL PARK AND PRESERVE
LUTHER BEAN MUSEUM, ALAMOSA
ALAMOSA NATIONAL WILDLIFE REFUGE
JACK DEMPSEY MUSEUM, MANASSA
CUMBRES & TOLTEC SCENIC RAILROAD, ANTONITO
SAN LUIS MUSEUM AND CULTURAL CENTER
STATIONS OF THE CROSS SHRINE, SAN LUIS
FORT GARLAND MUSEUM
FRANCISCO FORT MUSEUM
SPANISH PEAKS
HIGHWAY OF LEGENDS, CUCHARA PASS

LEFT: Sand Dunes National Park. **RIGHT:** the Valley is said to be a center of UFO activity.

the Santa Fe Trail connecting Franklin, Missouri with Santa Fe. Spanish-speaking people from New Mexico established Colorado's first permanent settlement in 1851 shortly after Mexico ceded the territory under the 1848 Treaty of Guadalupe Hidalgo. The US Army built Fort Massachusetts in 1852 to protect the village from Indian raids.

New Age Center

The most scenic way to approach the valley is from the north. US 285 climbs over **Poncha Pass** to CO 17, which arrows into the heart of the valley. At the hamlet of **Moffat**, County Road T veers due east to the town of **Crestone ❶**, nestled in the foothills of the Sangre de Cristos. The discovery

of gold lured hordes of prospectors to the mountains, and in 1880 Crestone was born. Ten years later, when the Denver & Rio Grande built a spur into town, the population swelled to 2,000. More gold was discovered in 1896, but the mines soon played out and within a decade the population dwindled to 100.

Real estate developers breathed new life into the place in the 1970s, with a scheme to subdivide a nearby ranch. As a tax write-off, they donated parcels of land to religious groups such as the Sri Aurobindi Center, the Naropa Institute and the Carmelite Sisters. The development failed, but the town became a New Age phenomenon, and there is now a variety of spiritual gatherings offered year-round.

According to a recent study, the Great Sand Dunes National Park is the quietest of all parks in the lower 48 states.

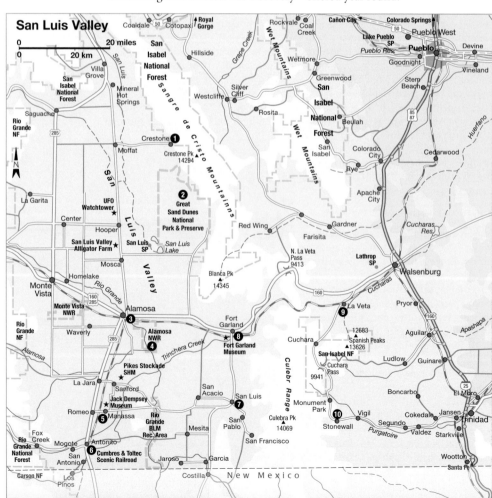

The world's biggest sandbox

From CO 17, turn east on Six Mile Lane toward **Great Sand Dunes National Park and Preserve** ❷ (11999 Hwy 150; tel: 719-378-6399; www.nps.gov/grsa; daily 24 hours, visitor center summer 8.30am–6.30pm, winter 9am–4.30pm; charge). A geological oddity, the dunes encompass 39 sq miles (101 sq km) of breathtaking sand formations that contrast with the snowcapped mountains behind them and the desert valley at their base. They are a remarkable sight – mounds of gleaming yellow sand heaped on one another in sculpted wind rows. Medano Creek slides out from the mountains in a long ripply wash, edging the dunes along their eastern rim for a mile or two, before bubbling out of sight.

A few hardy plants and animals manage to eke out an existence in this harsh place. Plants include blowout grass, Indian ricegrass and prairie sunflowers. Animals are even more scarce. Kangaroo rats – nocturnal creatures that extract moisture from seeds – live here, as do a half-dozen insects found nowhere else on earth. Peripheral animals – mule deer, elk, bobcat, coyote – skirt the edges of the dunes, leaving occasional tracks.

Around Alamosa

Southwest of the park is **Alamosa** ❸ (pop. 15,000), the biggest town in the San Luis Valley. Founded in 1878, when the Denver & Rio Grande chose the site for the terminus of its "chile line" to New Mexico, the town retains a certain workaday homeliness. About 2,500 undergraduates attend **Adams State College**, built in 1923 and home of the **Luther Bean Museum** (208 Edgemont Boulevard; tel: 719-587-7151; Tue–Fri 9am–4pm; free), featuring a beautiful 1930s interior and works by Hispanic, Indian and cowboy artists.

To the east of town, **Alamosa National Wildlife Refuge** ❹ (9383 El Rancho Lane; tel: 719-589-4021, http://alamosa.fws.gov) encompasses 11,169 acres (4,520 hectares) of wetlands in the floodplain of the Rio Grande. Meadows, oxbows and riparian corridors sustain song birds, water birds and raptors as well as deer, bea-

The surface temperature of the dunes at Great Sand Dunes National Monument reaches 140°F (60°C) in summer.

BELOW: Medano Creek meanders near the Dunes, attracting wildlife.

Great Sand Dune Formation

The Great Sand Dunes were most likely created by winds blowing northeast across the San Luis Valley. The winds carried the residue of glacial till deposited by the meandering Rio Grande. Whenever the river changed course, exposed sediments were swept across the valley to the Sangre de Cristos. Seeking a way over the barrier, the wind surged up through low mountain passes, transporting lighter particles but leaving heavier sand crystals at the foot of the mountains. Sand near the base of the formations, with a relatively high moisture content derived from snow and rain, is responsible for the remarkable stability of the dunes. By contrast, surface sand, chapped by wind and sun, is constantly molded into new and delicate patterns.

ver and coyote. In the spring and fall, some 20,000 sandhill cranes migrate through, along with a few rare whooping cranes. A 2-mile (3km) trail begins at the visitor center.

About 20 miles (32km) south of Alamosa via US 285 is the hamlet of **Manassa ❺**, birthplace of Jack "Manassa Mauler" Dempsey (1895–1983), the heavyweight boxing champion who started his career fighting in mining camp saloons. The **Jack Dempsey Museum** (412 Main Street; tel: 719-843-5207, http://museumtrail.org/jack dempseymuseum.asp; May–Sept Tue–Sat 9am–5pm; free) is housed in a log cabin on the main drag, and displays photographs of young Jack, and other memorabilia.

Tiny **Antonito**, situated farther south on US 285, is the terminus of the **Cumbres & Toltec Scenic Railroad ❻** (tel: 888-CUMBRES; www.cumbres-toltec.com; May–Oct Sat–Thur; charge), a 64-mile (103km) narrow-gauge line winds through the San Juan Mountains via Cumbres Pass to Chama, New Mexico. The line is a remnant of the Denver & Rio Grande's San Juan

Extension, constructed in 1880 to serve the mining camps of southwestern Colorado. Now the vintage locomotives haul tourists, most of whom opt for a six-hour, one-way train ride with a return by motorcoach. The train stops for lunch at the ghost town of **Osier**.

Hispanic heart

East of Manassa, CO 142 passes through the scrub desert of the San Luis Hills, one of the few elevated areas in this mostly flat valley. **San Luis ❼** (pop. 739), founded in 1851 by Hispanic immigrants from New Mexico, is the oldest town in Colorado. To protect themselves from hostile Indians, the settlers built an adobe *pueblo* around an easily defended plaza. Each family was allotted a narrow strip of land anchored at a stream and trailing back through meadows and woodlands, giving them access to water, grass and timber. Unlike Anglos elsewhere in the valley, who viewed water as a commodity belonging to whoever claimed it first, Hispanics utilized a traditional method of communal distribution. Colorado's first water collective, the San Luis People's Ditch, established in the 1850s, still parcels out irrigation allocations via a network of *acequias*, or irrigation ditches.

Of particular interest in town is the **San Luis Museum and Cultural Center** (401 Church Place; tel: 719-672-3611, http://museumtrail.org/sanluis-museum.asp; daily summer 10am–4pm, winter 9am–4pm; charge), built by the Works Progress Administration in the 1930s. It features murals and *santos* (sacred Spanish Colonial artworks) such as *retablos* (religious paintings on wood), *bultos* (carved figures) and a replica of a *morada*, or chapel, used as a meeting place by the secretive *penitente* sect. Across CO 159, a looping path leads to the top of La Mesa de la Piedad y de la Misericordia (Hill of Piety and Mercy) to the **Stations of the Cross Shrine** by celebrated local sculptor Huberto Maestas. The trail of

BELOW: a statue at the Jack Dempsey museum.

15 figures culminates at a lovely chapel with twin towers and a distinctive cupola. Miniatures (maquettes) of the figures are in the Vatican collection.

Sixteen miles (26km) north on CO 159, near the junction with US 160, is **Fort Garland ❽**. Named for Brigadier General John Garland, the fort was built in 1858 after an earlier post was abandoned. The 100-man garrison served a dual purpose: to protect settlers from Ute raids and provide a social and trading center in an otherwise desolate location. Kit Carson commanded the fort in 1866–7, his last military post. **Fort Garland Museum** (29477 CO 159; tel: 719-379-3512; www.museumtrail.org/fortgarlandmuseum.asp; Apr–Oct daily 9am–5pm, Nov–Mar Thur–Mon 8am–4pm; charge) displays a wide range of Indian, Mexican and Anglo artifacts as well as a sampling of Hispanic folk art.

Twin peaks

To the east, US 160 loops out of the San Luis Valley to the summit of **North La Veta Pass** (9,413ft/2,869 meters), before coasting down to the verdant folds of the **Cuchara Valley** at the foot of the **Spanish Peaks**. On a clear day they can be seen on the plains from the parapet of Bent's Old Fort, 80 miles (130km) away.

Follow CO 12 around the base of the peaks to a village named **La Veta ❾**, "The Vein," for the blades of volcanic rock that radiate from the mountains. The town's historic centerpiece is **Fort Francisco**, the first structure in the Cuchara Valley, built in the 1860s by Colonel John Francisco and Judge Henry Daigre. On the grounds stands a cottonwood planted by Colonel Francisco in 1878, which served not only as a shade tree but an impromptu gallows for 17 alleged bandits. **Francisco Fort Museum** (306 S. Main; tel: 719-742-5501; www.spanishpeakscountry.com; May–Sept Thur–Sat 11am–3pm, Sun noon–3pm; charge) displays artifacts from the period. Run by the Huerfano Historical Soci-

ety, the museum also offers educational programs.

CO 12, known as the **Highway of Legends**, winds to the summit of **Cuchara Pass** (9,941ft/3,030 meters), where meadows are filled with columbines and the surrounding mountains are blanketed with groves of aspen, fir, spruce and pine. Several lakes along the road have good fishing.

The road dips south into the leafy Purgatoire River watershed and the town of **Stonewall ❿**, named for the granite wall visible from the highway. A hideaway for fishing enthusiasts, Stonewall was established in the late 1860s by Juan Gutierrez, nephew of Gabriel Gutierrez, one of the founding fathers of nearby Trinidad.

CO 12 turns east at Stonewall and follows the Purgatoire River to the town of **Segundo,** with a gleaming white church named in honor of Ignatius. Ten miles (16km) farther on is **Cokedale** (pop. 139), a once bustling coal mining center founded in 1906 by the American Refining and Smelting Company. It is now a sleepy National Historic District. ❑

The Spanish Peaks have also been known as the Siamese Peaks, Mammas del Mundo (Breasts of the World) and Dos Hermanos (Two Brothers). They are 13,626ft (4,153 meters) and 12,683ft (3,866 meters) tall, respectively.

BELOW: an outcrop of the Spanish Peaks.

ROCKY MOUNTAINS

World-class skiing, Old West towns and back country adventure await travelers in the mountainous heart of Colorado

"I looked at the Alps, but they are nothing compared to the majestic grandeur of our wonderful Rockies," wrote painter Thomas Moran in 1911. Moran was among the first artists to see the Rocky Mountains while traveling to Yellowstone with the 1871 Hayden Survey. Both he and Albert Bierstadt, whose painting of Longs Peak for the Earl of Dunraven helped promote the Rocky Mountains as a national park, were forever changed after viewing the Rockies.

What could be more stirring than to glimpse the iconic Rockies, the backbone of America, for the first time, massed against the western horizon, backlit by a blood-red sunset? For Americans in the mid-1800s, the mountains represented the American Dream: a place to create a new life and maybe even strike it rich.

Hundreds of mining towns boomed overnight and busted just as quickly. Rocky Mountain National Park was set aside in 1915, just in time to attract Americans no longer able to travel to war-torn Europe. In the late 20th century, chunks of the remote San Juan Mountains were set aside as wilderness, luring mountain lovers to the little-known southern Rockies.

Interstate 70 in northern Colorado, Interstate 50 in central Colorado and US 160 in southern Colorado opened the whole state to tourism. The busy I-70 corridor between Denver and Glenwood Springs offers rapid access to natural attractions like Rocky Mountain National Park and St Mary's Glacier, and connects Denver foothill communities like Golden and Evergreen with Georgetown, Vail, Aspen and other famous former mine towns that have risen from the dead as ritzy ski resort and tourist towns, as well as the redrock canyon country on the Utah border.

Easier access to Durango via US 160, skirting the southern edge of the San Luis Valley and San Juans, has been a boon for the region. But mountain communities, such as Silverton, still slumber peacefully in the off season. That, for many visitors, is their main attraction. ❑

PRECEDING PAGES: golden aspen leaves in the autumn. **LEFT:** hikers set out for a jaunt around Maroon Lake. **TOP RIGHT:** Glendwood Caverns Adventure Park. **ABOVE LEFT:** old engine No. 482. **ABOVE RIGHT:** the historic Strater Hotel.

Maps on pages 196 & 206

ROCKY MOUNTAIN NATIONAL PARK

Straddling the Continental Divide, the park contains sky-scraping peaks, 150 lakes, rushing mountain streams, alpine tundra, pristine forests and an amazing array of wildlife

Denver
Colorado Springs

W hen Pope John Paul II journeyed to Denver in 1993, he asked to see **Rocky Mountain National Park ❶**. The pontiff's hiking outfit was a bit unusual – His Holiness wore a white cassock, gold pallium and sneakers with matching gold shoelaces – but the visit confirmed what lovers of the park already knew: Rocky Mountain is truly a religious experience. Like John Paul, millions of pilgrims have thrilled at this sea of mountains since the park was created in 1915. Many peaks soar over 12,000ft (3,660 meters). "There are higher peaks elsewhere," author Freeman Tilden wrote in 1951. "But for a sheer sense of towering density, of closely packed mountaintops, I know of nothing like this."

By the time Zebulon Pike set eyes on the Rockies in 1807, indigenous people had been venturing into the high country for at least 7,000 years. Mounted hunters of the Ute, Arapaho, Cheyenne and Shoshone tribes tracked deer and buffalo in the foothills and bighorn sheep on the alpine slopes. Late in the 19th century, a flood of trappers, miners and ranchers tried to tap the mountains' natural wealth. Mining camps such as Lulu City sprang up overnight and disappeared just as quickly.

Among the pioneers was a different breed, too – people like Enos Mills, (see *page 200)* who mined peace and rejuvenation from the mountains and made a living sharing them with others. Hailed as the "John Muir of the Rockies," Mills hatched the idea for the park and spent years rallying support and lobbying Congress, which finally gave its consent in 1915.

Estes Park and Trail Ridge Road

If you're coming from the east, start your trip in **Estes Park ❹**, a lively resort town adjacent to the park, with

Main attractions
ESTES PARK
TRAIL RIDGE ROAD
BEAVER MEADOWS VISITOR CENTER
MANY PARKS CURVE
TUNDRA COMMUNITIES TRAIL
ALPINE VISITOR CENTER
MILNER PASS
COLORADO RIVER TRAILHEAD
NEVER SUMMER RANCH
HORSESHOE PARK
OLD FALL RIVER ROAD
MORAINE PARK
SPRAGUE LAKE
GLACIER GORGE JUNCTION
BEAR LAKE
DREAM LAKE
LONGS PEAK
WILD BASIN

LEFT: Sprague Lake in Rocky Mountain National Park. **RIGHT:** Estes Park.

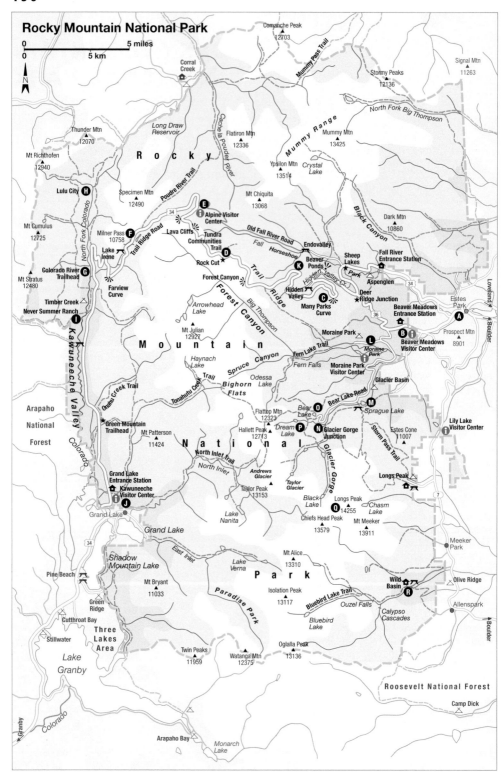

Rocky Mountain National Park

a bounty of restaurants, galleries, gift shops and lodging. The pioneers who settled this region are the focus of the **Estes Park Museum** (200 4th Street; tel: 970-586-6256; May–Sept Mon–Sat 10am–5pm, Sun 1–5pm, Nov–Apr Fri–Sat 10am–5pm, Sun 1–5pm; free) and the **MacGregor Ranch Museum** (off US 34; tel: 970-586-3749; June–Aug Tue–Fri 10am–4pm; free), an 1896 homestead and working ranch where visitors get a glimpse of life on the frontier in the late 19th century. **Estes Park Aerial Tramway** (420 E. Riverside Drive; tel: 970-586-3675; www.estestram.com; daily May–Sept 9am–6.30pm; charge) whisks passengers to the summit of Prospect Mountain for panoramic views of Longs Peak, the Continental Divide and Estes Park.

Enter the national park via US 36 for a tour of **Trail Ridge Road**, the park's main thoroughfare, arguably the most scenic drive in North America. Open seasonally from mid-May until the first heavy snowstorms blanket the interior in October, it features more than a dozen spectacular overlooks and exposes visitors to a large expanse of alpine tundra, one of the rarest ecosystems in the lower 48 states.

Starting at **Beaver Meadows Visitor Center B**, US 36 climbs gently through foothills scattered with ponderosa pine and sagebrush. At **Deer Ridge Junction**, Trail Ridge Road veers left and makes an abrupt ascent along **Hidden Valley Creek**, dammed in several places by beavers who usually emerge from their lodges in the early evening. The creek is also home to rare greenback cutthroat trout; a roadside exhibit provides information on them.

Just beyond, the overlook at **Many Parks Curve C** perches over deep valleys cut by Pleistocene glaciers more than 13,000 years ago. (Several small glaciers remain in Rocky Mountain, most straddling the eastern edge of the

Poppies grow well in the dry soil of Colorado.

BELOW: the ballroom of the Stanley Hotel is supposedly haunted.

The Stanley Hotel

The 138-room Stanley Hotel in Estes Park is one of America's most recognizable historic grand dames. It was built in 1909 by F. O. Stanley, inventor of the Stanley Steamer automobile, who moved to Estes Park in 1907 after being diagnosed with tuberculosis. Stanley constructed his European-style luxury hotel from timbers salvaged from the Bear Lake Burn and created an access road from Lyons, over which he brought his guests. The hotel has a reputation for being one of the most haunted hotels in America and served as the inspiration for Stephen King's novel *The Shining.* An on-site museum chronicles the careers of Stanley and his twin brother F. E., and the history of the hotel. For more information, tel: 970-586-3371 or visit www.stanley hotel.com.

TIP

Alpine tundra is an extremely fragile environment; it's imperative to stay on the trails at all times. Trampling delicate tundra plants can cause damage that takes decades, if not centuries, to repair.

Continental Divide in the park's central area.) Overhead, a red-tailed hawk or golden eagle may be scanning the land below, looking for an opportunity to snatch a small rodent or even a marmot sunning itself on a rock.

Trail Ridge Road passes through stands of fir and Engelmann spruce that are common in the subalpine zone and then, beyond the stunning overlook at **Forest Canyon**, enters alpine tundra. One of the highest overland routes on the continent, Trail Ridge Road stays above the tree line for 11 miles (18km), cresting at 12,183ft (3,713 meters) near **Lava Cliffs**.

Alpine tundra

A treeless, windblown realm, alpine tundra exists only in the highest reaches of the Rockies. For a closer look, walk the self-guiding **Tundra Communities Trail ◉** near **Rock Cut**. As you walk the trail, look closely for camouflaged ptarmigan, a member of the grouse family whose plumage changes from snowy white in winter to mottled brown in summer. You may also spy a water pipit foraging for insects, tiny pikas, or pudgy yellow-

bellied marmots scampering across a talus slope, or perhaps bighorn sheep, elk or mule deer grazing warily in a distant meadow.

Only the hardiest plants can survive in these arctic-like conditions. Stunted by wind and cold, gnarled whitebark pine hugs the ground; although no larger than bushes, some are as much as 200 or 300 years old. Silver-dollar-sized patches of lichen (actually an alga and fungus that grow symbiotically) can be centuries old as well. A bouquet of wild flowers – including lupines, yellow snow buttercups, shooting stars, daisies and blue Colorado columbines – send a blush through the meadows in late June and often last until the first snowfall of autumn. For more information about alpine tundra ecology, stop at the **Alpine Visitor Center ◉**, which is just a short drive from the Tundra Communities Trail.

Trail Ridge Road dips about 1,000ft (300 meters) in 4 miles (6km) and then, at **Milner Pass ◉**, crosses the Continental Divide. Known as the "backbone of America," the Divide has a profound effect on climate. Trapped

BELOW: a prospector in the Estes Park area in 1922.

behind mountain peaks, clouds blowing in from the Pacific Ocean dump rain and snow on the western slope, supplying the headwaters of the Colorado River. Half as much moisture falls east of the Divide, and incessant, drying winds tend to rob the land of what little water it receives. Naturally, there's a difference in vegetation and wildlife as well. The lush riparian environment of the western side sustains moose, river otter, Colorado River trout and a profusion of conifers. The more arid, eastern landscape is home to Abert's squirrel, endangered greenback cutthroat trout, ponderosa pine, prickly pear and wood lily.

From Milner Pass, the road zigzags several dizzying miles and then heads south toward the **Colorado River Trailhead G**, where you can start a moderate 2-mile (3km) hike to the tumbled-down cabin of Joe Shipler, a miner who tried his luck here in the 1870s. About 2 miles (3km) farther north, a few old shacks are all that remain of **Lulu City H**, where hundreds of prospectors, hearing stories of gold and silver strikes, came to make their fortunes in the early 1880s. The trail follows the North Fork of the Colorado River, which here is hardly more than a trickle. Believe it or not, this is the beginning of one of the mightiest rivers in the West – the same rushing waters that flow through the Grand Canyon several hundred miles away.

About 2 miles (3km) farther south, a short trail leads to the **Never Summer Ranch I**, a dude ranch founded in the 1920s and now operated as a "living-history" exhibit, complete with guides in period costume. The final stretch of Trail Ridge Road descends into Kawuneeche Valley to the **Kawuneeche Visitor Center J**. Coniferous forests grow thick here, and the Colorado River is fringed with aspens and willows that explode with glorious fall colors. Moose and elk are a common sight and birdwatching opportunities, especially for neotropi-

cal songbirds such as warblers, thrushes and finches, are excellent.

Just south of the park is **Grand Lake,** Colorado's largest natural lake and the highest yacht anchorage in the United States. Grand Lake drains into two large reservoirs, **Shadow Mountain Lake** and **Lake Granby**, making the area a haven for boaters, hikers and snowmobilers looking for a low-key, rustic getaway.

Horseshoe Park

There's plenty to see and do beyond Trail Ridge Road. If time allows, plan a side trip to **Horsehoe Park K**, a popular area for wildlife-watching northeast of Estes Park. From the visitor center, take US 36 into the park, then turn right at the junction with US 34 to **Sheep Lakes**, where naturally occurring mineral licks attract bands of bighorn sheep. The **Old Fall River Road**, a one-way unpaved lane open only in summer, starts at **Endovalley** and makes a 9-mile (14km) climb, much of it above tree line, to the **Alpine Visitor Center**. Notice the rocky debris scattered along the road: it

Fossils for sale at an Estes Park gift shop.

BELOW: Lake Granby, actually a reservoir, is one of three bodies of water that form the "Great Lakes of the Rockies."

The Colorado chipmunk can be identified by the dark and light stripes along it's side and back. They like to eat nuts and berries.

was deposited by a dam break in 1982 that sent a flood of mud, rocks and water downslope as far as Estes Park.

Bighorn sheep are frequently seen in this area. About 200 bighorns graze on the lush meadows and rocky slopes around Horseshoe Park. During the winter breeding season, males vie for dominance, using their massive corkscrew horns in dramatic head-butting contests. The report can be heard echoing through the mountains. Elk are frequently spotted here, too, never far from the forest edge.

Another option is to explore **Moraine Park** and **Bear Lake Road**, which leads into one of the most picturesque and heavily used regions of the park. The area is laced with interconnecting trails, and it's possible to spend a day or more hiking from one mountain lake to another and experiencing a variety of different life zones. Hikers can spend the morning wandering among tree-ringed glens and turquoise

lakes, and then make a push towards the Continental Divide, where glaciers send meltwater cascading down the eastern slope. Get your bearings at the **Moraine Park Museum**, where exhibits and a short interpretive trail explain the area's cultural and natural history, and then strike out on any number of possible tours.

A short drive to the **Cub Lake Trailhead** enables you to explore Moraine Park or to make the gentle 4-mile (6km) climb to **Cub Lake**, **Fern Falls** and **Fern Lake**; an extension trail makes a steep connection to the stark shoreline of **Odessa Lake**. Farther south, a free summer shuttle bus runs from Glacier Basin to the end of Bear Lake Road.

An easy nature trail around **Sprague Lake** makes a pleasant stroll through a storybook mountain setting. Farther down, a steep 4-mile (6km) round-trip takes hikers up to and around the forested shore of **Bierstadt Lake**. You'll find tougher hikes at **Glacier Gorge Junction** , which has branches that go to the foot of **Andrews Glacier** and **Taylor**

Nature Boy

Kansas-born Enos Mills was a sickly boy who came to live with relatives on their ranch in Estes Park and became enthralled by the great outdoors, climbing 14,256ft (4,345-meter) Longs Peak at the age of 15. Over the years, Mills worked as a snow observer and a forestry specialist and wrote several books about his experiences in the Rockies. Mills' mentor was naturalist John Muir. The two met during Mills' 1898 trip to San Francisco and remained friends until Muir's death in 1914.

Mills promoted Muir's message of conservation and was largely responsible for convincing Congress to set aside Rocky Mountain National Park in 1915. His cabin is now a small museum, south of Estes Park. Tel: 970-586-4706 for hours and directions.

Glacier via **Loch Vale** as well as a 5-mile (8km) scramble through **Glacier Gorge** to frigid **Black Lake**, well above tree line.

The most traveled and possibly most beautiful route is from **Bear Lake ⓞ** to **Dream Lake ⓟ**, which is cupped in a high-country basin with the snow-dusted summits of **Flattop Mountain** and **Hallett Peak** rising grandly from behind.

Longs Peak and Wild Basin

Farther south, an ascent of **Longs Peak ⓠ** is a challenge even to the most ambitious and physically fit hikers. At 14,255ft (4,345 meters), Longs Peak towers over the eastern side of the park; its flat summit and nearby **Chasm Lake** are considered by many to be the most magical destination in the park. And although technical equipment isn't necessary to make the climb, it's a big mistake to underestimate just how arduous the 16-mile (26km), 12-to-15-hour round-trip can be.

Hikers should be prepared for high winds, biting cold and a fair amount of hand-and-foot scrambling. It is essential to start your hike well before daybreak to avoid the dangerous afternoon lightning storms; many hikers stay at nearby **Longs Peak Campground** the night before. Greenhorns can inquire at the Colorado Mountain School in Estes Park about climbing lessons and guide services.

Finally, if you really want to escape the crowds, try the **Wild Basin ⓡ** region, off CO 7 just south of Longs Peak. Cut off from the rest of the park by a crescent of mountains, this isolated pocket of lakes and waterfalls is still recovering from a 1978 forest fire. In the early days, a park official tried promoting Rocky Mountain by dressing a woman, dubbed Eve, in animal skins and letting her wander around Wild Basin, much to the delight of reporters looking for a tantalizing story.

Hikers can spend a leisurely afternoon on the moderate, 3-mile (5km) trail leading to **Calypso Cascades** and **Ouzel Falls**, named after the tiny river-faring bird that naturalist John Muir found so enchanting. The trail branches a bit farther on, following a string of lakes into the highlands. ❑

Get off your earmuffs and hear the call of the jay, the splash of the jumping trout, the roar of a waterfall. Brush the dust of habit away from your eyes and see the lacery of the pine needles, the vivid coloring of the cliff or wildflower, the majesty of the peaks. In other words, take stock of the world in which you live.

Arthur C. Carhart, U.S. Forest Service, 1922

BELOW: the view of Longs Peak in Rocky Mountain National Park.

PEAK BAGGERS

Climbers flock to the Rockies to scale the state's 54 peaks that are over 14,000ft (4,270 meters), and wilderness stewardship programs attempt to clean up after them

The Colorado Rockies have 54 peaks over 14,000ft (4,270 meters), or "fourteeners," as they are known by climbers. Among the most storied peaks are Longs Peak and Pikes Peak at either end of the Front Range, where the Rockies meet the Plains. Pikes Peak, looming over Colorado Springs, is accessible to climbers from the 13-mile (21km) trail above the highway and Pikes Peak Cog Railroad Depot, the highest railroad in the world. The Maroon Bells-Snowmass Wilderness in the Elk range is close to Aspen and a popular destination for high-country lovers who enjoy its mirror lakes and wild flowers in summer. The Sangre de Cristo range creates a sheer, toothy skyline above the San Luis Valley. The range includes Colorado's fourth highest peak, 14,345ft (4,372-meter) Mount Blanca, sacred to the Navajo. Poncha Pass, a favorite fall color drive, separates the Sangres from the Collegiate Peaks in the Sawatch range. Of the 15 fourteeners, one peak, Mount Elbert is the highest in the state at 14,433ft (4,399 meters), and several are named for Ivy League colleges such as Harvard and Yale, hence their nickname. The San Juan Mountains, headwaters of the Rio Grande, are increasingly popular as a ski, hiking, and four-wheeling destination. Yankee Boy Basin near Ouray is the main trailhead for Mount Snefells Wilderness, also popular with the Jeep crowd.

LEFT: climbers should always take appropriate precautions before attempting a new climb.

ABOVE: straddling the Continental Divide at the top of Hallett Peak in Rocky Mountain National Park. The peak is easily accessible to non-climbers by driving along Flattop Mountain Trail.

ABOVE: evening comes early when the sun sets behind the mountains.

LEFT: hiking requires the appropriate equipment, including boots, poles, raingear, and a means of contacting help in case of emergency.

THE MIGHTY FOURTEENERS

Every year, an estimated 500,000 people visit the 54 four-teeners in Colorado. Concerned about increased visitors and impacts on fragile wilderness, in 1994 five outdoor organizations – Colorado Mountain Club, Outward Bound West, Volunteers for Outdoor Colorado, Rocky Mountain Field Institute, and Leave No Trace Center for Outdoor Ethics – joined with the US Forest Service to protect and preserve the state's fourteeners through active stewardship and public education. Using an all-volunteer staff, the Colorado fourteeners Initiative (CFI) has completed impact studies on all 54 fourteeners, identified the 35 most impacted peaks, and done trail maintenance on 18 fourteeners. Peaks that have received work to date are Mount Elbert, Mount Belford, Mount Oxford, La Plata Peak, Humboldt Peak, Huron Peak, Mount Harvard, Grays and Torreys Peaks, Missouri Mountain, Mount Bierstadt, Quandary Peak, Capitol Peak, Tabeguache Mountain, Mount Sneffels, Wetterhorn Peak, Mount Evans, Pyramid Peak, and Mount Massive. If you're interested in getting involved, volunteers are needed to carry out weekend field projects, become peak stewards, and assist in other ways, including collecting wild flower seeds to revegetate trampled areas. For information, contact. www.14ers.org.

ABOVE: Pikes Peak at sunrise. The pink tinge of the rocks comes not rom the sun, but rather from a large amount of potassium feldspar.

ABOVE: a mountain goat explores he terrain of the Rockies.

ABOVE: the Ouray Ice Festival is held each year in January.

RIGHT: trail maintenance is a big part of wilderness stewardship, an area where many Coloradans volunteer their time.

STEAMBOAT SPRINGS

Skiing is a way of life in this Northern Rockies town celebrated for its "champagne powder," Olympic athletes and Wild West atmosphere

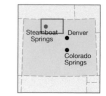

Steamboat Springs has a scenic setting on the Yampa River in the heart of Colorado's Northern Rockies. It's a cowboy-flavored ski town, which owes its down-to-earth Western feel to its ranching history and proximity to the Wyoming border. The mountains here seem gentler than those to the east and south, rising in swells from broad valleys, and cloaked in forests, meadows and alpine lakes. Nomadic Utes once summered in the valley of the Yampa River, which flows in relative tranquility through town before careening toward its confluence with the Green River. French fur trappers were the first Europeans to explore the area, and it was a party of such *coureurs de bois* who mistook the burbling of a hot spring for the sound of a steamboat, apparently giving the area its name.

Pioneer settlement

In 1875, American homesteader James J. Crawford staked a claim here, and soon a handful of pioneers formed the nucleus of a community they called Steamboat Springs. By the mid-1880s, the town had a newspaper, post office, general store and hotel, although travel and communication were regularly bogged down by heavy snow. Townspeople, cowboys and mail carriers struggled through the long, hard winters, sometimes using primitive

skis or snowshoes to get around. The mail came up from Wolcott, 60 rugged miles (96km) to the south – by wagon when the passes were clear, or by skis when the snow was too deep for horses. It was late 1908 before the railroad reached town, and no effort was made to keep primitive auto roads open year-round.

Through it all, the early settlers grazed livestock in lush meadows during the short, pleasant summers. They practically lived on horseback, at ease with the landscape, the animals

Main attractions
STEAMBOAT SPRINGS
OLD TOWN
TREAD OF PIONEERS MUSEUM
YAMPA RIVER BOTANIC PARK
OLD TOWN HOT SPRINGS
FISH CREEK FALLS
STEAMBOAT SKI AREA
HOWELSEN HILL
MEDICINE BOW-ROUTT NATIONAL FOREST
RABBIT EARS PASS
CLARK
YAMPA RIVER PRESERVE

LEFT: Steamboat Springs.
RIGHT: Olympic champion Billy Kidd.

There are more than a dozen natural hot springs in and around Steamboat Springs.

and the big sky overhead. Cowboys worked hard and played hard, and skis were used for winter recreation as well as for strictly utilitarian purposes. The *Steamboat Pilot*, the local newspaper, reported that the Hot Time Festival of 1898 featured an orchestral performance, a literary event, a dance, foot races and bronco riding. Rodeo was a summer tradition by the early 1900s, and it continues to this day during **Cowboy Roundup Days**, the centerpiece of the town's Fourth of July celebration for more than a century.

Historic heart

Get your bearings in **Steamboat Springs ❷** by first stopping for an orientation and brochures at the **Visitor Center** (125 Anglers Drive; tel: 970-879-0880; www.steamboat-chamber.com; late May–early Sept Mon–Sat 8am–6pm, Sun 10am–4pm, Sept–May Mon–Fri 9am–5pm, Sat 10am–3pm). **Old Town**, a tidy 27-block grid between Third and Eleventh Streets looks much as it did before the ski boom. **Routt County Courthouse** (522 Lincoln; tel: 970-870-6586), for example, stands

stolidly at the corner of 6th and Lincoln, its cream brick facade trimmed in sandstone and terracotta. The interior – hardly altered since its 1923 completion – houses a small collection of artifacts and historic photographs. The neighborhood's modest commercial buildings are mostly two or three stories, many sporting elaborate trim and cornices. Most are now occupied by fancy boutiques, galleries and restaurants, though quite a few still have a weathered charm.

Western outfitter F.M. Light & Sons (830 Lincoln Avenue; tel: 970-879-1822; www.fmlight.com), owned by the same family for four generations, is the town's oldest store, selling cowboy hats, boots, saddles and other gear since 1905. Just down the street, **Lyon's Corner Drug and Soda Fountain** (840 Lincoln Avenue; tel: 970-879-1114) is housed in a 1908 brick office building that has served as a pharmacy since 1920. Walk past the souvenirs to the old-fashioned soda fountain in the rear and you will feel as if you've stepped back in time.

Another way to turn back the clock is

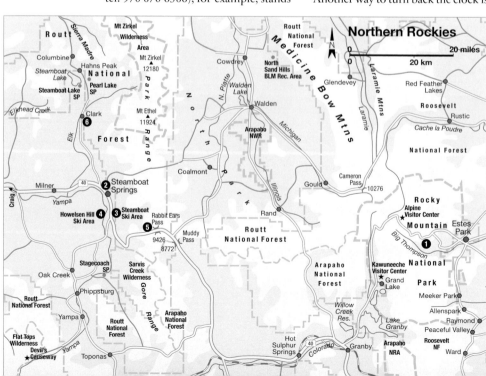

to visit the **Tread of Pioneers Museum** (800 Oak Street; 970-879-2214; www.treadofpioneers.org; Tue–Sat 11am–5pm; charge), a repository of rustic furnishings, Indian artifacts, ranching gear and other objects related to frontier life. Set in a 1908 Queen Anne-style house, the museum features exhibits of vintage skis (including those used by early mailmen), a collection of historic firearms, Ute Indian basketry, a stagecoach used in the 1890s to transport passengers from Wolcott, and a snowcat that operated between Steamboat and Hahn's Peak in the 1940s. Pick up a copy of the self-guided historic walking tour, which starts at the museum, then continue to the Beaux-Arts railroad depot that houses **Steamboat Springs Arts Council** (1001 13th Street; tel: 970-879-9008; www.steamboatspringsarts.com; Mon–Fri 10am–4pm, Sat–Sun noon–3pm). Pick up an *Art in Public Places* walking tour map, and combine the itinerary with the historic tour.

Water music

Even local hardbodies training for the popular **Steamboat Marathon, Half-Marathon, and 10k** in June use the gentle 4-mile (6km) **Yampa River Core Trail** for a quick run. It's equally popular for evening walks, family bike rides, and simply enjoying the sound of rushing water and perhaps stopping to identify wild flowers that grow along the bank. The trail connects with the west side of 6-acre (2.4-hectare) **Yampa River Botanic Park** (1000 Pamela Lane; tel: 970-879-4300; daily dawn–dusk; free). The park is laid out in 36 themed gardens, including the Garden for All Seasons, splashed with colorful blossoms from spring to late summer.

Also on the south end of downtown is **Old Town Hot Springs** (136 Lincoln Avenue; tel: 970-879-1828; www.steamboathotsprings.org; Mon–Fri 5.30am–10pm, Sat–Sun 8am–10pm; charge), a multi-use complex of eight hot spring pools, plus fitness facilities for both residents and visitors. Open year-round, with areas set aside for water slides, lap

swimming and peaceful soaking, it is a family favorite.

Take a short drive east on 3rd Street and follow the signs 4 miles (6km) to **Fish Creek Falls** (Fish Creek Falls Road; tel: 970-879-1870; www.fs.fed.us/r2; free), a thundering 283ft (86-meter) cascade and one of the town's most visited attractions. A flat, paved walkway leads to an overlook; a quarter-mile (500 meters) dirt trail snakes gently down to the base, then leads 6 miles (10km) through aspen groves, alpine meadows and steep switchbacks to Long Lake near the Continental Divide. A word of advice about visiting the falls: beat the crowd by arriving early in the morning or just before dusk, when alpen glow illuminates the scene.

In summer, when the sun goes down, Steamboat Springs' cultural scene heats up. **The Strings in the Mountains Music Festival** (tel: 970-879-5056; www.stringsinthemountains.org; charge), established in 1988 to foster an appreciation for fine music, presents live chamber music, jazz, folk, country and world music in 7-acre (3-hectare) Strings Festival Park at the entrance

Skipping stones on the Yampa River.

BELOW: visitors enjoy cool water and warm sunshine at the base of Fish Creek Falls.

Hot air balloonists prepare to take to the skies outside Steamboat Springs.

to the ski mountain, as well as a series of popular free noontime concerts at Yampa River Botanic Park. Also in the area is **Perry-Mansfield** (40755 CR 36; tel: 800-430-ARTS; www.perry-mansfield.org), the oldest performing arts school and camp in the nation. Theater and dance performances are staged on the rustic 76-acre (31-hectare) property north of town, from late June to early August and include student productions as well as workshops for professionals developing new work.

Winter sports

Steamboat's nickname, Ski Town USA, isn't an idle boast. With nearly 3,000 acres (1,200 hectares) of skiable terrain on three glorious peaks, **Steamboat Ski Area ❸** (2605 Mount Werner Circle, tel: 970-879-6111 info, 970-879-0740

reservations; www.steamboat.com; daily Nov–Apr), about 2 miles (3km) southeast of downtown Steamboat Springs, is one of the largest and most balanced ski resorts in the nation. The mountain massif snares an annual average of 335in (850cm) of snow so light and fluffy it inspired the marketing department to coin the phrase "champagne powder." Since 2007, facilities at the ski area have received a $23 million facelift. The resort village now includes improved walkways, lodging, restaurants, ski shops and other businesses. An outstanding childcare facility and children's ski school occupy prime space in the mountain village, and the beginner slopes, with dedicated lifts, are just steps away.

The main port of entry from the base complex is the eight-passenger Silver Bullet gondola, which leaves from the pedestrian promenade and climbs 2,200ft (670 meters) to a plateau called Thunderhead, where non-skiers can hang out and take in the view, eat at one of several restaurants in the rambling day lodge, or join a free naturalist-led snowshoe tour. From Thunderhead,

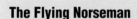

skiers and snowboarders drop down to Burgess Creek, then ride higher up on the Storm Peak chair-lifts or glide down to Priest Creek for the Sunshine Peak lifts. Wide trails of various pitches appeal to skiers and snowboarders of all abilities, while skiing through the Steamboat's widely spaced aspen trees delights powder hounds. Steamboat's upper mountain terrain hss the resort's fluffiest powder as well as some of its prettiest scenery and is a real mecca for tree-skiing aficionados. Continuing beyond Storm Peak, skiers and riders reach a parcel of intermediate and advanced terrain called Morningside Park. Tucked in behind Sunshine Peak is Pioneer Ridge, a snow-kissed bowl laced with a handful of medium-to-steep trails and still more glades.

Snowboarders gravitate to the 14-acre (5.7-hectare) terrain park, serviced by its own lift and hosting nearly a dozen terrain features, including Mavericks Superpipe, a 650ft (200-meter)-long halfpipe with 15ft (4.5-meter) walls, reputedly the longest in North America.

Steamboat, 160 miles (260km) from Denver, is too far away to be inundated with day-trippers, so it remains largely a multiday destination. The resort pioneered subsidized flights from major US cities as well as a landmark Kids Ski Free program. Families enjoy free lodging, lift tickets and rentals for children 12 and under, and even discounts on multiday lift passes for teens. Summer activities include mountain biking, hiking and picnicking. Steamboat Gondola ascends Mount Werner for gorgeous views of Yampa Valley (tel: 970-871-5252; late June–early Sept daily 10am–4pm; charge).

Overshadowed by Steamboat is **Howelsen Hill** ❹ (tel: 970-879-8499 for snow conditions), a smaller and older ski hill that in any other location would be the main attraction. Municipally owned and noted for ski jumps and groomed cross-country trails, Howelsen has been the training ground for generations of Steamboat's competitive skiers. Residents and visitors alike enjoy its short and demanding ski runs, night skiing, year-round ice skating and reasonable prices. In summer, Howelsen offers an alpine slide (a

With his Stetson and engaging manner, champion skier Billy Kidd is Mr Steamboat. He came west to race for the University of Colorado and won a silver medal in the 1964 Winter Games. Today, he remains Steamboat's most recognizable resident (see picture on page 205).

BELOW LEFT:
nestled amidst the mountains is Steamboat Springs.

The Flying Norseman

Planning a leap down Howelsen Hill? Remember to give credit to the man who made it – and Steamboat Springs – a skiing landmark. That would be Carl Howelsen, who came to America in 1905 after winning fame as a young skier in Norway. On this side of the Atlantic he thrilled crowds at summer outings with his ski-jump prowess on artificial turf and was billed as "The Flying Norseman" with the Barnum & Bailey circus. But he was born for the great outdoors and thus gravitated to Colorado.

In 1912, at Hot Sulphur Springs, he organized a winter carnival. His own 79ft (24-meter) leap was thrilling enough to give rise to an annual tournament, and he stirred similar enthusiasm at Steamboat Springs, where he built a rudimentary jump and taught the locals the art of skiing.

Thanks to Howelsen an enduring tradition was begun in 1914 – the Steamboat Springs Winter Carnival. For openers, Howelsen stunned the crowd with a prodigious leap of nearly 110ft (34 meters). Contests in the early years included ski jumping, cross-country skiing and an event that required contestants to climb the ¼-mile (½km) hill and slide back down.

A hill fashioned in 1915 was named for him. Howelsen returned to Norway in 1922, and died in 1955. He was among the first inductees into the Colorado Ski Hall of Fame.

Elk graze in the high country.

RIGHT: an old barn in Steamboat Springs. **BELOW RIGHT:** the gondola at Steamboat will whisk you to the top of the mountain.

sled-like contraption that speeds down a windy track), hiking trails and professional rodeo action at Romick Arena at the base of the slopes.

Back country adventures

For those who prefer warm weather, summer sports abound. The rafting season on the Yampa River – the last undammed river in the Colorado Basin – runs from about mid-May to early July, though spring runoff tends to produce the wildest rides in the first week of June. Outfitters in the area offer float trips ranging from a few hours of gentle tubing to a full-blown wilderness adventure taking in some of the most spectacular canyons in the West.

Steamboat is also a convenient starting point for back country journeys into **Medicine Bow-Routt National Forest** (tel: 970-879-1870), encompassing more than 2.2 million acres (890,300 hectares) of stunning alpine terrain laced with hiking trails and Jeep roads. Two areas are especially popular. **Rabbit Ears Pass** ❺, a broad "saddle" in the mountains about 12 miles

(19km) from town via US 40, accommodates motorized recreation (snowmobiles in winter, ATVs in summer) at the East Summit, while non-motorized users (Nordic skiers and snowshoers in winter, hikers and mountain bikers in summer) concentrate on the West Summit.

Farther afield, a drive north through the **Elk River Valley** (via CO 129) is an excursion into the rural past. New subdivisions quickly give way to ranchland. Just past the tiny hamlet of **Clark** ❻, about 18 miles (29km) north of Steamboat, you'll find **Seedhouse Road**, which offers access to numerous trails. To the north, nestled at the base of soaring Hahn's Peak, man-made **Pearl Lake and Steamboat Lake State Parks** (tel: 970-879-3922) offer fishing, boating and other water sports.

For those who really like to rough it, three wilderness areas – **Mount Zirkel**, **Flat Tops** and **Sarvis Creek**, totaling more than 440,000 roadless acres (178,000 hectares) – are nearby. The only hitch: motorized vehicles and bicycles are not permitted. The only way in is by foot or on horseback. ❏

Birding on the Yampa River

The Yampa River is significant for supporting a rare riparian forest type dominated by narrowleaf cottonwood, box elder and red-osier dogwood, home to a huge array of wildlife. It has been designated an Important Birding Area by the Audubon Society and supports numerous bird species, including bald eagles, bobolinks, Cooper's hawks, finches, great horned owls, red-tailed hawks, sandhill cranes, warblers, and woodpeckers. Two Nature Conservancy preserves in the Yampa Valley offer a close-up look at this important habitat. The 6,000-acre (2,428-hectare) Yampa River Preserve, 17 miles (27km) west of Steamboat Springs, is home to river otters, beaver, mink, and catbirds, and has a pleasant 2-mile (3km) trail through its Morgan Bottoms area. Carpenter Ranch, 20 miles (32km) west of Steamboat Springs, was pioneered in 1903 by J.B. Dawson, then leased beginning in 1925 and later owned by Farrington "Ferry" Carpenter. Ferry was a Harvard Law graduate and one of the area's most prominent citizens, serving as nearby Hayden's first attorney and as the first director of the federal Grazing Division, now the Bureau of Land Management. TNC operates the property as a working ranch, research and education center. It has listed ranch buildings, riparian areas, and the historic ranch house. Yampa River Preserve is open year round; Carpenter Ranch is open May–Sept Thur–Sat 9am–noon. For information, tel: 970-276-4626.

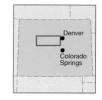

I-70 AND THE HIGH ROCKIES

A unique alpine freeway leads motorists over bridges and through tunnels, into a world of ski slopes, soaring peaks and gold-rush history

Denver
Colorado Springs

Sad but true, Colorado has no cruise ships. For many Denverites, the next best thing is a weekend trip on a segment of Amtrak's California Zephyr route that goes 200 miles (320km) west to Glenwood Springs (especially during the fall colors season, when seats are booked months in advance).

The only problem with such a trip is that travelers can't get off for detours into the surrounding Rocky Mountain high country. The solution, of course, is to drive. Admittedly, Interstate 70 is a fast, busy freeway. This guarantees that drivers will arrive at the hot springs with jangled nerves, but the rewards are great. Just about every exit along the way leads to a spectacularly scenic side trip. Glistening lakes and aspen forests, idyllic creekside parks and historic ghost towns – and even a ghost city or two – await adventurous motorists along this cross-section of Colorado's alpine heartland. For winter travelers, this is also the way to some of America's most famous ski resorts.

The numbered exits along I-70 indicate the distance from Colorado's western boundary. When taking the interstate through the Rockies, you can tell how far you are from downtown Denver by subtracting the exit number from 274.

Buffalo Bill and beer

Near the western edge of the Denver metro area, **Golden ❶** (I-70 exit 259) got its start as the gateway to the mountains during Colorado's 1859 gold rush and, two years later, became the territory's first capital. It is home to the 1874 **Colorado School of Mines**, where points of interest include the **Geology Museum** (1600 Maple Street; tel: 303-273-3823; www.mines.edu/geology_museum; Mon–Sat 9am–4pm, Sun 1–4pm; free), presenting gem and fossil specimens as well as walk-through replicas of a cave

Main attractions
GOLDEN
EVERGREEN
MORRISON
CENTRAL CITY
IDAHO SPRINGS
MOUNT EVANS SCENIC BYWAY
ST MARY'S GLACIER
GEORGETOWN
SOUTH PARK CITY
FAIRPLAY
EISENHOWER MEMORIAL TUNNEL
LOVELAND PASS
DILLON
FRISCO
BRECKENRIDGE
VAIL
GLENWOOD SPRINGS

LEFT: Glendwood Caverns Adventure Park.
RIGHT: the Day on the Prairie celebration at a Littleton school.

Pouring a tall one at the Coors Brewery sampling room.

and an old-fashioned gold mine. Also on campus, the **National Earthquake Information Center** (1711 Illinois Street; tel: 303-273-8420; www.neic.usgs. gov; free guided tours, by reservation only, Mon–Thur 9am–4pm) includes a chance to view seismographs that track tremors around the world.

Another unique Golden attraction, **Mother Cabrini Shrine** (20189 Cabrini Boulevard; tel: 303-526-0758; www.mothercabrinishrine.org; daily summer 7am–7pm, off-season until 5.30pm; free), offers a soul-soothing respite from the hectic traffic of I-70. The shrine commemorates St Frances (Francesca) Xavier Cabrini, the Italian nun who came to America in 1889, founded an orphanage in Denver and established this stonework complex in the forest as a summer camp for children. Her larger-than-life marble statue gazes out over Denver from the top of a 373-step "Stairway of Prayer." The main chapel at the site features magnificent stained-glass windows that depict key events in the saint's life, including a solo journey across the Andes and a miraculous healing.

Aficionados of vintage trains shouldn't miss the **Colorado Railroad Museum** (17155 W. 44th Avenue; tel: 800-365-6263; www.coloradorailway museum.org; daily 9am–5pm; charge). The 15-acre (6-hectare) site has dozens of locomotives and cars, tracks, switches and a museum housed in an 1880s-style depot.

Golden is best known for a more mundane attraction – the **Coors Brewery ❷** (13th and Ford streets; tel: 303-277-2337; www.coors.com; tours June–Aug Mon–Sat 10am–4pm, Sun noon–4pm, Sept–May Thur–Mon; free). Founded by Adolph Coors, a young German immigrant, in 1873, it's the world's largest single-site beer plant. From the public parking area at 13th and Ford streets, a shuttle bus takes visitors on a short guided tour of town en route to the plant, where they witness every phase of the beer-making process from blending specially grown barley malt, hops and Rocky Mountain spring water in huge copper kettles to canning the end result. (The aluminum beverage can, visitors learn, was invented by a member of the Coors

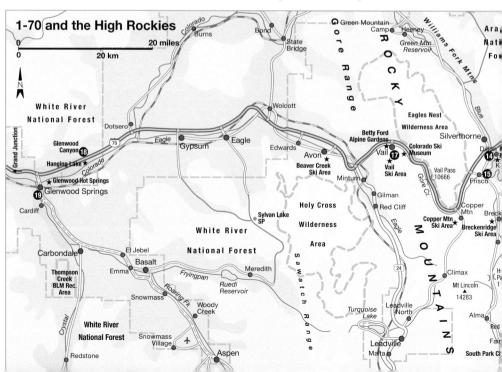

family.) The high point, so to speak, is a final stop at the sampling room.

Visitors are well advised not to do too much beer sampling before driving up **Lookout Mountain** to **Buffalo Bill Museum and Grave** ❸ (Lookout Mountain Road; tel: 303-526-0744; www.buffalobill.org; May–Oct daily 9am–5pm, Nov–Apr Tue–Sun 9am–4pm; charge). The paved road climbs 2,000ft (730 meters) in just 4.6 miles (7.7km), rounding dozens of curves, including seven tight switchbacks. Showman and dime-novel hero William F. "Buffalo Bill" Cody is said to have selected the mountain top as his gravesite for its panoramic vista overlooking the Great Plains. The long-fringed, beaded white buckskin outfit Cody wore in his Wild West show is on exhibit at the adjacent museum, along with several of his firearms and other memorabilia, and an exhibit about his changing attitude toward American Indians.

Buffalo Bill probably foresaw that his gravesite would become one of Colorado's top tourist sights. The scenic route up the mountain had been completed three years before he passed away in 1917, and near the summit, the now-defunct Lookout Mountain Resort was being promoted as "Denver's greatest future attraction." **Genesee Park** (tel: 303-370-6668, http://denvergov.org/parks/MountainParks/GeneseePark), the largest and oldest park in the 44-unit Denver Mountain Parks system, was also established around the same time to provide habitat for the city's small buffalo herd, the only one outside Yellowstone Park at that time, to save the American bison from the threat of extinction. Now flanked by subdivisions and bisected by I-70, the park still contains about 25 bison; a "buffalo only" tunnel lets them graze in pastures on either side of the interstate.

More than 70 vintage engines and cars are exhibited at Golden's Colorado Railroad Museum.

A passel of parks

Originally named Lariat Road, the road up Lookout Mountain is now one segment of the 40-mile (64km) **Lariat Loop Scenic Byway**, which leads motorists to three dozen more Denver Mountain Parks and Jefferson County Open Space Parks, covering a combined area of 40,000 acres (16,000 hectares). To follow Lariat Loop, con-

BELOW: a high school commencement ceremony at Red Rocks Amphitheater.

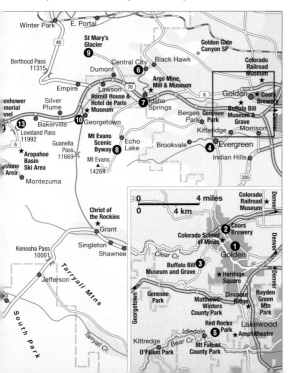

This type of sunflower is an arnica mollis, commonly known as a hairy arnica, and can be found growing in the wild throughout Colorado.

BELOW RIGHT:
Buffalo Bill Cody, a consummate showman, in an 1888 portrait.

tinue on Lookout Mountain Road as it winds down the south side of the mountain. Head west on Mount Vernon Canyon Road (US 40), the old highway that parallels I-70, to the historic El Rancho restaurant and lodge, and turn south there onto four-lane Evergreen Parkway (CO 74).

Large developments of identical condominiums and town houses fill the mountain sides for much of the way to **Evergreen** ❹, formerly an isolated ranching community until easy interstate access transformed it into an upscale Denver-area bedroom community. Vestiges of the town's past survive in the "historic district," as the original town's main (and only) street is known. Visitors can hike through the shady ponderosa forests of **Dedisse Park**, wander wild flower-strewn **Elk Meadows** or stroll around the shoreline of **Evergreen Lake**.

The real showplace of historic Evergreen is **Hiwan Homestead Museum** (4208 S. Timbervale Drive; tel: 720-497-7650; May–Sept Tue–Sun 11am–5pm, Oct–Apr noon–5pm; free), on the east end of town. The 17-room log man-

sion started as a barn in the 1890s and was expanded one room at a time over 25 years as the mountain retreat of Dr Josepha Williams, one of Colorado's first woman physicians, who operated a tuberculosis sanatorium in Denver. The furnishings are handmade and rather plain; the decor is enhanced by Dr Williams's collection of museum-quality Navajo rugs, Pueblo pottery and other American Indian artifacts, along with vintage photographs. Visitors may encounter children baking cookies in the old-fashioned kitchen – a traditional school field trip. Other vintage homes line Upper Bear Creek Canyon Road for several miles west of Evergreen Lake.

Red Rocks and dino tracks

Mountain parks appear one after another along the next segment of the Lariat Loop, following CO 74 as it narrows and winds east down Bear Creek Canyon from Evergreen to Morrison. The colorfully named **Lair o' the Bear Park** and a host of others, including **O'Fallon Park**, **Little Park**, **Corwina Park** and **Mount Falcon Park** were acquired by Denver or Jeffer-

Inventor of the Wild West

In 1872, at the ripe old age of 26, William "Buffalo Bill" Cody, already well known as a Pony Express rider, Army scout, Indian fighter and bison hunter, moved to Chicago to star in a stage play, *The Scouts of the Prairie*. The next season he produced his own play, which later evolved into Buffalo Bill's Wild West, a circus-like spectacular featuring hundreds of horseback riders, real-life Indians and herds of cattle, elk and bison.

The Wild West show toured the United States for nearly 40 years and played to enthusiastic crowds across Europe (including a performance for Queen Victoria's Golden Jubilee in 1887). Among its many stars were trick shooter Annie Oakley, "King of the Cowboys" Buck Taylor and, briefly, Sitting Bull. In 1890, the US Army called on Cody to return to the Western plains to help quell the "ghost dancer" uprising, but nearly two decades on the road had altered his attitude toward native people. He arrived in South Dakota with a group of Indians from his show and advocated on behalf of the Lakota Sioux, negotiating peace between the tribe and the Army.

William Cody died of kidney failure on January 10, 1917 and lay in state at the Colorado capitol. He is buried on Lookout Mountain overlooking the town of Golden.

son County and now form an almost unbroken strip along the silvery, gently rippling creek. Side roads cross stone bridges to give picnickers, hikers and anglers access to hidden side canyons.

To the north of the highway, just before reaching **Morrison**, is **Red Rocks Park ❺** (18300 W. Alameda Parkway; tel: 720-865-2494; www.red rocksonline.com), site of a 10,000-seat amphitheater built into sandstone out-croppings. The Beatles, Jimi Hendrix, Waylon Jennings and countless other big-name acts have performed here. A sunrise service is held on Easter morning. Farther north, near the intersection of CO 26 and 470, is **Dinosaur Ridge**, where a slab of sandstone is crisscrossed with dinosaur tracks laid down 100 million years ago at the edge of an inland sea. From Dinosaur Ridge, it's a short hop on CO 26 back to I-70.

Striking it rich... maybe

Central City ❻ is all about the past, or at least it used to be. No other town in the Colorado Rockies has had such a roller-coaster history as this one, situated a few miles north of I-70 via either CO 119 or the new Central City Park-way. Founded in 1859 as the epicenter of the gold rush, it was promoted by newspaper publisher Horace Greeley as "the richest square mile on earth." Within a few years, as placer gold prospecting gave way to large-scale industrial mining that employed droves of Welsh, Cornish and Chinese laborers, it became Colorado Territory's largest city, with a population of 30,000 – but only in the summer. Cut off from the outside world by snow, it dropped to 1,500 residents during the winter months.

Central City outlived most gold boomtowns, and its mines kept operating for decades, as the giant, colorful slag heaps attest. By 1900, though, its population had shrunk to a few dozen souls. The multistory brick and stone buildings along Central City's downtown streets endured, as did many of the Italianate mansions on the overlooking hillsides. The city was resurrected as a high-class tourist town in 1932, when the Central City Opera House reopened. It soon became the state's most popular ghost town, and the once-abandoned buildings were

Mountain biking is a popular summer activity at many winter ski resorts.

BELOW: Indian drummers set the beat at a Morrison powwow.

Fly fishermen will find an abundance of trout and other game fish in the icy streams of the Central Rockies.

transformed into curio shops. But by the 1980s, Central City's popularity had faded as a new generation of tourists headed for other revived mining towns deeper in the mountains instead. One by one, its stores and restaurants closed their doors for good.

In a last-ditch effort to rescue Central City and neighboring Black Hawk from decay, the Colorado state legislature legalized limited-stakes casino gambling in the three ghost towns in 1991. The results varied greatly between the towns. **Black Hawk**, with plenty of open space and relatively few historic buildings to preserve, has been transformed into a mini-Las Vegas, a strip of huge casino resorts and parking structures with few evident vestiges of the gold-rush days. In Central City, casinos displaced virtually every other business in town. Even the **Teller House** (120 Eureka Street) was turned into a casino/restaurant when the gambling boom hit. This elegant hotel was where silver baron Horace Tabor kept his mistress, Baby Doe; a second-story walkway used to connect it with Tabor's upstairs office in the opera house.

BELOW: aspens flourish in the high country.

The **Central City Opera House** (124 Eureka Street; box office tel: 303-292-6700; www.centralcityopera.org;), the second oldest in the country, built in 1878 and restored in 1932 after falling into disrepair, remains Central City's most thriving enterprise. It puts on three operas every summer as part of its popular music festival in an event as anticipated as the Santa Fe Opera season. Tickets go on sale months in advance.

At the upper end of Central City, most streets turn into unpaved forest roads leading to picturesque old ghost towns such as **Nevadaville** and **Apex**. The most dramatic of them, **County Road 279**, starts at the upper end of Spring Street. After passing **Russell Gulch**, an old mine camp now repopulated as a cluster of vacation cabins and artists' studios, motorists come to a hand-lettered sign that reads "**Oh My Gawd Road.**" The reason for the nickname soon becomes obvious as the road plunges down 8 miles (13km) of steep, edgy switchbacks, ending at Idaho Springs. Though well maintained, the route is not for the faint-hearted – or anyone driving a motor home.

Hidee Gold Mine

Central City isn't particularly child friendly, but one place the whole family is likely to enjoy is Hidee Mine, just outside Central City off Central City Parkway, one of the few mines in the area still operational. Former miner and mine owner Ed Lewandowski leads 1½-hour-long tours into the gold mine, a well-ventilated shaft where visitors can chip away at the mine's vein for souvenirs of gold ore. Lewandowski is an expert geologist and still works the vein. Mines in this area, all told, since 1859, have produced $1 billion in gold and silver. Dress warmly, as temperatures underground are cool, and don't wear open-toed shoes. Free tours are offered Apr–Oct daily 11am–5pm. For more information and reservations, tel: 720-548-0343 or email: info@hideegoldmine.com.

The highest highway

Located between I-70 exits 241 and 239, **Idaho Springs** ❼ has preserved its gold-rush heritage without the aid of legalized gambling. Mining has never entirely ceased there; though the gold played out before the end of the 19th century, rich deposits of uranium and valuable alloy metals such as tungsten and molybdenum were discovered in the surrounding rock. Today, several of the old mines offer tours. Premier among them is the **Argo Mine, Mill and Museum** (2317 Riverside Drive; tel: 303-567-2421; www.historicargotours.com; May–Sept daily 9am–6pm, call for off-season hours; tour charge), where visitors can also see the end of the remarkable tunnel that ran through solid rock all the way from Central City, providing ventilation, drainage and gold ore transportation for numerous mines along the way. Others that are open to the public include the still-operating, family-owned **Phoenix Gold Mine** (Trail Creek Road; tel: 303-567-0422; www.phoenixmine.com; daily 10am–6pm; tour charge) and the Colorado School of Mines' **Edgar Experimental Mine**

(365 8th Avenue; tel: 303-567-2911; www.mines.edu/edgarmine; June–Aug Mon–Fri tours by advance reservation at varied times; charge), where new mining techniques and equipment are tested.

Idaho Springs is the starting point for one of the area's most popular scenic drives, the **Mount Evans Scenic Byway** ❽ (tel: 303-567-3000, top 5 miles/8km Memorial Day–Labor Day, first 10 miles/16km until early Oct; charge). Billed as the highest paved automobile road in North America, the "highway" up the 14,240ft (4,340-meter) peak was built by the City of Denver beginning in 1917; the Pikes Peak Highway had been completed the year before, and Denver's mayor feared losing his city's tourist trade to Colorado Springs. From Idaho Springs, paved CO 103 climbs for 13 miles (21km) to **Echo Lake**, a quintessential alpine lake with a picnic area and a walking trail around the wooded shoreline. CO 5 turns off at the lake and runs above timber line for 14 miles (23km) to a parking lot ¼ mile (½km) from the summit, where visitors get a panoramic view that takes in Pikes Peak, Longs Peak and Rocky

Beware of the sun in Colorado. At higher elevations, it can be stronger than you think.

BELOW:
a mountain goat grazes on spring blooms.

Galleries, gift shops and restaurants occupy Georgetown's historic main street.

Mountain National Park. Descending to Echo Lake, motorists can return to Idaho Springs by the same route or continue on CO 103 along a ridgeline with magnificent views to Squaw Pass and then down to the Evergreen Parkway near I-70 exit 252.

A secret spot tucked away a few miles off I-70 exit 238, **St Mary's Glacier** ❾ is the southernmost true glacier in North America. The glacier itself is not visible from the road but can be reached by a 1½-mile (2.4km) trail that leads to St Mary's Lake, filled with ice water that melts from the glacier in summer and irrigates a river of lush greenery on its way to the lakeshore. Nearby, the forlorn old **St Mary's Lodge**, once a popular resort, waits for someone to come along and restore and reopen it, and a schoolhouse and other historic buildings remain in the old mining town of **Alice**, now sparsely repopulated with a hodgepodge of mobile homes, log vacation cabins and larger custom-built summer homes.

Steaming through history

The big sightseeing attraction at George-town ❿ (I-70 exit 228), the **George-town Loop Railroad** (1111 Rose Street; tel: 888-456-6777; www.george townlooprr.com; May–Sept daily, Oct Sat–Sun 9.45am–2.55pm; charge) offers the only narrow-gauge steam train excursion that can be taken easily as a day-trip from Denver. Though with only 4½ miles (7km) of track, the round-trip to **Silver Plume** takes just 80 minutes, it's one of the most thrilling excursions in the state, climaxing with a trestle that doubles back on itself 90ft (33 meters) above the floor of Devil's Gate Canyon. The trip includes an optional tour of the historic **Lebanon Gold Mine**, accessible only by train.

Georgetown's small historic district features ornate Victorian-era storefronts, many of which now house galleries and cafés. The highlight is the **Hotel de Paris** (6th and Taos streets; tel: 303-569-2311; June–Aug daily 10am–4.30pm, off-season Sat–Sun noon–4pm; charge), a museum that once ranked among the most elegant hostelries in the West. Of particular interest are the ornate former restaurant and the two "salesman's rooms"

Historic Georgetown

Lovers of vintage architecture and decor will appreciate Georgetown's historic preservation program, which started in 1971 with the restoration of the Hamill House, built in 1879 by William Hamill, a successful English silver mine owner, politician and banker. Challenging the notion that only the homes of the wealthy merit preservation, the five-part program has added other properties that now form the Georgetown/Silver Plume National Historic Landmark District. The Bowman-White House was owned by a professional man and mine owner; the Kneisel House belonged to a merchant; the Tucker-Rutherford Cottage was a miner's home; and the Johnson Cabin was an early prospector's log cabin. For more information, tel: 303-569-2840 or visit www.historicgeorgetown.org.

– extra-large guest rooms designed for traveling salesmen to display their wares, featuring desks that converted into beds at night as well as diamond dust mirrors, fireplaces and fine art.

Spectacular scenery compensates for potholed pavement, washouts and rocky unpaved stretches on the **Guanella Pass Road** (Forest Road 381), which winds up the steep mountain slope at the south end of town. Leveling off above 11,000ft (4,000 meters), the road takes motorists past alpine lakes, trailheads and recreation areas among the Douglas firs and aspen, finally rising above timber line for an eye-popping close-up view of the west side of Mount Evans. After about an hour's drive, it descends gently into **South Park**, joining US 285 about 28 miles (45km) east of Fairplay.

South Park is an expanse of high-altitude grasslands where herds of cattle graze and hay grows for shipment to other ranches throughout the state, flanked on all sides by 14,000ft (4,300-meter) peaks. The sole major tourist attraction is **South Park City** ⓫ (100 4th Street; tel: 719-836-2387; www.south

parkcity.org; daily June–Sept 9am–7pm, May and Oct 10am–6pm; charge), in the little mining town of **Fairplay**. The open-air museum is made up of 35 Gold Rush-era wooden structures – some on their original sites, others moved from abandoned mine camps nearby. They include an assay office, a mercantile store, a newspaper building, a pharmacy and, of course, a saloon, all fully furnished with 19th-century artifacts to give visitors a sense of what other Colorado ghost towns must have been like in their prime.

Eisenhower Memorial Tunnel

Before 1973, the Colorado Rockies posed a major obstacle that made winter travelers, from early-day pioneers to 20th-century long-haul truckers, seek easier east–west routes through Wyoming or New Mexico. It was not unusual for snow to close the route that is now I-70 for days at a time. The opening of the **Eisenhower Memorial Tunnel** ⓬ changed all that. Though the 1.7-mile (2.7km) tunnel under the Continental Divide trimmed only

A 1930s pickup truck collects dust among the remains of an old mining camp.

BELOW: the Gold Belt Tunnel near Silver Plume, about 1920.

*Flowers add a touch of
color to Breckenridge's
Victorian-style
architecture.*

about 9 miles (14km) from the old route over Loveland Pass, it made the four-lane interstate highway possible and thus reduced the driving time between Denver and Vail from four hours to 90 minutes.

Even for Coloradans, whose ancestors had been digging underground for more than a century, the tunnel (or "bore" in mining lingo) was a monumental undertaking, requiring $108 million and more than 1,100 laborers working in three shifts round the clock for five years. It carried traffic in both directions until 1979, when the parallel eastbound Johnson Memorial Tunnel (named not for the ex-president, as one might think, but for the former Colorado governor and senator who had promoted the project) was completed. Though technically only the westbound tunnel is named for President Dwight D. Eisenhower, Coloradans refer to both bores as the Eisenhower Tunnel.

Driving on high

If you enjoy mountain driving, check out what the tunnel bypassed by taking

US 6 over **Loveland Pass** **⑬**, a steep route that traverses rocky alpine tundra at an elevation of nearly 12,000ft (4,370 meters). The pass was named after William A.H. Loveland, the Golden railroad magnate who planned the first railroad over the Continental Divide to Leadville in 1878. (Loveland planned to build a tunnel where the Eisenhower Memorial Tunnel is today, but before completion Union Pacific bought out his railroad and rerouted it over the pass which now bears his name). At the top of the pass, a hiking trail leads up nearby Mount Sniktau ("Sniktau" was the pen name used by a popular *Rocky Mountain News* columnist in the 1870s) for a dramatic view of I-70 and the tunnel entrance, from high above. The highway also passes the Arapahoe Basin and Keystone ski areas before descending to rejoin I-70 at Dillon (exit 205).

In theory at least, the resort town of **Dillon** **⑭** has a past dating to 1883, when it got its start as a stagecoach stop. In reality, however, the original town was flooded in the 1960s by the construction of **Lake Dillon**, a large flood control reservoir at the confluence of the Blue and Snake rivers, and a new town with the same name was built along the north shore. Today the centerpiece of the bustling resort community is **Dillon Marina** (tel: 970-468-5100), which rents craft ranging from kayaks to sailboats, as well as party barges, for those who wish to explore the lake's 25-mile (40km) shoreline.

A few remnants of the area's history can still be found in **Frisco** **⑮**, on the lake's south shore at I-70 exit 203, where a cluster of 19th-century log homes, a chapel and a jail, along with an old schoolhouse that now serves as the town's museum, have been restored in **Frisco Historical Park** (Main and 2nd streets). The reigning queen of the Lake Dillon area, though, is Breckenridge, a world-class ski resort 10 miles (16km) from Frisco on CO 6.

Established during the 1859 gold rush, **Breckenridge** **⑯** never yielded

ore deposits large enough to warrant the kind of industrial-scale mining seen in Central City or Idaho Springs, but enough small strikes were made to attract a steady flow of small-time prospectors. Its reputation was assured when the largest gold nugget ever found in North America was unearthed there. Abandoned in the early 20th century, the town was revived in the 1960s as the nearest large ski resort to both Denver and Colorado Springs. Since most of Colorado's first generation of instructors and other ski slope personnel immigrated from older resorts in the Austrian, Bavarian and Swiss alps, Breckenridge soon developed a unique character that persists to this day, blending Old West architecture and Old World sensibilities.

In winter, Breckenridge's 1,441 acres (583 hectares) of ski slopes sprawl across three mountains known simply as Peak 8, Peak 9 and Peak 10. The town's strategy for staying alive during the off-season has been to develop public recreational facilities that include a year-round ice rink, a skateboard path, a mountain bike trail system and rid-

ing stables. A chair-lift takes fun-seekers up to the **Peak 8 Fun Park**, a sporty playground that offers an alpine slide, a rock climbing wall, bungie jumping, miniature golf and a large maze as well as hiking and biking trails. Still, Breckenridge can feel a little like a ghost town in summer, and travelers who eat dinner in one of its numerous good restaurants are likely to find that the staff outnumber the patrons.

Grand-scale skiing

Breckenridge ski resort, along with the smaller slopes at Keystone, Arapahoe Basin, Arrowhead and Beaver Creek, are now owned by Vail Resorts, Inc., making it the world's largest ski resort operator. For that matter, **Vail** ⓲ itself, the company's original resort, is Colorado's largest ski area – and the largest single-mountain ski complex in North America. Located 27 miles (44km) west of Lake Dillon at I-70 exit 176, the slopes span more than 5,000 acres (2,000 hectares) of skiable terrain served by 18 chair-lifts and a gondola; together, in peak ski season, they carry up to 61,000 skiers per hour up the mountain.

When the roads are full of snow and ice, you have to be creative in finding ways to commute: skis, sleds, and sometimes even snowshoes.

BELOW: panning for gold near Breckenridge.

The Colorado Ski Museum chronicles the development of the sport.

BELOW: taking the waters at Glenwood Hot Springs.

Vail's sheer size makes up for its lack of Old West heritage. The town did not exist before the beginning of Colorado's downhill skiing boom in 1962. That was when three old army buddies, who had discovered Vail's now-legendary Back Bowls while training with the 10th Mountain Division during World War II, obtained funding to develop the ski area in what up to then had been a sparsely populated ranching valley. With no historic buildings to preserve, they were free to invent their own architectural style. The result was **Vail Village**, a Disneyesque version of a Tyrolean town designed to look its best when the roofs and streets are covered with snow. In summer, shade trees along the Eagle River make for pleasant walking along paved paths between clusters of art galleries, restaurants and chic sportswear shops. Though Vail does have first-rate summer recreational facilities including golf courses, tennis courts, mountain bike trails and hiking access to the vast Eagles Nest and Holy Cross wilderness areas, the economic mainstay outside of ski season is conferences; its hotels offer prestigious venues

for everything from legal and medical association meetings to symposiums on international trade relations.

For travelers who are just passing through, two points of interest, both just off I-70 exit 176, make for unique sightseeing stops. The **Colorado Ski Museum** (231 S. Frontage Road; tel: 970-476-1876; www.skimuseum.net; June–Sept and Nov–Apr Tue–Sun 10am–5pm; charge) displays 19th-century wooden skis used to carry mail to snowbound mine camps, and traces the growth of Colorado's ski resorts. At the **Betty Ford Alpine Gardens** (530 S. Frontage Road; tel: 970-476-0103; www.bettyfordalpinegardens.org; daily dawn to dusk; free), idyllic walking trails meander among six themed gardens filled with flowers and herbs from the Rocky Mountains and other alpine ranges around the world, including the Peruvian Andes and the Himalayas of Nepal.

Enlightened highway

From the resort towns of the Vail Valley, I-70 follows the Eagle River down a long, gentle grade through open meadows and forested hills to its confluence

with the Colorado River headwaters at the tiny town of Dotsero and the upper end of **Glenwood Canyon** ⓲. The 19-mile (31km) route through the canyon was the last segment of I-70 to be converted into a four-lane divided highway. In earlier times, road builders might have simply hacked away at the cliff face to widen the roadbed, but by the early 1990s, when the $500 million project began, Colorado had enacted some of the nation's toughest environmental protection laws. Not only were the contractors prohibited from defacing the rock walls, but for every single piece of flora disturbed during construction they faced penalties ranging from $35 for a raspberry bush to $22,000 for a Douglas fir. The eastbound and westbound lanes were stacked one atop the other on pillars 80ft (24 meters) above the canyon floor, and a tunnel nearly a mile long was hollowed out of the cliff to conceal the roadway from hikers.

After a long hike, or even a long drive on the freeway, there's nothing better than to sink into the bathwater-temperature mineral water of **Glenwood Hot Springs** (401 N. River Road; tel: 970-945-6571; www.hotspringspool.com; June–Sept daily 7.30am–10pm, Oct–May 9am–10pm; charge), said to be the world's largest geothermal pool. Notables from President Theodore Roosevelt to gunslinger Doc Holliday came here to "take the waters." With the waning popularity of hot-springs health spas in the early 20th century, Glenwood Springs' grand hotels fell into disrepair, and for years the town's economy depended on its main agricultural crop – strawberries.

Sky-high room rates in Aspen, 45 minutes' drive away, have boosted the popularity of **Glenwood Springs** ⓳ as an affordable alternative, and the completion of the Glenwood Canyon Recreation Trail has assured this century-old resort town's status as one of Colorado's hottest "new" destinations. Opened in 1893, **Hotel Colorado** (526 Pine Street, tel: 970-945-6511; www.hotelcolorado.com) has been restored to its former grandeur, and the equally historic **Hotel Denver** (402 7th Street; tel: 970-945-6565) has been renovated in lavish Art Deco style. And, of course, there's always the train! ❏

The Hotel Denver in Glenwood Springs is just across the street from the train station, where in the early afternoon each day, a crowd of passengers steps down from the California Zephyr after a six-hour rail journey from Denver.

BELOW: Vail Village is modeled on European ski resorts.

Glenwood recreational trail

Glenwood Canyon Recreational Trail was created when I-70 replaced the former highway. The paved route rises only 400ft (146 meters) from the west end of the canyon at Glenwood Springs to the east end at Dotsero. Although most cyclists and rollerbladers start from the Glenwood Springs end of the trail, where rental bikes and other gear are available, four interstate exits provide access to trailheads along the route. The most popular trail goes to Hanging Lake, a fern-draped, aquamarine-hued pool perched high on the wall of a side canyon. Although the hike is only 1¼ miles (2km) long, it is quite steep, climbing nearly 1,000ft (365 meters), but there are pleasant resting points along the way, and the view from the top makes the effort worthwhile.

ASPEN AND THE CENTRAL ROCKIES

Once a scruffy mining camp, Aspen is now a chic
mountain resort patronized by the Beautiful People.
Welcome to the "Beverly Hills of the Rockies"

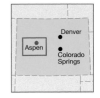

Although **Aspen** ❶ and Crested Butte are only 25 miles (41km) apart, the terrain in between is impassable to cars, requiring a drive of more than 200 miles (320km). This chapter combines two possible highway routes between the towns into a 450-mile (725km) loop tour. En route lie the deepest canyon, the highest mountain and the largest lake in Colorado. You will also discover a 19th-century miners' utopia, the place where the marble for the Lincoln Memorial was quarried, some of the state's best-preserved ghost towns and a historic hot springs resort.

As the central hub of the Rockies, the loop tour can be divided into segments that connect many other scenic routes, most notably Interstate 70 (*see page 213*), the San Juan Skyway (*see page 251*), and the San Luis Valley (*see page 185*). Whatever destinations you pick, your trip will take you through the heart of the Rockies.

The richest town in the Rockies

"This place is getting to be like Aspen," locals say in revived Victorian towns throughout the Rockies whenever a new bed and breakfast, café or art gallery opens – and they don't mean it in a good way. Yet, secretly, many small-towners would love to see their communities become "the next Aspen" – if only they could still afford to live there. Aspen is the prototype for every other former ghost town turned tourist resort.

In the silver boom of the 1880s, Aspen grew into a town of 12,000 people. Then, following the silver crash of 1893, it faded away until its population numbered just 350 and its brick buildings stood empty or collapsed. Gingerbread mansions with smashed windows could be bought up for a few hundred dollars in back taxes, if any-

Main attractions

ASPEN
MAROON BELLS NEAR SNOWMASS
ASHCROFT
REDSTONE
MARBLE
PAONIA
DELTA
BLACK CANYON OF THE GUNNISON NATIONAL PARK
GUNNISON
CRESTED BUTTE
PONCHA SPRINGS
BUENA VISTA
SALIDA
MOUNT PRINCETON HOT SPRINGS, NATHROP
LEADVILLE
INDEPENDENCE PASS

LEFT: the slopes of Aspen appear directly over the town. **RIGHT:** Leadville bartender.

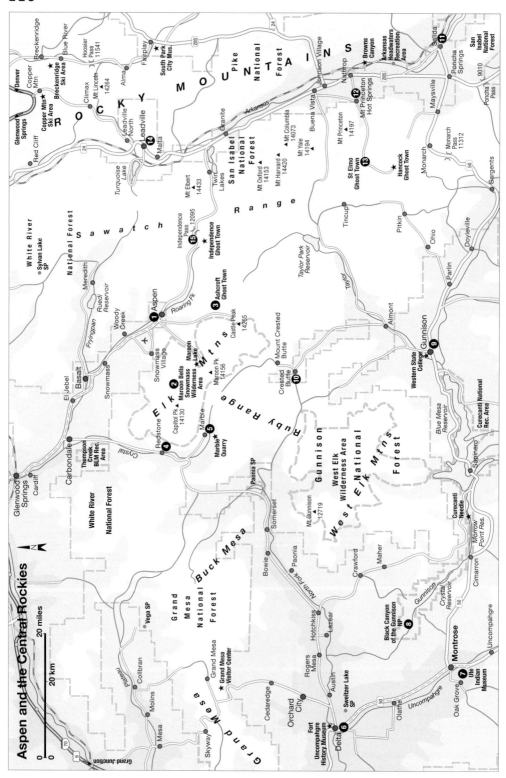

Aspen and the Central Rockies

body had wanted to own them. Aspen survived only because it was the seat of Pitkin County, which otherwise consisted entirely of national forest land.

Then, after World War II, something happened in Aspen that nobody could have predicted. Friedl Pfeifer, an Austrian ski instructor, announced plans to build Colorado's first ski resort. The idea was, of course, absurd. Few Americans skied and, before I-70 was built, Aspen itself was in one of the most remote places imaginable. Yet Pfeifer, with financial backing from Chicago cardboard box tycoon Walter Paepke, succeeded in building his ski slope, and in 1950 it was selected as the site of the World Alpine Ski Championships. In 1960, the first televised Winter Olympics introduced many Americans to the sport, and within five years the number of skiers in the US grew by a phenomenal 850 percent. Aspen experienced a boom unrivaled even in the old mining days.

Summer fun

Pfeifer and Paepke also anticipated a problem that has confronted every other ski resort town since: what to do during the eight months of the year when there's no snow. In 1950, the town garnered national attention with the Goethe Bicentennial Convocation, an alpine festival of philosophy and music, with Albert Schweitzer as keynote speaker – the only time he ever left Africa. Also featured were some of the nation's leading classical musicians, including pianist Arthur Rubinstein and the Minneapolis Symphony Orchestra. Though the Goethe connection was dropped the next year, the festival inspired the Aspen Institute of Humanistic Studies, the Aspen Music Festival and the Aspen International Design Conference, all of which continue to this day. Other prestigious summer celebrations have been added, including two jazz festivals and one of the largest dance festivals in the United States.

Visitors today approach Aspen along CO 82 from Glenwood Springs. The four-lane freeway up the **Roaring Fork Valley** runs between hillsides stacked high with multimillion-dollar homes and past the busy airport, its tarmac

The Treehouse Kids' Adventure Center in Snowmass includes a crawl-through fox den for hands-on learning.

BELOW: an Aspen gallery owner; there are more than 30 art galleries in town.

Aspen Ambience

Aspen is not really about sightseeing; it's about ambience. After Twentieth Century Fox acquired the Aspen Skiing Company in 1978 (it's now owned by the Crown family of Chicago), the town became Colorado's answer to California's Beverly Hills – a very expensive place where tourists are tolerated but outnumbered by the rich, famous and absolutely fabulous. You can shop for a painting that costs more than an automobile or take in a ballet. Go to a nightclub where it's hard to get in, then have sushi delivered to your suite at midnight. Learn to climb rock cliffs, ride whitewater in a kayak, or paraglide, but keep your eyes open for the beautiful people. Recent gossip has it that the billionaires have purchased so many homes in Aspen that there are none left for the mere millionaires.

A string ensemble serenades guests at the historic Hotel Jerome.

lined with Lear Jets. Arriving at last in the compact, lavishly refurbished historic district, the place to start sightseeing is the **Wheeler-Stallard Museum** Ⓐ (620 W. Bleeker Street; tel: 970-925-3721; www.heritageaspen.org; Tue–Sat 1–5pm; charge), a magnificent Victorian mansion in Queen Anne style built in 1888 by the founder of Macy's department store in New York. Period furnishings and historical photographs recall Aspen's history from the 1880s to the present day.

The museum is the starting point for guided and self-guided tours of the historic district. A highlight is beautifully restored **Wheeler Opera House** Ⓑ (320 E. Hyman Avenue; tel: 970-920-5770; www.wheeleroperahouse.com; May–Sept Mon–Sat 9am–5pm, Oct–Apr 11am–7pm; free guided tours), which offers a full schedule of performance events during the evening, and houses the town's visitor information center. Other historic district sights include the **Pitkin County Courthouse** Ⓒ (506 E. Main Street; tel: 970-920-5200), with its solid silver dome, and the elegant old **Hotel Jerome** Ⓓ (330 E.

Main Street; tel: 970-920-1000; www. hoteljerome.rockresorts.com).

Aspen can feel very heady. To get in touch with your natural self, head to one of the most scenic spots in the Rockies, photo-perfect **Maroon Lake**. The lake is located 10 miles (17km) south of Aspen at the end of Maroon Creek Road and mirrors the majestic **Maroon Bells**, twin 14,000ft (4,265-meter) peaks whose sheer, angular rock faces are stained red by iron oxide. A gentle trail leads around the lakeshore and past beaver ponds, and hikers can continue as far as Crater Lake at the base of the mountains.

Other trails lead deep into the **Maroon Bells-Snowmass Wilderness** ❷. In summer, the only way to reach Maroon Lake is by taking one of the shuttle buses that leave frequently from the **Rubey Park Transit Center** in downtown Aspen (Durant Street; tel: 970-925-8484; daily 8am–5pm).

Another vantage on Aspen's past awaits visitors to **Ashcroft** ❸, 12 miles (20km) south of town on Castle Creek Road. Only nine empty buildings remain at the site, a ghostly remnant of

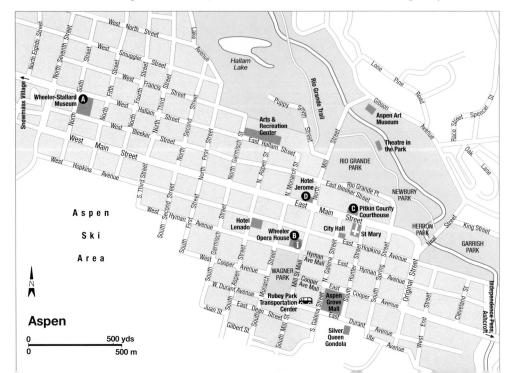

Aspen

a town that in its heyday was larger than Aspen. Friedl Pfeifer originally planned to build his ski area at Ashcroft, which might have changed its fate.

Redstone, coal and marble

Thirty miles (48km) north of Aspen on CO 82, CO 133 branches off to the left at Carbondale and meanders 17 miles (27km) down the peaceful two-lane highway to **Redstone ❹**, a hideaway town. It got its start in the 1880s as a company town for a coal mine owned by industrial visionary John Cleveland Osgood. Believing that a better living environment would make laborers more productive, Osgood built 84 Swiss-style chalets for his married mine workers and a rambling inn for the bachelors—among the first homes in Colorado to have electricity and indoor plumbing.

Osgood's own grandiose 42-room sandstone mansion, **Cleveholm Manor** (58 Redstone Boulevard; tel: 970-963-3463, tours Fri–Mon 1.30pm), otherwise known as Redstone Castle, is at the end of the town's main street. Eventually, Osgood lost his mining interests in a hostile takeover. The coal mine was closed down, the miners moved away, and Osgood and his new wife went into seclusion in their mansion in the otherwise abandoned village. Today, the town is still about the same size it was in Osgood's time and is inhabited mainly by artists and craftspeople who sell their creations in Aspen, Denver or elsewhere. The bachelor miners' lodge has been converted into the **Redstone Inn** (82 Redstone Boulevard; tel: 970-963-2526; www.redstoneinn.thegilmorecollection.com), a bed and breakfast inn.

Five miles (8km) up CO 133, a narrow paved road turns to the left and goes to the former ghost town of **Marble ❺**. The town was founded as a marble quarry and mill, which produced blocks of snow-white stone used for massive public sculptures, including the Tomb of the Unknown Soldier and the Lincoln Memorial. At the **Old Mill Site**, huge slabs and blocks of

marble lie haphazardly scattered from before the mill closed down in 1942. The small **Marble Museum** (412 W. Main Street; tel: 970-963-9815; www.marblehistory.org; May–Sept Thur–Sun 11am–4pm, Oct–Apr Sat–Sun; free), exhibits vintage photographs and memorabilia in the town's first high school, built in 1910.

Farm country

The charming little town of **Paonia** on the North Fork of the Gunnison River is the gateway to **Delta County**, one of the richest farming areas in Colorado. The area was once a broad floodplain, where during the spring run-off walls of water gushed through the Black Canyon of the Gunnison, inundating the valley and enriching the soil. The flooding halted with the completion of Blue Mesa Reservoir on the river above the canyon. Paonia and other North Fork Valley communities are gaining in popularity with outdoors lovers and creative people looking to escape the city. The award-winning Western environmental monthly *High Country News* (119 Grand Avenue; tel: 970-527-4898;

The small farm town of Paonia was named after the Latin word for peony in 1882 by its founder Samuel Wade, who brought peony root stock with him to Colorado. Peonies still grow in the town park.

BELOW: a few cabins are all that remain of Independence, a former gold-mining camp outside Aspen founded in 1879 and abandoned in 1899.

Boogie's Diner is one of dozens of interesting and trendy restaurants in the Aspen area.

BELOW: Chief Ouray and Chipeta. Ouray was recognized by the US government as chief of the Uncompahgre tribe.

www.hcn.org) is headquartered here, and organic farms, local food cafés, and lodgings are springing up fast.

CO 133 meets CO 92 at the crossroads hamlet of **Hotchkiss**. From here, it's 20 miles (32km) west to **Delta ❻**, a bland commercial center with an old-fashioned downtown main street, located at the confluence of the Uncompahgre and Gunnison rivers. The **Fort Uncompahgre History Museum** (205 Gunnison River Drive; tel: 970-874-1718; Apr–Oct Mon–Fri 9am–3pm; charge) is a rather disheveled replica of a trading post established in 1828 by fur trader Antoine Robidoux that became the first permanent settlement here.

Montrose, 21 miles (34km) south of Delta on US 50, anchors the north end of the popular San Juan Skyway Scenic Byway. It is the nearest city to both Ouray and Telluride and the gateway to Black Canyon of the Gunnison National Park and other natural areas that are luring an increasing number of new residents.

The top attraction in Montrose is the **Ute Indian Museum ❼** (17253 Chipeta Road; tel: 970-249-3098; Tue–Sat 9am–4pm; charge),known for its Ute artifacts and as a focal point of tribal celebrations on the West Slope. The museum sits on 8.65 acres (3.5 hectares) of land homesteaded by Ute Chief Ouray.

Chief Ouray was an impressive American Indian spokesman who led diplomatic missions to Washington, DC, and negotiated a government treaty that reserved the entire southwestern region of Colorado Territory for the Utes in 1873. He guided his people through the transition from nomadic hunting and trading to agriculture, becoming an excellent farmer himself. Visitors can view a poster-size photo of the signed treaty and learn how, eight years later when gold was discovered in the San Juan Mountains, the federal government broke the treaty and relocated the Northern Ute tribe to a reservation in Utah. Adjoining the museum is **Chief Ouray Memorial Park**. Ouray's beloved wife Chipeta is buried here; she is said to have started the colorful columbine gardens that still fringe the park's broad lawn.

Edge of the abyss

Eight miles (13km) east of Montrose on US 50 is the turn-off for the South Rim of **Black Canyon of the Gunnison National Park** ❽ (tel: 970-641-2337; www.nps.gov/blca; year-round; charge). The South Rim has a modest visitor center, a 7-mile (11km) long scenic drive that leads to 12 overlooks, picnic areas, a year-round campground (water May–Oct only), and a moderate rim trail suitable for all the family. There are no food outlets, lodging or other services in the park. The canyon itself couldn't be more dramatic. It is more than twice as deep as it is wide, with dark-hued, vertical walls of 1.7-billion-year-old granite and schist dropping an average 2,000ft (610 meters) from the rim to the river below and narrowing to as little as 40ft (12 meters) wide at river level. Adventurous visitors can obtain free wilderness permits from the visitor center to make the strenuous hike to the bottom, or raft or kayak through it.

Upriver, virtually all of the canyon was flooded to make the three reservoirs in **Curecanti National Recreation Area** (tel: 970-641-2337; www.nps.gov/cure). **Crystal Reservoir** and **Morrow Point Reservoir**, both long, slender lakes that seem more like big, lazy rivers, are out of sight of the main highway, have no boat ramps and are only open to kayaks, inflatables and other hand-carried boats. You can't miss **Blue Mesa Reservoir**: the highway follows its shoreline and crosses over it on a long bridge. Colorado's largest lake, it attracts boaters, water-skiers and windsurfers from all over the state. Its cold depths provide habitat for kokanee salmon and giant mackinaw trout.

Mountain bike heaven

The town of **Gunnison** ❾, close to the upper end of Blue Mesa Reservoir, is home to **Western State College**. With a student body of 2,400 and a total population of only 5,400, one would expect this college town to be livelier than it is. The economy focuses

on outfitting fishermen, hunters and horseback riders for expeditions into **Gunnison National Forest**, a 1.7 million-acre (690,000-hectare) expanse of evergreen woodlands and towering granite peaks that reaches north to the Maroon Bells. Long, rocky forest roads follow creeks up into the mountains and provide access to pack trails for the West Elk, Raggeds and Maroon Bells-Snowmass Wilderness Areas.

The paved route into the national forest, CO 135, begins as Main Street and winds north along the Gunnison River headwaters for 28 miles (46km) to **Crested Butte** ❿, a former ghost town turned ski resort. The town's location, surrounded by four 12,000ft (3,655-meter) peaks, makes for magnificent views at any time of year, and the midsummer wild flower displays on the mountain slopes are among the best in the Rockies. Unlike most other historic ski towns, the ski runs, chairlifts, lodges and a 252-room resort hotel at Crested Butte Ski Resort (www.skicb.com) are located 2½ miles (4km) away in the modern village of **Mount Crested Butte**. Built in 1881 as a coal

BELOW: an overlook at the Black Canyon of the Gunnison.

Steam is used to block or shape a hat at an Aspen cowboy shop.

BELOW: mountain biking on the plateau near Fruita.

mining town for the railroad that ran through Gunnison, historic Crested Butte was declared a National Historic District at the same time ski area development began, so no new construction is allowed in town. Refurbished and carefully preserved, it's a town of eccentric little bed and breakfasts, gourmet restaurants and art galleries in old miners' cabins and saloons.

Even more than for its skiing, Crested Butte is famed for mountain biking. Colorado's most popular summer sport was invented here in the early 1970s by Neil Murdoch, a young hippie who adapted an old newspaper bike for riding on Jeep roads and trails. He organized the first "fat tire" bike races over the mountains between Crested Butte and Aspen and promoted them into Fat Tire Bike Week, the largest mountain bike event in America, which takes place each year in June. Then in 1999 federal officers showed up in Crested Butte with a warrant charging that Murdoch was a fugitive living under a false identity, wanted for failure to appear in court on a drug charge 25 years before. Mur-

doch, then in his fifties and a pillar of the community, eluded the officers and disappeared. His whereabouts are still unknown. Visitors can learn about him and about a hundred others who have helped develop the sport at the **Mountain Bike Hall of Fame** (331 Elk Avenue; tel: 970-349-6817; www.mtnbike halloffame.com; June–Sept 10am–8pm, Dec–Mar noon–6pm; charge).

There are more than 50 designated mountain bike trails in and around Crested Butte. Bikes are for rent all over town in the same shops that rent skis in the winter; guided bike tours are also available.

Up the river

Back on the main highway, US 50 continues east for 61 miles (100km), climbing above timber line to cross the Continental Divide over 11,312ft (3,353-meter) **Monarch Pass**, with its small ski resort and its summertime aerial tram (tel: 719-530-5000; www.ski monarch.com; May–Sept daily 8.30am–5.30pm; charge), before intersecting US 285 at the crossroads village of **Poncha Springs**. Drivers following

the loop route back to Aspen will turn north here, but first, why not take a break and stroll around Salida, 5 miles (8km) farther east on US 50?

According to the *Colorado Historic Preservation Review*, **Salida** ⑪ (pop. 5,000) has "the finest collection of historically significant buildings in the state." The main street leads through a classic residential area with tidy lawns on its way downtown, where metal plaques identify 78 historic buildings, many of them beautifully restored and now serving as art galleries and excellent small restaurants and cafés serving local foods. Salida is increasingly becoming a hot art destination and affordable retirement town, but, like its neighbor **Buena Vista**, it's best known as a jumping-off point for all kinds of outdoor activities, from mountain biking and climbing the nearby mountains to camping, hiking, and fishing.

In a category all by itself is the superb whitewater rafting and kayaking on the **Arkansas River Headwaters Recreation Area** (307 W. Sackett Avenue; tel: 719-539-7289; daily 8am–5pm). During the **FIBArk Whitewater**

Festival in June, 10,000 people come to town to take part in the oldest, longest whitewater race in the world. The 150-mile (240km) long stretch of the Arkansas River that runs from above Buena Vista to Cañon City, below Salida, is the most heavily run whitewater river in the country. Depending on the year, 250,000 people or so run it in the two-month whitewater season. The rafting industry is worth $26 million to the local economy.

Returning to Poncha Springs and heading north on US 285, it's 16 miles (26km) to the tiny village of **Nathrop**, the starting point for whitewater rafting trips through **Browns Canyon**, the only segment of the upper Arkansas River that does not run alongside a highway. In fact, the steep-walled canyon is only accessible by back road at one point in its entire 10-mile (16km) length.

Directly across the highway from Nathrop, a road climbs to **Mount Princeton Hot Springs** ⑫ (15870 CR 162; tel: 719-395-2447; www.mtprinceton.com; year-round). The original spa resort dates to 1879, when a three-story hotel was built on the site by the wealthy owners

The Black Canyon of the Gunnison is named because of the extreme steepness of the canyon walls. It is difficult for light to penetrate to the bottom, and the rock walls often appear black in the daytime.

BELOW: the signpost at Monarch Pass.

BELOW: the Leadville Ice Palace in 1876.

of a nearby mine. The hotel's fortunes waxed and waned over the years, and in 1950, it was disassembled for lumber and shipped to Texas to build a housing subdivision. The current resort was built in 1960. It has been completely renovated by new owners and now includes not only the lodge but new cabins by the river. The lap pool, soaking pool and spa are open to the public and have a grand view of 14,197ft (4,327-meter) **Mount Princeton**.

Although the pavement ends at the hot springs, the road continues for 15 miles (25km) around the south face of Mount Princeton to **Saint Elmo** , one of the best-preserved ghost towns in the state. Established in 1878, the old mining camp grew into a town of 2,000 people before its mineral wealth ran out and it was abandoned. As of the 2000 census, it had a population of eight. More than two dozen weathered wooden buildings are still standing, including a saloon, the old county courthouse and jail, the church and an unusual two-story outhouse, as well as a general store, which has reopened and operates from May through October.

Mount Princeton is part of a mountain range known as the **Collegiate Peaks**. Motorists driving north on US 285 will also pass **Mount Yale**, **Mount Columbia**, **Mount Harvard** and **Mount Oxford**, all over 14,000ft (4,270 meters) tall. Mount Harvard and Mount Yale were named in 1869 by a professor who escorted a group of Ivy League geology students to Colorado and climbed the 9 peaks. The others were named by members of the Colorado Mountain Club after their alma maters. At the foot of the range is **Buena Vista**, an unremarkable town of 1,800 that is the main commercial center for **South Park**, a bowl of grasslands and hills that stretches between the Collegiates and the west face of Pikes Peak. The large facility on the southern outskirts of town is the Colorado State Reformatory, Buena Vista's largest employer.

Twenty-two miles (35km) north of Buena Vista at **Twin Lakes**, a cluster of lodges and cabins near the shores of two reservoirs, CO 82 turns off and climbs over the Continental Divide for the return trip to Aspen. Before tak-

Leadville's Frozen Asset

In 1876, following the silver bust three years earlier, boosters in Leadville decided to recruit unemployed miners to build the world's largest ice palace. Five thousand tons of ice blocks were hoisted onto a timber framework, then sprayed with boiling water to seal them together, creating an ice palace covering 5 acres (2 hectares) and reaching 90ft (27 meters) tall, with twin towers and an enormous arched doorway. Inside, glittering in the glow of electric lights, were a restaurant, an ice rink, a dance pavilion, a carousel, a casino and toboggan runs. Admission was 50¢ and, although sold out regularly, the ice palace was a financial disaster and was never repeated. A model of the palace is on display in the Leadville Heritage Museum (*see opposite*).

ing it, though, sightseers will want to detour another 15 miles (24km) north to Leadville, a famous mining town as different from Aspen as can be.

Living in the past

At an elevation of 10,152ft (3,094 meters), **Leadville** ⓮ claims the distinction of being the highest town in the United States. It got a fitful start during the "Pikes Peak or Bust!" gold rush of 1859, but it was not until major deposits of gold and silver were discovered there 20 years later that its population exploded from 1,200 to 45,000 almost overnight, making it one of the largest cities in the state. Though it deflated just as quickly when silver prices collapsed in 1893, large-scale mining continued at the nearby Climax Molybdenum Mine until 1980. Today, a large percentage of the town's 2,600 residents ride the daily workers' shuttle to hotel jobs in Vail, 37 miles (60km) away on the other side of the Continental Divide.

Leadville has its share of scenic beauty, as walkers, bikers and joggers can see for themselves along the paved 12½-mile (20km) **Mineral Belt Trail**, which loops around the outskirts of town. There's camping and a full range of water sports (but no marina) at nearby **Turquoise Lake**, a large reservoir with a wooded shoreline. But Leadville's main attraction is its history. This is the town where some of Colorado's most famous historical figures struck it rich, such as Horace Tabor and his two wives, Augusta and Baby Doe; and J.J. Brown and his "unsinkable" wife Molly *(see page 153)*.

The best introduction to the town's colorful past is the **Leadville Heritage Museum** (102 E. 9th Street; tel: 719-486-1878; www.leadville.com; May–Aug 10am–6pm, Sept–Oct 10am–4pm; charge). In addition to memorabilia from the gold and silver days, the museum features an exhibit about the US Army's 10th Mountain Division, whose soldiers on skis trained in the surrounding mountains before and during World War II. The founders of the ski resorts at both Aspen and Vail first came to the region as part of the division and returned after the war.

Another peek at local history awaits just up the street in the **Healy House** (912 Harrison Avenue; tel: 719-486-0487; May–Aug daily 10am–4.30pm, Sept–Oct Sat–Sun; charge), a gingerbread mansion built for a mining engineer. Guides in Victorian-era costumes show visitors through the period-furnished rooms. Behind the Healy House, and included on the same ticket, is **Dexter Cabin**, built of logs by a prospector who later became one of the district's first millionaires and converted it into a gentlemen's poker club.

The **National Mining Hall of Fame and Museum** (120 W. 9th Street; tel: 719-486-1229; www.mininghalloffame.org; daily May–Oct 9am–5pm, Nov–Apr 11am–4pm; charge), dubbed "the Smithsonian of the Rockies," traces the history of hard-rock mining from the gold rush days to the present. Mining equipment, models, ore samples and fluorescent minerals are on display, along with exhibits about pioneer miners and prospectors.

Dolls, furnishings and other household objects are collected at the Leadville Heritage Museum.

BELOW: Tabor Opera House Museum.

The Matchless Mine earned more than $10 million.

BELOW: Baby Doe Tabor. **RIGHT:** looking down on Snowmass.

Although Horace Tabor, Leadville's famed silver tycoon, is not remembered for his philanthropy as other mining millionaires like Molly Brown and Winfield Scott Stratton are, he did make public contributions in the form of opera houses in several of the region's larger towns. In his home town of Leadville, it was the **Tabor Opera House** (308 Harrison Avenue; tel: 719-486-8409; www.taboroperahouse.net; May–Sept Mon–Sat 10am–5pm; charge). When it was built in 1879, it was said to be the finest theater between St Louis and San Francisco. Today, restoration is ongoing, but the theater hosts a full roster of summer concerts on the stage where Oscar Wilde, John Phillip Sousa and the Metropolitan Opera Company appeared – and Harry Houdini disappeared. (The trap door he used still works.)

Leadville's must-see attraction, the **Matchless Mine Cabin** (E. 7th Street; tel: 719-486-3900; daily 9am–4.45pm; charge), may not be much to look at, but it fairly crackles with history. This was the site where grocer and town mayor Horace Tabor made the rich silver strike that made him one of the wealthiest men in Colorado – until the crash in silver prices following the repeal of the Sherman Silver Act in 1893 left him a pauper. He was working in a Denver post office when he passed away. Legend has it that his dying words to his second wife, Baby Doe, were "Hold onto the Matchless as it will pay millions again." Although in fact the Matchless had already been foreclosed by creditors, Baby Doe Tabor lived in a converted storage shed on the property for the last 36 years of her life, hoping to recover title to the mine. She died there at the age of 80 during a blizzard in 1935.

Visitors who are intrigued by Baby Doe's story can see her depicted in a one-woman show performed on summer evenings at the Healy House.

The view from the top

Returning south to Twin Lakes, motorists who turn onto CO 82 (closed in winter) find themselves headed directly toward a wall of peaks that appears impassable. The road scales the near-vertical granite face by switchbacks to 12,095ft (3,686 meter) **Independence Pass** ⑮, the highest mountain pass in the United States that can be reached by paved road. At the summit, a trail leads across alpine tundra strewn in summer with thousands of tiny wild flowers, to an overlook from which on a clear day you can see at least 18 "fourteeners" – peaks that stand more than 14,000ft (4,270 meters) above sea level.

At the center of this breathtaking panorama, toward the southwest, you can pick out the easily recognizable shapes of the Maroon Bells, at the heart of the wilderness that lies between Aspen and Crested Butte. On the other side of the highway stands the summit of **Mount Elbert**, at 14,433ft (4,400 meters) the highest mountain in Colorado. The fact that it doesn't look all that big emphasizes how high the pass summit is. From here, CO 82 makes a somewhat more gradual descent into Aspen, completing this grand tour of the central Colorado Rockies. ❑

WESTERN COLORADO

Breathtaking canyons, Indian ruins,
dinosaur bones and a scrappy frontier
spirit lure travelers to the Western Slope

The Western Slope is where the Rocky Mountains give way to the redrock Canyon Country of the Colorado Plateau, a 130,000 sq mile (337,000 sq km) region uplifted by faults and carved by rivers into a maze of valleys, canyons and weathered mesas. Distances are great but settlements are small. Here, farmers, ranchers, and miners have shaped a way of life that is quiet, down-home friendly and close to the land.

The earliest settlers were prehistoric Ancestral Puebloans in southwestern Colorado and, in the northwest corner, Fremont Indians, who combined elements of Pueblo culture with a nomadic hunter-gatherer way of life. Their successors were nomadic Utes, whose descendants today occupy the Ute Mountain Ute Reservation near Cortez, and reservations in Utah.

After explorer John Wesley Powell made his famous survey of the Colorado and Green rivers in 1869 and 1871, the Western Slope began to attract Anglo settlers. Set along the Colorado River in the shadow of verdant Grand Mesa, Grand Junction, renowned for fruit, is now an important wine-making region, and outdoors mecca. To the west, the spectacularly eroded landscape of Colorado National Monument hosts avid mountain bikers and scenic drivers while the carved canyons of the Colorado River lure river runners for trips all the way to Moab, Utah. You can visit dinosaur trackways in Fruita, then continue north through the oil-rich Piceance Basin to Dinosaur National Monument, famed for the bones at its Dinosaur Quarry.

The southwest corner holds Western Colorado's most famous attractions: the beautifully preserved 13th-century Ancestral Pueblo mesa-top *pueblos* and cliff dellings at Mesa Verde National Park and Hovenweep and Canyon of the Ancients National monuments. Durango, with its charming narrow gauge-railway, its college, and outstanding nearby natural and cultural history, permits easy forays to the parks and along the winding San Juan Skyway to revived mining towns like Ouray, Silverton, and Telluride. ❏

PRECEDING PAGES: the road approaching Mesa Verde National Park.
LEFT: sunset at the Colorado National Monument. **TOP:** Dinosaur Journey Museum.
ABOVE RIGHT: taking the Cliff House tour at Mesa Verde National Park.

SAN JUAN MOUNTAINS

Abandoned mines, historic railways, white-knuckle roads and a vast mountain wilderness testify to tough frontier life in the Southern Rockies

In the 1870s, the silver mining camp of Galena City, 9 miles (15km) west of Lake City, seemed to investor George Lee to be destined for great things. It was close to the biggest silver mining claims in the Galena Mining District. It would soon be linked to the other important mining towns of Ouray and Silverton by a road over the high passes of the western San Juans. And if transportation king Otto Mears, the Russian immigrant known as the "Pathfinder of the San Juans," had anything to do with it, a branch of the railroad wasn't far behind.

Like Mears, Lee not only wanted to be wealthy, he wanted to be powerful. He dreamed of becoming governor of Colorado and turning Galena City into his own personal fiefdom. He had the name of the mining camp changed to Capitol City in anticipation of its being crowned state capital, and brought in bricks from Pueblo to build a grand governor's mansion, complete with a formal ballroom and a small theater with an orchestra pit. Lee's dream seemed within reach in 1877, when big silver strikes brought prosperity to the smelters at Capitol City and the population grew to 400.

By 1893, though, the bottom had dropped out of the silver market and, with the boom-and-bust mentality of the times, miners quickly moved on to gold mining in other parts of Colorado. Capitol City went the way of thousands of mining towns in the San Juans, which have vanished in the mountain mists. Today, it's a ghost town, with only the remnants of the old post office and Lee's brick smelter visible amid the aspens and evergreens beside Henson Creek.

Silent ghosts

Capitol City is one of 11 town sites established between 1875 and 1885 on a 65-mile (105km) long back country

Main attractions
ANIMAS MUSEUM, DURANGO
DURANGO & SILVERTON NARROW
  GAUGE RAILROAD
SILVERTON
SAN JUAN SKYWAY SCENIC BYWAY
OURAY
ALPINE LOOP
ORVIS HOT SPRINGS, RIDGWAY
TELLURIDE
DOLORES RIVER CANYON
PAGOSA SPRINGS
CHIMNEY ROCK ARCHEOLOGICAL
  AREA
WOLF CREEK SKI AREA
SILVER THREAD SCENIC BYWAY
CREEDE
LAKE CITY

LEFT: a cold mountain near Telluride.
RIGHT: a Durango cowboy.

The San Juans attract extreme sports enthusiasts. Mountain bikers compete in the Iron Horse Classic, racing the narrow gauge train from Durango to Silverton, or undertake the "Death Ride" – the whole San Juan Skyway in one day!

byway through the western San Juans known as the **Alpine Loop Jeep Trail**. The rugged route (most of it requires a high-clearance, four-wheel-drive vehicle) crosses 12,800ft (3,900-meter) **Engineer Pass** and 12,620ft (3,846-meter) **Cinnamon Pass**, offering glimpses of silent ghost towns, glaciated 14,000ft (4,270-meter) peaks, and glorious **American Basin**, where you can frolic knee deep in Rocky Mountain columbines, the state flower.

The loop links three towns. On the eastern end, in the central San Juans, is pretty little Lake City, at the northern end of the Silver Thread Scenic Byway. At the western end are Ouray and Silverton, two former Victorian mining towns on the 236-mile (380km) San Juan Skyway Scenic Byway. All three

towns are typical of the New West, where hundreds of former mining towns have sprung back to life under the care of new residents looking for a sense of community and history away from mainstream America.

Getting around

The San Juan Mountains are in the Southern Rockies and occupy about one third of what is called the Western Slope. The huge province stretches from the headwaters of the Rio Grande and the Continental Divide in the north to the New Mexico–Colorado state line in the south, and from the San Luis Valley in the east to the Utah–Colorado line in the west. The San Juans have more thirteeners and fourteeners than anywhere else in the Rockies, and within

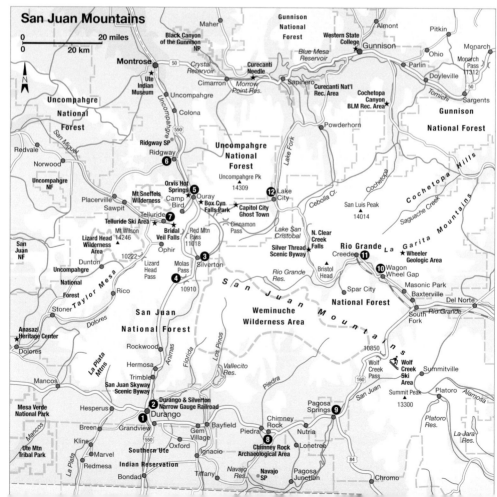

their boundaries are dozens of lesser ranges: the Needles and Grenadiers, the La Platas and La Garitas, and the Wilson Peaks and West Elks.

The vast majority of the country is public land managed by the National Park Service, Bureau of Land Management and US Forest Service. The Rio Grande, Uncompahgre, Gunnison and San Juan National forests encompass more than 2 million acres (4.1 million hectares) of the land mass. Easy access to public lands has made the San Juans a magnet for outdoor lovers. Horseback riding is popular throughout the southwestern corner, where almost every home has a corral and views of a mountain trail. The Rio Grande, San Juan, Gunnison and Dolores rivers, along with numerous high-country creeks and lakes, are renowned among fly fishermen for trout and other game fish. River runners choose from baby rapids on the Animas River and Class IV whitewater in the boulder-strewn Black Canyon of the Gunnison.

There's no more beautiful place than the San Juans in summer, when high mountain basins explode in eye-popping wild flower color beneath sharp granite peaks. Hikers have thousands of square miles to explore, on trails that range from easy day-hikes close to tiny mountain towns, to week-long backpacking trips in the Weminuche, Lizard Head and other wilderness areas. For a real San Juan experience, it's hard to beat a backpacking trip combined with a ride on the historic Durango & Silverton Narrow Gauge Railroad through the Animas River Canyon. By special arrangement, you can ride the train from Durango to the edge of the Weminuche Wilderness, then disembark and backpack directly into the mountains, as hundreds of passengers cheer you on your way. Now, that's a sendoff!

Crossroads town

Located at the junction of US 550 and US 160, **Durango ❶** (pop. 13,922) has a physically dramatic setting in the 6,500ft (2,000-meter) high desert, where the Southern Rockies and the Colorado Plateau meet. High red mesas and distant mountains enclose the town on three sides. Durango itself sits

WHERE

Keep an eye out for the strange landmark known as Lizard Head, south of Telluride off CO 145. This remarkable peak is rated in climbing circles as the ultimate challenge: the rock face goes straight up.

BELOW: the Durango Narrow Gauge Railroad Museum.

After years of decline, Durango's rail lines are busy again.

BELOW: guests at Durango's Strater Hotel have included Will Rogers and Western author Louis L'Amour, who wrote several novels while living there.

in a broad river valley created by the Animas River. The Rio de las Animas Perdidas (River of Lost Souls, named by Spanish explorers in the late 1600s) rises to the north in the San Juans near Silverton and has carved a deep canyon through the mountains. South of Durango, it parallels US 160 for a while, then heads south next to US 550 on its way to its confluence with the San Juan River.

Durango is the only sizeable town in southwest Colorado. It was founded by the railroad in 1880 and operated as a supply center and smelter town. After mining declined, many of the town's elegant Victorian brick and wood buildings were abandoned and Durango fell on hard times. Things changed in the 1950s, when **Fort Lewis College** relocated from Hesperus to Durango. It was just the shot in the arm this conservative company town needed, infusing Durango with a youthful energy and expanded vision that has brought the streets alive and ensured a healthy mix of businesses and cultural activities much of the year.

Many of the students who attend Fort Lewis College stay on as residents. Some have helped restore the numerous old redbrick buildings, "painted ladies" and "gingerbread" mansions, turning them into businesses, private residences and unique inns. One bed and breakfast, the 8,000 sq ft (740 sq meter), turreted **Gable House** (805 E. Fifth Avenue; tel: 970-247-4982), served as the town's hospital from 1913 to 1962.

A self-guided walking tour booklet describing many historic homes can be picked up at the **Animas Museum** (3065 W. 2nd Avenue; tel: 970-259-2402; www.animasmuseum.org; May–Oct Mon–Sat 10am–6pm, Nov–Apr Tue–Sat 10am–4pm; charge), which occupies the old schoolhouse; or the **Durango Area Tourism Office Association** (tel: 800-463-8726; www.durango.org), open daily in **Gateway Park**, a pleasant greenway next to the Animas River.

Durango's newest attraction is the expanded **Durango Discovery Museum** (133 Camino del Rio; tel: 970-259-9234; www.durangodiscovery. org; currently Wed–Sat 10am–5pm,

The Strater Hotel, Durango

In historic downtown Durango, everything stops for the Durango & Silverton Narrow Gauge Railroad, which makes an eight-hour daily round trip through the Animas Valley on the 45-mile (72km) line between Durango and Silverton. You'll have a grandstand view if you stay near the depot at the venerable Strater Hotel (699 Main Avenue; tel: 800-247-4431; www.strater.com), built in 1887 by Henry Strater at a cost of $70,000. The five-story redbrick building has 93 guest rooms, each furnished with period antiques, lace curtains, and old-fashioned beds. You'll find a good number of the local population in the lively Diamond Belle Saloon in the evening. The bar hasn't changed much in a century. A melodrama theater is located next door, adding to the authenticity.

Sun 1–5pm; charge). In March 2011, the hands-on scientific learning center opened in its new home in the 1893 Powerhouse, the oldest standing coal-fired, steam-generated AC current power plant in the country. The theme of the museum is Energy: Past, Present, and Future, and includes exhibits on man-made and natural ensergy generation as well as the Durango Discovery Kids program (formerly the Children's Museum).

Return of the railroad

Tourism is the other cornerstone of Durango's economy. After World War II, growing numbers of people began visiting nearby Mesa Verde National Park, the oldest and most popular archeological park in the country. Improved highways have helped connect this remote area with the rest of the Southwest and have boosted the population. The icing on the cake was the revival of the Durango & Silverton Narrow Gauge Railroad in 1991. The echo of the steam train whistle and puffy clouds of locomotive smoke and cinders rising above the valley gives

Durango a romantic charm rooted in an authentic past.

The **Durango & Silverton Narrow Gauge Railroad** ❷ (479 Main Avenue; tel: 970-247-2733; www.durangotrain. com; charge) operates May to October, with limited excursions in winter. Two trains leave early in the morning from the depot for a 3½-hour ride through Animas Canyon, which, for a while, parallels US 550, then heads into the mountains, clinging to the side of the Animas River Canyon, sometimes 400ft (120 meters) above the river. The steam train makes scheduled stops at the private resort of Tall Timber, Needleton and Elk Park (where you can get off and hike into the wilderness, by special arrangement), arriving in Silverton around noon. At 2.45pm, the train returns to Durango, but many people elect to ride a chartered bus home, shaving an hour off the return time.

You can banter with your neighbors and the train conductor if you ride the tightly packed, open-air gondolas, which are interspersed between parlor cars, throughout the train. If you opt for a gondola, wear dark clothing that

A cocktail waitress at the famous Diamond Belle Saloon at the Hotel Strater in Durango.

BELOW: the Durango & Silverton Narrow Gauge Railroad.

won't be ruined by flying cinders. And don't forget a jacket. Summer in the mountains means afternoon thunderstorms and chilly temperatures. Come prepared.

Silver by the ton

Like Durango, the 1874 mining town of **Silverton ❸** (pop. 550), established in an area called Baker's Park, has benefited from the train and its location on the San Juan Skyway. The whole of Silverton is a designated National Historic District, and there's plenty to see and do in the couple of hours you will spend here. Handlebars Saloon, with its parade of stuffed game animals on the walls, buffalo burgers and spit-and-sawdust atmosphere, is typical of many businesses in the historic Downtown, where residents spring into action to serve as many hungry customers in as short a time as possible each day.

Take time to stroll Blair Street, the old redlight district, and imagine what Silverton was like in its wilder days. Ex-miners lead tours of **Mayflower Gold Mill National Historic Site** (tel: 970-

387-0294; May–Oct) 2 miles (3km) east of town on SR 110.

You can also tour **Old Hundred Gold Mine** (tel: 970-387-5444; www.minetour.com; daily May–Oct 10am–4pm; charge), 3 miles (5km) beyond the Mayflower, where an electric train will take you to the heart of Galena Mountain on a narrated one-hour tour through the mine's various shafts and tunnels. Both mines offer gold panning in a stream as part of the tour. Many people find at least a small flake, which can be placed in a vial and taken home.

San Juan County Historical Society Museum (Greene Street; tel: 970-387-5838; www.silvertonhistoricsociety.org; May–Sept 9am–5pm, 10am–3pm through mid-Oct; charge), located in the four-story, 1902 sheriff's home next to the courthouse, at the north end of town, commemorates Silverton's more law-abiding past. The home doubled as the county jail, and you can still see cells and hammocks used by prisoners and view a variety of memorabilia, from Derringer guns to old toll road tickets. Admission

Silverton Rhubarb

The growing season lasts barely a couple of months at high-elevation Silverton, but one wild crop actually grows quite prolifically here without any help from gardeners – rhubarb, which can be found sprouting in gardens all over town in late June. Actually a vegetable not a fruit (only the stalk is edible; the leaves and root of the plant are toxic), rhubarb requires heavy sweetening before it can be the starring attraction in home-made pies, cobblers, crisps, and crumbles.

If you are a rhubarb fan, don't miss Silverton's famed International Rhubarb Festival over the Fourth of July weekend, where local chefs and enthusiasts compete to put rhubarb in as many dishes (and other products) as possible. Rhubarb beer, anyone?

includes entry to the new adjoining **Mining Heritage Center,** a recreation of the experience of hard-rock mining, complete with clammy tunnel and mining exhibits.

Silverton's small size and remoteness attract residents with an independent, creative streak. Ex-miners, artists, writers, psychologists, hikers, extreme snowboarders, ecologists, even snow scientists (this is prime avalanche country) rub elbows here in this quintessential mountain town far from the madding crowd.

This laid-back style is also a feature of Silverton's unadorned approach to outdoor activities. **Silverton Mountain Ski Area** (tel: 970-387-5706; www.silvertonmountain.com) and the inexpensive, family-oriented **Kendall Mountain Recreation Area** offer downhill and extreme skiing and snowboarding in one of the most natural settings in southwestern Colorado. In addition, miles of groomed trails beckon cross-country skiers, snowshoers, snowmobilers and sledders. In summer, hiking and mountain biking are just a chairlift ride away on Silverton Mountain. Jeeping is also popular on the Alpine Loop Jeep Trail and other mining routes. Get help planning a trip into the mountains, purchase maps and books, or sign up for an ecotour of the San Juans at the multiagency **Silverton Public Lands Center** (1246 Blair Street; tel: 970-387-5530; Mon–Fri 9am–5pm, Sat–Sun 10am–4pm).

Million dollar view

For drivers on the San Juan Skyway Scenic Byway, the descent to Silverton is dramatic. The Grenadier Mountains rise in the east as the road switchbacks down 10,910ft (3,325-meter) **Molas Pass ❹** into the Silverton valley, then climbs out again in a series of sharp twists and turns through the mountains. This has been called one of the most awe-inspiring scenic drives in the world, with good reason. The modern road follows the original single-track toll road built by Otto Mears in 1884,

using a route taken for centuries by Ute Indians. Not much has changed since. You will need to keep your eyes tightly on the road and pull off to admire the scenery; there are a number of steep dropoffs here. Those who suffer from vertigo may want to consider a different route.

The section between Silverton and Ouray is dubbed the **Million Dollar Highway**. It may have received its name because it cost a million dollars to build. Others say it's because gold ore was used in the roadbed. But more likely, it's because, as you climb the highest point, **Red Mountain Pass** (11,018ft/3,358 meters), the views make you feel like a million bucks, even if you don't have a penny.

Until the mines in the **Red Mountain Mining District** closed, there was much wealth to be had here. More than a hundred mines yielded 4 million ounces of gold, 21 million ounces of silver, and 12 million tons of lead, zinc and copper. Thomas Walsh, an Irish immigrant who struck it rich when he bought the Camp Bird Gold Mine in Ouray in 1896, was even able

In the 2010 census, the population of Silverton was registered as 527.

BELOW:
the mining town of Silverton is a National Historic Landmark District.

to buy his daughter Evalyn the Hope Diamond, the world's largest.

In the 1980s, the 17 sq mile (44 sq km) Red Mountain area became one of the first Superfund Cleanup sites in the country. It has undergone extensive reclamation by mining giant Idarado, and 10,500 acres (4,250 hectares) will eventually be acquired through the congressional Land and Conservation Fund and added to the adjacent San Juan and Uncompahgre National forests and Ouray County Parks for public recreation (www.fortlewis.edu/red mountainproject.com). Stop at the pullout just south of Ouray for views of mine shafts and the Treasury Tunnel Trestle, the eastern end of the tunnel linking the Idarado mine with the **Pandora Mine**, 2 miles (3km) from Telluride.

Alpine town

Ouray ❺ (pop. 400), named after the famous Ute chief, is often called the "Switzerland of America," and it's easy to see why. This charming little town, founded in 1875, is walled in on all sides by mountains that go straight up in the most extraordinary fashion,

leading to the Mount Snefells Wilderness in the west and the Weminuche Wilderness in the east. US 550 goes right through Ouray, where, since the 1970s, people have been buying modest miners' shacks and mining mansions and restoring both the infrastructure and a strong sense of community. After years of being boarded up, the 1886 **Beaumont Hotel** (505 Main Street; tel: 970-325-7000; www. beaumonthotel.com) reopened in 2003, following a painstaking $7 million private restoration. Its restaurant, the Tundra, has gourmet dining, and you will often find regional authors reading in the **Buckskin Booksellers store** (tel: 970-325-4044; www.buckskin booksellers.com), which specializes in Western literature.

The energetic volunteers who run the **Ouray County Museum** (420 6th Avenue; tel: 970-325-4576; May–Oct Mon–Sat 9am–6pm, Sun 1–6pm, call for off-season hours; charge) are proud of the fact that the Smithsonian Institution called their home town museum "The Best Little Museum in the West." Mining museums are

ubiquitous throughout the San Juans, but the Ouray Museum, housed in the 1887 brick hospital, is a cut above the rest. Each of the rooms of the old hospital offers a window to the past, recreating the Soda Fountain and General Store; Dr Spangler's Office; the Patients' Hospital Room: the Operating Suite; the Transportation Room; the Victorian Child's Play-room; and the Ute Indian room, dis-playing arrowheads and an old stuffed brown bear named Nemo.

Water seems to be everywhere in Ouray. Don't miss the waterfall in **Box Canyon Falls Park** (3rd Avenue; tel: 970-325-4464; 8am–dusk; charge), snugged into a canyon 20ft (6 meters) wide and 285ft (87 meters) high. This lovely misting fall is visited by rare black swifts in summer and is used by ice climbers in winter. The faulting that pushed up the San Juans some 25 million years ago has led to many hot springs in the Ouray area. Bathing in the million-gallon public hot springs pool on the north of town is your cheapest bet and a magical way of soothing away the kinks from the road.

Around Ridgway

Jeeping is big news in Ouray. Several outfitters offer tours of the nearby mountains, or you can rent a Jeep Wrangler with humungous tires and head out alone. The western entrance to Alpine Loop Jeep Trail, just south of town, starts off very rough and gets rougher on its ascent to Engineer Pass and Lake City. Even more popular are Yankee Boy Basin and Imogene Pass, west of town, which take you through the Mount Snefells Wilderness to Tel-luride. Imogene Pass is the most direct route to Telluride from Ouray but cer-tainly not the fastest. For that, you'll need to continue on US 550 to **Ridg-way ⑥** and turn left onto US 145.

Historic **Orvis Hot Springs** (tel: 970-626-5324; www.orvishotsprings.com; daily 9am–10pm; charge), located in a beautifully landscaped, rustic set-ting on US 550, a few miles south of Ridgway, offers the rare opportunity to bathe *au naturel* in seven bathing-suit-optional pools that range from 97°F to 105°F (36–41°C). There's a warm, homey feeling at this surpris-ingly affordable establishment, with a

Ouray is famous for its Ice Festival in January, an international gathering of ice climbing enthusiasts who climb frozen waterfalls in Ouray Ice Park.

BELOW: Ouray nestles in a narrow valley at an elevation of 7,760ft (2,365 meters).

kitchen, first-come, first-served private tubs, Dr Bronner's peppermint soap in the bathroom, beautifully renovated guest rooms and campsites. A bonus: Overnight guests can access the pools 24 hours.

If the open high country around Ridgway looks familiar, that's because it provided the backdrop for the 1969 Western movie *True Grit*, starring John Wayne. Quiet, unpretentious Ridgway has an interesting history. It was founded by railway pioneer Otto Mears, whose epic story in bringing the railroad to western Colorado is told through indoor and outdoor exhibits in the old railroad depot at the **Ridgway Railroad Museum** (150 Racecourse Road; tel: 970-626-5181; www.ridgwayrailroadmuseum.org; May–Oct daily 9am–4pm, Nov–Apr Mon–Fri 10am–3pm; free).

Mears also helped negotiate the 1873 Brunot Peace Treaty with Ute Chief Ouray that finally succeeded in banishing the majority of Utes to the Uinta Ute Reservation in northeastern Utah, leaving behind a a small number at the Ute Mountain Ute Reservation,

near Cortez, and the Southern Ute Reservation, headquartered at Ignacio, south of US 160.

The forced Ute exodus opened the way for mining in 1874, but you can still feel the American Indian presence throughout the San Juans in the colorful place names, in the spring Bear Dance held at Ignacio, the Council Tree Powwow site at Delta, and the impressive Ute Indian Museum, just south of Montrose.

Ridgway is a tight community, with a local farmers' market on Sunday mornings and down-home restaurants serving barbecue and Western fare. It's popular with celebrities who like its setting in an open mountain basin, the proximity to Durango and Telluride, and relative anonymity. Gulf War general Norman Schwartzkopf owns a home here, and designer Ralph Lauren has an enormous ranch west of town. Ridgway also has another celebrity connection: its **Billings Artworks** (tel: 970-626-3860; www.billingsartworks.com), run by Buffalo Bill lookalike John Billings and his son, is the gallery/foundry for the Grammy Awards.

When Butch Met Sundance

It's thought that they met at a horse race in the Cortez area. Harry Longabaugh had an eye for the ponies, having spent time on a cousin's ranch. Robert Leroy Parker, a wayward Mormon rancher's son from Utah, had a brother who worked nearby. By 1888, Parker, known to all as George "Butch" Cassidy, had joined forces with Cortez ranchers Matt Warner and Tom McCarty to race Warner's mare Betty, the fastest in the Four Corners. Now, with their winnings spent on drink and gambling, the men were looking for easy money.

Tom McCarty suggested robbing a bank. Warner, a seasoned outlaw, agreed. It was Cassidy who suggested the gold mining town of Telluride, one of his old haunts. Far from anywhere, the robbery would be easy to pull off. For good measure, he'd pay the marshal to leave town.

On June 24, 1889, Warner, Cassidy, McCarty and another man later identified as Longabaugh arrived in Telluride and proceeded to steal between $10,000 and $30,000 from the San Miguel Valley Bank. Shortly thereafter, Cassidy and some of the Wild Bunch had their photo taken and mailed to the bank, dressed to the nines. It included Longabaugh, who had been released from Sundance jail in Wyoming a month before the robbery. The legend of Butch Cassidy and the Sundance Kid had been born.

To Hell and back

There's little anonymity in **Telluride** ➐, but that's fine with folks there. Situated on the San Miguel River, in a dramatic box canyon in the mountains, the mining town began life as a mining camp in 1876. Most say it was named for its Tellurium, the non-metallic matrix that sometimes bears both gold and silver, although a few suggest the name was a play on the expression "to Hell you ride," an apt description of its early days.

With the arrival of the Rio Grande Southern Railroad, Telluride grew into a respectable and prosperous town with a formal hotel, the **Sheridan**, and an adjoining opera house that once presented Sarah Bernhardt, Lillian Gish and William Jennings Bryan. Far from other communities, Telluride's prosperity made it vulnerable. In 1889, Butch Cassidy and his gang of outlaws carried out their first robbery at the San Miguel Valley Bank.

Telluride was rediscovered in the 1970s, when a ski resort opened here. Today, there's no getting away from the hip quotient in Telluride. Expensive homes, condo developments, fancy restaurants, day spas, cyber cafés and an inordinate amount of real estate offices and glossy home-grown lifestyle magazines are much in evidence, and Tom Cruise, Oprah Winfrey and Sylvester Stallone are among the movie stars with homes here.

But, remarkably, Telluride has not sold out. That's largely due to the original homeowners in the 1970s – many of them lawyers – who purchased old buildings in the historic Downtown and immediately enacted tough preservation laws to prevent the runaway growth that has ruined another popular ski resort town: Aspen. Telluride proves that controlled growth doesn't have to mean monoculture. All the hallmarks of a real community are here: a lively Downtown of architecturally pleasing, old and new buildings; a variety of businesses; good social services and an interest in healthy living; people of all income levels, skin colors and nationalities; and a big heart (look for the free boxes of food Downtown). Beneath the welcome sign at the entrance to town is another sign stating "Citizen Rights Safe Zone." They really mean it.

This open-door policy is most visible in the arts. The year-round program of readings, lectures by scientists and other thinkers, and summer festivals (the most in the country) is more indicative of what you'd find in an arts town like Santa Fe. It's remarkable in a town of 2,360 people. Major festivals include Mountain Film over Memorial Day weekend; Telluride Blues and Brews, held the third weekend in September; and Telluride Film Festival, over Labor Day weekend.

Cheap fun

Although Telluride can be on the pricey side, you don't have to have big bucks to have a good time. Among free activities are the popular day hike 2½ miles (4km) east of town to view 365ft

With a year-round population of only 2,360, Telluride retains a friendly, small-town atmosphere.

BELOW: Telluride's Mountain Village is a great place for summer fun.

A Sioux dancer performs at a Durango powwow.

BELOW: at a height of 365ft (111 meters), Bridal Veil Falls outside Telluride is the highest in Colorado.

(111-meter) high **Bridal Veil Falls**, the highest in the state; the Friday afternoon **Farmers' Market** on South Oak Street; and the **Telluride Ski Gondola Ride** to **Mountain Village**, part of **Telluride Ski Resort** (565 Mountain Village Boulevard; tel: 970-728-6900; www.tellurideskiresort.com), which offers great views of the town.

Hiking and camping are, of course, the cheapest ways to get to know a place. You can hike for days in the 41,296-acre (16,712-hectare) **Lizard Head Wilderness**, southwest of Telluride, reached via CO 145 over 10,222ft (3,116-meter) high **Lizard Head Pass**. There are several, well-run US Forest Service campgrounds in the vicinity of **Ophir Pass** (the Matterhorn Campground has hot showers). From here, you have good views of the 14,000ft (4,270-meter) high **Wilson Mountains**, where some of *True Grit* was shot. In 1891, this area became the first in America to use commercially generated electricity, by Nicola Tesla's alternating current (AC) method, to process ore.

The San Juan Skyway loop continues south on CO 145 to rejoin US 160, following the beautiful Dolores River through its deep canyon to **Cortez** and **Mancos**. The 1879 mining town of **Rico** lived up to its Spanish name, meaning "rich," with one of the richest mines in Colorado history: the Enterprise. But no one got rich until the Rio Grande Southern Railroad blasted a route through the mountains in 1891, reducing by 90 percent the cost of hauling ore from Telluride and Rico to smelters at Durango. As you head south on CO 145, you follow the route of the railroad through the Dolores River Canyon. The **Railroad Museum** in **Dolores**, housed in the restored rail depot, has more information on the historic railroad and also displays one of the San Juan's famous "Galloping Goose" train cars, which were created in the 1930s from converted autos.

The central San Juans

There's lots to see and do on the San Juan Skyway loop. Perhaps too much. Things are much quieter east of Durango, on US 160. The highway leads through Pagosa Springs and over majestic Wolf Creek Pass, then turns north on the 75-mile (121km) **Silver Thread Scenic Byway** through the central San Juan Mountains on US 149. You'll find all the fascinating high-country mining history, outdoor activities and small-town charm of the San Juan Skyway here, but spread out on a much larger canvas.

Roughly halfway between Durango and Pagosa Springs, on US Forest Service-managed lands, is **Chimney Rock Archeological Area ❽** (Route 151; tel: 970-883-5389, visitors' cabin in season 970-264-2287; www.chimneyrockco.org; May–Sept 9.30am–4.30pm; guided tours by volunteers 9.30 am, 10.30am, 1pm and 2pm; charge), an essential for anyone interested in the

prehistoric archeology of southwest Colorado. These *pueblo* ruins, located close to the Piedras River, were excavated in the 1930s, then more extensively in the 1970s and 1980s by archeologists from the University of Colorado at Boulder.

Theories about Chimney Rock vary, but two different cultures appear to have occupied the site during the Classic Pueblo period. One group was composed of local people who had gradually worked their way up the river system from the Animas and Pinos Rivers to the Chimney Rock site above the Piedras River Valley in the 1000s. They seem to have been joined by a group with connections to Chaco Canyon, who built a Chaco outlier next to the twin Chimney Rocks in the 11th century. Their main purpose at Chimney Rock seems to have been to cut wood for use in construction at Chaco.

The presence of Chaco kivas and a great house next to a major landmark leads archeologists to believe that the community – probably mostly single men – was conducting ceremonies at the site. There is strong evidence that skywatching priests calculated the lunar standstill by tracking the passage of the moon and planets through the rocks.

Healing waters

Pagosa Springs ❾ has the largest public hot springs in the West. These pools were important to the Southern Ute people, whose reservation lies nearby, and to early Spanish explorers. The 150°F (67°C) waters are used to heat some of the town's buildings. A variety of developed pools at the attractive Springs resort, next to the river, have been cooled to between 96° and 105°F (36°–41°C) and are open to the public daily. Pagosa Springs (pop. 1,744) serves as the hub for a vast outdoor recreational industry, providing access to the **Wolf Creek Ski Area** (tel: 970-264-5639; www.wolfcreekski.com). This affordable family ski resort is easily accessible from Durango and sees the heaviest snow in Colorado (465ins/11.8 meters

a year on average). The rest of the year, it serves as a jumping-off point for hiking, rafting, snowmobiling, fishing and hunting trips.

Head over Wolf Creek Pass and drive north on US 149 to the headwaters of the Rio Grande and the heart of the San Juans. There's an opportunity to gas up and buy supplies at the junction community of **South Fork**, then you will quickly find yourself heading into the great open spaces of the Silver Thread Scenic Byway, which winds across the Continental Divide to the Gunnison River Valley.

The road parallels the Rio Grande through **Wagon Wheel Gap** ❿. The hot springs here were used by Utes, who also found special significance in the rock formations in the **Wheeler Geologic Area**, a few miles to the east, which at one time was preserved as a national park but has since been downgraded. After the Utes were removed to reservations in the mid-1870s, this area saw an influx of Eastern and European tourists, enticed by descriptions of the Upper Rio Grande Valley in books such as *Ingersoll's Crest*

The Pagosa Springs area made news on September 23, 1979, when a hunter killed a female grizzly bear in self-defense at the headwaters of the Navajo River. Some scientists believe that a breeding group of grizzlies remains in the area.

BELOW: you can enjoy the springs and the sunset at the same time.

Chaps await eager dudes at a San Juan guest ranch.

BELOW: these boats in Telluride are just waiting for a captain.

of the Continent and *Crofutt's Gripsack Guide*. The Barlow and Sanderson stagecoaches made daily runs between the towns of San Luis Valley, Lake City and Wagon Wheel Gap. By 1883, the Denver & Rio Grande Railroad was transporting tourists to the rail depot in town, and people were coming to "take the waters" at hot springs resort hotels. You can still see the historic bathhouse at the 4UR Ranch, one of a number of ranches that profited from tourism.

Where it's day all night

In 1890, Nicholas Creede and George Smith discovered a high-grade silver vein in Willow Creek, a tributary of the Rio Grande, and a late silver rush was on. Prospectors from all over Colorado hurried to the mining camp. Almost overnight, the new town of **Creede ⑪** grew to 10,000 residents, many of them occupying hastily constructed shacks in a series of settlements strung along the narrow valley. Silver fever was so high that people worked day and night, prompting local newspaperman Cy Warman to pen a ditty in 1892 with the refrain: "It's day all day in the day time, And there is no night in Creede."

Lawman Bat Masterson, ex-teacher Poker Alice Tubbs, conman Soapy Smith and other Wild West characters no longer stroll the streets of tiny Creede (pop. 400), but you half expect to run into them at places like the **Creede Hotel** (120 N. Main Street; tel: 719-658-2608; www.creede hotel.com), which has the best dining in town. The hotel is next door to the **Creede Repertory Theatre** (124 N. Main Street; tel: 719-658-2540; www.creederep.org), frequently cited as one of the best theater companies in Colorado. The **Underground Mining Museum** (407 N. Loma; tel: 719-658-0811; May–Sept daily 9.30am–3pm, Oct–Apr Mon–Fri; charge) authentically recreates a mine from the late 1800s. Don't leave without driving the 17-mile (27km) **Bachelor His-**

toric **Loop** through Creede's mining district, which begins in the canyon north of Downtown.

A growing number of bed and breakfasts, art galleries and other businesses attest to the fact that Creede has been discovered. Increasingly popular as a weekend getaway for hiking, fishing, skiing and exploring the outdoors, Creede's location off the beaten track has so far protected it. The small population includes ex-miners, artists and writers like Pam Houston, author of *Cowboys Are My Weakness*, who, a few years ago, fell in love with the San Juans and bought a ranch near town.

Land of lakes and forests

Once you get beyond Creede, you're in big country, where distant ranches and jewel lakes dot high-country moors and forested mountains managed by the Gunnison and Rio Grande National Forests and the Bureau of Land Management. Many people come to fly-fish the headwaters of the Rio Grande, reached by turning west from the main highway just before **Bristol Head**, a massive eroded headland that dominates the eastern horizon. Just beyond Bristol Head is **North Clear Creek Falls**, tumbling down a series of black, volcanic boulders into a narrow canyon. Archeologists have found evidence of paleo-hunter use from 10,000 years ago here, making it one of the highest-elevation Folsom sites known.

At the northern end of the Silver Thread Scenic Byway is **Lake City** ⓬, named for **Lake San Cristobal**, the second largest natural lake in Colorado, 3 miles (5km) south of town. The lake, a favorite with boaters, was created when the massive **Slumgullion Slide** blocked the Lake Fork of the Gunnison River. Lake City was a prominent Victorian supply town for mines in the Galena and Lake Mining Districts, growing from a single cabin built by toll road pioneer Enos Hotchkiss in 1874 into a town of 500 in the

1880s. Wagon roads, stagecoach service and the railroad helped Lake City grow and allowed it to make a quick transition from mining to tourism in the 1900s.

Today, Lake City's pristine setting, nestled in the shadow of 14,309ft (4,361-meter) high **Uncompahgre Peak**, draws thousands of vacationers. It is one of western Colorado's most scenic yet accessible towns and the only one in Hinsdale County, which is 97 percent public lands. The historic Downtown retains an authentic Victorian ambience and has one of the largest historic districts in Colorado. For more information, stop at the **Hinsdale County Visitor Center**, north of Downtown, which has maps, walking tour brochures, and information on public lands access, the nearby Alpine Loop Jeep Trail, and the ghost towns of **Carson, Sherman** and **Burrows Park**. CO 149 follows the Gunnison River north to its junction with US 50, where the tour ends along the shores of the dammed Gunnison River, now preserved as **Curecanti National Recreation Area**. ❑

Creede has been listed as one of the 100 Best Small Art Towns in the West and in 2010 won the Governor's Arts Award (with Telluride) for its support of the arts.

BELOW: taking a break next to the Indian Paintbrush on the Alta Lake Trail in Telluride.

MESA VERDE AND THE SOUTHWEST CORNER

Four states and a collage of ancient and modern cultures come together in a region that is home to one of the nation's great national parks

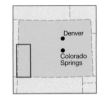

The southwestern region of Colorado is quite different in appearance and feeling from elsewhere in the state. Politically, it's an anomaly: the unique conjunction of four states – Colorado, New Mexico, Utah and Arizona – in an area known as the Four Corners. Geographically, it's the boundary between two geologic provinces: where the Southern Rockies bump up against the 130,000 sq mile (340,00 sq meter) Colorado Plateau, a mile-high uplift carved by wind and water into mazelike canyons, crumbling mesas and ebony-hued volcanic crags. But most of all it's a meeting place of cultures, both ancient and modern, with roots reaching far back into prehistory.

People have hunted, gathered and farmed on the mountains, river valleys and mesa tops of southwestern Colorado for thousands of years. Nowhere is this more evident than at Mesa Verde National Park, which, since 1906, has preserved 4,400 archeological sites, including 600 cliff dwellings, built by the ancestors of today's Pueblo people between AD 550 and 1300 atop a verdant mesa in the Mancos Valley. Thousands more sites lie on the adjoining Ute Mountain Ute Reservation and the surrounding Great Sage Plain. Mesa Verde National Park, Hovenweep National Monument and

Canyons of the Ancients National Monument are all part of the longer **Trail of the Ancients**, a scenic byway that winds through the Four Corners, visiting Indian reservations, museums, parks, archeological centers and miles of extraordinary scenery.

Cortez

The trail begins in the small ranching and farming town of **Cortez ❶**, a convenient base for exploring the area and well supplied with visitor facilities. Your first stop should be the **Cortez**

Main attractions

CORTEZ CULTURAL CENTER
MESA VERDE NATIONAL PARK
UTE MOUNTAIN UTE RESERVATION
ANASAZI HERITAGE CENTER
CANYONS OF THE ANCIENTS NATIONAL MONUMENT
HOVENWEEP NATIONAL MONUMENT
CROW CANYON ARCHEOLOGICAL CENTER
UNAWEEP-TABEGAUCHE SCENIC BYWAY
URAVAN
UNAWEEP SEEP RESEARCH NATURAL AREA
WHITEWATER

LEFT: Cliff House at Mesa Verde National Park. **RIGHT:** Anasazi Heritage Center.

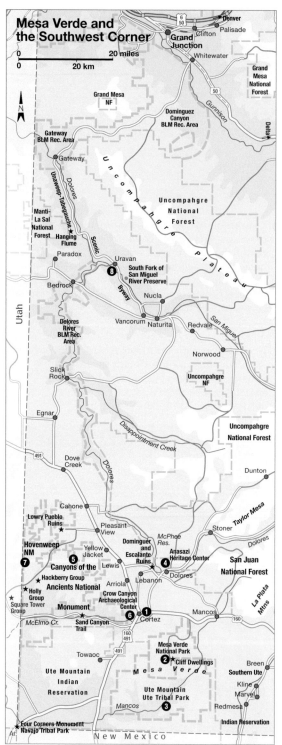

Mesa Verde and the Southwest Corner

0   20 miles
0   20 km

N

Cultural Center (25 N. Market Street; tel: 970-565-1151; www.cortezcultural center.org; May–Sept daily 10am–10pm, shorter hours off-season), run by the University of Colorado. Housed in a 1909 historic building in the Western-style Downtown, the center is a great place to get oriented to the area. Its museum has interpretive exhibits on the Basketmaker and Ancestral Pueblo people who lived in the Four Corners for 1,300 years, as well as some of the area's best interpretation of the contemporary Navajo and Ute Mountain Ute tribes, whose reservations lie to the south. Daily cultural presentations between Memorial Day and Labor Day include Native American storytelling and lectures, dances and day tours to archeological sites.

Ancient dwellings

Foremost among the archeological sites in the area is, of course, **Mesa Verde National Park ❷** (tel: 970-529-4465; www.nps.gov/meve; year-round; charge). Mesa Verde was the first national park to be set aside to preserve the works of mankind and remains a favorite with

Far View Lodge

If you want to splurge on a luxurious hotel room and a special dinner while visiting Mesa Verde National Park, Far View Lodge might just be the place (tel: 866-875-8456; mid-April–mid-Oct, reserve well ahead). Located across the street from the visitor center, the lodge looks like a plain motel from the outside, but don't judge too quickly. Every room has an extraordinary view of the San Juan Basin as well as a private balcony where you can enjoy the drama of the sudden summer thunderstorms that sweep across the desert. The Metate Dining Room has equally stunning views. The restaurant serves new Southwest cuisine featuring elk, bison, trout and other local delights – definitely a cut above standard park fare.

visitors, who regularly vote it America's top national park. Mesa Verde lives up to the hype. In few places in the Southwest do the works of man blend with a natural landscape of such beauty and rich resources. Moreover, it's a large park – some 54,000 acres (22,000 hectares) spread over the fingerlike Chapin and Wetherill Mesas – and there's a lot more here than Cliff Palace, which was discovered in 1888 by the Wetherill brothers.

There are numerous mesa-top pithouses – for example, the partially underground homes of choice for the Basketmakers, ancestors of the Ancestral Pueblo people who began to congregate in above-ground *pueblos* in the 700s. There are traces of fields, too, where residents once grew large quantities of corn, beans and squash. Standing in the cliff dwellings, you can just make out the chiseled toeholds in the vertical cliffs, where people once climbed up to their fields and down into the canyons to hunt mule deer, rabbits and other game. Mesa Verde's success stemmed largely from the people's skill in using all of the resources of their land and

their adaptation of new technologies, such as agriculture, basketweaving and pottery, learned through contact with people from the south.

Still, you have to wonder, what would it be like to spend a particularly snowy January here? Despite Mesa Verde's pronounced southward tilt and abundance of moisture, winter night-time temperatures, even in a south-facing *pueblo*, can't have been comfortable. Visit here in winter, and you'll find out. Although Cliff Palace, Balcony House and the ruins along the 12-mile (19km) Wetherill Mesa Road are closed, the Ruins Road on Chapin Mesa is kept clear year-round. Chances are you will have many of the ruins all to yourself.

This is when **Spruce Tree House Ⓐ**, the park's second largest ruin, behind **Park Headquarters** and **Chapin Archeological Museum Ⓑ** (daily Apr–Oct 8.30am–6.30pm, Nov–Mar 8am–5pm) comes into its own. Warm and dry under the overhang, you can linger in this lovely side canyon in the park's best preserved and most accessible ruin, watching rufous-sided towhees scratching in the duff below

Scientific studies abound at the Crow Canyon Archeological Center.

BELOW: the Sun Temple was incomplete when Mesa Verde was abandoned in the late 13th century. A sun dial at the site indicates that it may have been used to monitor the change of seasons.

BELOW: Long House, the second largest cliff dwelling at Mesa Verde, was occupied for about a century by 150 to 175 people.

pinyon pines laden with snow. The spirits of the Ancestral Pueblo people feel close at hand. You can easily imagine them, robed in warm cloaks of hide and feathers plucked from domesticated turkeys, anxiously observing the movements of the sun, moon and planets for signs of the winter solstice and warmer days ahead.

Far View

Winter travelers begin their visit at Chapin Archeological Museum, a great place to view examples of distinctive black-on-white pottery, bone and wood tools, yucca sandals and clothing and other artifacts. In summer, stop first at **Far View Visitor Center** Ⓒ (summer only 8am–5pm), 15 miles (24km) beyond the park entrance, to buy tickets for hour-long, ranger-led tours of **Cliff Palace** and **Balcony House** ruins on Chapin Mesa. After 5.30pm, tickets for next-day tours are available at Chapin Mesa Archeological Museum.

Those hoping to do the Chapin Mesa tours and the 90-minute tour of **Long House** Ⓓ, the park's second largest cliff dwelling, in one day should plan

carefully. It's a 45-minute drive to less developed Wetherill Mesa from here, on a winding road with stops at Long House, **Two Raven House, Badger House Community** Ⓔ and **Kodak House** Ⓕ, so named because Gustaf Nordenskiold, the Swedish archeologist who worked with Richard Wetherill, stashed his camera nearby. Visitor facilities at Badger House and Step House were badly burned in the 2000 Pony Fire, which swept across Wetherill Mesa. Recovery will take decades.

Another early archeologist (and later park superintendent), Jesse Walter Fewkes, named **Far View** (elev. 7,700ft/2,350 meters), one of a number of mesa-top *pueblo* communities that used Mesa Verde between AD 900 and 1300. From here, 100-mile (160km) vistas take in Ship Rock, the Chuska, Lukachukai, and Carrizo Mountains, and the Monument Valley Upwarp on the Navajo Reservation, south of the San Juan River. Sleeping Ute Mountain marks the Ute Mountain Ute Reservation to the west. To the northwest are the Abajo and La Sal Mountains adjoining Arches and Canyonlands

National Parks in Utah. And to the northeast are the La Plata Mountains, one of several ranges in the San Juan Mountains, near Durango, an alternative base for travelers in this area.

Cliff Palace

Mesa Verde architecture displays little of the elegant construction that characterizes the great houses and kivas at Chaco Canyon, to the south, which was abandoned long before these cliff dwellings were built. But as Chacoans began to move to the northern San Juan area, it seems logical that some of that culture's architectural ingenuity would have influenced Mesa Verdean masons. **Cliff Palace** ● is justifiably celebrated for its beauty and harmonious construction, and, as at Chaco, the effort that went into its planning suggests that these were public buildings for use by the whole community.

The minimal number of hearths and burials tells archeologists that Cliff Palace was occupied by a small population. Some were almost certainly priest astronomers who left behind red calendar markings on the smooth plas-

tered interior of one of the tower kivas. These are no mystery to contemporary descendants at pueblos like Santa Ana in New Mexico. Ritual leaders continue to use such markings to monitor the skies and plan annual crop ceremonies around the solstices.

Over on the other side of the mesa, **Balcony House** ●, a rare east-facing structure, has several shallow basins pecked into the floors of its rooms – also thought to be associated with astronomical observation. Like Cliff Palace, Balcony House is divided down the middle by a wall, suggesting a social division of some kind among its 50 estimated residents. A small *pueblo*, 600 dizzying ft (180 meters) above the canyon, Balcony House has an intimacy that will linger in the memory long after you leave Mesa Verde. The children won't forget it, either, as they scale ladders and squeeze through tunnels to enter and exit the *pueblo*.

As many as 5,000 people may have lived at Mesa Verde during the Classic or Pueblo III era (AD 1100–1300). In the Pueblo II era (AD 900–1100), the region was part of a vast trading net-

The Crow Canyon Archeological Center offers opportunities to volunteer, explore and research the people of the southwest.

A rusty sign directs visitors to a ranch in the Four Corners region.

BELOW: exploring Cliff Palace; T-shaped doorways are characteristic of Ancestral Puebloan construction.

work bringing items from as far away as Mexico and the Mississippi Valley for redistribution at Chaco Canyon. When Chaco collapsed, the people of Mesa Verde became more insular, perhaps in an effort to protect the attractive resources in their homeland and avoid the same fate as their neighbors to the south.

Defensive measures?

Archeologists are unsure why Mesa Verdeans began to build their pueblos in alcoves in the canyon walls in the 1200s. Some think that worsening drought and diminishing firewood and other natural resources forced the people to use creative new ways of survival. Cliff dwellings were well suited to the protected canyons of the Four Corners. They made good use of solar energy, and springlines seeping through the porous sandstone cliffs into the back of the alcoves offered a ready water source. People living there were hidden from view but could still climb to the mesa tops to work fields and travel into the dense pinyon-juniper and oak forests of the canyons to hunt and gather.

It's hard to escape the conclusion that the cliff dwellings were used to defend the population against an external danger, perhaps the burgeoning population on the Great Sage Plain or incoming Utes, Navajos and Apaches vying for Pueblo lands. No mass deaths have been found at Mesa Verde, but there are signs of ritual violence throughout the Four Corners. As a 24-year drought settled in, and powerful ceremonies failed to bring rain, one can imagine the despair that must have gripped the people of the Four Corners as the land that had always supported them failed. By 1300, Mesa Verde was empty. Today, some 24 pueblos, including the Hopi villages in Arizona, and Zuni, Acoma and the Rio Grande *pueblos* in New Mexico, trace their ancestors to Mesa Verde.

Exploring the Four Corners

As increasing numbers of people moved to Mesa Verde in the 1100s, space was clearly at a premium. Mesa-top sites at the head of narrow canyons in the northern San Juan region, which offered water, agricultural land and good places to build multistory *pueblos*, quickly began to fill up. Soon, people were spilling out all across the Four Corners in search of suitable places to live. A number of these sites have been restored and are open to the public. Often undeveloped, they offer a chance to escape the crowds at Mesa Verde and learn more about the people who once lived in the Four Corners.

A case in point is **Ute Mountain Ute Tribal Park ❸** (tel: 970-749-1452, tour reservations 800-847-5485; www.utemountainute.com/tribalpark; open seasonally), which adjoins Mesa Verde on the south. The Weminuche Ute who live on this small reservation are one of seven Ute hunter-gatherer bands that were living in the Four Corners by the 1400s. Forced onto a small reservation in southern Colorado in 1873, Chief Ignacio and 11 other Ute leaders were persuaded to lease Mesa Verde to the government for 10 years to pro-

tect it from pothunters. The Utes lost that land permanently in 1906, when President Theodore Roosevelt created Mesa Verde National Park. In 1911, the government took another 14,000 acres (5,700 hectares) from the Utes, including Balcony House. The part of Mesa Verde that remained under Ute control was set aside as a tribal park in the 1960s.

Today, the Ute Nation and the National Park Service work closely together to protect archeological sites, and in summer, for a fee, the Utes offer guided back country tours to sites in the tribal park. Easy half-day tours take in Ancestral Pueblo petroglyphs, scenic lands, Ute pictographic panels, geological land formations and surface sites. The more demanding full-day tour visits four well-preserved canyon cliff dwellings in Lion Canyon, reached by a 3-mile (5km) hike and climbing ladders to the cliffs. To sign up, call or stop at the tribal park visitor center. Check-in time is 8.30am for a 9am departure. Gas up and be prepared to drive your own car across the reservation: 40 miles (64km) for the half-day

trip and 80 miles (130km) for the full-day excursion. You should wear a hat, good shoes and sunscreen, and bring plenty of water and a lunch; these are not available on the tour. Gas, food and lodging are available at Towaoc and nearby Cortez.

Archaeology center

Several other archeological sites in the vicinity of Cortez make good day trips. Don't miss the attractive **Anasazi Heritage Center** ❹ (27501 Highway 184, Dolores; tel: 970-882-5600; www.co.blm.gov/ahc/hmepge.htm; daily Mar–Oct 9am–5pm, Nov–Feb until 4pm; charge), 10 miles (16km) north of Cortez, off CO 184. The Anasazi Heritage Center's museum will be a surprise to those accustomed to the dated exhibits often found at national parks. It was built by the Bureau of Reclamation to house 2 million artifacts that were excavated from the nearby Dolores River Canyon before it was lost forever under McPhee Reservoir. More than a million artifacts from excavations in the Four Corners have been deposited here, making it the single best research center in the area.

WHERE

The spot where Colorado, Utah, Arizona and New Mexico meet is preserved as Four Corners Monument Navajo Tribal Park (daily; charge). Navajo and Ute vendors sell foods and crafts at booths near the flapping flags of the survey marker.

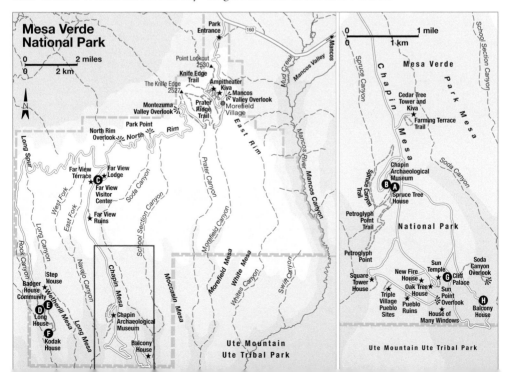

Hovenweep, a Ute word meaning "Deserted Valley," is less developed than Mesa Verde.

BELOW: archeologists excavate a site associated with the Crow Canyon Archeological Center.

Operated by the Bureau of Land Management, the center has an impressive museum that will appeal to children and adults alike. Interactive exhibits offer a variety of ways to understand why archaeology is important. Large photographs show step-by-step excavations of nearby sites. Computers allow you to make a virtual tour of an ancient *pueblo*. Smaller artifacts are located in drawers and can be opened and examined. You can even try your hand at grinding corn using a metate (grinding stone) and mano (hand stone). Pueblo women spent hours doing this each day. It's not as easy as it looks.

The Anasazi Heritage Center is the headquarters for 164,000-acre (66,000-hectare) **Canyons of the Ancients National Monument ❺**, located to the west on Cajone Mesa. This new BLM-managed national landscape monument contains the highest known density of archeological sites in the nation – 6,000 so far, and some areas have more than 100 cultural sites per square mile – spanning 10,000 years of use. It remains largely unknown and undeveloped, so it's important to stop at the Heritage Center (*see previous page*) and pick up information on visiting. The monument incorporates one previously excavated and restored site: **Lowry Pueblo National Historic Landmark**, a 40-room *pueblo*, with eight kivas and a rare great kiva that archeologists believe must have served as a ceremonial center. To reach Lowry, turn west onto County Road CC at the south end of Pleasant View and drive 9 miles (14km) to the site. Booklets for the self-guided wheelchair accessible trail are available at the trailhead.

CO 10 continues south through the monument. It's a lonesome place, with views across the Four Corners and south to Monument Valley. You can hike almost anywhere, but this is not a place for the uninitiated. It's easy to get disoriented. If you want to hike, your best bet is 6-mile (10km) **Sand Canyon Trail**, a one-way route from the monument south to Road G in McElmo Canyon. Although it's rugged, this is a popular trail, attracting some 17,000 hikers each year.

Dominguez and Escalante Ruins

The Anasazi Heritage Center in Dolores is located next to the Dominguez and Escalante ruins, named for the two friars who became the first Spaniards to travel through the region in 1776. These ruins are small but significant. The four-room Dominguez Ruin, built in AD 1123, contained the burial place of a female of high status who was interred with a variety of grave offerings, including 6,900 turquoise, jet and shell beads and a unique shell-and-turquoise frog pendant.

The larger Escalante Ruin, at the top of the hill, was built in 1129 by Chaco immigrants and is one of the northernmost of Chaco's many outliers. It was reoccupied by Mesa Verdeans in 1150, then again in 1200.

Digging in

Research in Sand Canyon has been carried out for a number of years by **Crow Canyon Archeological Center** ❻ (23390 Road K, Cortez, CO 81321; tel: 800-422-8975; www.crowcanyon.org; daily), a private institution located near **Sand Canyon Pueblo**, a few miles west of Cortez. Ongoing excavations here have established that 420-room Sand Canyon Pueblo, at the northern end of the trail, was one of the largest *pueblos* to be occupied in the final decades of occupation of the Mesa Verde region. It has 100 kivas and 14 towers. Field work at the smaller **Castle Rock Pueblo**, at the southern end of **Sand Canyon Trail**, revealed that the occupation there ended with a battle – one of the best documented examples of warfare from the ancient Southwest.

If you've ever wanted to know what archaeology is like on the ground, this is the place to find out. You can make a reservation to participate in the ongoing dig at Sand Canyon or accompany staff to a variety of archeological sites in the area. Longer residential courses include Cultural Exploration programs with leading Pueblo scholars and hands-on activities, such as weaving and ceramics with Native American artisans.

Although primitive camping on monument roads is permitted at Canyons of the Ancients National Monument, it has no developed camping facilities. However, there is an excellent little campground at nearby **Hovenweep National Monument** ❼ (tel: 970-562-4282; www. nps.gov/hove; daily; charge), one of those delightful, unexpected parks that remain relatively undiscovered.

Six 12th- and 13th-century Mesa Verde-style buildings, built in unusual round, square and D-shaped towers, line the rim of **Little Ruins Canyon** at this small national monument, between Blanding, Utah, and Cortez, Colorado. Two short rim trails lead from the new visitor center and campground to Square Tower Group, Hovenweep Castle and other structures used by prehistoric farmers.

River of sorrows

Although drought led Ancestral Pueblo people to abandon the Four Corners, the area around Cortez now supports

Sewemup Mesa on the Unaweep-Tabeguache Scenic Byway got its name for the outlaw practice of cutting off brands on rustled cattle, sewing them up with baling wire and rawhide, and rebranding them with another rancher's brand.

BELOW: Lowry Pueblo, Canyons of the Ancients National Monument.

numerous ranches and small farms. They raise bumper crops of beans, an important staple for ancient Pueblo people. Farming on this scale in the Cortez area is relatively recent. It was made possible by irrigation water brought onto the Great Sage Plain by the damming of the Dolores River, the "river of sorrows" named by early Spanish explorers. Finish up your tour by turning right on CO 141, just beyond **Dove Creek**, and following the pretty Dolores River as it winds north into the redrock country of western Colorado. CO 141 eventually reaches **Naturita**, the start of the spectacular **Unaweep–Tabegauche Scenic Byway**, which continues to **Whitewater**, just south of Grand Junction.

There's nothing sorrowful about this scenic byway, which may be the best-kept secret in Colorado. It's an absolute joy to drive the quiet highway through verdant mountains and soaring redrock canyons carved by the Dolores and San Miguel rivers. In the 1800s, these remote canyons were a favored hideout for cattle rustlers from Utah. One of these places, the evocatively named

Sewemup Mesa, is one of the most pristine ecological environments in western Colorado, encircled by 1,000ft (300-meter) high Wingate cliffs. The clifftops are home to peregrine falcons and golden and bald eagles, which fish the Dolores River from high ledges.

Uravan

Until it closed, **Uravan** ❽ was a major producer of uranium, radium and vanadium for the nuclear industry, processing 42 million lbs (19 million kg) of uranium and 220 million lbs (100 million kg) of vanadium between 1936 and 1984. A $70 million cleanup project is stabilizing the tailings above the old Joe Jr Mill. In 1888, the Montrose Placer Mining Company built a 13-mile (21km) hanging flume in the side of Dolores Canyon to bring water from the San Miguel River for gold processing at Mesa Creek Flats. Abandoned three years later, the disintegrating wooden flume can still be seen high above the river rapids.

North of here, CO 141 turns northeast away from the Dolores River, exiting at Whitewater on the northern end of the verdant Uncompahgre Plateau, which offers numerous recreational opportunities for hiking, mountain biking, camping and four-wheel-drive explorations. Beyond Gateway, the road passes through a magnificent valley, with redrocks on the west and high mountains composed of 1.7-billion-year-old rocks on the east. For anyone who loves canyons *and* mountains, it is simply heaven on earth. A New York capitalist, Lawrence Driggs, evidently thought so, too. Between 1914 and 1918, he hired local stone masons to construct a hunting lodge on 320 acres (130 hectares) of land near Gateway, using water from West Creek. The Driggses moved here in 1918 and stayed just a few weeks. The ruined mansion now sits abandoned and vandalized in a lush pasture near Unaweep Seep Research Natural Area, an important breeding ground for rare Nokomis fritillary butterflies. ❏

The Utes

Once nomadic, two remaining bands of Ute Indians live on reservations on Colorado's Western Slope: The Ute Mountain Ute, near Cortez and the Southern Utes, near Ignacio

The Utes, from the Spanish word *yuta*, were named by the first Spaniards to trade with them in Taos, New Mexico, around 1610. They call themselves the Nuche, or The People, and speak the same Uto-Aztecan language as the Aztecs, Hopis, Comanches, Paiutes and Shoshones, the latter their close relatives. They may have entered northwestern Colorado from the Great Basin – or, as some Utes believe, northern Mexico – between 500 and 800 years ago. Like their Archaic forebears, they were consummate hunter-gatherers. They began doing some informal farming after entering the canyon country of western Colorado, possibly after mingling with Fremont Indians in the area.

By historic times, there were six Ute bands in Colorado. The Mouache band's territory included the eastern Rockies, the San Luis Valley and northern New Mexico, where they mingled with the Kapote band. The Weminuche lived in the canyon country of the Four Corners. These three bands are known as the Southern Utes. The Kapote and Mouache bands now occupy the Southern Ute Reservation, east of Durango. The Weminuche live on the more traditional Ute Mountain Ute Reservation, south of Cortez.

The largest Ute bands occupied northwestern Colorado and were known as the Northern Utes. Chief Ouray's band – the Tabegauche or Uncompahgre Utes – lived in the Gunnison and Uncompahgre valleys, where they hunted atop 10,000ft (3,050-meter) high Grand Mesa and wintered near Montrose and Delta. North of the Tabegauche were the Parianuc or Grand Valley Utes, who lived along the Colorado River, and the Yampa band, who lived in the Yampa River Valley.

These two bands were renamed the White River Utes after Nathan Meeker established an Indian agency in Meeker. Tragedy struck Meeker, when in an effort to get Utes near Craig to take up farming, he plowed up their horse racetrack, triggering a fist fight, Army involvement, the massacre of soldiers,

Meeker, and eight of his men, and the taking of white women as hostages, a crisis that led to the White River Utes and Chief Ouray's band being forced to move to the vast Uintah Basin of east-central Utah in 1880. The bleak landscape had so few resources it was said even the birds wouldn't fly over it.

After accepting land allotments on the Southern Ute Reservation in 1863, the Mouache and Kapote bands led by chiefs Severo and Buckskin Charley were forced to become farmers, an activity scorned as women's work by the skilled hunters. Chief Ignacio and the Weminuche band held fast to a traditional way of life for decades, living in tents on the undeveloped Ute Mountain Ute Reservation until well into the 1930s.

Today, Colorado Utes have finally bowed to the inevitable and taken up Anglo pursuits, such as farming, ranching, construction, tourism, gaming and motel-keeping. Even so, traditional Ute gatherings still take place. The annual Chipeta Day, for example, is held every September at the Ute Indian Museum, south of Montrose, on Ouray's old farm, where his second wife Chipeta and her stepbrother John McCook are buried. It includes dancing, food, traditional beaded handicrafts, movies, silent auctions, and other activities. All three reservations still perform the Bear Dance every spring, a multiday event that celebrates the end of winter, a transition signified by a bear waking up from hibernation. ❑

RIGHT: Ignacio, leader of the Weminuche Utes, photographed in 1898.

COLORADO WINE COUNTRY

Warm, sunny days and cool nights create perfect grape-growing conditions on Colorado's Western Slope, jump starting the growth of more than 100 wineries throughout the state

Since Stephen Smith founded Grande River Vineyards in 1987, one of the largest grape-growing operations in Colorado, wine production has grown from some 279 liters to a million liters a year, contributing an estimated $42 million to the state economy and a further $20.6 million from increasingly popular wine-based tourism. Colorado has two areas that have been designated American Viticulture Areas (AVAs): the Grand Valley AVA, around Grand Junction, and the West Elks AVA, in the North Fork Valley of the Central Rockies between Paonia and Delta, both of which have the right growing conditions and make wine on-site. Two other regions make wine from grapes grown on the Western Slope: the Four Corners region, around Durango, and the Pikes Peak and Arkansas Valley of the Front Range. Of these, Grand Junction and its eastside suburbs of Palisade and Fruita, along the Colorado River, have by far the greatest number of wineries – 24 at last count. Conditions here favor Bordeaux-type red wines such as Merlot and Cabernet Sauvignon, while the North Fork is known for its whites and Rieslings. Increasingly, however, wine makers are blending grapes grown in both regions, so that these days you may also find excellent Rhones like Syrah and Chardonnays in Grand Junction and Pinot Noir, Pinot Gris and Cabernet Franc in the North Fork Valley.

ABOVE: Isabella Bird described finding wild grape vines growing on the mountain slopes near Estes Park in *A Lady's Life in the Rocky Mountains*, published in 1879.

ABOVE LEFT AND RIGHT: the vines at Garfield Estates in Palisade are self-rooted rather than grafted, and the soil is predominantly clay loam, which is rich in mineral content.

LEFT: the Colorado wine industry suffered a setback when the state went dry in 1916, four years before Prohibition.

CREATIVE WINE MAKERS

Wine, like art, is a creative medium, suited to artisans with an iconoclastic streak. Two such Colorado vintners both happen to have British roots and are winning international acclaim for their complex boutique wines. Sutcliffe Vineyards, in the Four Corners, is cultivated by John Sutcliffe, whose eclectic career has included a stint in the British Army, high-end restaurateur, cowboy, and now vintner. Sutcliffe Vineyards' pastoral acreage in Mancos Canyon near Cortez is about as idyllic as it gets, a perfect setting for the owner's gourmet wine dinners, guest stays and exploring nearby Pueblo ruins. Ex-Londoner Ben Parsons, whose Infinite Monkey Theorem Winery is housed in an old Quonset hut in the arts district of Denver, is equally passionate about the wine experience but the setting couldn't be more different. Parsons learned wine-making in Australia and the Western Slope but decided to strike out on his own to make wine that sings to his particular soul. His deep, fruity wines can be found at top Denver restaurants, where chefs have embraced this wine maker's passion for wines with a strong urban identity.

ABOVE: grapes are harvested using a combination of traditional manual labor and modern harvesting machines.

LEFT: a vineyard beneath the palisades in Mesa County. The town of Palisade is known mostly for it's peaches, but recent growth in the wine industry is making big news for oenophiles.

RIGHT: the Colorado Association for Viticulture and Enology was formed in 1982.

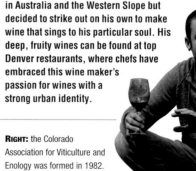

THE NORTHWEST CORNER

Dinosaur fossils, redrock canyons and raging rivers are just a few of the attractions in a rugged country where the intrepid John Wesley Powell unveiled the wonders of a great Western landscape

C olorado's least developed region, its northwestern corner, has begun to be discovered. This is due, in part, to cyclical oil, gas, uranium and coal mining booms that have periodically swelled the population and led to the construction of good highways and rail links. But mostly it's because of the presence of Dinosaur National Monument and the growth of recreation in the gorgeous Colorado redrock canyons surrounding Grand Junction (pop. 53,662), the main shopping center for the region and a logical base for explorations.

Junction, as locals call it, is located just north of the confluence of the Colorado and Gunnison rivers, in the majestic **Grand Valley**. With the forest-clad Rockies to the east and the mile-high Colorado Plateau to the west, the broad valley carved by the Colorado River has one of the loveliest settings of any city in the Southwest. To the north is Interstate 70 closely paralleling the imposing facade of the Book Cliffs. To the south is the Uncompahgre Plateau, the only place apart from the Continental Divide where two rivers – in this case the Uncompahgre and Dolores – divide and flow east and west, respectively.

On its northern end, the orange sandstone of the Uncompahgre Uplift has been carved by wind, water and ice into vertical cliffs, monuments and headlands that offer endless possibilities for recreation in **Colorado National Monument** and adjoining **McInnis Canyons National Conservation Area**.

Grand Mesa

Recreation is also plentiful on the forested volcanic plateau known as **Grand Mesa**, 35 miles (56km) east of Grand Junction. An outdoor-lover's paradise, 10,000ft (3,000-meter) high Grand Mesa is the highest flat-topped

Main attractions
GRAND MESA
PALISADE
CLIFTON
FRUITA
GRAND JUNCTION
COLORADO NATIONAL MONUMENT
MCINNIS CANYONS NATIONAL CONSERVATION AREA
CANYON PINTADO NATIONAL HISTORIC DISTRICT
DINOSAUR NATIONAL MONUMENT (UTAH)
HARPERS CORNER SCENIC DRIVE (COLORADO)
ECHO CANYON
CRAIG
MEEKER
RIFLE

LEFT: Grand Mesa National Forest.
RIGHT: Cross Orchards Historic Site.

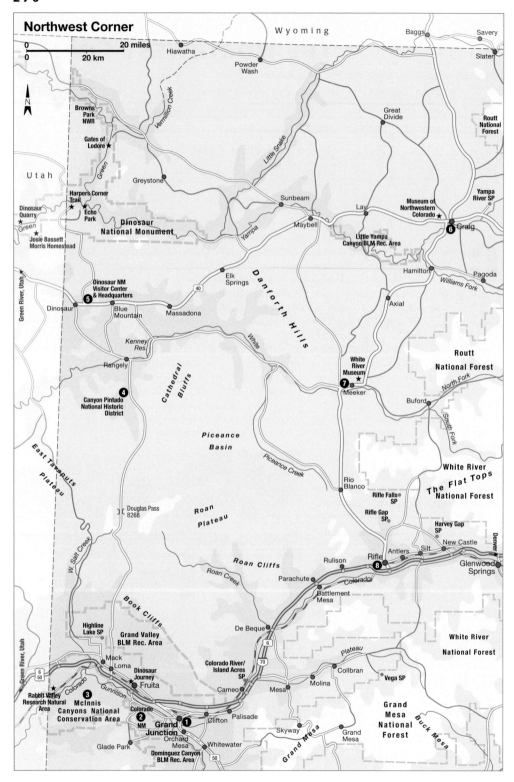

mountain in the world. Its cool forests, 200 sparkling lakes and numerous back country trails beckon to hikers, campers and fishermen all summer, when temperatures in the valley reach 100°F (38°C). In winter, "The Mesa," as it's called, becomes a haven for cross-country and downhill skiing, snowmobiling and other snow sports, and is a popular place for weekend geta,ways at rustic lodges with views all the way to the farmlands of the Uncompahgre and Grand Valley.

Located on the banks of the Colorado River, Grand Junction itself grew up around the railroad in 1881. It has been known as a commercial center ever since. Early settlers capitalized on the ready irrigation water and planted peach and apple orchards and vineyards, which today still thrive in the pretty suburbs of **Clifton, Palisade** and **Fruita.** Grand Junction's loveliest bed and breakfasts are located in these leafy communities, where you can spend lazy days strolling and bicycling, wine tasting, fruit picking, and admiring the spectacular cliffs surrounding the valley.

Sadly, **Grand Junction** ❶ itself, squeezed between I-70 on the north and the Colorado River on the south, seems to be losing the fight with urban sprawl. New housing developments and miles of "big box" superstores, chain hotels and restaurants on the wide avenues leading from I-70 have given the city a nondescript Anytown-USA appearance. This is a pity because there's lots to see and do in this historic city, once you get your bearings.

Grand Junction

Start in the restored historic Downtown, near the railroad station. In 1963, Junction received nationwide acclaim for its **Downtown Shopping Park**, an attractive, five-block Main Street redevelopment that features restored historic brick buildings housing shops, galleries and the city's best restaurants, breweries and cafés. One of the highlights of the Downtown is its innova-

tive **Art on the Corner** project, which was launched in 1984 and features life-size sculptures on annual loan to the city from local artists. A stroll along the tree-lined, curving streets makes for a fun art walk on a warm summer evening.

When Exxon dropped a multi-million-dollar oil-shale extraction project in nearby **Parachute** in 1984, Grand Junction fell on hard times, with nearly 15 percent of its homes vacant by 1989. But the city has worked hard to improve amenities, which has had a positive effect on its cultural institutions. The restored 1923 **Avalon Theatre** (645 Main Street; tel: 970-263-5700; www.tworiversconvention.com) is the linchpin of Downtown, hosting plays, concerts and other entertainment throughout the year. **Mesa State College**, founded in 1925 and located halfway between I-70 and Downtown, is a four-year liberal arts college. It is home to the stylish **Western Colorado Center for the Arts**, otherwise known as the **ART Center** (1803 N. 7th Street; tel: 970-243-7337; www.gjartcenter.org; Tue–Sat 9am–4pm; charge, Tue free),

Sunflowers nod in the breeze at a farm outside Grand Junction.

BELOW: Rifle Gap State Park.

Mountain bikers use Fruita, west of Grand Junction, as a jumping off point for some seriously scenic bike riding through the redrock canyons of Colorado National Monument and McInnis Canyons National Conservation Area.

BELOW: Red Rock Canyon Overlook, Colorado National Monument.

where you'll find historic and contemporary works by Western artists and special exhibitions all year.

Junction's main cultural institution, the **Museum of Western Colorado**, is the largest museum between Denver and Salt Lake City. It has three branches. Downtown's **History Museum** (5th Street and Ute Avenue; tel: 970-242-0971; www.museum ofwesternco.com; Apr–Oct Mon–Sat 9am–5pm, Nov–Mar Tue–Sat 10am–3pm; charge) is an accessible, modern museum featuring a one-room schoolhouse, a uranium mine, Indian pottery, guns and many other exhibits (look for the one on Alferd Packer, the infamous "Colorado Cannibal").

East of town, in **Clifton**, you'll find the open-air, **Cross Orchards Historic Site** (3073 F. Road; tel: 970-434-9814; Apr–Oct daily Tue–Sat 9am–4pm; charge). Cross Orchards is living history at its best, recreating traditional farm life in one of Colorado's largest apple orchards. Exhibits include a blacksmith shop, a bunkhouse, a barn and packing house, and the historic orchards, where you can buy fruit in

fall. Living-history demonstrations take place daily between April and October, and there are numerous special events, including arts and crafts workshops and displays of traditional farming methods.

The most popular branch of the museum for children is **Dinosaur Journey** (550 Jurassic Ct, Fruita; tel: 970-858-7282; May–Sept daily 9am–5pm, Oct–Apr Mon–Sat 10am–4pm, Sun noon–4pm; charge), west of town, in Fruita. Dinosaur Journey has a strong novelty feel, with its TV-generation exhibits and half-size robotic Dilophosaurus, Utahraptor, Apatosaurus and other dinosaurs. But it is also perfectly located to teach kids about real-life paleontology. Just up the street, at the east and west entrances to Colorado National Monument, are **Riggs Hill** and **Dinosaur Hill**, where paleontologists from the museum conduct ongoing fossil digs. **Rabbit Valley Research Natural Area,** 24 miles (39km) west of Grand Junction, is another area rich in dinosaur bones.

Colorado National Monument ❷ (tel: 970-858-3617; www.nps.gov/colm;

Browns Park

Browns Park is about 80 miles (130km) northwest of Craig, via a rough road that crosses a swing bridge over the Green River into Browns Park National Wildlife Refuge. The valley was a rendezvous point in the 1820s and 1830s, where mountain men traded with Comanche, Ute, Cheyenne, Arapaho and Navajo hunters. Homesteaders arrived in 1873, and by the 1880s, the valley's isolation attracted outlaws like Butch Cassidy and the Wild Bunch, who used it as a remote hideout from the law. The 44-mile (71km) section of the river between Little Hole Boat Launch and Little Swallows Canyon has easy Class I flatwater, several hiking trails and free campgrounds. Private whitewater river trips through Dinosaur National Monument are by lottery permit only. Annual deadline for applications is February 1.

daily June–Sept 8am–6pm, Mar–May, Oct–Nov 9am–5pm, Dec–Feb 9am–4pm; charge) is the top scenic drive in Grand Junction. From the west entrance at Fruita, 23-mile (37km) long **Rimrock Drive** winds onto 2,000ft (6,000-meter) high redrock cliffs on the south side of Grand Valley and is one of the most popular scenic mountain bike rides in an area famous for its biking. More than a dozen scenic vistas offer views of the Colorado River, Grand Junction, the Book Cliffs, Grand Mesa, and the eroded headlands, monument rocks and odd-shaped hoodoos of the monument. This landscape "felt like the heart of the world" to pioneer John Otto, who lived alone in the wild canyons. Otto built miles of trails through the area and helped get it set aside as a monument in 1911. He served as the park's first caretaker until 1927.

Campers can either spend the night in the park's pleasant campground near Saddlehorn Visitor Center, or turn south at East Glade Park Road and drive to a BLM campground within the 122,182-acre (49,445-hectare)

McInnis Canyons National Conservation Area ❸ (2815 H. Road, Grand Junction; tel: 970-244-3000; www.blm.gov/co/st/en/nca/mcnca.html). Designated in 2000, McInnis Canyons (formerly known as Colorado Canyons) is an extraordinary resource for Junction visitors and residents alike. You can hike a variety of trails in 75,439-acre (30,529-hectare) **Black Ridge Canyons Wilderness** (the sandstone arches of Rattlesnake Canyon are particularly memorable); mountain bike to Moab, Utah, on 137-mile (221km) **Kokopelli's Mountain Bike Trail**; and raft the canyons of the Colorado River from Loma Boat Launch through lovely **Ruby** and **Horsethief Canyons** to **Westwater Canyon** in Utah.

Dinosaur National Monument

Take your time making the three-hour drive along the winding scenic highway from Fruita through the **Book Cliffs** and **Piceance Basin** to reach Dinosaur National Monument, truly one of the best-kept secrets in the entire national park system. On your way, look out

BELOW: a museum-goer peruses contemporary art at the Museum of Western Colorado.

T. rex welcomes visitors to Fruita, home of Dinosaur Journey and the site of ongoing dinosaur excavation.

BELOW:
stopping for a closer look in Dinosaur National Monument.

for wild horses running in the Piceance Basin, part of several herds in the area managed by the Bureau of Land Management. Also of interest is the **Canyon Pintado National Historic District** , which preserves the entrancing rock art left behind by Fremont Indians who lived in this river valley more than a thousand years ago. At **Rangely**, SR 139 joins SR 64 and enters an austere desert landscape of pale crumbly shales weather-blasted by erosion. Oil and gas are the mainstays of this hot, dusty town of see-sawing oil derricks, oversized trucks and cowboy hats, where the only water in sight is the **Kenney Reservoir** on the **White River**, just north of town.

Blink and you may miss tiny **Dinosaur**, 18 miles (29km) north of Rangely, gateway to the Colorado side of Dinosaur National Monument. Your first stop should be **Dinosaur Welcome Center** (101 E. Stegosaurus Avenue; tel: 970-374-2205), at the junction of SR 64 and US 40, where staff will help you use your time wisely and pass on priceless insider tips on good places to take photos, view wildlife, hike little-known

trails, and even hang-glide – a popular sport on the cliffs above the serpentine canyons of Dinosaur. **Dinosaur National Monument Visitor Center and Headquarters** ❺ (4545 E. US 40, Dinosaur; tel: 970-374-3000; www.nps.gov/dino; daily; charge) is 2 miles (3km) east of the junction, on US 40, at the entrance to the Canyons section of the monument and has information and an audiovisual program on the park.

Remote and inaccessible, the Yampa River, which flows west to join the Green River in Echo Park in what is now Dinosaur National Monument, was a mystery to most early Americans. Fremont Indians and Utes had wandered there for centuries. The Spanish Dominguez-Escalante expedition of 1776 had passed to the south, through the fertile Colorado River valley, site of present-day Grand Junction, searching for a cross-country route to California from New Mexico. Fur trapper William Ashley was the first American to run the Green River in 1825, when rapids nearly destroyed his hide-covered bullboats.

But it wasn't until 1869 and 1871, when Major John Wesley Powell ran the length of the Green and Colorado rivers in the first government survey of the region, that Americans glimpsed the treasures at the heart of Colorado's wild canyonlands. The expedition passed through a lovely red-walled canyon on the Green River that Powell named the Gates of Lodore. Later, the men camped at a huge river bend, where the Yampa joined the Green River and snaked around an 800ft (240-meter) high sandstone wall shaped like a ship's prow. The distinctive formation (later dubbed Steamboat Rock) magnified the sound of the men's voices. Powell called it Echo Canyon.

Rivers and bones

In 1928, A.G. Birch, a reporter for the *Denver Post*, decided to take a trip down the Yampa River. For three weeks, headlines such as "Expedition to Risk Death in Wild Region" and "Post's Expedition is Nearing Perilous Trip Down

Canyon" captivated readers following Birch's adventures in the rugged, almost unknown Colorado canyon country bordering Utah and Wyoming.

"There is nothing like the Yampa River canyon that I have ever seen," he told his readers. "Imagine seven or eight Zion canyons strung together, end to end; with Yosemite Valley dropped down in the middle of them; with half a dozen 'pockets' as weird and inspiring as Crater Lake; and a score of Devil's Towers plumbed down here and there for good measure – then you will just begin to get some conception of Yampa Canyon."

Birch's message was clear. The canyons of northwestern Colorado merited national park status. The National Park Service took note, sending out surveyors who concurred with Birch that the area was worthy of inclusion in the park system. How to accomplish this during the lean years of the Depression was another matter. Finally, in 1938, President Franklin D. Roosevelt quietly added 200,000 acres (81,000 hectares) of Colorado canyon country to nearby Dinosaur National Monument.

Eighty-acre (32-hectare) Dinosaur National Monument had been set aside in 1915 to prevent the wholesale removal of an important quarry of dinosaur bones that had been found embedded in the fossil-rich Morrison Formation in 1909. But although the desert rocks surrounding the Colorado River in northeastern Utah held numerous dinosaur fossils, there were none deep in the billion-year-old canyons in northwestern Colorado, where the main features were extraordinary scenery, historic ranches and abundant wildlife.

Wall of Bones

If you have kids, you'll want to visit the **Dinosaur Quarry** on the Utah side of the monument first, then perhaps return to the Colorado side to spend time at the Canyons. In summer 2010, the visitor center and Wall of Bones closed so that the center could be rebuilt at a new location near the Dino-

saur Quarry. The former visitor center (a 45-minute drive from Dinosaur, 7 miles/11km north of Jensen, Utah) is being rehabilitated as an exhibition hall protecting the Wall of Bones. During construction, a **Temporary Visitor Center** (tel: 435-781-7700) is open 4 miles (6km) north of Jensen, Utah, on SR 149. Visitors can view fossils and exhibits and ride a shuttle to the ½-mile (1km) Fossils Discovery Trail to see unexcavated fossils still embedded in rock. The trail is open seasonally.

The Wall of Bones contains 1,500 bones of 10 different dinosaur species, including Camarasaurus, Stegosaurus, Diplodocus and Dryosaurus, first discovered here in 1909 by Carnegie Museum paleontologist Earl Douglass. Since then, excavations have uncovered more than 2,000 bones of dinosaurs embedded in the Morrison Formation. This is probably just a fraction of the number of dinosaurs that were entombed here when a catastrophic river flood wiped them out 150 million years ago.

This part of the monument sits on the Green River, below Split Mountain,

The Fight For Echo Park

Throughout the 1940s, out-of-the-way Dinosaur National Monument remained a well-kept secret, but in the early 1950s the park found itself at the center of a major controversy over government plans to construct huge dams at Echo Park and Split Mountain. The Sierra Club and more than 70 other environmental organizations formed an unprecedented alliance and successfully defeated the irrigation project. Many people still recall that their introduction to Dinosaur came through a flurry of outraged magazine and newspaper articles aimed at saving the park's canyons from immersion under a huge reservoir.

Backed by respected Western writers Bernard de Voto and Wallace Stegner, landscape photographer Philip Hyde and newly named "environmentalists" such as the Sierra Club's David Brower, Dinosaur became the poster child for a growing anti-development struggle in America. Nationwide support for saving wild lands in Dinosaur paved the way for the landmark 1964 Wilderness Act. Outdoor lovers came out to run the rivers they had saved and to camp at Echo Park, but the victory at Dinosaur was overshadowed in 1962 by the flooding of Glen Canyon, north of Grand Canyon, "The Place No One Knew," a defeat that cast a long shadow over the environmental movement. Dinosaur returned to obscurity. For another generation, it was just a park of old bones.

Hopi Kachina dolls at the Museum of Western Colorado. The dolls are not toys for children, but are effigies that embody the masked spirits of the Hopi tribe.

BELOW:
pottery at the Museum of Western Colorado.

a huge tilting, geological anticline with a plated profile that looks oddly like a stegosaurus (it's easy to get dinosaurs on the brain here). Geology is a big part of the story of Dinosaur. The park displays 23 different geological formations, the most complete geological record of any national park. That tops even the Grand Canyon.

The 22-mile (35km) **Tilted Rocks Scenic Drive** offers a closer look at Split Mountain and the Green River, both of which have campgrounds for hikers and river runners. Signs of human occupation can be seen all along this easily accessible road. A prehistoric rock shelter that was used by Paleo-Indians as long ago as 7,000 BC can be viewed at the start of the scenic drive; it has many examples of Fremont Indian art. At the end of the road, in Cub Creek, you'll find the fascinating **Josie Bassett Morris Homestead**. Morris was a pioneer who spent her early years in Browns Park, just north of Dinosaur park, and knew Butch Cassidy. She moved to Cub Creek a year before Dinosaur became a national monument and was well known locally. When she died in 1964, her homestead became part of the expanded park.

Canyon country

Morris wasn't the only homesteader drawn to Dinosaur's spectacular river canyon setting. In the early 1900s, Ralph Chew, originally from Blackburn in Lancashire, England, built a ranch on a tributary of the Green River, close to Echo Park, in the Canyons section of the park. The Chew family continues to ranch in Dinosaur, but the historic ranch, including a well-preserved chuck wagon, log cabins and corrals, is now part of the park and can be seen along the rugged, 13-mile (21km) drive down to Echo Canyon. The Chew Ranch is one of the highlights of the 23-mile (37km) **Harpers Corner Scenic Drive** to Harper's Corner in the eastern section of the park. It's easy to see what drew the Chews, the Mantles, the Ruples and other early ranchers: a sense of space, abundant grass, reliable water and plenty of game, from elk to deer to jackrabbits.

If you're here in summer and you have a four-wheel-drive, high-clearance vehicle, plan on spending at least one night in the popular campground at **Echo Park**, where history and landscape are at their most beguiling. This is one of the most beautiful canyon settings in the Southwest and a perfect place to tune into the ancient rhythms of rock, sky and river. Gentle breezes on the river brush across your face at night as you sleep, and rangers offer nightly skywatching and campfire talks, and morning hikes through the cottonwoods along the river. Next day, drive the **Yampa Bench Road**, east of Echo Park, which has a number of sights, including historic cabins, views of the river, and the Mantle Ranch, still a private holding here. Before leaving, continue to the end of the Harpers Corner Scenic Drive and hike the 2-mile (3km) **Harpers Corner Trail** for views of Whirlpool Canyon and the massive Mittens Fault in the Weber Sandstone.

Wild West

Finish your tour by returning to Grand Junction through the eastern portion of the Piceance Basin. You can take the fast route on US 40 to **Craig ❻**, a major coal-mining town. The main attraction in town is the interesting **Museum of Northwestern Colorado** (590 Yampa Avenue; tel: 970-824-6360; www.museumnwco.org; Mon–Fri 9am–5pm, Sat 10am–4pm; free), which displays one of the West's largest collections of gunfighter memorabilia.

A more scenic drive crosses the heart of the basin on SR 64, following the route of the pretty little White River, through Rangely to **Meeker ❼**. Meeker is a small, friendly, historic town surrounded by national forest, making it a popular outdoor-lover's getaway. It was named for a naive but well-intentioned missionary named Nathan Meeker, who came to the White River Ute Indian Agency in the 1870s. Meeker's plan to teach the Utes how to farm was met with stiff resistance from the tribe, whose beliefs taught them to live in harmony with what nature provided and forbade tilling the soil as a desecration of Mother Earth. The cultural clash ended tragically when Meeker plowed up the tribal racetrack, an important social area for this horse-loving people, and he and eight others were murdered, along with several soldiers. Unfortunately, their actions played right into the hands of government officials who, despite the intervention of Chief Ouray, used the massacre to justify removing the Utes from Colorado, thereby opening the way to white settlement.

You can learn more about this sad story at the **White River Museum** (565 Park Street; tel: 970-878-9982; daily Apr–Nov 9am–5pm, Dec–Mar 10am–4pm; charge) in Meeker, housed in an old log-cabin army barracks in the center of town. On the opposite side of the plaza is the Victorian **Meeker Hotel & Café** (560 Main Street; tel: 970-878-5255; www.themeekerhotel.com), built in 1896. The hotel's illustrious

guest list includes Teddy and Franklin Roosevelt, Gary Cooper, Billy the Kid and more recently Vice President Dick Cheney, who, like many outdoorsmen, enjoys hunting and fishing in **White River National Forest**.

SR 13 heads south for 39 miles (63km) to the small town of **Rifle ❽**, where you can pick up I-70 and return to Grand Junction or turn south to pick up the **Grand Mesa Scenic Byway**. A short detour to **Rifle Falls State Park** (5775 SR 325; tel: 970-625-1607, 5am–10pm; charge) offers one of the most delightful surprises on this tour. Exiting from nearby mountains, **East Rifle Creek** has created a lush year-round riparian oasis in a dry land, where water from the creek spills over a limestone cliff in the park, creating three waterfalls. In 1910, the waterfalls were used to power Rifle Hydroelectric Plant, the first in Colorado. A brief stroll takes you to the base of the falls, then a short, steep climb leads to the top. Rifle has a year-round campground that makes the perfect place to cool down before heading back to the sizzling Grand Valley. ❏

Ranchers have long been attracted to the Dinosaur region because of the wide open spaces.

BELOW:
Rifle Falls
State Park.

COLORADO

TRANSPORTATION

GETTING THERE
AND GETTING AROUND

From the United States

Two major interstates – the north–
south Interstate 25 and east–west
Interstate 70 – and several major US
highways that ring the western and
southern Rocky Mountains serve
Colorado, but distances between
major cities are so great, even within
the region, it frequently makes more
sense to fly in from elsewhere in the
US. For example, Albuquerque, in the
adjoining state of New Mexico, is
about an eight-hour drive from the
Denver Metro Area, even taking I-25
all the way and traveling at 75mph
(120kmh), the speed limit.

From more distant states,
including California, you will almost
certainly want to fly. Both nearby
Colorado Springs and Grand Junction
in Western Colorado have small
commuter airports served by regional
airlines, but even so, you are going to
find better prices if you fly into
Denver and rent a car to get where
you are going.

From Abroad

All major international airlines serve
Denver International Airport, one of
the busiest airports in the United
States, and this is invariably the
airport of choice for international
arrivals in Colorado, due to its
proximity to the Denver Metro Area
and competitive air fares and car
rental charges. As a major
international port of entry, you will be
asked to go through customs and
immigration in Denver.

By Air

Colorado is served by two major
airports – Denver and Colorado
Springs. The $4.3 billion **Denver
International Airport** (tel: 303-342-
2000; www.flydenver.com) opened in
1995, replacing the now defunct
Stapleton International Airport. The
facility is twice the size of Manhattan,
has a landing rate of 120 planes an
hour and is currently the sixth busiest
airport in the nation, able to
accommodate 50 million passengers
a year. The 1.4-million sq ft (130,000
sq meter) terminal building is a
distinctive architectural landmark.
The roof is constructed of a Teflon-
coated fabric shaped into 34 peaks,
which symbolize the Rocky Mountains
or – depending on who you ask – the
tepees of Arapaho and Cheyenne
Indians who once camped along the
South Platte River.

The following carriers serve Denver
International Airport:
Air Canada, tel: 888-689-2247; www.
aircanada.com
AirTran Airways, tel: 800-AIR-TRAN;
www.airtran.com
Alaska Air, tel: 800-ALASKAAIR; www.
alaskaair.com
American, tel: 800-433-7300; www.
aa.com
British Airways, tel: 800-247-9297;
www.britishairways.com
Continental, tel: 800-523-3273; www.
continental.com
Delta, tel: 800-221-1212; www.delta.
com
Frontier, tel: 800-432-1359; www.
frontierairlines.com
Great Lakes, tel: 800-554-5111;
www.greatlakesav.com
JetBlue, tel: 800-399-5838; www.
jetblue.com

Lufthansa, tel: 888-688-2345; www.
lufthansa.com
Mexicana, tel: 877-801-2010; www.
mexicana.com
United, tel: 800-864-8331; www.united.
com
US Airways, tel: 800-943-5436; www.
usairways.com

**Colorado Springs International
Airport** (tel: 719-550-1972; www.
springsgov.com) is served by American,
Continental, Delta, Frontier, and
United as well as **Allegiant Air**, tel:
702-505-8888; www.allegiant.com
Travelers wishing to visit western
Colorado can make connections to
Walker Field Airport (tel: 970-244-
9100; www.walkerfield.com) in Grand
Junction, which is served by:
Allegiant Air, American/American
Eagle, US Airways. Other carriers
include **Delta Connection/Skywest**,
tel: 800-453-9417; www.skywest.com;
United Express/Skywest, tel: 800-
241-6522; www.skywest.com.

A note about security: Stricter
airport security is expected to
continue indefinitely and will impose
some constraints on passengers and
visitors. Keep these guidelines in
mind as you prepare for your flight.
Check directly with your airline before
going to the airport. Make absolutely
sure your flight has not been
cancelled, rescheduled or delayed.

Allow plenty of time for check-in
prior to your scheduled departure
time. As much as two hours may be
required. Anticipate longer lines at
airline ticket counters, increased
security screening and other delays.
Your airline can advise you in
advance of how much extra time to
allow.

The Transportation Security Administration (TSA) is responsible for the passenger screening at the security checkpoint. For more information about screening policies, visit www.tsa.dot.gov.

New baggage restrictions allow only one carry-on bag and one personal item such as a purse, briefcase or laptop computer per passenger (laptops must be removed from their case and placed in a separate tray for screening). Many airlines now charge for checking bags. If you have more items than allowed, you will be asked to go back and check the extra items at the ticket counter. Full-body x-ray scanners and patdowns for those choosing not to – or unable to – go through the scanners were introduced at Denver International Airport by TSA.

By Train

Amtrak offers more than 500 destinations across the US. The trains are comfortable and reliable, with lounges, dining cars, snack bars and, in some cases, movies and live entertainment. Most routes offer sleeper cars with private cabins in addition to regular seating. Amtrak's California Zephyr runs from Chicago to San Francisco, with stops in Colorado at Fort Morgan, Denver, Winter Park, Granby, Glenwood Springs and Grand Junction. The Southwest Chief runs from Chicago to Los Angeles and stops at Lamar, Trinidad and La Junta.

Ask about two- or three-stopover discounts, senior citizens' and children's discounts, and Amtrak's package tours. International travelers can buy a USA Railpass, good for 15 to 30 days of unlimited travel on Amtrak throughout the United States.

Contact Amtrak (tel: 800-872-7245; www.amtrak.com) for detailed scheduling.

By Bus

One of the least expensive ways to travel in America is by interstate bus. The largest national bus company is **Greyhound**, tel: 800-231-2222; www.greyhound.com. The company routinely offers discounts such as go-anywhere fares. A Discovery Pass (available online at www.discoverypass.com) offers unlimited travel for 7, 15, 30 or 60 days. Greyhound serves more than 60 locations in Colorado, including Alamosa, Boulder, Cañon City, Colorado Springs, Denver, Durango, Englewood, Fort Collins, Fort Morgan,

Green Travel

For a low-impact vacation, take the train to Denver and get around using RTD light rail and bus. It's easy to reach small ski towns in the mountains by shuttle, or rent a hybrid vehicle to get there. Sightseeing trams operate in and around historic downtowns like Telluride and Aspen, and old mining towns like Durango and Georgetown have narrow-gauge scenic trains for excursions into the valleys. Ski resorts now compete with one another to operate sustainably by recycling, using longlife CFL bulbs and reducing water use. Many communities have weekly farmers' markets and eateries serving locally sourced food. You can even stay on a farm and pick your own food, if you like, or help restore habitat on a Nature Conservancy property or mountain trail. Ambitious bikers may want to sign up for the four-day, 238-mile (383km) Colorado Peace Ride along the narrow winding San Juan Skyway, a fundraiser for the Sophia Peace Center and Volunteers of America.

Frisco, Glenwood Springs, Grand Junction, Greeley, Gunnison, Idaho Springs, Pueblo, Salida, Silverton, Steamboat Springs, Vail and Winter Park. A rental car or other transportation is necessary to reach remote locations.

By Car

Colorado can be reached via three major interstate highways. I-25 heads north from New Mexico and climbs Raton Pass to enter southeast Colorado at Trinidad and continues north, with the Front Range on the left and the Plains on the right, all the way to Denver, then north into Wyoming. In Denver, I-25 is joined by I-70 from Kansas and I-76 from Nebraska. Busy I-70 forms the most traveled east–west route across the Colorado Rockies to Utah, providing access to major ski resorts like Breckenridge, Vail, Aspen, Steamboat Springs and the towns of Glenwood Springs and Grand Junction in northwestern Colorado. Elsewhere in Colorado, US highways wind around and through the Rockies. From Nebraska, US 50 passes through Lamar and La Junta, crosses I-25 at Pueblo and

continues west to Salida, Poncha Springs and Gunnison to connect with US 550 at Montrose, the main north–south route on the Western Slope. Between Durango and Montrose, US 550 is known as the San Juan Skyway Scenic Byway. From Montrose it continues north to Grand Junction. US 160 begins from I-25 at Walsenburg and passes through Alamosa and Monte Vista to Pagosa Springs and Durango in southwestern Colorado. US 285 enters southern Colorado south of Antonito and follows the Rio Grande Valley into the heart of the Rockies, passing Salida, Buena Vista and Fairplay to join I-70 at the main interchange south of Boulder, in Golden.

Getting Around

Its nickname says it all: Rocky Mountain State. Two-thirds of Colorado consists of high mountains, with a third of the state, on its east side, made up of the flat Great Plains. The major travel corridors are the paved all-weather highways of I-25, I-70, US 550/50, and US 160, which ring the mountains. **Mountain highways**, such as scenic US 285, make for pleasant driving through historic mining areas but are frequently challenging in winter due to heavy snowfall in the high Rockies.

Denver is the state capital and the main city in Colorado. Many first-time visitors are surprised to find out that Denver is not actually in the Rocky Mountain Front Range but sits on the flat Plains, about 25 miles (40km) east of the Rockies, with the high peaks of Rocky Mountain National Park in view to the west and the dusty plains spooling out to the east.

A modern city of skyscrapers, freeways, and malls, Denver is notable for its historic downtown buildings, museums, and parks and natural areas linked by an extensive trail system. The South Platte River, an urban waterway, passes through Denver. I-25, the main north–south route, passes close to the heart of downtown Denver and landmarks like Invesco Field. I-70 connects northeastern Denver with the Northern Rockies and is the main cross-mountain route for the state.

Because this is a farflung area, transportation is mainly by personal vehicle (highways are very clogged around Denver but quite pleasant, if more remote and mountainous, the farther you get away from the state capital). All major car rental companies are located at the airport, where rates are the best.

Shuttles run from Denver International Airport to Denver and communities in the Metro Area. Ski resorts also offer private mountain shuttles from the airport to resorts in the mountains. A public bus system is convenient for many commuters within the Denver area, and well priced if you are on a budget. Some cities, such as Trinidad and Durango, now have free trams linking attractions in their historic downtown core.

Light rail service links outlying communities within the Denver Metro Area with downtown Denver and may be an option if you are staying outside the downtown area.

To and From the Airport

Commuter shuttles pick up travelers at their home, office, or hotel throughout the Denver Metro Area and transport them at a reasonable cost via shared minivan to Denver International Airport, 23 miles (14km) northeast of the city, a journey that can take anything from a half-hour to an hour, depending on destination and time of day. **Denver Super Shuttle** (www.supershuttle.com/en DEN AirportShuttleDenver) is one such service. For more information, call 1-800-BLUEVAN. Some hotels also offer shuttles between the airport and Denver. Inquire on booking. Colorado **Mountain Express** (www.ridecme.com) links the airport with the ski towns of Vail, Beaver Creek, Breckenridge, Copper Mountain, Keystone, Aspen, and Snowmass. A number of companies offer **private limousine service** to pick you up or take you to the airport. Taxis run between the airport and the eight counties that make up Denver Metro Area. For those on a budget, **Skyride Public Bus Service** is the cheapest way to travel between the airport and downtown Denver. For more information about routes and schedules, tel: 303-299-6000.

By Air

The following towns in Colorado have commercial air service from small airports: Alamosa, Aspen, Colorado Springs, Cortez, Denver, Durango, Eagle, Fort Collins/Loveland, Grand Junction, Gunnison, Hayden, Montrose, Pueblo, and Telluride.

There are three small relief airports in the Denver suburbs of Aurora, Broomfield, Centennial. Many other towns have general aviation fields accessible by aircraft.

By Train

If you don't want to drive, you can travel through the scenic Northern Rockies to Glenwood Springs in Western Colorado on the California Zephyr from Union Station in downtown Denver. From there the train continues through Utah and Nevada to Emeryville, outside San Francisco in Northern California. (Note: Amtrak's Southwest Chief takes the Plains and desert route from Chicago and only stops at Trinidad, in extreme southeastern Colorado, before heading into New Mexico, Arizona, and Los Angeles, California.)

By Light Rail

Denver's **RTD Light Rail** (www.rtd-denver.com/light rail) serves Central, Southeast, and Southwest Denver. Scheduled trains stop at 36 stations between 5am and 1am. Scenic **narrow-gauge railroads** link small mining towns in the Central and South Rockies, including Durango & Silverton Narrow Gauge Railroad, Cumbres and Toltec Scenic Railroad, Cripple Creek and Victor Narrow Gauge Railroad, Georgetown Loop, and the Royal Gorge diesel train. The Pikes Peak Cog Railroad operates on Pikes Peak near Colorado Springs. Wilderness packers can arrange to ride the Durango & Silverton train and get off and hike back along parts of the 500-mile (805km) Colorado Trail.

By Bus

RTD bus service (www.rtd-denver.com) links Denver, Aurora and Boulder in concert with Denver's light rail system. Most larger Colorado cities, such as Grand Junction and Pueblo, have local bus services. A number of mining and ski resort communities operate sightseeing trams in their downtown historic districts, including Trinidad, Salida, Vail, Aspen, Telluride and Estes Park. Most buses in Colorado allow bicycles on the buses.

By Car

Driving is the most convenient way to travel in Colorado, especially outside

AAA Membership

Anyone spending a significant amount of time driving US highways is strongly advised to join the Automobile Association of America (AAA or Triple A). Benefits include emergency breakdown service, excellent road maps, travel literature and personalized trip planning, as well as discounts at motels like Best Western and other chains. Premier level offers towing up to 200 miles (320km) from breakdown site – important if you are in the middle of nowhere – and lockout, refueling and jump start service. Insurance is also available through the association, which has a reciprocal arrangement with some of the automobile associations in other countries. Tel: 800-874-7532 or visit www.aaa.com. In Denver: AAA 4100 E. Arkansas Drive, Denver CO 80222, tel: 800-222-4357.

the major cities. Major roads are well-maintained, although some back country roads may be unpaved. If you plan on driving into remote areas or in heavy snow, mud or severe weather, it's best to use a four-wheel-drive vehicle with high clearance. Jeeps are very popular for off-road travel in Ouray.

Maps and Information

Your greatest asset as a driver is a good road map. Maps can be obtained from state tourism offices, filling stations, supermarkets and convenience stores. Although roads are maintained even in remote areas, it is advisable to listen to local radio stations and to check with highway officials or police officers for the latest information on weather and road conditions, especially in winter or if planning to leave paved roads. Mountain passes are often closed by heavy snowfall in winter.

Driving in Remote Areas

If you plan to drive in uninhabited areas, carry a spare tire and extra water – at least 1 gallon (4 liters) per person per day. A cell phone is a good idea, too, though some areas may be out of range of the nearest communications tower.

Service stations can be few and far between in remote areas. Not every town will have one, and many close early. It's always better to have more fuel than you think you will need.

A word of caution: If your car breaks down on a back road, do not attempt to strike out on foot, even with water. A car is easier to spot than a person and provides shelter from the elements. If you don't have a cell phone or your phone doesn't work, sit tight and wait to be found.

Vehicle Rental

Car Rentals

Auto rental agencies are located at all airports, in cities and many large towns. In most places, you must be at least 21 years old (25 at some locations) to rent a car and you must have a valid driver's license and at least one major credit card. Drivers under 25 may have to pay an extra fee, as will additional drivers. Foreign drivers must have an international driver's license. Be sure that you are properly insured for both collision and personal liability. Insurance won't be included in the base rental fee. Insurance cost varies depending on the car and the type of coverage, but it is usually $15–35 per day. You may already be covered by your own auto insurance or credit card company, so check with them first.

Many companies offer unlimited mileage. If not, you may be charged an extra 10–25¢ or more per mile over a given maximum. Rental fees often vary depending on the time of year, location, how far in advance you book your rental, and if you travel on weekdays or weekends.

Inquire about discounts or benefits for which you may be eligible, including corporate, credit card or frequent-flyer programs.

Advantage, tel: 800-777-5500; www.advantage.com
Alamo, tel: 877-222-9075; www.alamo.com
Avis, tel: 800-230-4898; www.avis.com
Budget, tel: 800-527-0700; www.budget.com
Dollar, tel: 800-800-3665; www.dollar.com
E-Z, tel: 800-277-5171; www.e-zrentacar.com
Enterprise, tel: 800-261-7331; www.enterprise.com
Hertz, tel: 800-654-3131; www.hertz.com
National, tel: 800-222-9058; www.nationalcar.com
Thrifty, tel: 800-367-2277; www.thrifty.com

RV Rentals

No special license is necessary to operate a motor home (or recreational vehicle – RV for short), but they aren't

ABOVE: a pedi-cab peddles the Sixteenth Street Mall in Downtown Denver.

cheap. When you add up the cost of rental fees, insurance, gas and campsites, renting a car and staying in motels or camping may be less expensive.

Keep in mind, too, that RVs are large and slow and may be difficult to handle on narrow mountain roads. If parking space is tight, driving an RV may be extremely inconvenient. Still, RVs are very popular, and some travelers swear by them. For additional information about RV rentals, call the Recreational Vehicle Rental Association, tel: 703-591-7130; www.rvra.org.

Distances and Driving Times

Denver–Boulder: 29 miles/47km (0.5 hr)
Denver–Colorado Springs: 69 miles/111km (1.25 hrs)
Denver–Fort Collins: 65 miles/104km (1.25 hrs)
Denver–Estes Park: 65 miles/104km (1.5 hrs)
Denver–Glenwood Springs: 157 miles/253km (2.5 hrs)
Denver–Steamboat Springs: 166 miles/267km (3.5 hrs)
Denver–Aspen: 159 miles/256km (3.75 hrs)
Denver–Crested Butte: 228 miles/367km (4.75 hrs)

By Taxi

There are 16 cab companies in Denver. **Metro Taxi** (tel: 303-333-3333; www.metrotaxidenver.com) is the largest and most modern taxi service in town, while **Yellow Cabs** (tel: 303-777-7777; www.yellowtrans.com) operates a flat-rate service to the

airport from throughout the Denver Metro Area.

By Bicycle

Bicycle riding in Colorado verges on the obsessive for many people. This is the home of commuting long distances by bike on a network of trails throughout the Denver Metro Area, cycle touring on winding highways, road races like the Iron Horse Classic from Durango to Silverton, and fat tire festivals in mountain towns like Crested Butte, which invented the mountain bike. Bicycle Colorado (tel: 303-299-6000; www.bicyclecolo.org) is an excellent resource for cyclists.

On Foot

Lovely Boulder has one of the most extensive **Open Space** programs in the country, with 45,000 acres (18,210 hectares) of open space hike/bike trails, in and around the city, used by 5.3 million people a year, and Denver's **Lariat Loop** mountain parks, both offering amazing views of the Front Range. Trails around canyons in Mesa Verde, Hovenweep, Black Canyon of the Gunnison, Colorado National Monument, and the Harpers Corner section of Dinosaur are famed for their sweeping views as well as geology, natural history, and ruins. Multiday backpack trips in high country throughout the wild flower-strewn Rockies in summer offer endless possibilities to get away from people and connect with nature.

ACCOMMODATIONS

HOTELS, YOUTH HOSTELS, BED & BREAKFAST

Choosing Lodgings

Colorado offers a great variety of accommodations, ranging from rustic cabins with little in the way of amenities to extravagant resorts with a myriad of special features. Some places – inexpensive chain motels, for example – are suitable for a single night on the road. Others, such as golf resorts, spas and dude ranches are destinations in themselves and offer enough diversions to keep guests busy for a lengthy visit. It's always advisable to make reservations well in advance of the high season – winter in ski areas and summer in mountain resorts. Travelers in search of a bargain will find tempting off-season discounts.

Chain motels

Chains are reliable and convenient but lack character. You can usually depend on a clean, comfortable room for a reasonable cost. In general, prices range from $50 to $150 depending on location and additional amenities such as a pool, exercise room and restaurant.

Moderate to Expensive

Best Western, tel: 800-780-7234; www.bestwestern.com
Hilton, tel: 800-445-8667; www.hilton.com
Holiday Inn, tel: 800-465-4329; www.holidayinn.com
Hyatt, tel: 800-633-7313; www.hyatt.com
La Quinta, tel: 866-753-3757; www.lq.com
Marriott, tel: 888-236-2427; www.marriott.com
Radisson, tel: 800-201-1719; www.radisson.com
Ramada, tel: 800-272-6232; www.ramada.com

Sheraton, tel: 800-325-3535; www.starwoodhotels.com/sheraton/index.html
Starwood, tel: 888-625-5144; www.starwoodhotels.com
Days Inn, tel: 800-329-7466; www.daysinn.com
Econo Lodge, tel: 877-424-6423; www.econolodge.com
Howard Johnson, tel: 800-446-4656; www.hojo.com
Quality Inn, tel: 877-424-6423; www.qualityinn.com
Super 8, tel: 800-800-8000; www.super8.com
Travelodge, tel: 800-578-7878; www.travelodge.com

Hotels

Larger and generally more comfortable than motels, hotels are designed for upscale business travelers and tourists, and are usually situated in a central area with easy access to attractions and public transportation. Nearly all have at least one restaurant and bar and such amenities as a pool, a fitness center, meeting facilities, room service, a gift shop and an extensive lobby. Some, such as Embassy Suites or AmeriSuites, offer one- or two-bedroom suites (some with kitchenettes) that are suited for long stays or families. Always look for new or newly renovated properties as these will be in the best condition and have the most up-to-date facilities.

Resorts

Luxury, relaxation and recreation are emphasized at resort properties, most of which have large, sumptuous rooms, suites or cottages, fine dining, extensive grounds with manicured landscaping, and such recreational facilities as ski slopes, golf courses, tennis courts and elaborate pools as

well as health and beauty spas. A minimum stay of two or three nights is sometimes required.

Bed and breakfasts

B&Bs tend to be more homey and personal than hotels. In many cases, you're a guest at the innkeeper's home. Some are historic houses or inns decorated with antiques, quilts, art and various period furnishings; others offer simple but comfortable accommodations. Before booking, ask if rooms have telephones or televisions and whether bathrooms are private or shared. Ask about breakfast, too. The meal is included in the price but may be anything from a few muffins to a multicourse feast. Guests may be served at a common table, a private table or in their rooms. For more information contact:
Above Denver Lodging Association
www.abovedenverlodging.com
Bed and Breakfast Innkeepers of Colorado
Tel: 800-265-7696; www.bbonline.com/co/bbic

Campgrounds

Campsites in Colorado's most popular parks may be reserved ahead of time – essential during the busy summer season. For reservations at campgrounds operated by the National Park Service and US Forest Service, log on to www.recreation.gov. Reserve in Colorado State Parks by logging on to www.reserveamerica.com or by calling tel: 800-678-2267 or 303-470-1144.

Reservations may be made up to six months in advance.

Bed and Breakfast Inns of Glenwood Springs
www.glenwood-springs-inns.com
Colorado West Bed and Breakfasts – Fruita, Grand Junction, Palisade
www.coloradowestbnb.com
Bed and Breakfasts of the Pikes Peak Area
PO Box 342, Manitou Springs, CO 80829; tel: 888-835-8900; www.pikespeakareabnbs.com
Breckenridge Bed and Breakfast Association
PO Box 8046, Breckenridge, CO 80424; www.colorado-bnb.com/breckinns
Denver Bed and Breakfast Guild
2147 Tremont Place, Denver, CO 80205; tel: 303-296-6666 or 800-432-4667; www.denverbedbreakfast.com

Summit County Bed and Breakfast Association
www.summitcountybnbs.com

Guest ranches

Guest, or dude, ranches range from working cattle operations with basic lodging to full-fledged "resorts with horses" that have swimming pools, tennis courts and other amenities. Most ranches offer horseback riding lessons, guided pack trips, entertainment like rodeos, square dances and storytellers, and plenty of hearty food. If traveling with a family, be sure to ask about a children's program. For more information and an extensive list of dude ranches contact:

Colorado Dude and Guest Ranch Association
PO Box D, Shawnee, CO 80475; tel: 866-94-CDGRA; www.coloradoranch.com
Dude Ranchers Association
PO Box 2307, Cody, WY 82414; tel: 307-587-2339; www.duderanch.org

Camping

Most tent and RV sites in national and state parks and forests are available on a first-come, first-served basis. Campgrounds fill early during the summer season. Contact the parks for information on availability. Fees are usually charged for campsites. Back country permits may be required for wilderness camping.

ACCOMMODATIONS LISTINGS

THE EASTERN PLAINS

Fort Collins

Edwards House Bed and Breakfast
402 W. Mountain Avenue, Fort Collins, CO 80521
Tel: 970-493-9191
www.edwardshouse.com
Set in a leafy residential area a few minutes from Colorado State University and an hour by car from both Denver and Rocky Mountain National Park, this classic Denver Four-Square house has eight guest rooms with gas fireplaces, antique furnishings, four-poster queen-size beds, and bathrooms with claw-foot tubs or whirlpools. Complimentary breakfast is included. **$–$$**

Loveland

Cattail Creek Inn
2665 Abarr Drive, Loveland, CO 80538
Tel: 970-667-7600, 800-572-2466
www.insite.com
This large contemporary bed and breakfast is set on Cattail Creek Golf Course, with views of Lake Loveland and the Rocky Mountains. Eight guest rooms are spacious and comfortably appointed; some feature a fireplace, deck and/or whirlpool tub. All rooms have a private bath and cable television. Gourmet breakfast. **$$**

Sylvan Dale Guest Ranch
2939 N. County Road 31D, Loveland, CO 80538
Tel: 970-667-3915 or 877-667-3999
www.sylvandale.com
Situated on the banks of the Big Thompson River in the Rocky foothills, this 3,000-acre (1,200-hectare) dude ranch offers cattle round-ups, overnight pack trips, birdwatching, fishing and all the horseback riding you can handle. Guests stay in cabins, rental houses and a central lodge. Single-night, "bunk & breakfast" rates are available. **$–$$$**

Pueblo

Abriendo Inn
300 W. Abriendo Avenue, Pueblo, CO 81004
Tel: 719-544-2703
www.abriendoinn.com
This grand 1906 Craftsman-style bed and breakfast has been in business since 1989. It features 10 attractive rooms with elegant furnishings. Some rooms have whirlpool tubs, refrigerators, microwaves, VCRs and fans; all rooms have private baths televisions, phones and free Wi-fi. Full breakfast. A nice romantic getaway. **$–$$**

Stratton

Claremont Inn
800 Claremont Drive, Stratton, CO 80836
Tel: 888-291-8910
www.claremontinn.com
Much more than a bed and breakfast, this lavish inn was built in 1995 in the style of a European mansion. Ten plush guest rooms are designed in various styles, from rustic Western to British Colonial. A restaurant features gourmet bistro-style cuisine. Guests can watch movies in an on-site theater, join a cooking class, or partake in an elaborate murder mystery evening. Full breakfast is included. **$$**

Trinidad

Tarabino Inn
310 E. 2nd Street, Trinidad, CO 81082
Tel: 719-846-2115 or 866-846-8808
www.tarabinoinn.com
A charming, well-priced Victorian country inn in historic Trinidad. Two suites are furnished with four-

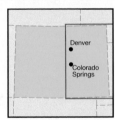

posters and carved beds, fresh white linens and private clawfoot tubs. Two smaller rooms have the same fresh feel, but share a bath. Full breakfast. **$–$$**

BELOW: a guest ranch.

PRICE CATEGORIES

Price categories are based on the average cost of a double room per night:
$ = under $110
$$ = $110–250
$$$ = more than $250

DENVER

Brown Palace Hotel

321 17th Street, Denver, CO 80202
Tel: 303-297-3111 or
800-321-2599
www.brownpalace.com
The Palace has served as the Denver headquarters of presidents, princes, socialites and other celebrities for more than a century. Designed in Italian Renaissance style by Frank E. Edbrooke, architect of the State Capitol, the hotel was completed in 1892 at a cost of $1.6 million. Its splendor rivaled even the finest Eastern hotels, impressing guests with a red granite and sandstone facade, soaring eight-story atrium, golden onyx pillars and stained-glass ceiling. The Victorian-style guest rooms are equally impressive and a recent renovation has left them outfitted with all the digital-age amenities upscale travelers have come to expect. Amenities include several restaurants and bars, a fitness room, laundry service and concierge. **$$$**

Castle Marne Bed and Breakfast

1572 Race Street, Denver, CO 80206
Tel: 303-331-0621 or
800-926-2763
www.castlemarne.com
This unusual family-run inn occupies a stone castle. Built in 1889 by noted architect William Lang and listed in the National Register of Historic Places, the inn offers nine guest rooms appointed with antiques and fine repro-

ductions; some have a jacuzzi or hot tub. The three-room Presidential Suite, which features a private solarium with a two-person whirlpool tub, is especially elaborate. A gourmet breakfast is served in the formal dining room; afternoon tea and candle-light dinners are also available. **$$–$$$**

Hostel of the Rocky Mountains

1530 Downing Street, Denver, CO 80218
Tel: 303-861-7777
www.innkeeperrockies.com
Cheap, safe and set in a good location. Those are the principal benefits of this downtown hostel, frequented mostly by students and backpackers. Each dormitory room has three or four beds; a few private rooms are also available. Guests will also find a laundry and kitchen. Breakfast is included. **$**

Hotel Teatro

110 14th Street, Denver, CO 80202
Tel: 303-228-1100 or
888-727-1200
www.hotelteatro.com
Topping several lists of Denver's best hotels, this luxury boutique hotel is located across from the Performing Arts Center. It combines contemporary style with a flair for the dramatic. Props and costumes from plays staged at the Center are displayed in the lobby and other public spaces. Guest rooms are decorated in subtle tones, with 12ft (4-meter) high

ceilings, cherry wood armoires, desks and headboards in modern European style, down comforters and fine fabrics; suites are available. Acclaimed chef Kevin Taylor runs two restaurants at the hotel: Restaurant Kevin Taylor and Prima. Extras include a fitness center and complimentary shuttle service in the downtown area. **$$–$$$**

Oxford Hotel

1600 17th Street, Denver, CO 80202
Tel: 303-628-5400 or
800-228-5838
www.theoxfordhotel.com
Though not quite as grand as the Brown Palace, this Victorian-era hotel – also designed by architect Frank Edbrooke – embodies the high-flying aspirations of the Gilded Age. Most rooms are furnished with French and English antiques; some units reflect the Art Deco style of the 1930s. Facilities include a spa and health club, two restaurants, including the popular McCormicks Fish House, the Deco-style Cruise Room bar and two art galleries. Located near Union Station in the heart of LoDo. **$$–$$$**

Queen Anne Urban Bed and Breakfast Inn

2147–51 Tremont Place, Denver, CO 80205
Tel: 303-296-6666 or
800-432-4667
www.queenannebnb.com
Set on Benedict Fountain Park in the Clement Historic District, within walking distance of the Capitol and 16th Street Mall, these two 19th-century houses offer a soothing environment away from the hectic city. There are 14 guest rooms, including four two-room suites, with period antiques, private baths, desks, modem lines and air conditioning. A full breakfast and evening wine tasting are included. **$$–$$$**

Sheraton Denver Downtown Hotel

1550 Court Place, Denver,

CO 80202
Tel: 303-893-3333
www.sheratondenverdowntown.com
The former Adams Mark Hotel Denver is now managed by Starwood properties and recently received a $70 million renovation of its 1,231 guest rooms and 82 suites. It is set in the heart of downtown Denver with all the expected amenities: four restaurants, a nightclub, and a variety of recreational activities including a health club with sauna and fitness equipment. **$$–$$$**

Westin Tabor Center

1672 Lawrence Street, Denver, CO 80202
Tel: 303-572-9100
www.starwoohotels.com/westin
This modern high-rise managed by Starwood is notable for its refined contemporary style and central location in LoDo, and the Denver Performing Arts Complex. The 430 guest rooms (including 15 suites) are newly decorated in soothing tones of beige, gray and white, with ample space, comfy bedding and a large desk. The fourth-floor pool has excellent views of the Rocky Mountains. Other amenities include a heated indoor pool, fitness facility, racquetball courts, meeting facilities, V's Lounge, break-fast in the Augusta restaurant and fine dining in The Palm steakhouse. **$$–$$$**

BELOW: the elegant Brown Palace Hotel.

BOULDER AND ENVIRONS

The Alps Boulder Canyon Inn
38619 Boulder Canyon Drive, Boulder, CO 80302
Tel: 303-444-5445
www.alpsinn.com
This idyllic hideaway in Boulder Canyon, 10 minutes from Downtown, is housed in a former stagecoach stop built in the late 19th century. Beautifully restored and expanded, the inn features large rooms furnished with British antiques, fireplaces, queen beds, down comforters and private bathrooms with either a clawfoot or whirlpool tub; many have patios or porches with mountain views. A gourmet breakfast is included. Hiking, biking and fishing are available. **$$–$$$**

Boulder International Hostel
1107 12th Street, PO Box 1705, Boulder, CO 80306
Tel: 303-442-0522
www.boulderhostel.com
There's a nice intellectual vibe and sense of global community at this sprawling hostel, which has 400 beds in 250 rooms. Choose either private rooms ($49–55) or dorm rooms ($27). Dorm beds do not come with linen, so bring a sleeping bag or be prepared to rent linen from the hostel. All bathrooms are shared. Dorm guests must have out-of-state identification. Located in the University Hill

District, two blocks from the University. Free Wi-fi. **$**

The Bradley
2040 16th Street, Boulder, CO 80302
Tel: 303-545-5200 or 800-858-5811
www.thebradleyboulder.com
A very lovely, peaceful inn, just one block from Pearl Street. Walls are decorated with contemporary art from some of Boulder's finest art galleries. The 12 elegant rooms have Aveda spa toiletries and jacuzzi tubs: balconies and fireplaces in some rooms; guest privileges at a local fitness club. Gourmet breakfasts of quiche or eggs cooked to order, fresh-baked bread and fruit. Daily wine-and-cheese hour. **$$**

Briar Rose Bed and Breakfast
2151 Arapahoe Avenue, Boulder, CO 80302
Tel: 303-442-3007
www.briarrosebb.com
Reminiscent of an English country house, this peaceful, green inn offers nine rooms with antique furniture, queen beds and private bathrooms; a few have fireplaces. A complimentary organic breakfast is served in the dining room or on the sun porch. Afternoon tea daily, complete with excellent loose-leaf tea. The University of Colorado and Pearl Street Mall are within a 15-minute walk. **$$**

Colorado Chautauqua Association

900 Baseline Road, Boulder, CO 80302
Tel: 303-952-1611
www.chautauqua.com
In 1898, Texas educators involved in the national Chautauqua movement joined with local Boulder leaders to create a summer colony devoted to educational enrichment, spiritual enlightenment and physical health. That spirit of improvement and cultural richness is still evident at this 26-acre (10-hectare) park, where overnight guests stay in attractive but simple cottages. Each unit has a private or shared kitchen; daily housekeeping is not provided. Reserve early; cottages are booked well ahead by returning vacationers. Some units may be available for long-term rental off-season, if you inquire. **$$–$$$**

Foot of the Mountain Motel
200 W. Arapahoe Avenue, Boulder, CO 80302
Tel: 303-442-5688
www.footofthemountainmotel.com
This tiny 1930s cabin resort, opposite Eben Fine Park in Boulder Canyon, is one of the great finds for travelers who enjoy natural surroundings, reasonable prices and a friendly family atmosphere. Pine-clad cabins are old and have shared walls but meticulously clean and attractive. There are two suites. Each cabin has a small desk with

views of the mountainside (watch for foxes, deer and other wildlife), television, phone, refrigerator and private bathroom; the office will heat up meals for you in its microwave. Off-season weekly rates with reduced housekeeping available. **$**

Hotel Boulderado
2115 13th Street, Boulder, CO 80302
Tel: 303-442-4344 or 800-433-4344
www.boulderado.com
A city landmark since 1909, the hotel features a dramatic atrium with a stained-glass ceiling, a cantilevered staircase and a plethora of Victorian touches. Of the 160 rooms and suites, those in the original building have the most character, with antiques and period reproductions. The new annex is comfortable and well-appointed but doesn't have the same personality. Amenities include a business center, Q's restaurant and the always lively Catacombs Blues Bar, the oldest in town. **$$–$$$**

COLORADO SPRINGS AND ENVIRONS

Colorado Springs

Antlers Hilton Colorado Springs
4 S. Cascade Avenue, Colorado Springs, CO 80903
Tel: 719-955-5600
www.antlers.com
This 292-room downtown high-rise hotel is a cut above the usual chain operation, with such extra features as a day spa, health club, indoor pool, beauty salon and

marble-trimmed lobby plus a casual grill and Judge Baldwin's brew pub. Large, well-appointed rooms have a few nice touches left over from the two previous Antlers, both destroyed. The first was built in 1883 by Colorado Springs founder William Jackson Palmer. Visitors wanting extra space and comfort should ask for one of the seven executive suites. **$$–$$$**

The Broadmoor
1 Lake Avenue, Colorado Springs, CO 80906
Tel: 719-577-5775 or 866-837-9520
www.broadmoor.com
A landmark since 1918, the Broadmoor is a 3,000-acre (1,200-hectare) resort at the base of Pikes Peak. Designed in the style of a grand Italian villa, with marble staircases, tile floors, chandeliers,

fountains and a priceless art collection, the resort encompasses more than 25 buildings, a full-service spa, three golf courses, tennis facilities, a lake, an indoor and outdoor pool, 20 shops, a theater, and a wide range of activities, including horseback riding, biking, boating and children's programs. Accommodations in the main lodge have the most character. Those in the outer buildings tend to be a bit more contemporary in style. Nine restaurants and three bars offer an array of dining and drinking options. The Penrose Room is among the city's finest. Sunday brunch in the Terrace Dining Room is a lavish affair. All this luxury doesn't come cheap, but those with a taste for the good life will find it here. Dramatic discounts are sometimes offered in winter. **$$$**

Cheyenne Mountain Resort
3225 Broadmoor Valley Road,
Colorado Springs, CO 80906
Tel: 719-538-4000 or
800-588-0250
www.cheyennemountain.com
The 316 rooms and suites at this upscale resort are clustered in eight lodges on 217 landscaped acres (89 hectares) at the base of Cheyenne Mountain. The main lodge reflects the rugged style of Rocky Mountain architecture with massive wood beams, cedar shakes and rough-sawn siding. Guest rooms are spacious, most with queen beds, internet access and private decks or balconies. There is an 18-hole golf course, indoor and outdoor pools, indoor and outdoor tennis courts, basketball courts, a fitness center and a 35-acre (14-hectare) lake for swimming, sailing and bass fishing. Two fine restaurants, a pub and lounge. **$$$**

Old Town Guesthouse
115 S. 26th Street,
Colorado Springs, CO 80904
Tel: 719-632-9194 or
888-375-4210
www.oldtown-guesthouse.com
This three-story redbrick building, built in 1997, blends in perfectly with its historic surroundings. The eight rooms are individually decorated. A special guest room offers disabled-friendly lodging. All floors are accessible by elevator. Amenities include gourmet breakfast, fireplaces, hot tubs, and Wi-Fi. **$–$$**

Manitou Springs

Cliff House at Pikes Peak
306 Canon Avenue,
Manitou Springs, CO 80829
Tel: 719-785-1000 or
888-212-7000
www.thecliffhouse.com
Built in 1874, this turreted grande dame is a national historic landmark that has hosted Theodore Roosevelt, Clark Gable and Thomas Edison in its time and simply oozes history and elegance. It was closed for many years, following a fire in 1982, and reopened in 1999 after a meticulous restoration and reconstruction of areas that were burned in the fire. It has 54 beautiful rooms and suites and a fine-dining restaurant operated by executive chef Scott Savage. You wouldn't expect a four-star hotel this enchanting to come cheap, but look for sweeping discounts online. **$$–$$$**

El Colorado Lodge
23 Manitou Avenue,
Manitou Springs, CO 80829
Tel: 719-685-5485 or
800-782-2246
www.elcolorado.net
A good budget choice for families, this charming 4-acre (1.6-hectare) historic property offers more than 20 adobe *casitas* decorated in Southwestern style at rock-bottom rates. Each *casita* has one to three bedrooms and most have a corner kiva fireplace. The lodge has the largest heated swimming pool in Manitou Springs as well as a basketball court, shuffleboard court, playground, an enormous barbecue grill and picnic pavilion. Built in 1926, El Colorado had the dubious distinction of being the first lodging in town to offer sheets on the beds. **$**

Victoria's Keep
202 Ruxton Avenue, Manitou Springs, CO 80829
Tel: 719-685-5354 or 800-905-5337
www.victoriaskeep.com
Lovers of Victorian style will enjoy this meticulously restored and decorated 1892 Queen Anne bed and breakfast. Six frothy rooms and suites are furnished with four-poster beds, period antiques, Oriental rugs and chintz comforters and wallpaper. Each has a private bathroom, fireplace and air conditioning; suites have a large sitting area and whirlpool tub. Full breakfast and afternoon tea are included. Very good value. **$–$$**

SAN LUIS VALLEY

Antonito

Conejos River Guest Ranch
25390 Highway 17, Antonito, CO 81120
Tel: 719-376-2464
www.conejosranch.com
Set on the Conejos River in Rio Grande National Forest, this down-home guest ranch has an unpretentious lodge with eight bed and breakfast rooms, most with lodgepole pine beds, and six fully equipped cabins. A restaurant on the premises specializes in hearty Western fare like smoked chicken and barbecued ribs. Chuckwagon meals are occasionally served around a campfire by the river. Activities include horseback riding, pack trips, fishing, hunting, snowmobiling and cross-country skiing. **$**

Medano

Zapata Ranch
5303 CO 150, Medano, CO 81146
Tel: 719-378-2356
www.zranch.org
Owned by The Nature Conservancy, managed through a unique partnership with the Duke and Janet Phillips family, a third-generation ranching family, this 103,000-acre (40,500-hectare) working ranch, 12 miles (19km) from Great Sand Dunes National Park, welcomes guests for multiday stays to learn about the historic ranching lifestyle in the San Luis Valley. Lodging is rustic but comfortable, with handcrafted furniture and Navajo rugs. Guests can participate in naturalist workshops or seminars, join a nature walk for a look at rare birds, including migrating sandhill cranes and white-faced ibis, join a volunteer project, ride horses into the park or help doctor the ranch's buffalo or cattle herd. Fees are American Plan, including meals, accommodations and program activities; there is usually a three-night minimum, but the ranch may be willing to accommodate shorter stays with notice. **$$$**

Moffat

Joyful Journey Hot Springs Spa
28640 CR58 EE, Moffat, CO 81143
Tel: 719-256-4328 or
800-673-0656
www.joyfuljourneyhotsprings.com
An unexpected joy in the northern San Luis Valley, 30 miles (48km) south of

Salida and 50 miles (80km) north of Alamosa, Joyful Springs offers hourly soaking in 98°F to 108°F (37°F to 42°F) developed artesian hot springs and massages and other body therapies. A range of overnight accommodations are available at reasonable prices. The attractive rooms in the retreat and conference center have saltillo tile floors, lodgepole pine beds and other Southwest touches. The comfy circular yurts have beds and robes and are quite private. Or you can play Cowboys and Indians and stay in a tipi or camp in the campground. No private bathrooms in yurts, tipis and campsites; guests bathe in the bathhouse. Continental breakfast and unlimited soaks included in the overnight rate. **$**

Mosca

Great Sand Dunes Lodge
7900 Highway 150, Mosca, CO 81146

Tel: 719-378-2900
www.gsdlodge.com
What you'll find here is basic motel lodging ¼-mile (½km) from the park entrance. Each of 10 large rooms has two queen beds, a television and a private bathroom. Hummingbird feeders attract dozens of tiny hummers. Indoor pool. **$–$$**

South Fork

Arbor House Inn
PO Box 995, 31358 Highway 160, South Fork, CO 81154
Tel: 719-873-5012 or 888-830-4642
www.arborhouseinnco.com
In a mountain setting bordering Rio Grande National Forest about 45 minutes west of Alamosa, this attractive contemporary house has five guest rooms with private bathrooms, satellite televisions, and theme decor. A suite has a sitting area, fireplace, two-person whirlpool and private entrance. A full breakfast is included. **$$**

ROCKY MOUNTAIN NATIONAL PARK AREA

Estes Park

Alpine Trail Ridge Inn
927 Moraine Avenue, Estes Park, CO 80517
Tel: 970-586-4585 or 800-233-5023
www.alpinetrailridgeinn.com
Independently owned motel right next to the entrance to Rocky Mountain National Park with 48 comfortable rooms. Open May through October. **$–$$**

Aspen Lodge at Estes Park
6120 Highway 7, Estes Park, CO 80517
Tel: 970-586-8133 or 800-332-6867
www.aspenlodge.net
Less a dude ranch than a resort with horses, this grand lodge (the largest log structure in Colorado and the only one at the base of Longs Peak) has both hotel-style rooms and cabins (without kitchens). Activities include horseback riding, sleigh and wagon rides, square dancing, hiking, mountain biking, fishing, cross-country skiing, ice skating and a myriad of children's programs. All meals are served at an on-site restaurant. Multiple-night stays may be required in summer. Bed and breakfast or inclusive American Plan. **$–$$$$**

Baldpate Inn
PO Box 700, 4900 Highway 7, Estes Park, CO 80517
Tel: 970-586-6151
www.baldpateinn.com
Set on Twin Sisters Mountain about 7 miles (11km) north of Estes Park, this old-fashioned mountain lodge, built in 1917, has 12 guest rooms and four cabins, furnished in rustic Grandma's attic style. Some lodge rooms share bathrooms. All cabins have fireplaces and require a two-night minimum stay. Room rates include a full breakfast. **$$**

Stanley Hotel
333 Wonderview, Estes Park, CO 970-577-4000 or 800-976-1377
www.stanleyhotel.com
This grande dame was built in 1909 by F. O. Stanley, inventor of the Stanley Steamer automobile, and is listed in the National Register of Historic Places and a member of the Historic Hotels of America. The 138 guest rooms range from nicely modernized classic, historic and de luxe rooms and spacious suites to a five-room Presidential Cottage. The hotel is set atop a hill with outstanding views of Estes Park and Longs Peak. Amenities include a heated pool, tennis courts, shops, a grand ballroom and restaurants. **$$–$$$**

YMCA of the Rockies Estes Park Center
2515 Tunnel Road, Estes Park, CO 80511
(See Snow Mountain Ranch, Grand Lake entry below)

Grand Lake

Coyote Ridge Bed and Breakfast
PO Box 1703, Route 34, Grand Lake, CO 80447
Tel: 970-887-1650
www.coyoteridgebb.com
Seven miles (11km) from Rocky Mountain National Park, this contemporary mountain lodge has three rooms with private bathrooms – two with fireplaces – and lovely views over Lake Granby. Full breakfast is included. **$**

Rapids Lodge
PO Box 1400, Hancock Street, Grand Lake, CO 80447
Tel: 970-627-3707
www.rapidslodge.com
This log hotel – one of the oldest in the area – is set on the Tonahutu River 3 miles (5km) from the west entrance of Rocky Mountain National Park. Seven lodge rooms are furnished with a funky mix of country furniture. New suites and condominiums have fireplaces, kitchen facilities and living areas. A restaurant is on the premises. **$$–$$$**

Snow Mountain Ranch
1101 County Road 53, Granby, CO 80446
Tel: 800-777-9622
www.ymcarockies.org
Owned and operated by the YMCA, Snow Mountain Ranch and YMCA of the Rockies Estes Park are set on several hundred scenic

acres on either side of Rocky Mountain National Park. Guests have a choice of simple group and family lodge rooms or fully equipped cabins, many with fireplaces. Recreational opportunities include canoeing, horseback riding, volleyball, basketball, roller skating, a climbing gym, and a wide variety of children's programs. A great choice for families. **$–$$$**

BELOW: Stanley Hotel, Estes.

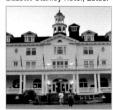

PRICE CATEGORIES

Price categories are based on the average cost of a double room per night:
$ = under $110
$$ = $110–250
$$$ = more than $250

STEAMBOAT SPRINGS

Hotel Bristol
PO Box 774927, 917 Lincoln Avenue,
Steamboat Springs, CO 80477
Tel: 970-879-3083
www.steamboathotelbristol.com
Friendly, characterful hotel
with 24 rooms. Family
rooms will accommodate
four people. **$–$$**

**Sheraton Steamboat
Resort**
2200 Village Inn Court, Steamboat
Springs, CO 80477
Tel: 970-879-2220 or 800-325-3535
www.starwood.com
This slope-side resort, now
managed by Starwood
Properties, has received a
$20 million renovation. Its
spacious, attractively
redesigned guest rooms
and suites now feature calm

decor, Sheraton Sweet
Sleeper beds, 32in (81cm)
flat-panel TVs, in-room
refrigerators and private
balconies. Condominiums
are available on the top
floor of the hotel. There's a
retail shopping area, a
fitness center, spas and a
ski shop. Non-smoking
throughout. **$$$**

**Steamboat Central
Reservations**
2305 Mount Werner Circle,
Steamboat Springs, CO 80487
Tel: 970-879-0740 or
877-783-2628
www.steamboat.com
This company handles
bookings for several ski-in/
ski-out accommodations,
ranging from standard hotel

rooms to condominiums.
$$–$$$

**Vista Verde Guest and Ski
Ranch**
PO Box 465, Steamboat Springs,
CO 80477
Tel: 970-879-3858, 800-526-7433
www.vistaverde.com
A classic guest ranch, set on
500 mountainous acres
(200 hectares) north of
Steamboat Springs and
surrounded by Routt
National Forest and Zirkel
Wilderness. Guests stay in
lodge rooms or log cabins
decorated in rustic style with
western art and handmade
log furniture. Each cabin has
a hot tub and wood-burning
stove. Summer activities are
focused on horseback riding

in Routt National Forest, and
fly fishing, mountain biking,
and hiking. Winter activities
include sleigh rides, snow
shoeing and cross-country
on groomed back country
trails. Meals range from
hearty country fare to fine
dining. Cooking classes and
wine tastings are available.
American Plan. **$$$**

THE I-70 CORRIDOR AND THE HIGH ROCKIES

Breckenridge

Barn on the River
303 North Main Street,
Breckenridge, CO 80424
Tel: 970-453-2975 or
800-795-2975
www.breckenridge-inn.com
A classic timber-frame
building with five view
rooms decorated with
country antiques. Located in
a quiet riverside setting, but
only a few steps from
historic Main Street. **$$**

Breckenridge Ski Resort
PO Box 1058, Breckenridge,
CO 80424
Tel: 970-496-4700, 800-536-1890
www.breckenridge.com
Vail Management runs many
properties, including ski-in/
ski-out condominium units
and the rustic, 71-room
Breckenridge Mountain
Lodge at the south end of
Main Street. Great Divide
Lodge, a full-service hotel at
the base of the mountain,
has 208 rooms with sitting
areas and large-screen
televisions. A ski shop is on
the premises. Village at
Breckenridge Resort, at the
base of the mountain next to
the Quicksilver Super 6 lift,
has standard rooms that
sleep up to four, studio

units, and condominiums.
Features include a heated
pool, exercise rooms, nine
restaurants and taverns,
and a shopping complex.
$$–$$$

**Poirrier's at the
Wellington**
200 N. Main Street, PO Box 5890,
Breckenridge, CO 80424
Tel: 970-453-9464, 800-655-7557
www.inntravels.com/usa/co/poirriers
The four guest rooms at this
Victorian inn have queen-
size beds, private baths with
whirlpool tubs, and bal-
conies with mountain views.
The restaurant has an
extensive wine list. **$$–$$$**

Copper Mountain

Copper Mountain Resort
209 Ten Mile Circle, PO Box 3001,
Copper Mountain, CO 80443
Tel: 888-219-2441 reservations
www.coppercolorado.com
Resort lodgings, just steps
from the lifts, include a bed
and breakfast, hotels, con-
dominiums and private
homes with up to five bed-
rooms. The resort's newest
property, Copper Springs
Neighborhood, is next to the
Super Bee ski lift. Guests at
all lodgings have use of the
Copper Mountain Athletic

Club, which has an indoor
pool, workout room and
steam room. **$$$**

Frisco

**Galena Street Mountain
Inn**
First Ave and Galena Street,
PO Box 417, Frisco, CO 80443
Tel: 970-668-3224
www.colorado-bnb.com/galena
This popular Mission-style
inn, now under new man-
agement, has recently
remodeled its guest rooms.
There's not a Victorian doily
or tchotchke in sight;
instead, the interior features
soothing light colors and
sturdy but attractive
furnishings. All 15 guest
rooms have 32in (81cm)
flat-screen televisions,
hypoallergenic down
comforters, private
bathrooms and mountain
views. Rates include a
healthy breakfast bar of
home-made granola, home-
made breads, fruit, and
daily breakfast entrée.
Communal hot tub. A free
shuttle transports guests to
Copper Mountain or Breck-
enridge, about 15 minutes
away. Frisco's Main Street is
within walking distance. **$$**

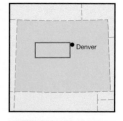

Minturn

Minturn Inn
442 Main Street, PO Box 186,
Minturn, CO 81645
Tel: 970-827-9647 or
800-646-8876
www.minturninn.com
Guests have a choice: they
can opt to stay at a 1915
hewn log home on the
town's Main Street, just
behind the Inn, or in a
contemporary lodge on the
banks of the Eagle River.
Both buildings have guest
rooms designed in attractive
Rocky Mountain style,
featuring exposed beams,
log walls, antler chandeliers,
hand-crafted log beds, down
comforters, and, in some
cases, large stone fire-
places. Some rooms have
whirlpool tubs for two and
private decks or patios.
Amenities include on-call

massage therapists, an exercise room, a complimentary breakfast, sauna and snow-shoes, The property is adjacent to White River National Forest and a five-minute drive to Vail and Beaver Creek Resorts. **$–$$$**

Vail

Beaver Creek Resort
PO Box 7, Vail, CO 81658
Tel: 970-496-4900 or
800-608-4849
www.beavercreek.com
Beaver Creek has properties ranging from inns and hotels to five-bedroom town house condos; most offer ski-in/ski-out convenience. The Charter, a European-style mountain lodge 100yds/meters from the Elkhorn ski lift, has two-bedroom condominiums with fireplace and balconies. Amenities include a ski rental shop and children's game room. Park Hyatt Beaver Creek Resort and Spa (www.beavercreek-hyatt.com) has 276 rooms with mountain or valley views, an elaborate fitness spa, an indoor-outdoor pool, and several restaurants and bars. **$$$**

ASPEN AND THE CENTRAL ROCKIES

Aspen

Hotel Jerome
330 E. Main Street, Aspen, CO 81611
Tel: 970-920-1000 or
877-412-ROCK
www.hoteljerome.com
This beautifully restored luxury hotel – built in 1889 and listed in the National Register of Historic Places – is now managed by Rock Resorts. It has 94 spacious rooms and suites with period furnishings, fluffy down comforters, feather pillows and high-thread-count sheets, flat-screen televisions and high-speed internet access. Known for first-rate service, the hotel offers a fitness room, heated outdoor pool and jacuzzi, ski and airport transfers and concierge service. Fine dining in the Garden Terrace and casual meals in the Library, and the popular J-Bar. **$$–$$$**

Hotel Lenado
200 S. Aspen Street, Aspen, CO 81611
Tel: 970-925-6246 or
800-321-3457
www.hotellenado.com
Distinctive postmodern architecture sets this boutique inn apart from the usual Victorian-flavored inns one finds in former mining towns. A 28ft (8.5-meter) -high contemporary stone fireplace dominates the great room. The 19 guest rooms are furnished with elaborate four-poster or carved beds, down comforters, terry cloth robes, high-end CD players, cable television with video or DVD players, cherry wood armoires, air conditioning and private bathrooms.

Some rooms also have wood-burning stoves, wet bars, balconies and whirlpool tubs. A rooftop deck (with hot tub) has good views of the town and surrounding mountains. A Whitaker Park location makes it convenient to downtown attractions and the ski areas. **$$–$$$**

Inn at Aspen
38750 Highway 82, Aspen, CO 81611
Tel: 970-925-3900 or
800-222-7736
www.innataspen.com
The only ski-in/ski-out property at the base of Buttermilk Mountain, the inn has 122 queen studios with balconies, kitchenettes, and refrigerators; junior and king suites; and king- and queen-size rooms. There's an outdoor heated pool, hot tub, health spa, and a free shuttle to the airport and village. **$$–$$$**

Saint Moritz Lodge and Condominiums
334 W. Hyman Avenue, Aspen, CO 81611
Tel: 970-925-3220 or
800-817-2069
www.saintmoritzlodge.com
This in-town motel, a block and a half from the public ski shuttle, offers hostel rooms, standard motel rooms, and one- to two-bedroom condos with fireplaces. There's a heated pool and sauna. **$–$$$**

St Regis Aspen
315 E. Dean Street, Aspen, CO 81611
Tel: 970-920-3300 or
866-716-8135
www.stregisaspen.com
A luxurious hotel located at the foot of Aspen mountain. The spa offers a comprehensive range of massage, body treatments and water therapy. Impeccable and friendly service. Fine contemporary Mediterranean dining in the in-house restaurant. There are 179 elegantly styled guest rooms and suites. **$$$**

Buena Vista

Los Manos Bed and Breakfast
22889 CR 371, Buena Vista, CO 81211
Tel: 719-395-4567
www.losmanosbandb.com
A nature lover's dream, this luxurious green bed and breakfast, 4 miles (6km) from Buena Vista, may be the most beautiful sustainable building you ever stay in. It is custom built from straw bale/adobe construction and is off the grid, located on 15 acres (6 hectares) surrounded by 400 acres (162 hectares) of pinyon forest, with glorious views of the Collegiate Peaks beyond. It has two soothingly decorated suites with log furniture, sleeper sofas, entertainment center with DVD/VCR player, satellite TV and Wi-fi access. Each suite is self-contained with its own entrance and patio. Home-cooked gourmet breakfast. Both owners are massage therapists and offer in-room massage to guests. **$$**

Crested Butte

Lodge at Mountaineer Square
620 Gothic Road, Mt Crested Butte, CO 81225
Tel: 970-349-4000 or
800-810-7669
www.skicb.com

Crested Butte's newest lodging is a lofty contemporary building in the heart of the ski village near the ski lifts. The attractive lodge offers deluxe king and studio, one-, two-, three- and four-room suites. Rooms feature elegant rustic furnishings, Serta Sleeper beds, high-thread-count sheets, flat-screen televisions, DVD/VCRs, complimentary Wi-fi, among other things. Small-plate contemporary dining in the on-site restaurant, Django's, is a big draw with locals as well as visitors. **$$–$$$**

Remington Management Group
PO Box 1249, Crested Butte, CO 81224
Tel: 970-349-2133 or
800-950-2133
This company manages 144 rooms in motel, resort and condominium rental properties, including Crested Mountain North, which has two- and three-bedroom condos 60yds/meters from one of the Crested Butte ski lifts. **$$–$$$**

PRICE CATEGORIES

Price categories are based on the average cost of a double room per night:
$ = under $110
$$ = $110–250
$$$ = more than $250

Leadville

Ice Palace Inn Bed and Breakfast
813 Spruce Street, Leadville, CO 80461
Tel: 719-486-8272 or 800-754-2840
www.icepaceinn.com
Built partly with lumber from Leadville's original Ice Palace – a 19th-century curiosity constructed largely of ice – this bed and breakfast has five toasty guest rooms decorated in period style with antiques and reproductions. All have private bathrooms, television, VCRs and fireplaces. A full breakfast and afternoon tea are included in the room rate. **$–$$**

Nathrop

Mount Princeton Hot Springs Resort
Nathrop, CO 81236
Tel: 719-395-2447 or 888-395-7799
www.mtprinceton.com
A refurbished historic hot springs resort in the mountains, northwest of Poncha Springs, with cliffside and poolside rooms in the lodge and attractive new log cabins by the river. Pool and on-site spa. Restaurant. A lovely retreat. **$$**

Paonia

Fresh & Wyld
1978 Harding Road, Paonia, CO 81428
Tel: 970-527-4374
www.freshandwyld.com
Stay in a charming farmhouse in the North Fork Valley surrounded by heirloom apple orchards, organic gardens and chickens. The seven comfy guest rooms glow with warm non-toxic paint schemes, stripped floorboards and rugs, and beds have cozy comforters and quilts. Upstairs rooms and suites have shared baths, the two downstairs rooms have private baths. This is a popular spot to meet locals, who come for the bounteous organic Sunday Brunch; guests enjoy a full organic breakfast from the farm daily. On-site cooking and gardening classes and workshops; gift shop. **$$**

Redstone

Redstone Inn
82 Redstone Boulevard, Redstone, CO 81623
Tel: 970-963-2526
http://redstoneinn.thegilmorecollection.com
This Swiss-style, turn-of-the-century resort is in the former home of the founder of Redstone, an historic coal mining village hidden away among red cliffs. A variety of rooms and suites, including sloping dormer rooms, are attractively furnished in traditional style with loads of character. A separate chalet has two bedrooms. On-site restaurant features everything from elk to fish and chips. Complimentary breakfast Mon–Wed; order off-menu in the Grill Thur–Sun. Open year round. **$–$$$**

Snowmass

Silvertree Hotel
100 Elbert Lane, Snowmass Village, CO 81615
Tel: 970-923-3520 or 800-837-4255
www.silvertreehotel.com
The village's only full-service hotel has more than 250 non-smoking rooms and suites, many with balconies overlooking the slopes. Amenities include dining in Brothers' Grille, a heated pool, whirlpool, sauna, massage service, health club and airport shuttle. **$$–$$$**

Snowmass Mountain Chalet
115 Daly Lane, Snowmass Village, CO 81615
Tel: 970-923-3900 or 800-843-1579
www.mountainchalet.com
This four-story ski-in/ski-out lodge has 64 standard and de luxe hotel rooms. There's an outdoor heated pool and an indoor sauna and fitness center. Rates include a full breakfast and light lunch. **$$–$$$**

SAN JUAN MOUNTAINS

Durango

Gable House Bed and Breakfast
805 E. 5th Avenue, Durango, CO 81301
Tel: 970-247-4982
www.durango.org
This huge, sprawling, three-story Queen Anne home in downtown Durango was built in 1892 and is on the National Register of Historic Places. It was a mansion home, a mercantile building, a private sanitorium and a hospital before being beautifully restored as a comfortable bed and breakfast by current owner and hostess extraordinaire Heather Bryson in the 1970s. There are six antique-filled rooms, two with balconies and shared baths. The large, comfortable lounge and formal dining room are decorated with Southwestern art and antiques. **$$**

General Palmer Hotel
567 Main Avenue, Durango, CO 81301
Tel: 970-247-4747 or 800-523-3358
www.generalpalmerhotel.com
Set in downtown Durango near the train station, this gracious, mid-sized Victorian hotel is fully restored with period furnishings and lots of Old West ambience. Rooms range in size and price; bridal suites have two-person whirlpools and wet bars stocked with Champagne. Amenities include cable television, air conditioning, phones with data ports, concierge service and a complimentary Continental breakfast. **$$**

Rochester Hotel and Leland House
721 E. Second Avenue, Durango, CO 81301
Tel: 970-385-1920 or 800-664-1920
www.rochesterhotel.com
This tastefully refurbished 1927 brick apartment building has 10 suites with kitchen facilities and private baths with Aveda toiletries. Decor features photos, memorabilia and framed written biographies of historic figures associated with the place. A gourmet breakfast is served at the newly renovated adjacent Rochester Hotel, which has 15 luxury rooms, a distinctive neon sign outside and serves afternoon tea daily in the lounge. Complimentary bicycles available for guest use. **$$–$$$**

Strater Hotel
699 Main Avenue, Durango, CO 81301
Tel: 970-247-4431 or 800-247-4431
www.strater.com
This Victorian belle has been providing fine accommodations since 1887. The

hotel features museum-quality antiques, period decor, 93 comfortable rooms and its own melodrama theater and saloon, the Diamond Belle, one of the most famous honky-tonks in the West. Fine dining is available. **$–$$**

Ouray

Beaumont Hotel
505 Main Street, Ouray, CO 81427
Tel: 970-325-7000 or
888-447-3255
The Beaumont Hotel reopened in 2003 after being closed for 39 years, following an award-winning, multimillion-dollar renovation that returned the hotel to its former Victorian splendor. Twelve elegantly decorated rooms have been completely updated with heating and air conditioning, large private baths, internet access and televisions with DVD players. The hotel also features a full-service salon, three retail boutiques and the acclaimed Tundra restaurant, offering fine dining and an extensive wine list. **$–$$**

China Clipper Bed and Breakfast
525 Second Street, Ouray, CO 81427
Tel: 970-325-0565 or
800-315-0565
www.chinaclipperinn.com
This three-story contemporary Victorian, now under new ownership, offers 13 guest rooms, with queen beds, private baths, satellite television, ceiling fans and phones with voice mail and data ports. Some have special features such as jacuzzis for two, decks, fireplaces or large bay windows. A full breakfast is served in the formal dining room or on the front porch. Wine and cheese are served in the afternoon. **$$**

Historic Western Hotel
210 Seventh Avenue, Ouray, CO 81427
Tel: 970-325-4645

www.historicwesternhotel.com
Just off Main Street, this clapboard, false-front hotel offers simple period accommodations at hostel rates in an authentic Old West atmosphere. The hotel has 14 rooms and two suites, some with shared bathrooms. **$**

St Elmo Hotel
426 Main Street, PO Box 667, Ouray, CO 81427
Tel: 970-325-4951 or
866-243-1502
www.stelmohotel.com
Victoriana rules at this turn-of-the-century bed and breakfast inn in the center of Ouray's historic district. Nine snug, cheery guest rooms sport floral print wallpaper and comforters, sturdy straight-backed chairs or sofas and private bathrooms (although some have only a shower). Complimentary breakfast buffet and afternoon wine and cheese are included in the rate. The popular fine-dining Bon Ton restaurant and the Buen Tiempo Mexican restaurant are on the ground floor. **$–$$**

Silverton

Inn of the Rockies at the Historic Alma House
220 E. Tenth Street, Silverton, CO 81433
Tel: 970-387-5336 or
800-267-5336
www.innoftherockies.com
Built in 1898, this eclectic Victorian has 10 guest rooms, each furnished with antiques and named after a mine in the area. Rooms are provided with a history and photographs of their respective mine. Some rooms have

shared bathrooms. Full breakfast is included. **$–$$**

Wyman Hotel and Inn
1371 Greene Street, PO Box 780, Silverton, CO 81433
Tel: 970-387-5372 or
800-609-7845
www.thewymanhotelandinn.com
Built in 1912 and listed on the National Register of Historic Places, this former commercial building has thick sandstone walls, floor-to-ceiling arched windows and cathedral ceilings. All rooms are furnished with period antiques, king- or queen-sized beds and down comforters and are equipped with televisions, VCRs, telephones and private bathrooms. Several rooms have two-person whirlpool tubs. Included in the rate is a gourmet breakfast, afternoon tea, wine and cheese, and videos. **$–$$**

Telluride

Inn at Lost Creek
119 Lost Creek Lane, Mountain Village, Telluride, CO 81435
Tel: 970-728-5678 or
888-601-5678
www.innatlostcreek.com
This exclusive ski-in/ski-out mountain inn has just 32 chic studios and suites with fireplaces, marble bathrooms and whirlpool tubs. All rooms have kitchenettes and washer-dryers. There's a rooftop spa, bistro dining and a great room with a massive stone fireplace. Top rated for a unique stay. **$$$**

New Sheridan Hotel
231 W. Colorado Avenue, Telluride, CO 81435
Tel: 970-728-4351 or
800-200-1891

www.newsheridan.com
Built in 1895, the New Sheridan is situated in the heart of Telluride's historic district. Sensitively restored and modernized to retain the Victorian ambience but offering more amenities. Furnishings are tasteful, with Egyptian cotton sheets, flat-screen televions, iPod stations and high-speed internet access. Guests enjoy a complimentary full breakfast, a fitness room and two rooftop hot tubs. The hotel has the oldest bar in town. **$$$**

San Sophia Luxury Properties
300 W. Colorado Avenue, PO Box 1825, Telluride, CO 81435
Tel: 970-728-3001 or
800-537-4781
www.sansophia.com
Set in the center of Telluride and Mountain Village, the San Sophia Collection is a portfolio of luxury condos, private residences and hotel rooms offering a variety of elegant guest accommodations in the Gondola area and downtown historic Telluride. **$$–$$$**

Telluride Mountainside Inn
PO Box 2288, 333 S. Davis Street, Telluride, CO 81435
Tel: 888-728-1950
www.telluridemtnsideinn.com
This affordable mountain inn is just a few steps from the Coonskin ski lift in Telluride, which provides access to cross-country skiing and snowshoe trails. The 79 rooms have private baths; some have kitchenettes and fireplaces. One-bedroom condos and a luxury riverside unit are also available. **$–$$**

MESA VERDE AND THE SOUTHWEST CORNER

Cortez

Holiday Inn Express
2121 E. Main Street, Cortez, CO 81321
Tel: 970-565-6000 or
800-626-5652
www.coloradoholiday.com
This pleasant hotel a short drive from Mesa Verde

National Park is a cut above the usual chain operation, with an attractive two-story lobby and generous rooms with cable television, VCRs, refrigerators and high-speed internet access. If you're traveling with children, ask for a "kidsuite," which features log bunk beds and

an Old West theme. Amenities include an indoor pool, sauna, fitness center and complimentary breakfast buffet. **$$**

Kelly Place
14663 Road G, Cortez, CO 81321
Tel: 970-565-3125 or
800-745-4885
www.kellyplace.com/home.html

Amateur archeologists will love this place. It's a rustic bed and breakfast in McElmo Canyon about 10 miles (16km) west of Cortez. More than 25 documented archeological sites have been discovered on the 100-acre (40-hectare) property. Guests are welcome to explore them on their own or strike out into neighboring Canyon of the Ancients National Monument. The main lodge is an adobe building with seven guest rooms decorated in rustic Southwestern style. All rooms have private baths and queen-size beds. Three adobe cabins, some with kitchenettes, fireplaces and whirlpool tubs, are also available. Activities include horseback riding, overnight pack trips, and guided botany and archeology hikes. A full complimentary breakfast is included in the rate. Wi-fi in the main lodge. **$**

Sutcliffe Vineyards
12202 Road G, Cortez, CO 81321
Tel: 970-565-0825
www.sutcliffewines.com
A unique opportunity to stay on a working vineyard hosted by British vintner and ex-restaurateur John Sutcliffe whose wines feature on top wine lists in Colorado and beyond. Choose from an eccentric 54ft (16-meter) -high tower that sleeps one to two, or the Yellow House, an adobe building that accommodates two couples. Breakfast is included in the overnight rate; a three-course dinner cooked personally by John Sutcliffe and featuring food raised on the farm is available for an extra $50 per person. The wine tasting room is open Thur–Sun noon–5pm. Reservations for vineyard stays should be

made well ahead as lodging books up fast. **$$–$$$**

Mancos

Sundance Bear Lodge
38890 Highway 184, Mancos, CO 81328
Tel: 970-533-1504 or 866-529-2480
www.sundancebear.com
There are three lodging options at this site, about 10 miles (16km) from Mesa Verde: two lodge rooms, a fully equipped log cabin and a three-bedroom guesthouse. Though the elaborate amenities typical of larger operations are absent, accommodations are comfortable and prices are reasonable. **$$–$$$**

Mesa Verde

Far View Lodge
1 Navajo Hill Road, Mesa Verde,

CO 81330
Tel: 800-449-2288
Situated near the top of Mesa Verde, this park lodge offers 150 guest rooms, decorated with Southwest furnishings and featuring balconies and 100-mile (160km) vistas. The Metate dining room is known for its contemporary Native American food, featuring corn, beans, squash, game, wild salmon and other fare. Tours of the nearby cliff dwellings are available. **$$**

BELOW: Mesa Verde.

THE NORTHWEST CORNER

Fruita

Stonehaven Inn
798 N. Mesa Street, Fruita, CO 81521
Tel: 970-858-0898 or 800-303-0898
www.stonehavenbed.com
Built in 1908, this Victorian inn is on the national historic register. It has five characterful rooms and suites, three with queen beds, two with twin beds. The Honeymoon Suite is the most lavish, with gas fireplace and jacuzzi tub, and the two-room Monument Suite has an old-fashioned tin ceiling and an extra room; both rooms have bathrooms. The other two rooms share bathrooms. Porch, hot tub, full breakfast. Views of the Book Cliffs, and a great jumping-off point for cycling to Colorado National Monument. **$–$$**

Grand Junction

Grand Vista Hotel
2790 Crossroads Boulevard at Horizon Drive, Grand Junction,

CO 81506
Tel: 970-241-8411 or 800-800-7796
www.grandvistahotel.com
This six-story high-rise in central Grand Junction has large, well-equipped rooms with whirlpool tubs and cable television. Other amenities include an indoor pool, spa, health club privileges, and restaurant. **$**

Los Altos Bed and Breakfast
375 Hill View Drive, Grand Junction, CO 81507
Tel: 970-256-0964 or 888-774-0982
www.losaltosgrandjunction.com
The 360-degree views from this lofty bed and breakfast inn make it one of the most scenic places to bed down for the night in the Grand Valley. All seven rooms and suites have queen beds, attractive furnishings, private baths and vistas. Beautiful gardens, full breakfast, free Wi-fi. **$$**

Meeker

Meeker Hotel

560 Main Street, Meeker, CO 81641
Tel: 970-878-5255
www.themeekerhotel.com
This historic inn in the center of Meeker has a long history and has welcomed many famous people since it was built in the late 19th century. The restaurant feeds hungry hunters, and you can stay the night in one of 24 freshly renovated regular rooms or suites; several studios have full kitchen facilities. Ask about staying in the Theodore Roosevelt Room, which was occupied by Teddy Roosevelt. **$–$$**

Palisade

Colorado Wine Country Inn
777 Grande River Drive, Palisade, CO 81526
Tel: 970-464-5777 or 888-855-8330
www.coloradowinecountryinn.com
Set amid 20 acres (8 hectares) of vineyards 10 miles (16km) east of Grand Junction, in the heart of the Grand Valley's Wine Country, this charming new

Denver

inn has been winning rave reviews among wine lovers as a great base for wine touring. The 80 well-appointed rooms all have flat-screen televisions, microwaves and refrigerators. Full breakfast, afternoon wine reception, tapas and light dining nightly in the Tapestry Lounge, pool, fitness center, business center, and spa. Book well ahead for Wine Fest in mid-September. **$$**

PRICE CATEGORIES

Price categories are based on the average cost of a double room per night:
$ = under $110
$$ = $110–250
$$$ = more than $250

E ATING OUT

RECOMMENDED RESTAURANTS, CAFÉS, & BARS

What to Eat

As a ranching state, Colorado is of course big on beef. Steakhouses are found just about everywhere, and even run-of-the-mill restaurants can be relied upon to serve decent steaks and burgers.

But there's more to Colorado cuisine than meat and potatoes. Innovative chefs have given a creative twist to native Rocky Mountain ingredients, including game meats such as bison, venison and elk. Colorado lamb is a popular item, too, as is local trout.

Don't be confused by the delicacy known as Rocky Mountain oysters. They're not shellfish at all but the testicles of calves, bison or sheep, usually sprinkled with breadcrumbs and fried.

Visitors are also sometimes confused about the meaning of the word café. In cities and large towns, café is usually used in the European sense – a coffee bar that serves pastries, breads and light meals. In rural areas, however, the word generally refers to a small family-run restaurant or diner, the kind of place

you might stop for burgers and pie but not cappuccino.

Brewpubs are also a source of some confusion. Are they breweries? Bars? Restaurants? Well, yes, all three. And they are not to be mistaken for microbreweries, which make beer that is consumed mostly off-site.

As for ethnic foods, you'll find a wide variety in urban areas and resorts, a narrower choice in small towns. The one exception is Mexican food, which, along with hamburgers and pizza, is available just about everywhere.

R E S T A U R A N T   L I S T I N G S

THE EASTERN PLAINS

Fort Collins

Bisetti's Italian Restaurant
120 S. College Avenue, Fort Collins, CO 80524
Tel: 970-493-0086
www.bisettis.com
This old-fashioned family-owned Italian restaurant specializes in northern Italian favorites such as lasagna, *manicotti*, veal *saltimbocca* and a variety of pasta dishes. **$**

Coopersmith's Pub and Brewing
5 Old Town Square, Fort Collins, CO 80524
Tel: 970-498-0483
www.coopersmithspub.com
Wood-fired pizza, calzone

and a variety of interesting sandwiches are paired with freshly brewed beers and a selection of single malt scotch at one of northern Colorado's oldest brew-pubs. **$**

Cozzola's Pizza North
241 Linden Street, Fort Collins, CO 80524
Tel: 970-229-5771
Some say this is the best pizza in town. A choice of savory crusts and sauces with plentiful toppings. **$**

Egg & I Restaurant
2809 S. College Street, Fort Collins, CO 80524
Tel: 970-223-5271
www.eggandirestaurants.com
A great chain for breakfast (there's also a branch in

Estes Park); the chefs at this local favorite whip up a variety of specialty egg dishes, pancakes, French toast, home-made soups and sandwiches. **$**

Jay's Bistro
135 W. Oak Street, Fort Collins, CO 80524
Tel: 970-482-1876
www.jaysbistro.net
Choose from fresh oysters, Maine lobster, or individually made-at-your-table pan-roasted soup. That's just for starters. Live jazz Wednesday through Saturday. **$$**

Silver Grill Café
218 Walnut Street, Fort Collins, CO 80524
Tel: 970-484-4656

This Western-style café is the oldest restaurant in northern Colorado. It dishes out delicious home-style food in generous portions, with a Mexican twist. Specialties include hefty breakfast burritos, *huevos rancheros*, tamales, stacks of pancakes and giant cinnamon rolls. Open for breakfast and lunch. **$**

PRICE CATEGORIES

Price categories indicate the rough cost of dinner for one excluding beverages, tax and tip:
$ = under $20
$$ = $20–40
$$$ = more than $40

Greeley

Fat Albert's
1717 23rd Avenue, Greeley,
CO 80634
Tel: 970-356-1999
www.fat-alberts.com
Salads, thick sandwiches,
burgers and a variety of
steak, chicken and seafood
dishes are on the menu at
this family-style restaurant.
It's worth a stop for pie and
coffee. **$**

Trinidad

El Capitan Restaurant
321 State Street, Trinidad,
CO 81082
Tel: 719-846-9903
This is one of those places
that does two ethnic
cuisines well. Diners can
choose from Mexican
dishes such as burritos,
enchiladas, and
chimichangas or Italian
classics like spaghetti and
meatballs. **$**

**Nana & Nano's Pasta
House**
418 E. Main Street, Trinidad,
CO 81082
Tel: 719-846-2696
Stop for a big bowl of pasta
at this family-oriented Italian
restaurant. Pasta dishes are
served with salad and meatballs or sausage. **$**

DENVER

Bistro Vendôme
1420 Larimer Square, Denver,
CO 80202
Tel: 303-825-3232
www.bistrovendôme.com
Classic French bistro-inspired
menu, regularly changing.
You can't go wrong with the
steak au poivre and pommes
frites. Sit outside in the
romantic courtyard under a
shady canopy of trees. **$$**

The Broker
821 17th Street, Denver, CO 80202
Tel: 303-292-5065
www.thebrokerrestaurant.com
This is a good place for
romantic dining – in a
genuine bank vault. Fine
steak and seafood are the
specialties of the house...
that is, bank. **$$$**

Buckhorn Exchange
1000 Osage Street, Denver,
CO 80204
Tel: 303-832-0880
www.buckhornexchange.com
Denver's oldest restaurant
serves buffalo and elk in an
Old West setting. **$$–$$$**

Chop House & Brewery
1735 19th Street, Denver,
CO 80203
Tel: 303-296-0800
www.chophouse.com
Just the place for carni-
vores. Choose from filet
mignon, pepper-crusted NY
strip and a herb-crusted
rack of lamb. Sides include
jumbo shrimp and oven
roasted asparagus. As you
would expect there is a fine
selection of hand-crafted
ales, brewed on-site. **$$**

D Bar Desserts
1475 E. 17th Avenue, Denver,
CO 80218
Tel: 303-861-4710
www.dbardesserts.com
Fun foods on small plates
dominate at Food Network,
star and top pastry chef
Keeghan Gerhard's novel
contemporary eatery. Along
with wraps and salads, side
dishes like fries and avocado
halves are main attractions
here with the addition of
spices and sauces. The
creative Plated Desserts are
the focal point though. Try
Baby Charmel – chocolate
caramel tart, sauteed baby
bananas, rum cream and
caramel ice cream – or the
Molten Chocolate Thingy
(don't ask... just eat). **$**

Jax Fish House
1539 17th Street, Denver, CO 80202
Tel: 303-292-5767
www.jaxfishhousedenver.com
Located in the former home
of Jack Kerouac in LoDo, Jax
is one of Denver's top-
ranked fish restaurants. The
chef sources produce at
Cure Farms and other local
purveyors. **$$–$$$**

Lola
1575 Boulder Street, Denver,
CO 80211
Tel: 720-570-8686
www.loladenver.com
Named one of America's top
places to drink tequila (100
varieties are served in the
bar), Lola has a coastal
Mexican-inspired menu
cooked by award-winning
chef, Jamey Fader. The fresh
guacamole is prepared at
your table. The indoor/
outdoor bar has great views
of the city. **$–$$**

**McCormick's Fish House
& Bar**
1659 Wazee Street, Denver,
CO 80202
Tel: 303-825-1107
www.mccormickandschmicks.com
A longtime popular seafood
spot, McCormick's has more
than 30 varieties of fresh
fish and seafood, as well as
prime meats and pasta.
$–$$

Morton's of Chicago
1710 Wynkoop Street, Denver,
CO 80202
Tel: 303-825-3353
www.mortons.com
Steaks don't come any finer
than Morton's prime aged
beef. Snappily attired waiters
give a theatrical presentation
of the day's choices,
including a few seafood
dishes. There's an excellent
wine list and first-rate
martinis. Dark wood paneling
and celebrity photos give the
place a clubby, and decidedly
masculine, ambience. Buzzy
atmosphere in the heart of
LoDo. **$$–$$$**

Palace Arms
Brown Palace, 321 17th Street,
Denver, CO 80202
Tel: 303-297-3111
Seventeenth-century
antiques give the ring of
authenticity to the Napo-
leonic decor at this hotel
restaurant, which is popular
for its fine contemporary
dining. The award-winning
wine list features 900-plus
selections. **$$–$$$**

Panzano
909 17th Street, Denver, CO 80202
Tel: 303-296-3525
www.panzano-denver.com
Located in the stylish Hotel
Monaco near 16th Street
Mall, Panzano occupies an
elegant dark-paneled room
with private booths and
ceiling murals. Chef Elise
Wiggins highlights organic
and locally sourced foods in
her northern Italian cuisine.
Try an award-winning Caesar
salad or pancetta-wrapped
shrimp, followed by Bear
Mountain Ranch steak or
grass-fed veal scaloppini.
Gluten-free available. **$$**

Red Square Euro Bistro
1512 Larimer Street, Denver,
CO 80202
Tel: 303-595-8600
www.redsquarebistro.com
Located in downtown Denver,
the menu at Red Square has
Asian and French overtones
with some Russian
influences. The vodka bar
features 100 vodkas from
around the world. **$$–$$$**

Restaurant Kevin Taylor
Hotel Teatro, 1106 14th Street,
Denver, CO 80202
Tel: 303-820-2600
Outstanding contemporary
cuisine artfully fusing
Southwest and Asian flavors
from a nationally acclaimed
chef, served in an elegant
dining room in the Hotel
Teatro. Seasonal prix-fixe
menu and à la carte menu
available. **$$$**

Rioja
1431 Larimer Street, Denver, CO
Tel: 303-820-2282
www.riojadenver.com
Well located near Larimer
Square, Denver's top-rated
restaurant has talented chef
Jennifer Jasinski at the
helm, turning out imagi-
native Mediterranean-
inspired dishes that riff on
local ingredients. Try the
duo of seasonal soups or a
flight of local artisan goat
cheese, followed by Colo-
rado lamb two ways or
seared nori-wrapped sea
scallops. The dessert
beignets rival those at Café
du Monde in New Orleans.
$$

Rocky Mountain Diner
800 18th Street, Denver, CO 80202
Tel: 303-293-8383
www.rockymountaindiner.com

An old-fashioned diner with wooden booths and a long lunch counter, this cozy eatery in downtown Denver satisfies patrons with a Rocky Mountain version of comfort food – buffalo meatloaf, venison chili, charred rib-eye, mashed potatoes drowned in gravy, and heaping slices of chocolate cake. It has one of the largest selections of Bourbon in Denver. **$–$$**

Root Down
1600 W. 33rd Street, Denver, CO 80211
Tel: 303-993-4200
www.rootdowndenver.com
A fun neighborhood restaurant in a renovated lube shop with a commitment to reduce, reuse, and recycle, Root Down takes sustain-

able to a new level. Globally influenced omnivore locavore dishes include gluten-free and raw options. Try Colorado buffalo sliders, country-fried tofu or roasted Petaluma chili chicken and a creative soft "mocktail" made with juices, soda, spices and agave. **$$**

Strings
1700 Humboldt Street, Denver, CO 80210
Tel: 303-831-7310
www.stringsrestaurant.com
Upscale American dining in a recently redecorated uptown restaurant. Creative dishes include braised veal cheeks with harissa aioli, tangerine gremolata and creamy polenta. Try the lighter bar and patio menu featuring happy-hour specials. **$$$**

Sushi Den
1487 S. Pearl Street, Denver, CO 80210
Tel: 303-777-0826
www.sushiden.net
Hip, high-tech decor meets traditional, beautifully presented Japanese cuisine at this popular restaurant. The emphasis is on sushi, of course, but the tempura, noodle dishes, dumplings, sukiyaki and other selections are equally good. **$$**

Wolfe's Barbeque
333 E. Colfax Avenue, Denver, CO 80203
Tel: 303-831-1500
www.wolfesbbq.samsbiz.com
Barbecue purists will be in pig heaven at this bustling rib joint on Capitol Hill, where politicians rub elbows with the people. Even vegetarians

will be happy. The smoked tofu is surprisingly good. **$**

Wynkoop Brewing Co.
1634 18th Street, Denver, CO 80202
Tel: 303-297-2700
www.wynkoop.com
Denver's first brewpub is housed in the cavernous J. S. Brown Mercantile Building in LoDo. There's a billiards club upstairs, a comedy club downstairs and about a dozen microbrews on tap. The dinner menu is weighted toward hearty fare, with entrées such as grilled elk medallions, buffalo rib-eye, lamb sirloin, shepherd's pie and bangers and mash as well as several interesting sandwiches, salads and pasta dishes. **$$**

BOULDER AND ENVIRONS

Black Cat Farm Table Bistro
1964 13th Street, Boulder, CO
Tel: 303-444-5500
www.blackcatboulder.com
Chef-owner Eric Skokan goes one step farther in sourcing local produce: he grows it himself on his own farm in nearby Niwot. Beets, carrots, and other veggies are starring attractions at this earthy bistro, paired with Skokan's note-perfect rendition of slow-cooked pork shoulder and other entrées. The national buzz on Black Cat and other top-ranked local eateries is one reason why Boulder was voted "Most Foodie Town in America" by *Bon Appetit* in 2010. **$$$**

Dushanbe Teahouse
1770 13th Street, Boulder, CO 80302
Tel: 303-442-4993
World cuisine, from Persian tamarind shrimp to Tibetan Kongpo beef are served in this enchanting teahouse from Tajikistan. **$**

Frasca Food and Wine
1738 Pearl Street, Boulder, CO 80302
Tel: 303-442-6966
www.frascafoodandwine.com
This friendly neighborhood

northern Italian restaurant has won its place atop many Best of Denver Area lists the old-fashioned way: building relationships with local farmers and ranches, sourcing the freshest local ingredients, then allowing their true colors to shine through with careful cooking techniques and wine pairings. Less is more is remarkably hard to pull off, but James Beard Award winner Lachlan McKinnon-Patterson does it nightly. Prix fixe. **$$–$$$**

Hapa Sushi Grill and Sake Bar
1117 Pearl Street, Boulder, CO 80302
Tel: 303-473-4730
Artfully prepared sushi, tempura and other Japanese specialties are the attraction at this restaurant, which leaves aside the usual kitschy decor for an airy, high-tech look. **$$**

Flagstaff House Restaurant
1138 Flagstaff Drive, Boulder, CO 80302
Tel: 303-442-4640
www.shopflagstaffhouse.com
Set on Flagstaff Mountain, with glorious views of the city below, the Flagstaff has long been the go-to place

for upscale Continental cuisine. The menu changes daily, but diners can usually count on a succulent rack of lamb, buffalo filet mignon and such seafood dishes as rainbow trout with crisp polenta cakes, tuna tartar and fresh halibut with scallops. Desserts are truly decadent; the wine list is extensive. **$$–$$$**

The Kitchen Café
1039 Pearl Street, Boulder, CO 80302
Tel: 303-544-5973
www.thekitchencafe.com
This hip community café takes the concept of Farm to Table quite literally, offering a set chalkboard menu of 20 seasonal dishes and encouraging diners to sit together at community tables and share food, family style. Local growers have a starring role on the menu, which features wholesome yet delectable dishes such as wood-roasted vegetables, a wheatberry risotto, seared Colorado trout, Long Farm pork loin and Colorado lamb with harissa. For those watching the pennies, lunch menu items are reduced at Community Hour, 3–5.30pm. **$$**

Lucile's Creole Café
2124 14th Street, Boulder, CO 80302
Tel: 303-442-4743
www.luciles.com
The award-winning breakfast is the specialty at this popular Creole restaurant. Eggs Benedict, etouffee, poached eggs with shrimp and creamed spinach, and pan-fried trout with eggs and béarnaise sauce are just a few of the options. Whatever you decide, don't miss sampling the warm, sugar-dusted beignets. Expect to wait for a table on weekends. **$**

The Mediterranean Restaurant
1002 Walnut Street, Boulder, CO 80302
Tel: 303-444-5335
www.themedboulder.com
The colorful tiled decor and relaxing atmosphere in this airy restaurant on the Mall is authentically Iberian – you

PRICE CATEGORIES

Price categories indicate the rough cost of dinner for one excluding beverages, tax and tip:
$ = under $20
$$ = $20–40
$$$ = more than $40

might as well be vacationing on the Mediterranean than in the foothills of the Rockies. No wonder it comes out over and over as Boulder's most popular restaurant, and it's most reasonably priced one for a social night out. The large menu features entrées such as lamb brochettes, braised pork chops, paella, woodfired pizza, pasta, rice dishes and a selection of fish prepared as you like it with choice of sauce. Hot and cold tapas such as prosciutto wrapped asparagus,

poached shrimp, eggplant and goat cheese are on the menu and also served daily at Happy Hour (3–6.30pm) and won't break the bank. **$–$$**

Red Lion
38470 Boulder Canyon Drive,
Boulder, CO 80302
Tel: 303-442-9368
www.redlionrestaurant.com

Long known for game dishes such as boar tenderloin and venison satay, the Red Lion also serves excellent steaks, seafood, and such imaginative specials as pecan-

crusted lamb and coconut-crusted red snapper. The hexagonal dining room has lovely mountain views. Good wine list. **$$–$$$**

Salt the Bistro
1047 Pearl Street, Boulder, CO
Tel: 303-444-SALT
www.saltboulderbistro.com

In true locavore style, chef Bradford Heap works with local growers to source ingredients for such small plates as roasted local beet carpaccio and entrées like late summer vegetable tasting. **$$**

Walnut Brewery and Restaurant
1123 Walnut Street, Boulder,
CO 80302
Tel: 303-447-1345
www.walnutbrewery.com

Set in a century-old brick building, this spacious brewpub serves good food in a lively setting. Pub favorites include smoked fish and chips, buffalo fajitas and vegetarian enchiladas. Sandwich platters, pasta, salads and a selection of beef and poultry entrées are also available. **$**

COLORADO SPRINGS AND ENVIRONS

Colorado Springs

The Blue Star
1645 S. Tejon Street,
Colorado Springs, CO 80905
Tel: 719-632-1086
www.thebluestar.net
A very popular upscale eatery with a Mediterranean and Pacific Rim-inspired menu. **$$–$$$**

Le Bistro
1015 W. Colorado Avenue,
Colorado Springs, CO 80904
Tel: 719-634-0400
www.lebistrocs.com
For affordability, flair and service, it would be hard to top this pretty 1894 cottage on the west side of Colorado Springs. The excellent contemporary cuisine is French, though the chefs aren't afraid to experiment with other traditions. The menu changes often, but appetizers may include wild mushroom tart, duck pate or pistou. Entrées range from beautifully presented chicken breast Niçoise, tagliatelle fruits de mer and roast leg of Colorado lamb to sauteed Colorado rainbow trout Grenobloise, almost all under $20. The desserts are heavenly, and the wine list is first-rate. **$–$$**

Margarita at Pine Creek
7350 Pine Creek Road,
Colorado Springs, CO 80919
Tel: 719-598-8667
www.coloradoeats.com/margarita
An intriguing adobe building with clay tiles and mosaic

tables is the setting for fine Mexican creations prepared with an imaginative twist. A large patio has views of Pikes Peak. The wine list isn't terribly extensive but is thoughtfully selected. Live music. **$$**

Mollica's Italian Market
985-A Garden of the Gods Road,
Colorado Springs, CO 80907
Tel: 719-598-1088
www.mollicas.com
Home-made sausages and meatballs, fat sandwiches, abundant salads and a variety of ravioli, *manicotti*, and lasagna are the bill of fare at this informal deli and market. A good spot for a quick and hearty meal. **$**

Nemeth's El Tejon
1005 S. Tejon, Colorado Springs,
CO 80903
Tel: 719-471-0240
www.coloradoeats.com/El_Tejon
You'll find a familiar line-up of Mexican dishes at this well-known and loved family-owned restaurant, which has been serving top-shelf fajitas, enchiladas, chile rellenos and a variety of seafood and steak dishes for more than four decades.
$

Pepper Tree
888 W. Moreno Avenue,
Colorado Springs, CO 80905
Tel: 719-471-4888
www.peppertreecs.com
Old-fashioned, buttoned-down elegance is the style at this hilltop restaurant with sweeping views of the

city. Waiters/chefs in tuxedoes prepare your meal at table-side. The menu sticks with a tried-and-true formula. Entrées such as steak Diane, filet mignon, Chateaubriand, and the house specialty, pepper steak, are excellent though not particularly innovative. **$$$**

Phantom Canyon Brewing Co.
2 E. Pikes Peak Avenue,
Colorado Springs, CO 80903
Tel: 719-635-2800
www.phantomcanyon.com
Set in the 1901 Cheyenne Building in downtown Colorado Springs, this brewpub offers creditable dinner entrées as well as typical pub fare. A variety of ales are brewed on the premises, and there's a spacious billiard parlor with 12 pool tables and a bar on the second floor. **$–$$**

Walter's Bistro
1606 S. 8th Street,
Colorado Springs, CO 80906
Tel: 719-630-0201
www.waltersbistrocs.com
Sophisticated without being stuffy, this newly renovated contemporary dining restaurant offers fine food, exemplary service, and a menu that features excellent seafood. Look for carefully prepared entrées such as grilled filet mignon, pan-seared sea scallops, and pan-roasted Alaskan halibut. **$$–$$$**

Manitou Springs

Cliff House
306 Canon Avenue,
Manitou Springs, CO 80829
Tel: 719-685-3000
www.thecliffhouse.com
A beautifully restored Victorian resort at the base of Pikes Peak is the setting for this elegant restaurant overseen by award-winning chef Scott Savage. The dining room is decked out in crystal, china and crisp damask linens. The menu features duck crêpes and grilled quail as well as pan-roasted Colorado striped bass, cedar plank salmon, and a filet mignon stuffed with black truffle and topped with blue cheese. The wine list has more than 550 selections. **$$**

Craftwood Inn
404 El Paso Boulevard,
Manitou Springs, CO 80829
Tel: 719-685-9000
www.craftwood.com
Housed in a Tudor-style building with glorious views of Pikes Peak, this eatery serves robust Colorado cuisine with a light touch. The game dishes are particularly interesting. Try bison tenderloin, elk steak, wild boar teriyaki, pecan-crusted venison, caribou strip loin or pheasant en croute as well as several beef and seafood dishes. There are usually a few vegetarian selections, too. **$$–$$$**

SAN LUIS VALLEY

Alamosa

Bauer's Campus Café
435 Poncha Street, Alamosa,
CO 81101
Tel: 719-589-4202
Coeds at Adams State College flock to this little eatery for king-sized cinnamon rolls and cheap, bountiful breakfasts with good green chile. **$**

Bistro Rialto
716 Main Street, Alamosa,
CO 81101
Tel: 719-589-3039
www.bistrorialto.com
Look for the old movie sign above this popular Italian restaurant. Hearty pastas, calzones and pizzas offer soothing comfort food. **$**

El Charro Café
421 6th Street, Alamosa, CO 81101
Tel: 719-589-2262
Hispanic culture is deeply rooted in the San Luis Valley. Immigrants from New Mexico

were among the first settlers. Mexican restaurants in the area serve authentic, inexpensive food, and El Charro is one of the better choices – a simple, family-run place with first-rate eats at rock-bottom prices. **$**

Milagro's Coffeehouse
529 Main Street, Alamosa,
CO 81101
Tel: 719-589-9299
For road warriors, there's nothing more welcome than the sight of an attractive little hometown coffee house serving good coffee drinks (locally roasted Bongo Billy's coffee) and loose-leaf teas, homemade pastries and cakes, and light meals like quiche that are also light on the budget. Used bookstore in the back. **$**

Oscar's Restaurant
710 Main Street, Alamosa, CO 81101
Tel: 719-589-9230
Customers squeeze into

vinyl booths for belly-busting portions of enchiladas, *chimichangas, tostadas, flautas* and burritos smothered in red or green chile. Try a bowl of *menudo*, an aromatic soup made of tripe, hominy and chile. **$**

San Luis Valley Brewing Company
631 Main Street, Alamosa,
CO 81101
Tel: 719-581-BEER
www.slvbrewco.com
Try a refreshing San Luis Valley Hefeweizen, Mexican style light beer, IBA, amber ale or oatmeal stout, homemade root beer and black cherry cream soda at this microbrew pub and sports bar. Average but filling pub food of the burger, pizza and pasta variety. **$**

True Grits
100 Santa Fe Street, Alamosa,
CO 81101
Tel: 719-589-9954

No, it's not a restaurant dedicated to the cornmeal gruel known in the South as "grits." This steakhouse – a good place for T-bones and locally grown potatoes – is a virtual shrine to John Wayne, star of the film *True Grit*. Movie memorabilia and other Duke-iana are displayed on just about every surface. **$–$$**

Antonito

Dos Hermanas Restaurant
435 Main Street, Antonito,
CO 81120
Tel: 719-376-5589
Antonito's favorite eatery serves generous helpings of fresh-tasting Mexican food. Enjoy fresh steaks, fajitas, enchiladas, burritos, and other rib-sticking dishes loaded with chile and beans. Famous for its margaritas. **$**

ROCKY MOUNTAIN NATIONAL PARK AREA

Allenspark

Fawn Brook Inn
357 Route 7, Allenspark, CO 80510
Tel: 303-747-2556
www.fawnsbrookinn.com
This rustic lodge features a changing menu of elegantly presented, Austrian-influenced game, duck, veal and seafood. Expensive but worth it. Reservations recommended. **$$**

Estes Park

Dunraven Inn Restaurant
2470 Highway 66, Estes Park,
CO 80517
Tel: 970-586-6409
www.dunraveninn.com
Diners can choose from traditional Italian entrées like veal parmigiana, ziti and chicken cacciatore, char-broiled steaks or seafood at this family restaurant. The bar is plastered with thousands of $1 bills left by satisfied customers. **$–$$**

Ed's Cantina & Grill
362 E. Elkhorn Avenue, Estes Park,

CO 80517
Tel: 970-586-2919
www.edscantina.com
Open for breakfast, lunch, and dinner, this boisterous eatery dishes out hefty burritos and other Mexican staples as well as two-fisted burgers, barbecued ribs, bratwurst, buffalo stew and sandwiches. **$**

Estes Park Brewery
470 Prospect Village Drive,
Estes Park, CO 80517
Tel: 970-586-5421
www.epbrewery.com
The formula is simple here. Start with a mug of freshly brewed beer, then add a selection of tried-and-true bar food – pizza, wings, burgers and sandwiches. A few full dinners are also on the menu, including barbecued chicken breast and "brewhouse" sirloin. **$**

Molly B Restaurant
200 Moraine Avenue, Estes Park,
CO 80517
Tel: 970-586-2766
www.estesparkmollyb.com
Good family value, this

friendly local favorite offers a variety of nicely done entrées, including grilled trout, chicken Marsala, strip steak, sandwiches, and burgers. The menu's vegetarian section caters to the tastes of herbivores with vegetarian lasagna, pasta primavera and other choices. Breakfast and lunch only. **$**

Mountain Home Café
547 E. Wonderview, Estes Park,
CO 80517
Tel: 970-586-6624
Open only for breakfast and lunch, this home town diner is a perennial favorite in Estes Park. Good Mexican/American dishes, from omelets and other egg dishes, biscuits and gravy and apple strudel pancakes at breakfast to tamales and juicy hamburgers at lunch. **$**

Notchtop Bakery and Café
457 E. Wonderview, Estes Park,
CO 80517
Tel: 970-586-0272
Hearty breakfasts like Green Eggs and Ham made of organic and natural ingre-

dients, good coffee on tap, and free Wi-Fi; open for breakfast, lunch and dinner. You can also get locally brewed beer. Located in a strip mall, but don't let that put you off. **$**

Pura Vida
160 1st Street, Estes Park,
CO 80517
Tel: 970-586-3686
www.puravidaestes.com
Here's something a little different: Costa Rican food. Think healthy Mexican but with the addition of fried plantains and yucca and interesting sauces. Loads of authentic atmosphere, great prices. Specialties include gallo pinto, *casada tipico*, *salsa lizano, tico* rolls with plum sauce. Lunch buffet. **$**

PRICE CATEGORIES

Price categories indicate the rough cost of dinner for one excluding beverages, tax and tip:
$ = under $20
$$ = $20–40
$$$ = more than $40

Grand Lake

Caroline's Cuisine at Soda Springs Ranch
9921 US 34, No. 27, Grand Lake, CO 80447
Tel: 970-627-9404
www.sodaspringsranch.com
"Rustic elegance" sums up the style of this mountain getaway, a good stop for a romantic dinner. The menu changes often, but entrées often include apple brandied shrimp, pepper-glazed pork, duck enchiladas,

steak Diane and prime rib. The wine list is not extensive but is carefully chosen. There's a kids' menu. **$$**

Back Street Steakhouse
604 Marina Drive, Grand Lake, CO 80447
Tel: 970-627-8144
Set in the Daven Haven Lodge near the west entrance to Rocky Mountain National Park, this rustic steakhouse serves hearty "mountain cuisine," including juicy steaks, oven-roasted prime rib, ruby red

trout, Jack Daniels pork chops and elk medallions. For those with smaller appetites, lighter entrées include lemon ginger chicken and seafood crêpes. **$$**

Fat Cat Café
916 Grand Avenue, Grand Lake, CO 80447
Tel: 970-627-0900
A local favorite for satisfying fresh breakfasts and lunches. Many home-cooked favorites like biscuits and gravy and

coconut cream pie. Get there early or wait in line. **$**

Sagebrush BBQ & Grill
1101 Grand Avenue, Grand Lake, CO 80447
Tel: 970-627-1404
www.sagebrushbbq.com
Barbecued ribs, hot sausage, beef brisket and a selection of steaks, burgers and fish (salmon, trout, and catfish) are the attractions at this casual country restaurant. There are even a few vegetarian dishes.
$–$$

STEAMBOAT SPRINGS

Bistro Cv
345 S. Lincoln Avenue, Steamboat Springs, CO 80487
Tel: 970-879-4197
www.bistrocv.com
Locally sourced food, creative contemporary small plates, stand alone or grouped as prix-fixe choices, and contemporary less-is-more takes on fresh, seasonal meat, fish and organic produce. These are what make Bistro Cv a popular choice for a special meal and one of Steamboat's top eateries.
$$–$$$

Café Diva
1855 Ski Time Square, Steamboat Springs, CO 80487
Tel: 970-871-0508
www.cafediva.com
Eat with the seasons at this top-notch locavore favorite, where the owners are also

your sommeliers. In fall, try the "deconstructed" chicken cassoulet; free-range pheasant in winter; elk tenderloin in spring; or the red quinoa and roasted carrot cakes or wild Alaskan halibut in summer. Fresh. Local. Delicious. **$$–$$$**

Harwig's
911 Lincoln Avenue, Steamboat Springs, CO 80477
Tel: 970-871-1980
www.lapogee.com
Housed in the same building as L'Apogée and run by the same people, Harwig's offers a more casual, less expensive option. The menu encompasses a wide range of ethnic foods, including dim sum, jambalaya, Thai curry, and a variety of "fusion" dishes. Customers can order from L'Apogée's extensive wine list. **$–$$**

BELOW: at your service.

Hazie's
2305 Mt Werner Circle, Thunderhead Lodge, Steamboat Springs, CO 80477
Tel: 970-871-5150
It's up, up, and away to this elegant restaurant, perched atop Thunderbird Peak and reached via the Silver Bullet Gondola. Sweeping views of Steamboat Springs, the ski area and the surrounding mountains complete an evening of fine dining. A four-course gourmet feast features expertly prepared Continental cuisine. A special place for a special occasion. **$$–$$$**

La Montaña
Après Ski Way and Village Drive, Steamboat Springs, CO 80477
Tel: 970-879-5800
www.lamontanasteamboat.com
Mexican, Tex-Mex, and Southwestern cuisine is given a creative spin at this popular restaurant at the base of the ski slopes. Try the grilled buffalo loin, Southwestern blue corn enchiladas with goat cheese and peppers, braised chicken mole, or pepita-crusted tuna. The bar is from the 1904 St Louis World's Fair. **$$**

L'Apogée
911 Lincoln Avenue, Steamboat Springs, CO 80477
Tel: 970-879-1919
www.lapogee.com
The fine French cuisine at this romantic restaurant is exceeded only by a wine list of some 750 labels.
$$–$$$

Riggio's
1106 Lincoln Avenue, Steamboat Springs, CO 80477
Tel: 970-879-9010
An airy contemporary space is the backdrop at this lively eatery, which features gourmet pizza, light pastas, elaborate salads and nicely prepared standards such as veal scallopine, *saltimbocca*, chicken cacciatore and *manicotti*. **$–$$**

Steamboat Smokehouse
912 Lincoln Avenue, Steamboat Springs, CO 80487
Tel: 970-879-6926
www.steamboatsmokehouse.com
This spirited place promises "authentic hickory-smoked Texas BBQ" and that's exactly what it delivers. Join the crowd for rib-sticking helpings of pork ribs, brisket, smoked turkey and corned beef, with mashed potatoes, coleslaw, beans and other traditional side dishes. There are even a couple of vegetarian dishes. **$**

Tugboat Grill and Pub
1860 Ski Time Square, Steamboat Springs, CO 80487
Tel: 970-879-7070
The rustic Old West decor, including a 19th-century cherry wood bar, recalls Steamboat's former life as a ranching center. Set at the base of the ski mountain, this is a good spot to tank up on burgers, chicken wings, sandwiches, steak, pan-fried trout or pasta before or after hitting the slopes. **$**

I-70 CORRIDOR AND THE HIGH ROCKIES

Breckenridge

Blue Moose Restaurant
540 S. Main Street, Breckenridge,
CO 80424
Tel: 970-453-4859
There's little ambience to speak of, but breakfast and lunch at this local favorite are guaranteed to satisfy. The menu includes eggs and pancakes as well as steaks, sandwiches, burritos, and a variety of vegetarian dishes. **$**

Breckenridge Brewery & Pub
600 S. Main Street, Breckenridge,
CO 80424
Tel: 970-453-1550
www.breckbrew.com
More than half a dozen hand-crafted ales are served with burgers, nachos, fish and chips, shepherd's pie, and other pub grub at this lively brewpub in central Breckenridge. **$**

Poirriers's Cajun Café
244 S. Main Street, Breckenridge,
CO 80424
Tel: 970-453-1877
Etouffee, gumbo, po' boys, crawfish and other Cajun dishes are the specialties of the house at this festive eatery, decked out in Mardi Gras masks and other reminders of the Big Easy. **$**

Relish
137 S. Main Street (on the Riverwalk), Breckenridge,
CO 80424
Tel: 970-453-0989
www.relishbreckenridge.com
Chef-owner Matt Facklish specializes in tasty, locally sourced New West cuisine that comforts even as it sparks the imagination. "Spaghetti and meatballs" features elk and lamb meatballs; organic Colorado "pot-pie" is served open face with sweet potatoes; and buffalo hanger steak is served on skewers. **$$-$$$**

Empire

Peck House
83 Sunny Avenue, Empire,
CO 80438
Tel: 303-569-9870
This restaurant, housed in one of the oldest hotels in Colorado, recalls the days when such inns were tiny islands of refinement in the wild and woolly mining towns of the Central Rockies. The chefs emphasize substance over style, with traditional beef, poultry and seafood entrées for dinner and a savory assortment of gourmet dishes for Sunday brunch. **$$**

Georgetown

Happy Cooker
412 Sixth Street, Georgetown,
CO 80444
Tel: 303-569-3166
A small, cheery house in Georgetown's historic district is the setting for this good-natured restaurant specializing in European waffles, home-made breads, soup, chile, a variety of vegetarian entrées, and scrumptious desserts. **$**

Mountain Buzz Café
1200 Argentine Street, Georgetown,
CO
Tel: 303-569-2020
The bill of fare is all marked up on a chalkboard at this homey little café. Egg breakfasts in the morning, and a good selection of thin-crust pizza, paninnis, and other sandwiches for lunch and dinner. A good coffee refueling spot anytime. **$**

Idaho Springs

Café Aimee
1614 Miner Street, Idaho Springs,
CO
Tel: 303-567-2333
A sweet café with a strong Francophile feeling. They serve breakfast and lunch. Try a mini croissant, the stuffed portabello mushroom baguette with gruyere cheese, or perhaps a Mediterranean omelet. Closed Tue. **$**

Morrison

Café Prague
209 Bear Creek Avenue
Tel: 303-697-9722
www.cafepraguerestaurant.com
Café Prague specializes in Bohemian and German dishes such as roast duck with potato pancakes and red cabbage, roast pork with sauerkraut and bread dumplings, and desserts like apple strudel and Bohemian crêpes. **$**

The Fort
19192 Highway 8, Morrison,
CO 80465
Tel: 303-697-4771
www.thefort.com
Coloradans come from far and wide to eat at this restaurant, set in a re-created adobe fur-trading post, which serves food and drink of the early American West. Start with a Hailstorm (Colorado's first mixed drink, a prickly pear Margarita), rattlesnake cakes or bison marrow bones, followed by a buffalo steak, elk medallions or charbroiled quail. The adobe bricks were made on-site; hand-hewn beams and fireplaces complete the Western atmosphere. **$$$**

Vail

Kelly Liken Restaurant
12 Vail Road, Vail, CO 81657
Tel: 970-479-0175
Seasonal American cuisine with a frequently changing menu using locally grown ingredients. Kelly was a semifinalist on the 2010 season of Top Chef on Bravo TV, where she proved her creativity. Her signature dish is potato-crusted trout filets with toasted pecans and raisins. Make sure to leave room for the sticky bun sundae. The wine list is extensive and over 30 wines are offered by the glass. Reservations are recommended. **$$-$$$**

The Little Diner
616 W. Lionshead Circle, Vail,
CO 81657
Tel: 970-476-4279
The local favorite for breakfast, the starring attraction here are eggs done every which way. Try the eggs Benedict. Good fuel for a day on the slopes. **$**

Montauk Seafood Grill
549 E. Lionshead Circle, Vail,
CO 81657
Tel: 970-476-2601
Fish is flown in daily for this fine seafood restaurant and raw bar. Most entrées are grilled over an open flame and served with light sauces. Two or three beef or poultry dishes are also on the menu. Appetizers and side dishes like lobster, calamari, garlic French fries, and wasabi mashed potatoes are worthy companions to the main course. **$$**

Sweet Basil
193 E. Gore Creek Drive, Vail,
CO 81657
Tel: 970-476-0125
Set on a creek in the heart of Vail Village, this classy, low-key bistro offers American cuisine with Asian and Mediterranean accents. Be prepared for flavorful dishes such as rack of Colorado lamb, and Dungeness crab soufflé. The Saturday and Sunday brunch are delightful. The wine list isn't gigantic but is thoughtfully compiled. Reservations are highly recommended. **$$-$$$**

Terra Bistro
352 E. Meadow Drive, Vail,
CO 81567
Tel: 970-476-0700
www.terrabistrovail.com
Located inside the Vail Mountain Lodge and Spa, Terra Bistro has a light, healthy approach to seasonal eating, emphasizing local and organic foods inspired by the Southwest, Mediterranean and Asia by way of the Rocky Mountains. Try the apricot-glazed Colorado lamb loin or perhaps Alaskan halibut grilled in a banana leaf. Sides include healthy edamame, kale and other greens. Open for dinner (and breakfast in season). **$-$$$**

PRICE CATEGORIES

Price categories indicate the rough cost of dinner for one excluding beverages, tax and tip:
$ = under $20
$$ = $20–40
$$$ = more than $40

ASPEN AND THE CENTRAL ROCKIES

Aspen

Bonnie's
Above Lift 3, Aspen Mountain
Tel: 970-544-6252
This popular free and home-made lunch spot packs out around noon, so try to get there before then, or after 1.30pm. Try the excellent artichoke chile pesto pizza, white bean chili, and finish with apple strudel featuring local apples. **$**

Jimmy's
205 S. Mill Street, Aspen, CO
Tel: 970-925-6048
www.jimmysaspen.com
"Fierce American food" in a white tablecloth dining atmosphere is the owner's description of this Contemporary American restaurant open for breakfast, lunch, and dinner. Known for its locally raised meats and seafood and extensive tequila menu. A Sunday Blues Brunch is served in the bar. **$–$$$**

Matsuhisa Aspen
303 E. Main Street, Aspen, CO 81611
Tel: 970-544-6628
www.matsuhisaaspen.com
Stellar chef Nobu Matsuhisa mixes Japanese cuisine with world influences at this reservations-only restaurant, a popular spot for Aspen's celebrity crowd. The sushi is otherworldly, but don't pass up an opportunity to taste one of Matsuhisa's masterful fusion dishes. **$$–$$$**

Syzygy Restaurant and Ute City Bar
520 E. Hyman Avenue, Aspen, CO 81611
Tel: 970-925-3700
www.syzgyrestaurant.com
Live jazz provides a fittingly cool backdrop for this contemporary nouvelle restaurant, where diners enjoy beautifully presented dishes such as lemon-cured salmon, sesame-crusted snapper and seared beef tenderloin. The wine list has more than 600 French, Italian and American labels. **$–$$$**

Woody Creek Tavern
2858 Upper River Road, Woody Creek, CO 81656
www.woodycreektavern.com
Home base for the counter-culture in the Aspen area since gonzo Rolling Stone journalist Hunter S. Thompson's first set up shop here in the 1980s, this funky tavern is still a local landmark for extremely good food at rock-bottom prices and excessive drinking and socializing. Huge portions (even the appetizers are designed to be shared) span the gamut from naturally raised chicken, low-fat Limousin beef, trout and tilapia to organic salads and soups, sandwiches, and excellent Mexican fare like tamales and burritos. **$–$$**

Buena Vista

Bongo Billy's Café
1713 S. Highway 24, Buena Vista, CO 81211
Tel: 719-395-2634
www.bongobillyscafe.com
A great place to rub shoulders with the locals and get something healthy and delicious to eat. The main attraction here is the café's own locally roasted Bongo Billy's coffee, roasted right here in Buena Vista and available in bulk in the café. The home-made fare – from all-natural, unrefined ingredients – is pretty good, too: muffins, scones, cookies, brownies and fruit bars, cakes and pastries. At lunch time, there's a daily selection of soups, croissant sandwiches, quiches, and salads. There's another branch in nearby Salida. **$**

Crested Butte

Le Bosquet
525 Red Lady Avenue, Crested Butte, CO 81224
Tel: 970-349-5808
Fine French cuisine is the specialty at this pleasant restaurant. Signature dishes include rack of lamb, hazelnut chicken and salmon

with ginger glaze. **$$**

The Dogwood Cocktail Cabin
309 Third, Crested Butte, CO
Tel: 970-349-6338
www.thedogwoodcocktailcabin.com
Here's a thing to behold: real ale, Champagne, and creative cocktails in a remodeled 1890s miner's cabin as you munch on kabobs, edamame and other hors d'oeuvres. Try the Beetnik, a beet-infused vodka martini. Hot drinks, too. If that isn't enough to intrigue you, check out their delightful website. Only in fun and funky downtown Crested Butte! **$**

Django's Restaurant and Wine Bar
Mountaineer Square, Mt Crested Butte, CO
Tel: 970-349-7574
www.djangos.us
Small plate dining reaches its happy apotheosis in Colorado at Django's restaurant, the brainchild of Kate and Chris Lazoulis whose magic in the kitchen has enchanted thousands of diners with such intriguing creations as cocoa butter caramel seared scallops with haricot verts and Meyer lemon confit. The restaurant offers an exceptional wine list, featuring southern European wines. Located in an airy, contemporary space in the courtyard of Mountaineer Square. Worth the hype, and then some. **$–$$**

Ginger Café
313 3rd Street, Crested Butte, CO 81224
Tel: 970-349-7291
An innovative Asian bistro with Thai, Vietnamese, and Indian selections that features produce from farms just over Kebler Pass in Hotchkiss and Paonia. Where else are you going to try peach lavash, a cracker-bread topped with impressive Avalanche goat cheese made in Basalt, peaches, Colorado honey, chives, and truffle oil? **$–$$**

Soupçon
127 Elk Avenue, Crested Butte, CO

Tel: 970-349-5448
www.soupconcrestedbutte.com
Delightful Provençal-inspired gourmet dining in an old 1891 miner's cabin. A knowledgeable, talented chef in the kitchen and exceptional local ingredients to draw on, such as beets from Hotchkiss and cherries from Paonia, are a recipe made in heaven. Try home-made smoked salmon or pulled duck purses followed by double elk chop. A good place to push the boat out. Dinner only. **$$$**

Leadville

Golden Burro Café & Lounge
710 Harrison Avenue, Leadville, CO 80461
Tel: 719-486-1239
Down-home grub at rock-bottom prices is the attraction at this Western style café. Massive breakfast burritos, meat loaf, pork chops, chicken fried steak and mashed potatoes with gravy are almost as good as mom's. **$**

The Grill Bar & Café
715 Elm Street Leadville, CO 80461
Tel: 719-486-9930
www.thegrillbarcafe.com
A local favorite for Mexican food, this casual bar and restaurant wins kudos for its green chile, stuffed *sopaipillas* and potent Margaritas. There are great mountain views from the rear patio. Expect to wait for a table on weekends. **$**

Paonia

Flying Fork Café and Bakery
Corner 3rd and Main, Paonia, CO
Tel: 970-527-3202
www.flyingforkcafe.com
Talented chef-owner Kelly Steinmetz has created a cosy home town restaurant that people flock to from far and wide for elegantly prepared made-from-scratch Italian food using local ingredients and lots of care. In the few years it has

been open, Flying Fork has also become a popular community gathering palce for some "chat and chew" over delicious baked goods and morning coffee. Kelly makes sensational artisan breads, and New York-style bagels are available on Sunday mornings. **$–$$**

Salida

The Laughing Ladies
128 W. 1st Street, Salida, CO
Tel: 719-539-6209
www.laughingladiesrestaurant.com
The husband-and-wife chef team honed their skills in top Napa Valley restaurants before landing in Salida and

earning a reputation for producing the best food in town. The emphasis is on simple, elegant New American cuisine made from scratch using local ingredients and the freshest seafood and natural meats. For dinner, try the Cabernet braised lamb shanks or

buffalo tri tip. Vegetarian entrées include a delectable roasted squash/portobello mushroom enchilada with local goat cheese and *pico de gallo*. The couple also owns and operates the Downtown Bakery and Delicatessen, Salida's only artisanal bakery. **$–$$**

SAN JUAN MOUNTAINS

Durango

Francisco's Restaurante y Cantina
619 Main Avenue, Durango, CO 81301
Tel: 970-247-4098
www.franciscosdurango.com
The Garcia family has been satisfying residents and visitors alike for more than 30 years at this spirited restaurant, specializing in platters freighted with such Mexican staples as enchiladas, *chile rellenos*, fajitas, and *carne adovada* as well as a selection of steak, chicken and seafood. **$**

Gazpacho New Mexico Restaurant
431 E. 2nd Avenue, Durango, CO 81301
Tel: 970-259-9494
Fiery New Mexican cooking is the specialty at this friendly spot. Recommended is the *carne adovada*, Santa Fe style blue enchiladas (stacked instead of rolled), and the eponymous "cold field soup," or gazpacho. Several tasty vegetarian dishes round out the menu. **$**

Ken & Sue's
636 Main Avenue, Durango, CO 81301
Tel: 970-385-1810
Casual and creative, the chefs at this sophisticated little place turn out "New American" interpretations of longtime favorites: herb-seared chicken breast, potato-crusted salmon, grilled pork and filet mignon as well as a few Asian dishes such as spring rolls and Thai shrimp with coconut, curry and basmati rice. **$–$$**

Season's Rotisserie and Grill
764 Main Avenue, Durango, CO 81301
Tel: 970-382-9790
www.seasonsofdurango.com
A warm, welcoming American grill housed in a historic building right in the heart of Durango. The chefs lean heavily on meat, cheese, and organic produce grown in the Animas Valley. Try Foxfire Farm lamb loin, free-range chicken with sugar snap peas from James Ranch, or a vegetarian warm tomato Belford tart using a Dutch-style farmstead cheese only available locally and made at James Ranch's Dairy. **$–$$**

Steamworks Brewing Company
801 E. Second Avenue, Durango, CO 81301
Tel: 970-259-9200
www.steamworksbrewing.com
This spit-and-sawdust Durango brewpub is a favorite local watering hole. Eight microbrews on tap, including stouts, lagers and IPA. There's an extensive pub grub menu. **$**

Silverton

Handlebars Restaurant & Saloon
117 E. 13 Street, Silverton, CO 81433
Tel: 970-387-5395
Beer, burgers and barbecue are the staples at this old-time eatery and "museum," crammed to the gills with 19th-century mining equipment and mounted animals. Other interesting choices include buffalo chili, cream of green chile soup and chicken pot pie. **$**

San Juan Grill
1250 Greene Street, Silverton, CO 81433
Tel: 970-387-9918
Located in the historic Teller House, the San Juan Grill serves up heaping plates of the best food in Silverton. The menu changes seasonally and draws on local and organic ingredients whenever possible. At breakfast, fuel up with a huge burrito with green chile. Melting spare ribs are a popular choice on the dinner menu. Open for breakfast, lunch and dinner. **$–$$**

Silverton Brewery and Restaurant
1333 Greene Street, Silverton, CO 81433
Tel: 970-387-5033
www.silvertonbrewing.com
Exceptional award-winning microbrewed beers at this popular small town brewery will make you feel as light-headed as the high country around you. Fine if you've arrived by narrow-gauge train and are taking the train or coach back to Durango. Watch out on the narrow, steep San Juan Skyway if you're driving. The Red Mountain ale is popular, and they also make seasonal beers like a Belgian Wit, flavored with coriander and orange peel. **$**

Telluride

Cocina de la Luz
123 E. Colorado Street, Telluride, CO 81435
Tel: 970-728-9355
www.lacocinatelluride.com
A simply superb homey little Mexican place serving traditional dishes like

flautas, burritos, enchiladas, and tacos made using fresh, organic ingredients plus home-made tortillas. The healthiest Mexican food this side of Mexico. **$**

Cosmopolitan
300 W. San Juan Avenue, Telluride, CO 81435
Tel: 970-728-1292
www.cosmotelluride.com
This elegant restaurant is located in the Hotel Columbia. Chef/owner, Chad Scothorn has created an innovative menu. Choose from the Colorado lamb rack with butternut squash truffle risotto, green beans and garlic jus or the barbecued salmon with crispy yams, sweetcorn broth and bacon-braised spinach. There are over 200 vintage wines on the wine list. **$$–$$$**

La Marmotte
150 San Juan Avenue, Telluride, CO 81435
Tel: 970-728-6232
www.lamarmotte.com
The style and attitude of a French country bistro comes alive at this 100-year-old brick building, the town's old ice storage house. Start with goat cheese ravioli and beet salad or a foie gras terrine, then try a lovely seafood stew, filet mignon or sauteed scallops with mushroom flan. Or try a taste of everything by ordering the full four-course menu. **$$**

PRICE CATEGORIES
Price categories indicate the rough cost of dinner for one excluding beverages, tax and tip:
$ = under $20
$$ = $20–40
$$$ = more than $40

MESA VERDE AND THE SOUTHWEST CORNER

Cortez

Francisca's Fine Mexican Food
125 E. Main Street, Cortez,
CO 81321
Tel: 970-565-4093
Prepare yourself for fiery enchiladas, *carne adovada*, fajitas, tamales and other New Mexican dishes at this friendly, family-run cantina, the top local choice for

BELOW: sharing the gossip over something sweet.

dinner out. Cool off your mouth with a first-rate Margarita or *sopaipilla* (puffy fried dough) drizzled with honey. **$**

Main Street Brewery
21 E. Main Street, Cortez,
CO 81321
Tel: 970-564-9112
Hand-crafted beer is the main attraction at this brew-pub, but the food is pretty good, too. There's the usual assortment of pizza, wings, burgers, bratwurst and sandwiches as well as more substantial choices such as prime rib and Rocky Mountain trout. **$**

Nero's
303 W. Main Street, Cortez,
CO 81321
Tel: 970-565-7366
Home-made pasta is only half the story at this attractive little eatery. In addition to northern Italian specialties are thick steaks, grilled chicken and seafood. **$–$$**

Silver Bean Coffee Company
410 W. Main Street, Cortez,
CO 81321

Tel: 970-946-4404
This drive-through coffee kiosk is housed in a 1969 Airstream trailer. The coffee here is strong enough to get you through the day. A local favorite is the Frozen Flamingo, a coffee drink with vanilla, Ghiradelli chocolate and whipped cream. It's named in honor of the coffee shop's mascot who sports seasonal attire on the "lawn" outside the trailer. **$**

Mancos

Millwood Junction
Highway 160 and Main Street,
Mancos, CO 81328
Tel: 970-533-7338
www.millwoodjunction.com
Don't let the rustic exterior fool you. Waiting inside this barn-like building about 7 miles (11km) east of Mesa Verde National Park are some of the best steak and seafood dishes in the Four Corners area. Other choices include barbecued ribs, blackened catfish, lobster, roasted chicken and pork

tenderloin. A large salad bar should satisfy the vegetarians in your party. **$–$$**

Mesa Verde

Far View Lodge
1 Navajo Hill Road, Mesa Verde National Park, CO 81330
Tel: 970-533-1944
The lodge's Metate Room not only has some of the best views in the Southwest but offers a well-executed menu of heritage foods interpreted with a contemporary twist. Food at the Far is above the standard fare. Executive chef Brian Puett was awarded the Colorado Chefs Association's Award of Culinary Excellence in 2010 in recognition of his achievement here. Try the bison shepherd's pie, the turkey Napoleon or the marinated grilled quail and you can imagine yourself as a hunter tracking game through Mesa Verde in the fall and winter and spit-roasting it on the fire. **$–$$**

THE NORTHWEST CORNER

Fruita

Hot Tomato Pizza
124 N. Mulberry Street, Fruita,
CO 81521
Tel: 970-858-1117
www.hottomatocafe.com
Refuel after a long day of bike riding around Colorado National Monument at this fun home town pizza joint. The owners are bikers themselves. **$**

Grand Junction

Crystal Café & Bake Shop
314 Main Street, Grand Junction,
CO 81501
Tel: 970-242-8843
Freshly baked breads and pastries are only the beginning at this popular café, where residents and visitors line up for breakfasts of pancakes, French toast and a variety of ome-

lets. Lunch runs to the lighter side, with salads, soups and sandwiches. Dinner is served Thursday to Saturday. **$**

Il Bistro Italiano
400 Main Street, Grand Junction,
CO 81501
Tel: 970-243-8622
www.ilbistroitaliano.com
Italian-born Brunella Gualerzi and her husband, Ron Hall, former longtime manager of the Winery, run this hot northern Italian bistro. Brunella's home-made pastas and traditional sauces are authentically Italian recipes centered on local ingredients found on the Western Slope. Look for Jumpin' Good Goat cheese from Buena Vista and local tomatoes, fruit and wine to play starring roles on the seasonal menu. **$$**

Winery Restaurant

642 Main Street, Grand Junction,
CO 81501
Tel: 970-42-4100
www.winery-restaurant.com
Widely regarded as the best restaurant in town, the Winery stakes its reputation on straightforward preparations of classic Western dishes – prime rib, salmon, rack of lamb, pork chops, roast chicken and more. **$$$**

Meeker

Meeker Café
560 Main Street, Meeker,
CO 81641
Tel: 970-878-5255
This old-fashioned Western café inside the historic Meeker Hotel is the best place in town to rub elbows with the locals while digging into burgers, steaks, mashed potatoes, pie and other down-home, rib-

sticking fare. **$**

Palisade

Slice of Life Bakery
105 W. 3rd Street, Palisade,
CO 81526
Tel: 970-464-0577
"Baking the world better, one batch at a time," this long-established home town bakery specializes in fresh-baked pastries and pies using all local ingredients, including Western Slope flour, Palisade-grown fruits and walnuts, and local honey. Closed Mon. **$**

PRICE CATEGORIES

Price categories indicate the rough cost of dinner for one excluding beverages, tax and tip:
$ = under $20
$$ = $20–40
$$$ = more than $40

A CTIVITIES

THE ARTS, FESTIVALS, NIGHTLIFE, SHOPPING, OUTDOOR ACTIVITIES, & CHILDREN'S ACTIVITIES

THE ARTS

From world-class contemporary and historic art museums and theaters representing a variety of cultures in Denver, Colorado Springs and Aspen, to potteries and galleries among the Colorado River communities in Grand Junction, and quirky artist spaces and repertory theater in restored mine towns like Crested Butte, Salida, Ouray and Creede – the Rocky Mountain state is passionate about art. And it's not all located indoors. Grand Junction's popular Art on the Corner project places sculptures throughout the historic downtown area, and Denver Botanic Garden recently hosted a temporary installation of Henry Moore sculptures.

American Indian art is also well covered and can be viewed at various locations throughout the state, including Koshare Indian Kiva and Museum in La Junta *(see page 143)*, Ute Museum in Montrose *(see page 232)*, and in Mesa Verde National Park *(see page 262)*, and the Anasazi Heritage Center *(see page 267)*.

Visual Arts

Art and Soul Gallery
1615 Pearl Street, Boulder, CO 80302; tel: 303-544-5803; www.art andsoul.com
Boulder's premier contemporary art gallery for the last decade is in a light, bright space on the Mall.
Denver Art Museum
100 W. 14th Avenue Parkway, Denver, CO 80204-2788; tel: 720-865-5035; www.denverartmuseum.org

Colorado's premier art museum featuring Western landscape and contemporary art, and national touring exhibits.
Four Winds Gallery
118 F Street, Salida, CO 81201; tel: 719-539-6075; www.fourwinds gallery-colorado.com
Paintings by artist and gallery owner Linda Frances, whimsical ceramic teapots and mugs by Damian Radice, and jewelry, photography, and art prints by various artists in the Arts District.
Telluride Gallery of Fine Art
130 E. Colorado Avenue, Telluride, CO 81435; tel: 970-728-3300; www.telluridegallery.com
In business 25 years, Telluride Gallery of Fine Art is the oldest gallery in the region and shows local, national, and international contemporary artists.
Western Colorado Center for the Arts
1803 N. 7th Street, Grand Junction, CO 81501; tel: 970-243-7337; www.gjartcenter.org
This art center on the campus of Mesa State College in Grand Junction is a focal point for arts in the community.

Theater

Arts Theater of the West
721 Santa Fe Drive, Denver, CO 80204; tel: 303-595-3800
Two theaters stage well-known plays, musicals and original works.
Avenue Theater
2119 E. 17th Avenue, Denver, CO 80203; tel: 303-321-5925
Top-rated theater; often produces comedies.
Creede Repertory Theater
124 N. Main Street, Creede,

CO 81130; tel: 719-658-2540; www.creederep.org
Known statewide for 45 years for its excellent rotating summer repertory offerings in the remote mining town of Creede in the San Juan Mountains.
Denver Performing Arts Complex
14th and Curtis streets, Denver, CO 80204; tel: 303-893-4100 or 800-641-1222; www.denvercenter.org
The complex encompasses four city blocks and eight theaters, seating more than 10,000 people. It is the second-largest such center in the country after Lincoln Center in New York.
Germinal Stage Denver
2450 W. 44th Avenue, Denver, CO 80211; tel: 303-455-7108; www2.privatei.com/~gsden
Highly regarded small theater producing traditional and experimental plays.

Opera

Central City Opera House
400 S. Colorado Boulevard, Ste 530, Denver, CO 80246; tel: 303-292-6700 or 800-851-8175; www.central-cityopera.com
Three operas are presented during the summer at this historic Victorian opera house in the former mining town of Central City.
Opera Colorado
695 S. Colorado Boulevard, Ste 20, Denver, CO 80246; tel: 303-778-1500; www.operacolorado.org
Denver's premier opera company stages three works a year, attracting stars such as Placido Domingo. Its major season is in Boettcher Concert Hall is in April and May, with other presentations in The Buell.

Classical Music

Boulder Philharmonic
2590 Walnut Street, Boulder,
CO 80302; tel: 303-449-1343;
www.boulderphil.org
Guest performers and the Boulder
Ballet round out a season of
symphonic and chamber music.

Colorado Springs Philharmonic
Plaza of the Rockies, 111 S. Tejon
Street, Ste 102, Colorado Springs,
CO 80906; tel: 719-575-9632;
http://csphilmonic.org
The symphony presents a repertoire
of classical works and pops at the
Pikes Peak Center.

Colorado Symphony Orchestra
1000 14th Street, Ste 15, Denver,
CO 80202; tel: 303-623-7876 or 877-
292-7979; www.coloradosymphony.org
Performs classical, pops and family
concerts at Boettcher Concert Hall
(Sept–June), as well as summer
concerts in City, Washington and
Sloan Lake parks.

Grand Junction Symphony
225 N. 5th Street, Ste 120,
Grand Junction, CO 81501; tel: 970-
243-6787; www.gjsymphony.org
The symphony appears at venues
throughout the region.

Dance

Cleo Parker Robinson Dance
119 Park Avenue West, Denver,
CO 80205; tel: 303-295-1759;
www.cleoparkerdance.org
A multicultural dance organization
that performs at the Buell Theater.

Colorado Ballet
1278 Lincoln Street, Denver,
CO 80203; tel: 303-837-8888;
www.coloradoballet.org
Classical ballet company with fall,
winter and spring seasons at the Buell
Theater.

Colorado Springs Dance Theater
PO Box 877, Colorado Springs,
CO 80901; tel: 719-630-7434;
www.csdance.org
A mixed bag of styles from classical to
experimental are presented at the
Pikes Peak Center.

Film

Bluebird Theater
3317 E. Colfax Street, Denver,
CO 80206; tel: 303-377-1666;
www.bluebirdtheater.net
Movie classics and musicals on
Sunday nights. Live music Wed–Sat.

Historic Park Theatre
130 Moraine Avenue, Estes Park,
CO 80517; tel: 970-586-8904;
www.historicparktheatre.com

One of the oldest movie theaters in
the country and home to September's
Estes Film Festival.

Mayan Theater
110 Broadway, Denver, CO 80203;
tel: 303-744-6799
Landmark theater showing foreign,
independent and art films.

Nugget Theatre
207 W. Colorado Avenue, Telluride,
CO 81435; tel: 970-728-3030;
www.nuggettheatre.com
A 1930s "picture palace" that shows
movies and is a venue for the Telluride
Film Festival.

Concert Venues

**Arvada Center for the Arts and
Humanities**
6901 Wadsworth Boulevard, Arvada,
CO 80003; tel: 720-898-7200;
www.arvadacenter.org
With both indoor and outdoor venues,
the center is host to touring theater
companies, children's theater, dance,
and pop and classical concerts.

Boulder Theater
2034 14th Street, Boulder,
CO 80302; tel: 303-786-7030;
www.bouldertheater.com
Headliner gigs with top jazz, rock,
country and pop entertainers. The
National Public Radio show *E-Town* is
also broadcast from the theater.

Chautauqua Community Hall
900 Baseline Road, Boulder,
CO 80302; tel: 303-442-3282;
www.chautauqua.com
Well-known musicians perform
throughout the summer. The hall is
host to film festivals, too.

Colorado Springs World Arena
3185 Venetucci Boulevard, Colorado
Springs, CO 80906; tel: 719-520-7469
or 866-464-2626; www.worldarena.com
The largest venue in southern
Colorado presents touring bands as
well as horse shows, car shows, and
other events.

Coors Amphitheater
6350 Greenwood Plaza Boulevard,
Englewood, CO 80111; tel: 800-279-
4444; www.tickco.com
This 7,500-seat outdoor venue
presents rock, jazz, classical, and
country music performances.

Ogden Theater
930 W. 7th Street, Denver, CO 80204;
tel: 303-832-1874; www.ogdentheater.net
Local and touring bands.

Paramount Theater
1621 Glenarm Place, Denver,
CO 80202; tel: 303-623-0106;
www.paramountdenver.com
This fabulous Art Deco theater
presents pop concerts, top-name acts
and other events.

Pepsi Center
Off Speer Boulevard and Auraria
Parkway; tel: 303-405-8555
(information) or 303-405-1111 (box
office); www.pepsicenter.com
State-of-the-art venue for large
concerts.

Pikes Peak Center
190 S. Cascade Avenue, Colorado
Springs, CO 80903; tel: 719-520-
7469; www.pikespeakcenter.com
The calendar at this venue is filled
with classical and pop music as well
as touring theater and dance
companies.

Red Rocks Amphitheater
18300 W. Alameda Parkway,
Morrison, CO 80465; tel: 720-865-
2494; www.redrocksonline.com
Spectacular outdoor venue set amid
rock outcroppings. Summer concerts
range from symphonies to rock, jazz
and pop.

Vilar Center for the Arts
68 Avondale Lane, Beaver Creek,
CO 81620; tel: 970-845-8497 or
888-920-2787; www.vilarcenter.org
This 530-seat theater presents a
variety of year-round performances,
such as jazz, comedy, dance, film,
musicals, drama and family shows.

Wheeler Opera House
320 E. Hyman Street, Aspen,
CO 81611; tel: 970-920-5770;
www.wheeleroperahouse.com
A wide range of performances are
staged at this historic theater,
including classical, pop, jazz, opera,
and dance.

FESTIVALS

January

**National Western Stock Show and
Rodeo**
Denver Coliseum, 4600 Humboldt
Street; tel: 720-865-2474; www.national
western.com
The Coliseum is host to one of the
country's biggest rodeos and the
world's premier livestock show, where
more than 10,000 animals are shown
and sold.

Ouray Ice Festival
Ouray Ice Park, tel: 970-4288;
www.ourayicefestival.com
Ice climbing on frozen waterfalls in
Ouray, climbing pro clinics, and gear
swaps. First week of January.

February

Winter Carnival
Steamboat Springs, tel: 877-754-
2269; www.steamboatchamber.com

The oldest winter festival in the West, with ski competitions and entertainment.

March

Denver Powwow
Denver Coliseum; tel: 303-934-8045; www.denvermarchpowwow.com
The Coliseum has dancing, drumming and food at one of the largest American Indian gatherings, with tribes from across North America.

Frozen Dead Guy Days
Nederland, tel: 303-258-3936 or 800-221-0044
A winter festival of arts, snowshoe races, a Frozen Dead Van Smash, and a midnight visit to the cabin housing the frozen remains of a dead Norwegian.

St. Patrick's Day Parade
Tel: 800-233-6837; www.denverstpatricks dayparade.com
This Rocky Mountain version of St Patrick's Day, with stagecoaches, horses and marching bands in downtown Denver, is the second largest in the country after New York City's.

April

Fruita Fat Tire Festival
Tel: 970-858-7220; www.fruitamountain bike.com
Mountain biking event on the famous Kokopelli Trail.

Greater Prairie Chicken Viewing Tour
Wray, tel: 970-332-3484; www.wray chamber.net/prairiechicken2.html
Early morning tours with wildlife experts to view the greater prairie chicken mating dance on the eastern plains (March 26–April 25).

May

Bolder Boulder
Tel: 303-444-7223; www.bolderboulder.com
A Memorial Day tradition, this race through the streets of Boulder attracts runners from around the world, with music and a great party atmosphere on the sidelines.

Cinco de Mayo
Civic Center Park
Colorado's largest Hispanic celebration, with mariachi bands, dancers, entertainment, crafts and great food.

Downtown Art and Jazz Festival
Grand Junction, tel: 970-245-9697; www.downtowngj.org
Music and fine art by local and out-of-state artists.

ABOVE: snowboarding through the fresh powder.

Iron Horse Bicycle Classic
Durango, tel: 970-259-4621; www.iron horsebicycleclassic.com
A 47-mile (77km) road race for ranked and non-ranked racers with 5,500ft (1,680 meters) of elevation gain over two 11,000ft (3,350-meter) passes. Held over the Memorial Day weekend, the event includes in-town criteriums, circuit races, road races, tours, BMX races, dual slaloms, team trail rides and mountain bike races.

June

Aspen Music Festival
Tel: 970-925-9042; www.aspenmusic festival.com
Masters and students come together for two months of teaching, learning and performing, June through August.

Colorado Music Festival
Boulder, tel: 303-449-1397; www.coloradomusicfest.org
Classical concerts four nights a week for seven weeks, beginning in June, at the open-air Chautauqua Auditorium.

Colorado Shakespeare Festival
Boulder, tel: 303-492-0554; www.coloradoshakes.org
Held outdoors at the Mary Rippon Theater on the University of Colorado campus; through August.

Fat Tire Festival
Crested Butte, tel: 970-349-6817; www.ftbw.com
The country's oldest mountain bike event features races, clinics and guided tours.

FibARK
Salida, tel: 877-772-5432; www.fibark.com
Nationally known kayaking event attracts thousands for races on the Arkansas, plus music and food. Coincides with Salida Art Walk (www.coloradoheadwaters.com), which kicks off with a Friday night Art Walk to 12 downtown galleries.

Food and Wine Classic at Aspen
Tel: 877-900-WINE; www.foodandwine.com/promo/classic-in-aspen
A three-day extravaganza featuring nationally known celebrity chefs and culinary talents from Colorado.

Jazz Aspen Snowmass
Tel: 970-920-4996; www.jazzaspen.org
Four days of top jazz, R&B and blues musicians.

Pikes Peak International Hill Climb
Manitou Springs, tel: 719-685-4400; www.usaracing.com/ppihc
This famous auto race follows a serpentine, 12-mile (19km) gravel road to the summit of Pikes Peak. There are 156 hairpin turns with no guardrails. Vehicles include stock cars, sport cars, diesel trucks and motorcycles.

Platte River Rendezvous
Denver, Confluence Park, tel: 800-233-6837
A week-long Mountain Man festival with costumed actors, celebrating Denver's founding.

Renaissance Festival
I-25 exit 172, Larkspur, tel: 303-688-6010 or 877-259-3328; www.colorado renaissance.com
Costumed characters re-create a 16th-century village, with jousting contests, music and crafts; held in a forest south of Denver every weekend from mid-June through July.

Telluride Bluegrass Festival
Tel: 800-624-2422; www.bluegrass.com/telluride
Established acts and emerging talent perform at this popular event.

July

Bravo! Vail Valley Music Festival
Tel: 970-827-5700; www.vailmusic festival.org
A month-long celebration of orchestral and chamber music, with performances by local and visiting musicians.

Collegiate Peaks Music Festival
Buena Vista, tel: 800-492-9114;
www.collegiatepeaksmusicfestival.com
Home-brewed beer and bands, from
jazz to bluegrass, in the clean
mountain air.

Crested Butte Wild Flower Festival
Tel: 800-455-1290; www.crestedbutte
wildflowerfestival.com
The proclaimed Wildflower Capital of
Colorado celebrates the return of the
flowering season with hikes and
photography workshops.

August

Palisade Peach Festival
Tel: 970-464-7458; www.palisadepeach
fest.com
Celebrate Palisade's famous peaches
with farmers, vendors, arts and crafts
booths, and music.

Pikes Peak or Bust Rodeo
Colorado Springs, tel: 719-635-1101,
exit 1; www.coloradospringsrodeo.com
Buckaroos from around the country
compete at the state's biggest rodeo.

Pikes Peak Marathon
Manitou Springs, tel: 719-473-2625;
www.pikespeakmarathon.org
Competitors in this half marathon
follow the 13-mile (21km) Barr Trail to
the summit of Pikes Peak. A full
marathon to the summit and back is
run the next day.

Telluride Jazz Celebration
Tel: 970-728-7009; www.telluride
jazz.com
Three days of hot jazz with top artists.

September

Colorado Mountain Wine Festival
Palisade, tel: 970-464-0111 or 800-
704-3667; www.coloradowinefest.com
Vineyard tours, wine tasting and
gourmet food are featured at this
festival in Colorado's Wine Country.

**Longs Peak Scottish-Irish Highland
Festival**
Estes Park, tel: 970-586-6308 or
800-90ESTES; www.scotfest.com
One of the largest Celtic festivals in
the US, with bagpipe bands, Irish
dancing, folk music and Highland
games.

Pearl Pass Ride
Crested Butte, tel: 970-349-6817;
www.mtnbikehalloffame.com
The world's oldest mountain bike
event is a two-day, 38-mile (61km)
ride from Crested Butte to Aspen via
12,700ft (3,870-meter) Pearl Pass.

A Taste of Colorado
Denver, tel: 303-295-6330; www.ataste
ofcolorado.com
Free entertainment, rides and great
food from 75 of the state's best

restaurants; held Labor Day weekend
in Civic Center Park.

Telluride Blues and Brews Festival
Tel: 866-515-6166 or 970-728-8037;
www.tellurideblues.com
The festival features three days of
world-renowned musicians
performing live on the Town Park
stage and samples of beer from 50
choice microbreweries.

Telluride Film Festival
www.telluridefilmfestival.com
Film fans screen new works,
rediscovered classics and tributes,
and attend lectures and other events
with film-makers and actors.

October

Denver International Film Festival
Tel: 303-595-3456, exit 250; www.
denverfilm.org
New films are screened at various
venues around the city.

Great American Beer Festival
Denver, Currigan Exhibition Hall;
tel: 303-447-0816 or 888-822-6273;
www.greatamericanbeerfestival.com
The nation's largest beer festival,
with samples of more than 1,700
lagers, stouts, ales, chile beers and
designer brews.

November

**Catch the Glow Holiday Celebration
and Evening Parade**
Estes Park, tel: 800-443-7837;
www.estesparkcvb.com/events
The traditional day-after-Thanksgiving
lighting celebration in downtown
Estes Park features carolers, pony
rides, hay rides, Santa, and the
45-minute Catch the Glow Parade.

Polar Express
Durango & Silverton Narrow Gauge
Railway; tel: 888-872-4607;
www.durangotrain.com

Retelling of the famous children's
Christmas tale, hot chocolate and
gifts for children from Santa on
magical holiday train rides between
Durango and Silverton, November to
December.

December

Blossoms of Light
Tel: 720-865-3500;
www.botanicgardens.org
Thousands of twinkling lights
decorate the gardens, many forming
gigantic flowers.

Winter Wildland
Cheyenne Mountain Zoo, Colorado
Springs, tel: 719-633-9925; www.cm
zoo.org
Lights, holiday characters, and gift
making for the animals each night,
beginning one week before Christmas.

NIGHTLIFE

As you'd expect in a state of former
rowdy mining towns, Coloradans know
how to kick up their heels. Quirky
bars, microbrew pubs and taverns
serving locally made wine and whisky
and creative home-grown cocktails;
home town festivals; and art walks
are the main entertainment in the
isolated high country, where ranchers
rub shoulders with artists and
outdoors lovers. The scene is more
sophisticated at ski resorts like
Telluride, Aspen, Vail, Breckenridge,
and Steamboat Springs – haunted by
Hollywood celebrities making deals
over après-ski hot toddies in chic
restaurants. In the small farm and
ranch towns of the Western Slope,
early to bed, early to rise rules. The
Denver Metro Area is the main place
to get a big-city nightlife fix. On the

BELOW: whitewater kayaking is becoming increasingly popular.

agenda are arena concerts and major sporting events at places like Red Rocks and Coors Arena, pub crawls at the state's largest collection of microbreweries, midnight snacks at the latest hot celeb chef eatery, martini lounges, and clubbing in Larimer Square and LoDo – Denver's hip hang-out spot.

SHOPPING

Colorado shopping runs the gamut. In the rapidly expanding Denver Metro Area along I-25 and towns like Grand Junction off I-70, you'll find the usual big-box stores in rather nondescript malls, of which 16th Street Mall, Cherry Creek Mall and Larimer Square in Denver are by far the swankiest and most memorable. At high-end resorts in Aspen, Vail, Steamboat and elsewhere, you'll find exclusive designer boutiques selling knick-knacks and fine art for those with deep pockets. Pearl Street Mall, an attractive outdoor pedestrian-only street mall in downtown Boulder, has a mix of quirky shops selling ethical and ethnic gear to suit the city's mainly green residents; fun and hip restaurants, and street entertainment, as well as a popular nearby farmers' market, making it an excellent low-key shopping venue for the mall-adverse. Most enjoyable are the funky boutiques and galleries selling one-of-a-kind arts and crafts in former mining cabins and brick buildings in old mining towns like Salida, Creede, Ouray, Crested Butte, Paonia, Durango, and Telluride in the Central and Southern Rockies, and historic downtown Grand Junction in the Colorado River valley, where you may score an antique, a Western souvenir, a quirky teapot, some silver jewelry or perhaps a piece of beautiful woven fiber art.

OUTDOOR ACTIVITIES

At lower elevations on the eastern plains and along the Colorado River, winter, spring, and fall are the best times for mountain biking, trail running, hiking, camping, and viewing praries chickens, bighorn sheep, bison elk, and other game. The state's fourteeners are not clear for backpacking, camping and climbing until July, and then only briefly before cold temperatures arrive. Summer is a good time to

ABOVE: fly fishing near the Spanish Peaks in southern Colorado.

enjoy kayaking and river rafting on the Colorado, Yampa, Green, Gunnison, and Arkansas rivers. With snow on the ground, a good part of the year, it's no wonder that skiing is so popular, especially the big, set snowfalls of spring. New sports include ski joring, using horses, which has become popular in Georgetown and Silverton, ice racing with Jeeps in Georgetown, and ice climbing in Ouray.

Cycling

Opportunities abound for mountain and road biking in Colorado. Several organizations provide information on trails, races, and group tours and other events. The **Rocky Mountain Cycling Club** (www.rmccrides.com) promotes cycling throughout the state. Regional cycling clubs include the **Denver Bicycle Touring Club** (www.dbtc.org); **Fort Collins Cycling Club** (www.fccycleclub.org); **PEDAL Bicycling Club of Loveland** (www.pedal club.org); **Team Evergreen** (www.teamever green.org); **Front Rangers Cycling Club** (www.frontrangers.org); **Boulder Cycling** (www.bouldercyclingclub.com); and **Spanish Peaks Cycling Association** (www.spcycling.org).

Kayaking, Canoeing, and Rafting

Colorado offers an abundance of both whitewater and flatwater paddling. For information on routes and conditions, consult the agency that manages the river or lake. Other sources of information are paddling clubs and outdoor-gear retailers. For more information, contact the **Colorado Whitewater Association** (PO Box 5074, Englewood, CO 80155; http://coloradowhitewater.org), **High Country River Rafters** (PO Box

317, Wheat Ridge, CO, 80034; www. hcrr.org), **Rocky Mountain Canoe Club** (www.rockymountaincanoeclub.org), **Rocky Mountain Sea Kayak Club** (PO Box 100643, Denver, CO 80250; 303-988-4822; www.rmskc.org), **Poudre Paddlers Canoe and Kayak Club** (www.poudrepaddlers.org), the **Pikes Peak Whitewater Club** (www. pikespeakwhitewaterclub.com). **Arkansas Headwaters Recreation Area** (www. sangres.com/colorado/state-parks/arkansas-headwaters).

Fishing

Fishing is permitted year-round in Colorado, but a license is required. Licenses can be purchased at sporting goods stores, tackle shops and in some Wal-Marts. For more information, contact the **Colorado Division of Wildlife** (6060 Broadway, Denver, CO; tel: 303-297-1192; www. wildlife.state.co.us). Fishing on the Ute Indian reservations requires tribal permits.

Golf

There are scores of public and private golf courses as well as full-fledged golf resorts throughout the state. For information on course location and facilities, tournaments and other special events, contact the **Colorado Golf Association** (5990 Greenwood Plaza Boulevard, Ste 130, Greenwood Village, CO 80111; tel: 303-366-4653; www.cogolf.org), or the **Colorado Gold Resort Association** (2110 S. Ash Street, Denver, CO 80222; www. coloradogolfresorts.com)

Hiking

Lower-elevation trails can be found in Comanche National Grasslands on the plains, a good place for birding, and along the Front Range in places like Boulder, which has more Open Space than almost any city in the nation. Hikers and climbers acclimated to elevation may be interested in climbing Colorado's fourteeners. As soon as the trails clear in places like Rocky Mountain National Park, hikers take to the trails, both easy and strenous to view sawtoothed mountains, glaciers, lakes, wildlife, and historic cabins. Hiking at 10,000ft (3,048 meters) and above guarantees shortness of breath due to low oxygen and thin air. Acclimate gradually and take it slow and expect to be more tired than usual. Drink plenty of water and eat high-energy food.

Tennis

Public tennis courts are available in just about every city and large town in Colorado, although avid players may find it more convenient to stay at a hotel with courts. Contact the city or county Parks and Recreation Department for locations and hours. For information on tournaments, lessons and leagues, contact the **Colorado Tennis Association** (www.coloradotennis.com).

Skiing

There are two dozen ski resorts in the Colorado Rockies, offering some of the world's best skiing. Most are redeveloped mining towns that have gained international cachet among the smart set. The best known are **Aspen-Snowmass** (www.aspensnowmass.com), **Vail** (www.vail.com), **Telluride** (www.tellurideskiresort.com), **Breckenridge** (www.breckenridge.com), **Crested Butte** (www.skicb.com) and **Steamboat Springs** (www.steamboat.com), the latter famed for its Champagne powder and cowboy sensibility. Resorts such as **Durango Mountain** (www.durangomountainresort.com) are aimed at families. On the other hand, remote **Silverton Mountain** (www.silvertonmountain.com) is decidedly non-traditional and geared toward extreme skiers and snowboarders who want a challenge.

SPECTATOR SPORTS

Coloradans enjoy spectator sports – from major league football, basketball, baseball and hockey to auto racing and horse and dog racing. The National Football League **Denver**

National Park Passes

Most parks charge an entrance fee, usually $10–25, which allows unrestricted vehicle entry for a car and up to four passengers for one week. If you plan on visiting several parks on your vacation, or to return within a year, you should buy **America the Beautiful Annual Pass** ($80), available at any park that charges an entrance fee (the park you choose will benefit directly from the sale, an added incentive). You can also purchase the pass by logging on to www.store.usgs.gov/pass or by telephoning 888-ask-usgs. The pass offers access to all public lands managed by the National Park Service, US Forest Service, US Fish and Wildlife Service, Bureau of Land Management and Bureau of Reclamation.

Broncos (www.denverbroncos.com) play September to December at Invesco Field at Mile High. The National Baseball League **Colorado Rockies** (www.rockies.mlb.com) play April to October at Coors Field. The National Basketball Association **Denver Nuggets** (www.nba.com/nuggets) play at the Pepsi Center. And the Stanley Cup-winning **Colorado Avalanche** (www.coloradoavalanche.com) play at the Pepsi Center. Auto racing is popular at a number of tracks in Colorado, including **Pikes Peak International Raceway** in the shadow of the famous Pikes Peaks. There are also tracks in Morrison, Erie, Fort Morgan, Pueblo, Denver, Commerce City, and Olathe. Horse and dog racing take place on tracks in Aurora, Colorado Springs, Pueblo, and Commerce City.

TOURS AND OUTFITTERS

A good tour guide can help orient you quickly. Colorado has a large number of tour companies and outdoor outfitters geared toward general tourism and specialty travel. Here are a few suggestions.

Tour Operators

Classic Golf Tours
3045 S. Parker Road, Ste 201, Aurora, CO 80014; tel: 303-751-7200 or 800-359-7200; www.classicgolftours.com
A full-service tour operator specializing in golf packages.
Colorado Sightseer
6780 W. 84th Circle, Ste 60, Arvada, CO 80003; tel: 303-423-8200 or 800-255-5105; www.coloradosightseer.com
Customized sightseeing tours throughout the state.
Discover Colorado Scenic Tours and Guide Service
11930 W. 62nd Plaza, Arvada, CO 80004; tel: 800-641-0129
Personalized tours for groups and

individuals, with an emphasis on historic sites and national parks.
Geo Tours
1201 Buttonwood Drive, Fort Collins, CO 80525; tel: 303-756-6070, 800-660-7238
Tour packages designed for outdoor enthusiasts with a desire for adventure.
Gray Line of Denver
PO Box 17646, Denver, CO 80217; tel: 800-348-6877; www.coloradograyline.com
The company offers a menu of bus tours in the Denver and Colorado Springs areas, including Rocky Mountain National Park, Garden of the Gods and Royal Gorge.
Kindred Spirits Tour and Travel
PO Box 416, Empire, CO 80438; tel: 303-912-7114 or 877-589-8860
Customized packages with a focus on adventure and natural history.
Mesa Verde Tours
109 S. Main Street, PO Box 277, Mancos, CO 81328; tel: 970-247-8533; www.mesaverdetours.net
The park concessionaire offers tours from May to mid-October.
A Private Guide
820 S. Monaco Parkway, Unit 100, Denver, CO 80224; tel: 303-758-8149; www.aprivateguide.com
Transportation and touring company offering custom itineraries for groups of all sizes.

Outdoor Adventure

Action Adventures Vail/Timberline Tours
PO Box 131, Vail, CO 81658; tel: 970-476-1414 or 800-831-1414
The premier rafting and rock climbing outfitter in the Vail area.
Adrift Adventures
500 E. 6000 South Jensen, UT 84035; tel: 800-824-1050; www.adrift.com
River rafting trips for the whole family on the Yampa River through Dinosaur National Monument, as well as the Gunnison and Arkansas rivers in Colorado.

Adventures Out West
1680 S. 21st Street, Colorado Springs, CO 80904; tel: 719-578-0935, 800-755-0935; www.adventure soutwest.com
Balloon flights in the Colorado Springs region.

Adventure Bound Expeditions
Tel: 800-423-4668; www.raft-colorado.com
Two- to seven-day guided whitewater trips through Dinosaur National Monument on the Green and Yampa Rivers.

Bill Dvorak Kayak and Rafting Expeditions
17921 US Highway 285, Nathrop, CO 81236; tel: 800-824-3795; www.dvorakexpeditions.com
Raft trips up to a week or more on rivers throughout the Southwest. Many trips combine rafting with mountain biking, horseback riding, rock climbing, Jeep tours, and fishing.

Clear Creek Rafting Co.
350 Whitewater Road, PO Box 3178, Idaho Springs, CO 80452-3178; tel: 800-353-9901; www.clearcreekrafting.com
Arkansas River trips through Royal Gorge, Bighorn Sheep Canyon and Brown's Canyon

Colorado River Runs
Star Route, Box 33, Bond, CO 80423; tel: 800-826-1081; www.colorado riverruns.com
Full- and half-day guided rafting on the Arkansas and Eagle rivers.

Echo Canyon River Expeditions
Tel: 800-755-ECHO (3246); www.raft echo.com
Arkansas River trips in the Royal Gorge region and wilderness trips on the Piedra River and in Gunnison Gorge.

Highside Adventure Tours
Tel: 800-997-3448; www.rafting colorado.com
Raft trips on the Arkansas, Colorado and Clear Creek rivers.

Mild to Wild Rafting
Tel: 800-567-6745; www.mild2wild rafting.com
Float trips on five Colorado rivers.

Mile Hi Rafting
Tel: 303-567-0717; www.milehi rafting.com
Guided trips on the Yampa, Clear Creek, and Arkansas rivers.

Outlaw Rivers and Jeep Tours
Tel: 877-259-1800; www.outlaw tours.com
Float trips in southwest Colorado plus Jeep tours to ghost towns and abandoned mines.

River Runners Rafting Resort
24070 CR 301, Buena Vista, CO 81211; tel: 888-723-8923 (central reservations)

Rafting on the Arkansas and Colorado rivers, including trips through Royal Gorge and Brown's Canyon.

Rocky Mountain Outdoor Center and Headwaters Outdoor
228 N. F Street, Salida, CO 81201; tel: 719-539-4680 or 800-255-5784; www.rmoc.com
Adventure school on the Arkansas River, with instruction on kayaking, ice and rock climbing, mountain biking and wilderness first aid. Children's programs are available.

NATIONAL PARKS & SITES

Colorado's most visited national park is **Rocky Mountain**, as much for ease of access from the Front Range communities as for its sweeping grandeur and glorious 10,000ft (3,050-meter) elevation scenic drive. In the southwest corner, **Mesa Verde** and nearby **Hovenweep** and **Canyons of the Ancients** National Monuments are equally famed for their thousands of Ancestral Pueblo archeological sites. In the northwest corner, **Dinosaur National Monument** preserves a dinosaur quarry and the Yampa River canyons, and **Colorado National Monument** has dramatic redrocks sculpted by the Colorado River. Even the quiet southeastern Plains have gems: **Bent's Old Fort National Historic Site**, a former mountain man rendezvous on the Santa Fe Trail, and **Comanche National Grasslands** and **Pawnee Buttes**, famed for their exceptional birding.

Environmental Ethics

Remember the old saying: "Take nothing but pictures, leave nothing but footprints." The goal of low-impact/no-impact backpacking is to leave the area in the same condition as you found it, if not better. If you're camping in the back country, don't break branches, level the ground or alter the landscape in any way. Make fires in designated places only. Otherwise, use a portable camping stove. When nature calls, answer with a trowel: dig a hole 6ins (15cm) deep and at least 200ft (60 meters) from water, campsites and trails. Take away all trash, including toilet paper. Ziplock bags and Dr. Bronner's eco-friendly peppermint soap are a camper's best friend.

In between are a handful of lesser-known gems. **Florissant Fossil Beds National Monument**, near Colorado Springs, is known for its fossils. **Great Sand Dunes National Park and Preserve**, in the wildlife-rich San Luis Valley, protects the country's tallest sand dunes. **Black Canyon of the Gunnison National Park**, carved into schist by the Gunnison River, rivals the Grand Canyon for extraordinary depth, scenic rim views, wildlife and whitewater. Except for Rocky Mountain and Black Canyon of the Gunnison, which are snowbound in winter, all the parks may be visited year round. For more information on Colorado's national parks, log on to www.nps.gov.

CHILDREN'S ACTIVITIES

Colorado is a child-friendly place. The Denver area has numerous activities, from **Denver Children's Museum** to both the **Denver Zoo** and **Cheyenne Mountain Zoo** in Colorado Springs.

Mining towns in the Rockies offer gold mine tours and ever-popular rides on scenic railroads, including Durango to Silverton, Cumbres and Toltec in the San Luis Valley, the Georgetown Loop and Royal Gorge. Grand Junction, in the northwestern corner, is a dinosaur center, where kids can sign up to participate in a nearby dig with **Dinosaur Journey** in Fruita or view a wall of dinosaur bones at **Dinosaur National Monument**.

Ski resorts all have special children's programs in winter and many have all-terrain parks; in summer, there are often tram rides up the mountain. Festivals throughout the year are fun for the whole family, from **Cinco de Mayo** celebrations in Denver to harvest festival fun in the North Fork Valley.

Families will also enjoy visiting farms and ranches to see their food being grown first hand. The peach harvest in Palisade is a good time to ride bikes along the Colorado, or you can visit the goats who produce the milk for **Jumpin' Good Goat Cheese** in Buena Vista in the Central Rockies.

The ultimate Colorado vacation, of course, is a stay on a **dude ranch**. Most have special programs catering to children, including horsemanship and ranch skills and chuckwagon dinners in the evening with homespun cowboys.

A HANDY SUMMARY OF PRACTICAL INFORMATION, ARRANGED ALPHABETICALLY

A dmission charges

Admission is usually charged at both private and public museums and attractions, and national and state parks. As a rule, entrance fees are $10 or under per person, although very popular sites, such as Rocky Mountain National Park and special traveling exhibits at nationally known museums, may charge as much as $20. Museums often offer free or reduced entrance fees certain days or evenings.

Consider buying **multi-site passes** for attractions in Denver, if available. Local visitor centers and state welcome centers can assist you with planning and many also offer discount coupons, with excellent deals on local attractions, hotels and dining.

Anyone planning to visit several national parks is strongly advised to buy an $80 **America the Beautiful Pass** that allows unlimited entry to federally managed public lands across the US for a year. Passes are available at the entrance gate to national parks that charge admission, and through the internet. For more information, see page 316.

B udgeting for Your Trip

In early 2009, the dollar strengthened considerably against the pound and euro, so several unbroken years of rock-bottom prices for European travelers abruptly ended. Even so, the US remains a good buy for travelers, especially those traveling around by auto, where the main cost will be car rental, gas, lodging and food, and you can search out bargains en route. You can save considerably if you camp, stay in budget motels, eat in hometown cafés like the locals, and purchase food direct from farm stands and farmers' markets for picnics, easy to do in Colorado, one of the top ranching and agricultural states in the country. Boulder Farmers' Market, for example, has an extraordinary selection of prepared foods, including wine.

Allow $80–100 a day for good-quality motels for two people; really memorable hotels and bed and breakfasts tend to run $125–175 per night and offer a good way to connect quickly with the local scene. Lodgings that are self-contained destinations will be the most expensive and, in Colorado, include ski-in and ski village resort condos and hotels, small boutique and restored grande dame hotels in historic downtowns and national park gateway communities like Estes Park and Durango. Lavish resorts and dude ranches are in a category by themselves. Dude ranches, in particular, operate on a multi-day, all-in American Plan basis, including lodging, food and all activities. At the other end of the spectrum, you'll find an array of attractive campgrounds throughout Colorado for $16–25 a night; hostels are often a great budget choice in Colorado (there are excellent ones in Boulder and Salida) and tend to run from $30–50, depending on whether you bunk in a dorm or have a private room. Bare-bones motel lodgings can be found for less than $50; reliable chain motels are in the $60–80 range (look for AAA discounts and online deals at chains like Best Western and La Quinta).

You can probably get away with $30 per day per person for food, if you stick to basic diners, cafés, markets, farm stands and inexpensive restaurants, especially ethnic ones, and make breakfast your main meal, eating more lightly for lunch and dinner and avoiding alcohol. Don't worry, though: If the high-elevation Rocky Mountain air doesn't get you high, you can always tour Colorado's many fine microbreweries, wineries, and distilleries to enjoy free and low-cost tastings of Colorado microbrew ales, wines and even whiskey (Stranahan's Distillery in Denver).

Meals in better restaurants cost a lot more *(see Restaurant section)*, but if you're determined to visit a famous high-end establishment and don't have the cash, one insider trick is to eat lunch there: you'll find many dinner menu items at much lower prices and still get to say that you've eaten in a hip eatery.

Budget at least $3 per gallon for gas costs for your rental car; most economy vehicles get over 30 miles (48km) per gallon, but if you plump for the four-wheel-drive (a good idea in winter), you'll likely get only around 20 miles (32km) per gallon. Inexpensive or free trams, light rail, buses and other public transportation are available in Denver and other cities, such as Trinidad and Grand Junction, as well as ski resort towns.

ABOVE: children play in an old-fashioned sack race in Canon City.

C hildren

Two things about traveling with children: first, be prepared and second, don't expect to cover too much ground – think quality not quantity. Take everything you need, along with a general first-aid kit and those wonderful all-purpose traveler's aids: wet wipes and Ziplock baggies. Away from the Front Range and ski resort towns, Colorado is primarily a state of remote mountain towns, with limited supplies and often no nearby hospital. If you need baby formula, special foods, diapers or medication, carry them with you. Games, books and crayons help kids pass the time in the car. Carrying snacks and drinks in a day pack will come in handy when children (or adults) get hungry on the road.

Colorado's Front Range communities, ski resort towns like Aspen, and Western Slope communities like Grand Junction and Durango have museums and activities geared toward families. Away from towns, make sure that mountains, back country areas and parks are suitable for kids. Are there abandoned mine shafts, steep stairways and trails, cliffs or other hazards? Is a lot of walking necessary? Are food, water, shelter,

bathrooms and other essentials available at the site? Everyone should be careful of dehydration in this high-elevation state by drinking plenty of water before and during outdoor activities and eating high energy foods. Don't push children beyond their limits. Rest often and allow for extra napping. Good advice for grown-ups on vacation, too.

Climate

When to Visit

Colorado is a popular four-season state for tourism. It spans a wide range of climate and life zones, but generally has sunny skies, low humidity and limited precipitation. Climate varies widely with elevation. Climbing 1,000ft (300 meters) is equivalent to traveling 300 miles (500km) northward. Conditions atop the highest peaks are akin to those in the Arctic. There are even a few permanent ice fields like St Mary's Glacier, the southernmost glacier in North America.

CLIMATE CHART

Denver

☐ Maximum temperature
☐ Minimum temperature
— Rainfall

Colorado enjoys 295 days of sunshine annually. The climate is semi-arid. Yearly precipitation ranges from 16ins (41cm) on the eastern plains and 14ins (36cm) in the Front Range to less than 10ins (25cm) on the Western Slope. Most rain falls in brief, intense thunderstorms during the summer season, when small streams, dry washes and narrow canyons are prone to flash floods. Violent electrical storms are common on mountain peaks during summer afternoons. Nights in the mountains can be chilly even in July and August, and winds are often brisk, so bring a sweater or jacket. Snow, hail, and sleet are possible at the highest elevations at any time of year.

The spring thaw usually begins in March, though snow lingers well into July on the highest peaks and passes. Summer weather begins in late June or early July. Autumn begins in September, a lovely period of sunny days, chilly nights and spectacular colors on the Rockies' forested slopes. Winter sets in by late November, though ski areas such as Arapahoe Basin and Loveland sometimes open as early as late October (with the aid of snow-making machines) and close in June.

Average high temperatures in summer reach 88°F (31°C) in **Denver** (elev. 5,280ft/1,609 meters), 94°F (34°C) in **Grand Junction** (elev. 4,586ft/1,398 meters), and 80°F (27°C) in **Aspen** (7,773ft/2,369m). Nights are crisp and pleasant, usually ranging from 45°F (7°C) to 65°F (18°C).

Winter is very chilly but often sunny, with average lows of 16°F (-9°C) in Denver and Grand Junction, and 6°F (-14°C) in Aspen. Annual snowfall in Denver is typically 45 to 65ins (114–65cm), though warm spells between storms reduce large accumulations. Annual snowfall in excess of 300ins (760cm) is common in the ski areas around Aspen. Winter storms roll into Colorado from the Pacific, lose moisture over the desert Southwest, and then dump piles of the light, dry powder for which the Rocky Mountains are famous.

What to Wear

With few exceptions, Western dress is informal and geared toward practical clothing for enjoying the outdoors. A pair of jeans or slacks, a polo or button-down shirt, and boots or shoes are appropriate at all but the fanciest places and events. Shorts and light shirts are suitable for most situations in the warmer months, though. Year round, be sure everyone wears sunscreen with an SPF of at least 30, polarized eye protection, a broad-brimmed hat protecting the neck, layered clothing with sleeves and legs that can be rolled down as sun protection, and sturdy hiking sandals or boots that secure the foot for walking on rough ground – no flip-flops or flimsy shoes.

If you're hiking, a thin, inner polypropylene sock and a thick, outer sock will help keep your feet dry and comfortable. Blisters or sore spots can develop quickly. Cover them with moleskin or surgical tape, available at most pharmacies or camping supply stores. Bring a warm cover-up and rain shell; even in summer, high-country weather can be cool and suddenly rainy.

Crime and Safety

A few common-sense precautions will help keep you safe while traveling in Colorado. For starters, know where you are and where you're going. Whether traveling on foot or by car, bring a map and plan your route in advance. Don't be shy about asking for directions. Most people are happy to help.

Don't carry large sums of cash or wear flashy or expensive jewelry. Lock unattended cars and keep your belongings in the trunk. If possible, travel with a companion, especially after dark.

Carry a cell phone. Few items are more useful if you are lost, have had an accident, need to report an emergency, or your car has broken down.

If involved in a traffic accident, remain at the scene. It is illegal to leave. If you have no cell phone, or no signal, find a nearby telephone or ask a passing motorist to call the police, then wait for emergency vehicles to arrive.

Driving under the influence of alcohol carries stiff penalties, including fines and jail. Wearing seat belts is required. Children under four must be in a child's safety seat.

Customs Regulations

Everyone entering the United States must go through US Customs, often a time-consuming process. To speed things up, be prepared to open your luggage for inspection and keep the following restrictions in mind. You may bring in duty-free gifts worth up to $800 (American citizens) or $100 (foreign travelers). Visitors over 18 may bring in 200 cigarettes and 50 cigars (not Cuban) or 2kg of tobacco. Those over 21 may bring in 34fl. oz (1 liter) of alcohol. Travelers with more than $10,000 in US or foreign currency, traveler's checks or money orders must declare these upon entry. Among prohibited goods are meat or meat products, illegal drugs, firearms, seeds, plants and fruits. For a breakdown of customs allowances, write to US Customs Service, PO Box 407, Washington, DC 20044; tel: 877-227-5511; www.cbp.gov.

Electricity

Standard electricity in North America is 110–115 volts, 60 cycles AC. An adapter is necessary for most appliances from overseas, with the exception of Japan.

D isabled Travelers

The 1995 Americans with Disabilities Act (ADA) brought sweeping changes to facilities across America. Accommodations with five or more rooms must be useable by persons with disabilities. Older and smaller inns and lodges are often wheelchair accessible. For the sight-impaired, many hotels provide special alarm clocks, captioned TV services and security measures. To comply with ADA hearing-impaired requirements, many hotels have begun to follow special procedures; local agencies may provide TTY and interpretation services.

Check with the hotel when you make reservations to ascertain the degree to which the hotel complies with ADA guidelines. Ask specific questions about bathroom facilities, bed height, wheelchair space and availability of services.

Many major attractions have wheelchairs for loan or rent; most national parks today also offer paved "barrier-free" or "accessible" trails. Some provide special visitor publications for disabled visitors and interpreters and visitor guides. The Society for Accessible Travel and Hospitality (tel: 212-447-7284; www.sath.org) publishes a quarterly magazine on travel for the disabled.

E mbassies

Australia: 1601 Massachusetts Ave NW, Washington DC 20036, tel: 202-797-3000.
Canada: 501 Pennsylvania Ave NW, Washington, DC 20001, tel: 202-682-1740.
Great Britain: 3100 Massachusetts Ave NW, Washington, DC 20008, tel: 202-462-1340.
Ireland: 2234 Massachusetts Ave NW, Washington, DC 20008, tel: 202-462-3939.
New Zealand: 37 Observatory Circle NW, Washington, DC 20008, tel: 202-328-4800.

ABOVE: photographing wild elk in Rocky Mountain National Park.

Emergencies

Dial 911 (the operator will put you through to the police, ambulance or fire services). The call is toll free anywhere in the US, including on cell phones. If you can't get through, **dial 0** for an operator. In national parks, it's best to contact a ranger.

Etiquette

When traveling in Colorado, you'll notice a big difference in tone among people who live in the fast-paced, highly developed, modern urban communities strung out along the Front Range, which feels very like California, where many residents are from; and the slower-paced, more tightly knit rural mountain communities and farm and ranch towns on the Western Slope whose residents tend to be more conservative and courtly and polite in their manners.

The first rule of travel is to blend in and take your cue from local etiquette. This is particularly true should you happen to visit the Ute Mountain Ute Indian Reservation just south of Cortez, or the Four Corners Navajo Tribal Monument, where you'll meet Navajo and Ute people. Indian reservations are sovereign lands, with their laws and moral code, and call for unique sensitivity and cultural awareness to avoid giving offense.

Follow all Indian regulations and do not presume anything while on the reservation. Travel as lightly among people as you would on sensitive lands.

G ay and Lesbian Travelers

GLBT travelers will find few problems traveling in Colorado, even in more far-flung rural areas or conservative Colorado Springs, home to Focus on the Family and other religious groups. This is, after all, a state that prides itself on its international sophistication and embrace of diversity and political correctness. For GLBT resources, check out the Gay and Lesbian Yellow Pages (tel: 800-697-2812; www.glyp.com). In Colorado, contact Gay, Lesbian, Bisexual and Transgender Services (tel: 303-733-7743; www.glbtcolorado.org). PrideFest takes place in Denver in mid-June.

H ealth and Medical Care

Precautions

Insurance: It's vital to have medical insurance when traveling. Although hospitals are obligated to provide emergency treatment to anyone who needs it whether or not they have insurance, you may have to prove you can pay for treatment of anything less than a life-threatening condition. Know what your policy covers and have proof of the policy with you at all times or be prepared to pay at the time service is rendered.

Flash floods: Sudden downpours – even those falling miles away from your location – can fill canyons and dry river beds with a roaring torrent of water and mud that will sweep away everything in its path. Travelers should be especially careful during the summer "monsoon" season. Avoid hiking or driving in *arroyos* or narrow canyons, and never try to wade or drive across a flooded stream. If rain begins to fall or you see rain clouds in the distance, move to higher ground. It's impossible to outrun or even outdrive a flash flood. Take action before the water level begins to rise.

Sunburn: Even a couple of hours outdoors can result in sunburn, so protect yourself with a high-SPF sunscreen and polarized sunglasses. The elderly and the ill, small children and people with fair skin should be especially careful. Excessive pain, redness, blistering or numbness mean you need professional medical attention. Minor sunburn can be soothed by a cool bath.

Dehydration: Drink plenty of liquids and, if outdoors, carry bottles of water and something to eat. The rule of thumb in arid conditions is 1 gallon (4 liters) of water per person per day. Don't wait to get thirsty – start drinking as soon as you set out.

Drinking water: All water from natural sources must be purified before drinking. *Giardia* is found throughout the West, even in crystal-clear water, and it can cause severe cramps and diarrhea. The most popular purification methods are tablets or filters (both available from camping supply stores) or by boiling water for at least three minutes.

Cactus: To avoid being pricked, stay on trails and wear long pants and

Abandoned Mines

Exercise caution around old buildings and abandoned mines. Structures may be unstable and the ground may be littered with broken glass, nails and other debris. Mine shafts are particularly dangerous. Never enter a mine shaft or cave unless accompanied by a park ranger or other professional.

sturdy boots.

Hypothermia: This occurs when the core body temperature falls below 95°F (35°C). At altitude, combinations of alcohol, cold and thin air can produce hypothermia. Watch for drowsiness, disorientation and sometimes increased urination. If possible get to a hospital, otherwise blankets and extra clothing should be piled on for warmth. Don't use hot water or electric heaters and don't rub the skin. The elderly should be especially careful in extremely cold weather.

Frostbite: Symptoms of frostbite, which occurs when living tissue freezes, include numbness, pain, blistering and whitening of the skin. The most immediate remedy is to put frostbitten skin against warm skin. Simply holding your hands for several minutes over another person's frostbitten cheeks or nose may suffice. Otherwise, immerse frostbitten skin in warm (not hot!) water. Refreezing will cause even more damage, so get the victim into a warm environment as quickly as possible. Check other members of your party. If one person is hypothermic or frostbitten, others may be too.

Altitude sickness: People traveling from sea level may feel uncharacteristically winded at elevations as low as 6,000 or 7,000ft (1,800–2,100 meters). The sensation usually passes after a few days. Symptoms, including nausea, headache, vomiting, extreme fatigue, light-headedness and shortness of breath, intensify over 10,000ft (3,000 meters). Although the symptoms may be mild at first, they can develop into a serious illness. Move to a lower elevation and try to acclimatize gradually.

Lightning: In Colorado, lightning is the number one life-threatening weather hazard. In the past 10 years there has been an average of three deaths and 15 injuries from lightning each year. Stay alert for fast-changing weather conditions. It doesn't have to be raining where you are for lightning to be a threat. Avoid being the tallest object in the area, and stay away from other tall objects such as a small group of trees. If hiking in the mountains, go early in the day, before thunderstorms develop. Above tree line, there are few places to take cover. If you are in the mountains when a storm is moving in, descend from high points. If you can't get away from an exposed area, make yourself as small as possible, crouching down or perching on a small rock with insulation such as a poncho or foam pad under you, your feet touching

ABOVE: an alligator farm in the San Luis Valley.

rock and your hands clasped around your knees. Never seek shelter under a lone tree, in a shallow cave, or under a rock overhang.

Insects and Animals

Snakes: Of the 25 species of snakes in Colorado, the Western rattlesnake and the massasauga are the only venomous species. The Western rattlesnake appears in most habitats throughout the state. The massasauga is limited to the southeastern grasslands. There are six basic ways to distinguish these two venomous snakes from their non-venomous relatives: 1) rattles at the end of the tail; 2) fangs in addition to their rows of teeth; 3) facial pits between the nostrils and eyes; 4) vertical and elliptical pupils that may look like thin lines in bright light (non-venomous snakes have round pupils); and 5) a broad triangular head and narrow neck. Only about 3 percent of people bitten by a rattlesnake die, and these are mainly small children. Walk in the open when possible, proceed with caution among rocks, sweep grassy areas with a long stick before entering, avoid dark or overgrown places where snakes might lurk, shake out bedding or clothing that has been lying on the ground, and wear sturdy hiking boots. Snakes often lie on roads at night because of the residual heat radiating from the pavement, so use a flashlight if walking on a paved road after dark. Keep your hands and feet where you can see them, and don't let children poke under rocks or logs.

Snakebite kits are good psychological protection, but there is some question over how effective they really are. The most useful snakebite kit consists of car keys, and coins for calling a hospital. If bitten, remain calm so as not to increase circulation and spread the venom faster, remove rings, watches, bracelets and other articles that may constrict swelling below the bite area, if possible, wash the wound with soap and water, immobilize the bite area and keep it below the heart, and get to a hospital immediately. Do not wait for the pain to become severe. The use of an approved anti-venom is the most effective treatment. Do not use a tourniquet, make an incision at the bite site, suck out the venom with your mouth, or pack the limb in ice.

Insects: Bees are abundant, which should concern only those allergic to the sting. Those with severe allergies should carry an EpiPen or other form of emergency treatment, especially if hiking in remote areas. The bite of a black widow spider or tarantula and the sting of a scorpion's tail can pack a punch but are rarely a serious health threat to adults. Scorpions are nocturnal, so use flashlights if you walk barefoot at night. They often hide in recesses, dark corners and wood piles and like to crawl into protected places, so shake out clothes or sleeping bags that have been on the ground and check your shoes before slipping them on in the morning.

Insurance

Most visitors to the US will have no health problems during their stay. Even so, you should never leave home without travel insurance to cover both yourself and your belongings. Your own insurance company or travel agent can advise you on policies, but shop around since rates vary. Make sure you are covered for accidental death, emergency medical care, trip cancellation and baggage or document loss.

Internet

Many public libraries, copy centers, hotels and airports offer high-speed (DSL) or Wireless (Wi-fi) email and internet access, either on their computers or your laptop. At Starbucks coffee houses, for example, you must first purchase a T-Mobile Hot Spot pass or Boingo Pass (currently about $10 a day), before being able to log on; other coffee houses and restaurants offer free Wi-fi as a customer incentive. Services providers such as Earthlink (www.earthlink.net) and Hotmail (www.hotmail.com) offer Web mail accounts that will enable access while traveling. The modems of many foreign laptops, handheld computers and smart-phones won't work in the US. You may need to purchase a global modem before leaving home or a local PC-card modem once you arrive in the US. For more information, log on to www.teleadapt.com.

Maps

Accurate maps are indispensable in Colorado, especially when leaving primary roads. Road maps can be found at bookstores, convenience stores and gas stations. Free maps are also available by mail from state or regional tourism bureaus and in person at visitor centers, tourism offices and state welcome centers. Free city, state and regional maps as well as up-to-date road conditions and other valuable services are available to members of the **Automobile Association of America** (AAA).

Maps of national parks, forests and other public lands are usually offered by the managing governmental agency. Good topographical maps of national parks and forests are available from **Trails Illustrated**, PO Box 3610, Evergreen, CO 80439, tel: 303-670-3457 or toll-free 800-962-1643; www.natgeomaps.com/trailsillustrated. These maps are often found in bookstores. Extremely detailed topographical maps are available from the **US Geological Survey**, PO Box 25286, Denver Federal Center, Denver, CO 80225, tel: 303-236-7477; www.usgs.gov/sales.html. Like maps from Trails Illustrated, USGS maps are often available in higher-end bookstores and shops that sell outdoor gear.

Media

Newspapers

In this rapidly expanding era of electronic publishing and free information on the worldwide web, print media has undergone a massive contraction. Yet most communities still publish print editions of newspapers, as well as electronic editions, and the opinions and endorsements of columnists and editorial boards continue to play an important role in community life. Colorado's top newspaper is the *Denver Post*. Other Colorado newspapers include the *Aspen Daily News*, the *Colorado Springs Gazette*, the *Colorado Tribune* in Pueblo, *The Daily Sentinel* in Grand Junction, the *Durango Herald*, the *Estes Park Trail Gazette*, the *Telluride Daily Planet*, and *Vail Daily*. *High Country News*, headquartered in Paonia, is an award-winning environmental journal.

Magazines

Several Colorado lifestyle magazines are worth checking out for their regional articles on interesting destinations and local people, as well as restaurant listings and a calendar of events: *5280: Denver's Mile-High Magazine, Zone 4: Living in the High Country West, Aspen Magazine, Colorado Homes and Lifestyles Magazine, Mountain Living Magazine* and *Telluride Magazine*.

Money Matters

Currency

The basic unit of American currency, the dollar ($1), is equal to 100 cents. There are four coins, each worth less than a dollar: a penny or 1 cent (1¢), a nickel or 5 cents (5¢), a dime or 10 cents (10¢) and a quarter or 25 cents (25¢).

There are several denominations of paper money: $1, $5, $10, $20, $50 and $100. Each bill is the same color, size and shape; be sure to check the dollar amount on the face of the bill.

It is advisable to arrive with at least $100 in cash (in small bills) to pay for ground transportation and other incidentals.

Automatic Teller Machines (ATMs)

ATMs are the most convenient way to access cash and are widely available throughout the state. They are usually found at banks, shopping malls, supermarkets, service stations, convenience stores and hotels. ATM, or debit, cards may also be used at a growing number of grocery stores and gas stations, much as credit cards are.

Traveler's Checks

Foreign visitors are advised to take US dollar traveler's checks since

exchanging foreign currency – whether as cash or checks – can be problematic. A growing number of banks offer exchange facilities, but this practice is not universal.

Most shops, restaurants and other establishments accept traveler's checks in US dollars and will give change in cash. Alternatively, checks can be converted into cash at the bank.

Credit Cards

These are very much part of daily life in the US. They can be used to pay for pretty much anything, and it is common for car rental agencies and hotels to take an imprint of your card as a deposit. Rental companies may oblige you to pay a large deposit in cash if you do not have a card.

You can also use your credit card to withdraw cash from ATMs. Before you leave home, make sure you know your PIN (personal identification number) and find out which ATM system will accept your card. The most widely accepted cards are Visa, MasterCard, American Express, Diners Club, and Discovery.

Money may be sent or received by wire at any **Western Union** office (tel: 800-325-6000) or **American Express Money Gram** office (tel: 800-543-4080).

Public Holidays

On public holidays, post offices, banks, most government offices and a large number of shops and restaurants are closed. Public transport usually runs less frequently.

New Year's Day: January 1
Martin Luther King, Jr's Birthday: The third Monday in January
Presidents Day: The third Monday in February
Good Friday: March/April – date varies
Easter Sunday: March/April – date varies
El Cinco de Mayo: May 5
Memorial Day: Last Monday in May
Independence Day: July 4
Labor Day: First Monday in September
Columbus Day: Second Monday in October
Election Day: The Tuesday in the first full week of November during presidential election years
Veterans Day: November 11
Thanksgiving Day: Fourth Thursday in November
Christmas Day: December 25

Tipping

Service workers in restaurants and hotels depend on tips for a significant portion of their income. With few exceptions, tipping is left to your discretion and gratuities are not automatically added to the bill. In most cases, 15–20 percent is typical for tipping waiters, taxi drivers, bartenders, barbers and hairdressers. Porters and bellmen usually get $1 per bag.

O pening Hours

Standard hours for business offices are Monday–Friday 9am–5pm. Many banks open a little earlier, usually 8.30am; a few open on Saturday morning. Post offices are usually open Monday–Friday 8am–5pm and Saturday 8am–noon. Most stores and shopping centers are open weekends and evenings.

P hotography

Even in this era of instant-view digital cameras, film is still widely available throughout the US. Business centers and discount chains often offer rapid development or conversion of digital to paper prints. Colorado, in particular, is spectacularly photogenic. Some of the most rewarding photography is of mountain vistas and lakes in places like Rocky Mountain National Park, Maroon Bells and the redrock country around Grand Mesa. Seek out wildlife events such as the elk rut in Rocky, sandhill cranes wintering in San Luis Valley or Prairie chicken dances in Comanche National Grasslands. Old mining towns in the central and southern Rockies make particularly haunting subject matter. Everywhere in Colorado, you'll find unique and colorful festivals and sporting events. Photography workshops are held throughout Colorado. One of the more spectacular locations is Crested Butte, which offers photography workshops during its summer Wild Flower Festival. Several well-known photographers live in the old town and maintain galleries there.

Postal Services

Even the most remote towns are served by the US Postal Service. Smaller post offices tend to be limited to business hours (Mon–Fri 9am–5pm), although central, big-city branches may have extended weekday and weekend hours.

Stamps are sold at all post offices. They are also sold at some convenience stores, filling stations, hotels and transportation terminals, usually from vending machines.

For reasonably quick delivery within the US at a modest price, ask for priority mail, which usually reaches its destination within two or three days.

For overnight deliveries, try US **Express Mail** or one of several domestic and international courier services:
FedEx, tel: 800-238-5355
DHL, tel: 800-345-2727
United Parcel Service, tel: 800-742-5877

Poste Restante

Visitors can receive mail at post offices if it is addressed to them, care of "General Delivery," followed by the city name and (very important) the zip code. You must pick up this mail in person within a week or two of its arrival and will be asked to show a valid driver's license, passport or some other form of picture identification.

R eligious Services

Some 65 percent of Coloradans define their religious preference as Christian, mostly Protestant but with a fair number of Evangelical Christians and Roman Catholics. Far fewer define themselves as Jewish or Muslim, and a quarter of Coloradans state no religious preference at all. Colorado Springs is home to a number of conservative religious groups, including Focus on the Family, an activist anti-abortion group. Two well-known churches may be visited in the area: the Cadet Chapel on the US Air Force Academy, well known for its interesting modern architecture; and Chapel on the Rock, a historic Roman Catholic church on the grounds of the Saint Malo Retreat Center near Allenspark. An Easter Sunrise service at Red Rocks Amphitheater is a popular annual event, attended by thousands.

Boulder is a center of alternative health and spirituality and home of Naropa University, a well-regarded educational institution that includes Tibetan Buddhist meditation and other spiritual practices in its curriculum. Theravadan and Zen Buddhist meditation centers and retreats in the mountains associated with Naropa are very popular. Well-known international teachers of Buddhism and Tibetan lamas are frequently in residence at the centers in Boulder and Front Range communities.

T ax

Like most states, Colorado levies a flat sales tax on goods and services. It varies from city to city but is a lot lower than in many states. The general rate in Denver County is 3.62 percent, 4 percent on food and liquor, and 7.25 percent on auto rentals of less than 30 days; in Western Slope communities it is around 2 percent.

Telephones

In this era of cell phones, you'll find fewer public telephones in hotel lobbies, restaurants, drug stores, garages, road side kiosks, convenience stores and other locations. The cost of making a local call from a payphone for three minutes is 25–50 cents. To make a long-distance call from a payphone, use either a prepaid calling card, available in airports, post offices and a few other outlets, or your credit card, which you can use at any phone: dial 800-CALLATT, key in your credit card number, and wait to be connected. In many areas, local calls have now changed to a 10-digit calling system, using the area code. The main area codes in Colorado are as follows: Denver Metro Area, including Boulder – 303 and 720; Southeastern Colorado, including Colorado Springs and Pueblo – 719; the rest of the state is 970.

Watch out for in-room connection charges in more up-market hotels; it's cheaper to use the payphone in the lobby. Ditto: wireless and broadband internet connections in your room: many hotel lobbies offer free wireless but charge for it in guest rooms, Inquire ahead.

Dialing Abroad

To dial abroad (Canada follows the US system), first dial the international access code 011, then the country code. If using a US phone credit card, dial the company's access number below, then 01, then the country code.

Sprint, tel: 10333
AT&T, tel: 10288.

Country codes:

Australia	61
Austria	43
Belgium	32
Brazil	55
Denmark	45
France	33
Germany	49
Greece	30
Hong Kong	852
Israel	972
Italy	39
Japan	81
Korea	82
Netherlands	31
New Zealand	64
Norway	47
Singapore	65
South Africa	27
Spain	34
Sweden	46
Switzerland	41
United Kingdom	44

Western Union (tel: 800-325-6000) can arrange money transfers and telegrams. Check online (www.western union.com) or a phone directory or call information for numbers of local offices.

Fax machines are available at most hotels and motels. Printers, copy shops, stationers and office-supply shops may also have them, as well as some convenience stores.

Time Zones

The continental US is divided into four time zones. From east to west, later to earlier, they are Eastern Standard Time, Central Standard Time, Mountain Standard Time, and Pacific Standard Time, each separated by one hour. Colorado is on Mountain Standard Time (MST), seven hours behind Greenwich Mean Time. On the first Sunday in April, Coloradans set the clock ahead one hour in observation of daylight savings time. On the last Sunday in October, the clock is moved back one hour to return to standard time.

Tourist Information

The state tourism office, www.colorado. com, has in-depth online information about visiting Colorado, including sections on arranging travel to Colorado from the UK, Italy, France, Germany and Japan. The website has feature articles on special-interest tours, from microbreweries and wineries to visiting and staying on farms and ranches, connecting with the art scene, volunteer opportunities for environmental cleanup and taking part in sports and other special events.

Colorado Welcome Centers are located at the state line. They are staffed by volunteers who can give you maps, brochures, discount coupon books and sound advice on your stay and have restrooms, water, and often hot coffee. Most

ABOVE: golfers take advantage of Colorado's natural beauty and good weather.

communities have visitor centers that offer information and trip planning. When visiting national parks, be sure to stop at the visitor center or ranger station first. Rangers there can help you get the most out of your time in the park. Colorado has 25 spectacular scenic and historic drives designated by the government as scenic byways. Check out www.byways.org to find out more.

Colorado Tourism Offices

Alamosa Visitor Information Center
Cole Park, Alamosa, CO 81101; tel: 800-BLU-SKYS; www.alamosa.org

Aspen Chamber Resort Association
425 Rio Grande Place, Aspen, CO 81611; tel: 970-925-1940; www.aspenchamber.org

Aurora Chamber of Commerce
14305 E. Alameda, Ste 300, Aurora, CO 80014; tel: 303-344-1500; www.aurorachamber.org

Beaver Creek Ski Area
PO Box 7, Vail, CO 81658; tel: 970-496-4900; http://beavercreek.com

Boulder Convention and Visitors Bureau
2440 Pearl Street, Boulder, CO 80302; tel: 303-442-2911; www.bouldercoloradousa.com

Breckenridge Chamber of Commerce
311 S. Ridge, Breckenridge, CO 80424; tel: 970-496-4700 or 800-536-1890; www.breckenridge.com

Buena Vista Chamber of Commerce
343 Highway 24 S, Buena Vista, CO 81211; tel: 719-395-6612 or 800-311-0605; www.fourteenernet.com

Buttermilk Ski Area
PO Box 1248, Aspen, CO 81612; tel: 800-525-6200; www.aspensnowmass.com/buttermilk

Cañon City Chamber of Commerce
403 Royal Gorge Boulevard, Cañon City, CO 81215; tel: 719-275-2331 or 800-876-7922; www.canoncitychamber.com

Castle Rock Chamber of Commerce
420 Jerry Street, Castle Rock, CO 80104; tel: 866-441-8508; www.castlerock.org

Central City Visitors Center
141 Nevada, Central City, CO 80427; tel: 303-582-5251; www.centralcitycolorado.us

Colorado Springs Visitors Bureau
104 S. Cascade, Colorado Springs, CO 80903; tel: 719-635-7506 or 800-368-4748; www.visitcos.com

Colorado Travel and Tourism Authority
1672 Pennsylvania Street, Denver, CO 80203; tel: 303-832-6171 or 800-265-6723; www.colorado.com

Cortez Chamber of Commerce
928 E. Main Street, Cortez, CO 81321; tel: 970-565-3414; www.cortezchamber.org

Craig Chamber of Commerce and Moffat County Visitor Center
360 E. Victory Way, Craig, CO 81625; tel: 970-824-5689 or 800-864-4405; www.craig-chamber.com

Creede-Mineral Chamber of Commerce
PO Box 580, Creede, CO 81130; tel: 719-658-2374 or 800-327-2102; www.creede.com

Crested Butte Chamber of Commerce
PO Box 1288, Crested Butte, CO 81224; tel: 970-349-6438; www.cbchamber.com

Cripple Creek Chamber of Commerce
PO Box 430, Cripple Creek, CO 80813; tel: 877-858-4653; www.cripple-creek.co.us

Delta County Visitor Bureau
PO Box 753, Delta, CO 81416; tel: 970-874-2100; www.deltacountycolorado.com

Denver Metro Chamber of Commerce
1445 Market Street, Denver, CO 80202; tel: 303-534-8500; www.denverchamber.org

Denver Metro Visitors Bureau
1555 California Street, Ste 300, Denver CO 80210; tel: 303-892-1112 or 800-233-6837; www.denver.org

Durango Visitors Bureau
111 S. Camino del Rio, Durango, CO 81302; tel: 970-247-3500 or 800-463-8726; www.durango.org

Estes Park Convention and Visitors Bureau
500 Big Thompson Avenue, Estes Park, CO 80517; tel: 970-577-990 or 800-44-ESTES; www.estesparkcvb.com

Evergreen Chamber of Commerce
28065 Highway 74, Ste 201, Evergreen, CO 80437; tel: 303-674-3412; www.evergreenchamber.org

Fort Collins Visitors Bureau
19 Old Town Square, Ste 137, Fort Collins, CO 80524; tel: 970-232-3840 or 800-274-3678; www.ftcollins.com

Glenwood Springs Chamber of Commerce
1102 Grand Avenue, Glenwood Springs, CO 81601; tel: 970-945-6589; www.glenwoodchamber.com

Golden Chamber of Commerce
1010 Washington Avenue, Golden, CO 80402; tel: 303-279-3113; www.goldencochamber.org

Grand Lake Chamber of Commerce
928 Grand Avenue, Grand Lake, CO 80447; tel: 970-627-3402 or 800-531-1019; www.grandlakechamber.com

Gunnison-Crested Butte Tourism
PO Box 314, Gunnison, CO 81230; tel: 800-814-7988; www.gunnisoncounty.com

Lake City Chamber of Commerce
PO Box 430, Lake City, CO 81235; tel: 970-944-2527 or 800-569-1874; www.lakecityco.com

Lakewood Chamber of Commerce
1667 Cole Boulevard, Bldg 19, Ste 400, Lakewood, CO 80401; tel: 303-233-5555; www.westchamber.org

Leadville Chamber of Commerce
809 Harrison Avenue, Leadville, CO 80461; tel: 719-486-3900 or 888-532-3845; www.leadvilleusa.com

Loveland Chamber of Commerce
5400 Stonecreek Circle, Loveland, CO 80538; tel: 970-667-6311; www.loveland.org

Manitou Springs Chamber of Commerce
354 Manitou Avenue, Manitou Springs, CO 80829; tel: 719-685-5089 or 800-642-2567; www.manitousprings.org

Mesa Verde Visitor Bureau
PO HH, Cortez, CO 81321; tel: 800-530-2998; www.mesaverdecountry.com

Monte Vista Chamber of Commerce
947 1st Avenue, Monte Vista, CO 81144; tel: 719-852-2731; www.monte-vista.org

TRANSPORTATION · ACCOMMODATIONS · EATING OUT · ACTIVITIES · A – Z

Montrose Visitor and Convention Bureau
1519 E. Main, Montrose, CO 81402; tel: 970-249-5000 or 800-873-0244; www.visitmontrose.com

Monument Chamber of Commerce
300 Highway 105, Monument, CO 80132; tel: 719-481-3282; www.tri lakes.net

Ouray Visitors Bureau
1230 Main Street, Ouray, CO 81427; tel: 970-325-4746 or 800-228-1876; www.ouraycolorado.com

Pagosa Springs Chamber of Commerce
PO Box 787, Pagosa Springs, CO 81147; tel: 800-252-2204; www.pagosa-springs.com

Pueblo Chamber of Commerce
302 N. Santa Fe Avenue, Pueblo, CO 81002; tel: 719-542-1704 or 800-233-3446; www.pueblochamber.org

Silverton Chamber of Commerce
414 Greene Street, Silverton, CO 81433; tel: 970-387-5654 or 800-752-4494; www.silvertoncolorado.com

Snowmass Village Resort Association
130 Kearns Road, Snowmass Village, CO 81615; tel: 866-352-1763; http://snowmassvillage.com

South Fork Chamber of Commerce
PO Box 1030, South Fork, CO 81154; tel: 719-873-5512 or 800-571-0881; www.southfork.org

Sterling Chamber of Commerce
PO Box 1683, Sterling, CO 80751; tel: 970-522-5070 or 866-522-5070; www.logancountychamber.com

Summit Chamber of Commerce
PO Box 5450, Frisco, CO 80443; tel: 970-668-2051; www.summitchamber.org

Telluride Visitor Services
PO Box 653, Telluride, CO 81435; tel: 970-728-3041 or 888-605-2578; www.visittelluride.com

Vail Valley Tourism Bureau
101 Fawcett Road, Ste 240, Vail, CO 81657; tel: 970-476-1000; www.visitvailvalley.com

Winter Park Chamber of Commerce
PO Box 3236, Winter Park, CO 80482; tel: 970-726-4118; www.playwinter park.com

Tour Operators and Travel Agents

Even if you are planning on doing the driving yourself, you may want to hook up with a local tour operator to let someone else show you around for a few days. You can locate a US tour operator by checking listings on the websites of the **US Tour Operator Association** – USTOA (www.ustoa) and the **National Tour Association** (www. ntaonline.com) or by contacting the

ABOVE: kids explore at Dinosaur Journey in western Colorado.

visitor center at your destination for official listings. In Colorado, contact Tour Colorado (tel: 888-311-TOUR; www.tourcolorado.com)

Top tour operators serving all of the US include **Tauck Tours** (tel: 800-788-7885; www.tauck.com), **Abercrombie and Kent** (tel: 800-554-7016; www.abercrombieandkent.com), both of which specialize in luxury tours. The **Smithsonian Institution** (tel: 877-338-8687; www.smithsonian journeys.com) offers educational tours to sites of archeological, historical and scientific interest, such as Mesa Verde National Park, guided by authorities in the field.

Specialty tour operators offer guided trips tailored to your interests, from walking tours of historic downtowns and gold mines to balloon trips and visits to the state's numerous wineries and microbreweries. Outfitters offer guided trips of the outdoors. The possibilities in outdoorsy Colorado are virtually limitless, including fishing, hunting, river rafting, horseback riding, skiing, rock climbing, mountain biking, and Jeep touring. Heritage and agricultural tourism are growing in popularity in Colorado, and include tours of archeological sites on the Ute Mountain Ute Reservation with native guides; learning ranch and farm skills from cowboys and farmers on the Western Slope; and taking part in paleontological digs near Dinosaur National Monument.

See "Activities" pages 315–17 for a list of Tour and Outdoor Adventure Operators.

V isas and Passports

A machine-readable passport, a passport-sized photograph (note: the size required in Britain is different

from that in a US passport), a visitor's visa, proof of intent to leave the US after your visit, and (depending upon your country of origin) an international vaccination certificate, are required of most foreign nationals for entry into the US.

Visitors from the UK staying less than 90 days no longer need a visa (visa waiver); however, as of January 12, 2009, non-US residents from VWP countries are required to submit information about themselves online to the Department of Homeland Security and be pre-approved for travel to the US at least three days before they travel. It is compulsory for short-term visitors to the US to register via the website of the Electronic System for Travel Authorization (www.esta.us/travel_authorization.html) before traveling.

Vaccination certificate requirements vary, but proof of immunization against smallpox or cholera may be necessary.

US citizens traveling by air between the US, Canada, Mexico, the Caribbean, and Bermuda must present a current passport: a birth certificate and photo ID are no longer valid proof.

Up-to-date details on entry requirements and machine-readable passports may be found on the US State Department's website: www.travel.state.gov/visa/visa_1750.html.

Extensions of Stay

Non-US citizens should contact US Immigration and Naturalization Service at 425 I Street, Washington DC 20536; tel: 202-501-4444 or 888-407-4747

Weights and Measures

Despite efforts to convert to metric, the US still uses the Imperial System of weights and measures.

FURTHER READING

Nonfiction

History

Colorado: A History of the Centennial State, by Carl Abbot, Stephen J. Leonard and David McComb. Modern urbanization, multiculturalism, boosterism and Colorado history.

Colorado: Yesterday & Today, by Joseph Collier and Grant Collier. The descendant of 19th-century photographer Joseph Collier examines Colorado through photographs.

Denver: From Mining Camp to Metropolis, by Stephen J. Leonard and Thomas J. Noel offers a thorough examination of the Mile High City, then and now.

Eccentric Colorado: A Legacy of the Bizarre and Unusual, by Kenneth Jessen. Weird and wonderful lore about life in the Colorado Rockies.

I Never Knew That About Colorado: A Quaint Volume of Forgotten Lore, by Abbott Fay. Entertaining collection of little-known facts about Colorado.

A Lady's Life in the Rocky Mountains, by Isabella Lucy Bird. Memoir of a 19th-century Englishwoman's life exploring the Colorado Rockies, alone and on horseback.

Money Mountain: The Story of Cripple Creek Gold, by Marshall Sprague. Truth is more fantastic than fiction in this enjoyable look at Cripple Creek history.

The Rockies, by David Lavender. The standard history on the Rockies by the late Colorado historian.

Roof of the Rockies: A History of Colorado Mountaineering, by William M. Bueler. Details fourteener summit climbs with photos.

Stampede to Timberline: The Ghost Towns and Mining Camps of Colorado, by Muriel Sibell. Oral histories of pioneers.

Utes: A Forgotten People, by Wilson Rockwell. The most complete history of the Utes available.

Culture and Current Events

The Beast in the Garden: A Modern Parable of Man and Nature, by David Baron. A mountain lion attack in Colorado prompts the writer to explore human–wildlife relations.

Culinary Colorado: The Ultimate Food Lover's Guide, by Claire Walter. An encyclopedic tour of Colorado's food culture.

Deep in the Heart of the Rockies, by Ed Quillen. Wit and wisdom from a *Denver Post* columnist.

No Easy Answers: The Truth Behind Death at Columbine, by Brooks Brown and Rob Merritt. One of the better treatments of the tragic Columbine High School shooting.

Perfect Murder, Perfect Town: The Uncensored Story of the JonBenet Murder and the Grand Jury's Search for the Final Truth, by Lawrence Schiller. An investigation into the unsolved murder of a six-year-old child.

When I Was Cool: My Life at the Jack Kerouac School, by Sam Kashner. A memoir of the author's experiences as a student at Boulder's Naropa University.

Whiteout: Lost in Aspen, by Ted Conover. A memoir of the author's

Send Us Your Thoughts

We do our best to ensure the information in our books is as accurate and up-to-date as possible. The books are updated on a regular basis using local contacts, who painstakingly add, amend and correct as required. However, some details (such as telephone numbers and opening times) are liable to change, and we are ultimately reliant on our readers to put us in the picture.

We welcome your feedback, especially your experience of using the book "on the road". Maybe we recommended a hotel that you liked (or another that you didn't), or you came across a great bar or new attraction we missed.

We will acknowledge all contributions, and we'll offer an Insight Guide to the best letters received.

Please write to us at:
Insight Guides
PO Box 7910
London SE1 1WE
Or email us at:
insight@apaguide.co.uk

experiences as a low-wage worker in high-rent Aspen. A revealing look at celebrity culture and the transformation of a former mining town.

Travel

100 Classic Hikes in Colorado, by Scott S. Warren. A good trail companion.

Colorado Close-Up, text by Conger Beasley, photos by J.C. Leacock. Nature essays and photos by a Colorado writer/photographer team.

Colorado's Fourteeners: From Hikes to Climbs, by Gerry Roach. Ambitious hikes over 14,000ft (4,270 meters).

Colorado Scenic Byways: Taking the Other Road, text by Susan Tweit, photos by Jim Steinberg. Awardwinning celebration of Colorado's back roads by a naturalist and photographer.

Colorado Wildlife Viewing Guide, by Mary Taylor Young. Watchable wildlife in Colorado.

Complete Guide to Colorado's Wilderness Areas, text by Mark Pearson, photos by John Fielder.

Guide to Colorado Wildflowers, by G.K. Guennel. Identify columbines and more.

Roadside Geology of Colorado, by Halka Chronic. An excellent series on state geology.

Fiction

Angle of Repose, by Wallace Stegner. A reflective, Pulitzer Prize-winning work by a master of serious Western literature.

Centennial, by James A. Michener. A An intergenerational epic set mostly on the plains of eastern Colorado.

Eventide, by Kent Haruf. The lives, loves and trials of a small town on the high plains of Colorado.

On the Road, by Jack Kerouac. Much of Kerouac's Beat Generation classic takes place in Denver.

Blinded, by Stephen White. A mystery series set in Boulder, Colorado.

The Serpents Trail: A Maxie and Stretch Mystery, by Sue Henry. This installment of the series takes place in and around Grand Junction, Colorado.

Art and Photo Credits

INDEX

Main references are in bold type

W y o m

Browns Park NWR

Sierra Madre

Mt Zirkel Wilderness Area

North Sand Hills BLM Rec. Area

Medicine Bow Mtns

Laramie Mtns

★ Gates of Lodore

Steamboat Lake SP

Pearl Lake SP

Echo Park

Dinosaur National Monument

Yampa River SP

Routt National Forest

Arapaho NWR

Na

Craig

Yampa

Steamboat Springs

North Park

Ro Mou Nat Pa

Little Snake

Elkhead Creek

Vermillion Creek

Little Snake

Stagecoach SP

Routt NF

Lake Granby

Danforth Hills

Little Yampa Canyon BLM Rec. Area

Routt National Forest

Yampa

Routt NF

Arapaho NF

Arapaho National Forest

Arapal NWR

White

Cathedral Bluffs

★ Canyon Pintado National Historic District

Roaence Creek

Sheep Mtn 12241

Colorado

Gore Range

Williams Fork Mtns

Arapaho National Forest

Na

Roan Plateau

White River National Forest

Rifle Falls SP

Eagle

Eagles Nest Wilderness Area

Silverthorne

Blue

Roan Creek

Rifle Gap SP

Harvey Gap SP

Avon

Vail

Dillon Res.

Rifle

Colorado

Glenwood Springs

White River Sylvan Lake SP National Forest

Holy Cross Wilderness Area

Ta

Highline Lake SP

Carbondale

Fryingpan

Turquoise Lake

South Park

Grand Valley BLM Rec. Area

Colorado River/ Island Acres SP

White River National Forest

Thompson Creek BLM Rec. Area

Aspen

Leadville

S. Platte

McInnis Canyons NCA

Fruita

Grand Junction

Vega SP

Grand Mesa National Forest

Maroon Bells Snowmass Wilderness Area

Sawatch Range

Spinne

Colorado NM

Grand Mesa

Buck Mesa

Castle Peak 14265

Mt Harvard 14420

Grand Mesa NF

Dominguez Canyon BLM Rec. Area

Delta

Gunnison National Forest

Taylor Park Reservoir

Pike National Forest

Gunnison

Sweitzer Lake SP

West Elk Wilderness Area

Taylor

Arkansas Headwaters SP

Uncompahgre National Forest

Black Canyon of the Gunnison NP

Blue Mesa Reservoir

Gunnison

Arkans Headw Rec. A

Montrose

Morrow Point Res.

Curecanti Nat'l Rec. Area

San Miguel

Uncompahgre

Lake Fork

Cebolla Cr.

Tomichi

Cochetopa

Gunnison National Forest

Hills

Sangre de San Luis

Dolores River BLM Rec. Area

Ridgway SP

Cochetopa

Sar Isl

Uncompahgre NF

Mt Sneffels Wilderness

Uncompahgre National Forest

Uncompahgre Pk 14309

San Luis Peak 14014

La Garita Mountains

Saguache Creek

San Luis Valley

Disappointment Creek

Dolores

Lizard Head Wilderness Area

Taylor Mesa

Rio Grande

Rio Grande Res.

Rio Grande

San Luis SP

McPhee Res.

Uncompahgre National Forest

San Juan Mountains

Weminuche Wilderness Area

Rio Grande

Monte Vista

Canyons of the Ancients NM

San Juan National Forest

Vallecito Res.

Monte Vista NWR

Alamosa

Al N

Ute Mountain Ute Indian Reservation

Mesa Verde National Park Mesa Verde

La Plata Mtns

Animas

Floride

Platoro Res.

La Jara Res.

Alamosa

Mancos

Ute Mtn Ute Tribal Park

Durango

Southern Ute Indian Reservation

Los Pinos

Navajo Res.

Navajo SP

New